Maria Lipman (ed.)

RUSSIAN VOICES ON POST-CRIMEA RUSSIA

An Almanac of *Counterpoint* Essays from 2015–2018

Bibliografische Information der Deutschen Nationalbibliothek
Die Deutsche Nationalbibliothek verzeichnet diese Publikation in der Deutschen Nationalbibliografie; detaillierte bibliografische Daten sind im Internet über http://dnb.d-nb.de abrufbar.

Bibliographic information published by the Deutsche Nationalbibliothek
Die Deutsche Nationalbibliothek lists this publication in the Deutsche Nationalbibliografie; detailed bibliographic data are available in the Internet at http://dnb.d-nb.de.

ISBN-13: 978-3-8382-1251-7
© *ibidem*-Verlag, Stuttgart 2020
Alle Rechte vorbehalten

Das Werk einschließlich aller seiner Teile ist urheberrechtlich geschützt. Jede Verwertung außerhalb der engen Grenzen des Urheberrechtsgesetzes ist ohne Zustimmung des Verlages unzulässig und strafbar. Dies gilt insbesondere für Vervielfältigungen, Übersetzungen, Mikroverfilmungen und elektronische Speicherformen sowie die Einspeicherung und Verarbeitung in elektronischen Systemen.

All rights reserved. No part of this publication may be reproduced, stored in or introduced into a retrieval system, or transmitted, in any form, or by any means (electronical, mechanical, photocopying, recording or otherwise) without the prior written permission of the publisher. Any person who does any unauthorized act in relation to this publication may be liable to criminal prosecution and civil claims for damages.

Printed in the EU

Soviet and Post-Soviet Politics and Society (SPPS) Vol. 204
ISSN 1614-3515

General Editor: Andreas Umland,
Institute for Euro-Atlantic Cooperation, Kyiv, umland@stanfordalumni.org

Commissioning Editor: Max Jakob Horstmann,
London, mjh@ibidem.eu

EDITORIAL COMMITTEE*

DOMESTIC & COMPARATIVE POLITICS
Prof. **Ellen Bos,** *Andrássy University of Budapest*
Dr. **Gergana Dimova,** *University of Winchester*
Dr. **Andrey Kazantsev,** *MGIMO (U) MID RF, Moscow*
Prof. **Heiko Pleines,** *University of Bremen*
Prof. **Richard Sakwa,** *University of Kent at Canterbury*
Dr. **Sarah Whitmore,** *Oxford Brookes University*
Dr. **Harald Wydra,** *University of Cambridge*

SOCIETY, CLASS & ETHNICITY
Col. **David Glantz,** *"Journal of Slavic Military Studies"*
Dr. **Marlène Laruelle,** *George Washington University*
Dr. **Stephen Shulman,** *Southern Illinois University*
Prof. **Stefan Troebst,** *University of Leipzig*

POLITICAL ECONOMY & PUBLIC POLICY
Dr. **Andreas Goldthau,** *Central European University*
Dr. **Robert Kravchuk,** *University of North Carolina*
Dr. **David Lane,** *University of Cambridge*
Dr. **Carol Leonard,** *Higher School of Economics, Moscow*
Dr. **Maria Popova,** *McGill University, Montreal*

FOREIGN POLICY & INTERNATIONAL AFFAIRS
Dr. **Peter Duncan,** *University College London*
Prof. **Andreas Heinemann-Grüder,** *University of Bonn*
Prof. **Gerhard Mangott,** *University of Innsbruck*
Dr. **Diana Schmidt-Pfister,** *University of Konstanz*
Dr. **Lisbeth Tarlow,** *Harvard University, Cambridge*
Dr. **Christian Wipperfürth,** *N-Ost Network, Berlin*
Dr. **William Zimmerman,** *University of Michigan*

HISTORY, CULTURE & THOUGHT
Dr. **Catherine Andreyev,** *University of Oxford*
Prof. **Mark Bassin,** *Södertörn University*
Prof. **Karsten Brüggemann,** *Tallinn University*
Dr. **Alexander Etkind,** *University of Cambridge*
Dr. **Gasan Gusejnov,** *Moscow State University*
Prof. **Leonid Luks,** *Catholic University of Eichstaett*
Dr. **Olga Malinova,** *Russian Academy of Sciences*
Dr. **Richard Mole,** *University College London*
Prof. **Andrei Rogatchevski,** *University of Tromsø*
Dr. **Mark Tauger,** *West Virginia University*

ADVISORY BOARD*

Prof. **Dominique Arel,** *University of Ottawa*
Prof. **Jörg Baberowski,** *Humboldt University of Berlin*
Prof. **Margarita Balmaceda,** *Seton Hall University*
Dr. **John Barber,** *University of Cambridge*
Prof. **Timm Beichelt,** *European University Viadrina*
Dr. **Katrin Boeckh,** *University of Munich*
Prof. em. **Archie Brown,** *University of Oxford*
Dr. **Vyacheslav Bryukhovetsky,** *Kyiv-Mohyla Academy*
Prof. **Timothy Colton,** *Harvard University, Cambridge*
Prof. **Paul D'Anieri,** *University of Florida*
Dr. **Heike Dörrenbächer,** *Friedrich Naumann Foundation*
Dr. **John Dunlop,** *Hoover Institution, Stanford, California*
Dr. **Sabine Fischer,** *SWP, Berlin*
Dr. **Geir Flikke,** *NUPI, Oslo*
Prof. **David Galbreath,** *University of Aberdeen*
Prof. **Alexander Galkin,** *Russian Academy of Sciences*
Prof. **Frank Golczewski,** *University of Hamburg*
Dr. **Nikolas Gvosdev,** *Naval War College, Newport, RI*
Prof. **Mark von Hagen,** *Arizona State University*
Dr. **Guido Hausmann,** *University of Munich*
Prof. **Dale Herspring,** *Kansas State University*
Dr. **Stefani Hoffman,** *Hebrew University of Jerusalem*
Prof. **Mikhail Ilyin,** *MGIMO (U) MID RF, Moscow*
Prof. **Vladimir Kantor,** *Higher School of Economics*
Dr. **Ivan Katchanovski,** *University of Ottawa*
Prof. em. **Andrzej Korbonski,** *University of California*
Dr. **Iris Kempe,** *"Caucasus Analytical Digest"*
Prof. **Herbert Küpper,** *Institut für Ostrecht Regensburg*
Dr. **Rainer Lindner,** *CEEER, Berlin*
Dr. **Vladimir Malakhov,** *Russian Academy of Sciences*

Dr. **Luke March,** *University of Edinburgh*
Prof. **Michael McFaul,** *Stanford University, Palo Alto*
Prof. **Birgit Menzel,** *University of Mainz-Germersheim*
Prof. **Valery Mikhailenko,** *The Urals State University*
Prof. **Emil Pain,** *Higher School of Economics, Moscow*
Dr. **Oleg Podvintsev,** *Russian Academy of Sciences*
Prof. **Olga Popova,** *St. Petersburg State University*
Dr. **Alex Pravda,** *University of Oxford*
Dr. **Erik van Ree,** *University of Amsterdam*
Dr. **Joachim Rogall,** *Robert Bosch Foundation Stuttgart*
Prof. **Peter Rutland,** *Wesleyan University, Middletown*
Prof. **Marat Salikov,** *The Urals State Law Academy*
Dr. **Gwendolyn Sasse,** *University of Oxford*
Prof. **Jutta Scherrer,** *EHESS, Paris*
Prof. **Robert Service,** *University of Oxford*
Mr. **James Sherr,** *RIIA Chatham House London*
Dr. **Oxana Shevel,** *Tufts University, Medford*
Prof. **Eberhard Schneider,** *University of Siegen*
Prof. **Olexander Shnyrkov,** *Shevchenko University, Kyiv*
Prof. **Hans-Henning Schröder,** *SWP, Berlin*
Prof. **Yuri Shapoval,** *Ukrainian Academy of Sciences*
Prof. **Viktor Shnirelman,** *Russian Academy of Sciences*
Dr. **Lisa Sundstrom,** *University of British Columbia*
Dr. **Philip Walters,** *"Religion, State and Society", Oxford*
Prof. **Zenon Wasyliw,** *Ithaca College, New York State*
Dr. **Lucan Way,** *University of Toronto*
Dr. **Markus Wehner,** *"Frankfurter Allgemeine Zeitung"*
Dr. **Andrew Wilson,** *University College London*
Prof. **Jan Zielonka,** *University of Oxford*
Prof. **Andrei Zorin,** *University of Oxford*

* While the Editorial Committee and Advisory Board support the General Editor in the choice and improvement of manuscripts for publication, responsibility for remaining errors and misinterpretations in the series' volumes lies with the books' authors.

Soviet and Post-Soviet Politics and Society (SPPS)
ISSN 1614-3515

Founded in 2004 and refereed since 2007, SPPS makes available affordable English-, German-, and Russian-language studies on the history of the countries of the former Soviet bloc from the late Tsarist period to today. It publishes between 5 and 20 volumes per year and focuses on issues in transitions to and from democracy such as economic crisis, identity formation, civil society development, and constitutional reform in CEE and the NIS. SPPS also aims to highlight so far understudied themes in East European studies such as right-wing radicalism, religious life, higher education, or human rights protection. The authors and titles of all previously published volumes are listed at the end of this book. For a full description of the series and reviews of its books, see www.ibidem-verlag.de/red/spps.

Editorial correspondence & manuscripts should be sent to: Dr. Andreas Umland, Institute for Euro-Atlantic Cooperation, vul. Volodymyrska 42, off. 21, UA-01030 Kyiv, Ukraine

Business correspondence & review copy requests should be sent to: *ibidem* Press, Leuschnerstr. 40, 30457 Hannover, Germany; tel.: +49 511 2622200; fax: +49 511 2622201; spps@ibidem.eu.

Authors, reviewers, referees, and editors for (as well as all other persons sympathetic to) SPPS are invited to join its networks at www.facebook.com/group.php?gid=52638198614
www.linkedin.com/groups?about=&gid=103012
www.xing.com/net/spps-ibidem-verlag/

Recent Volumes

196 Anke Giesen
„Wie kann denn der Sieger ein Verbrecher sein?"
Eine diskursanalytische Untersuchung der russlandweiten Debatte über Konzept und Verstaatlichungsprozess der Lager-gedenkstätte „Perm'-36" im Ural
ISBN 978-3-8382-1284-5

197 Alla Leukavets
The Integration Policies of Belarus and Ukraine vis-à-vis the EU and Russia
A Comparative Case Study Through the Prism of a Two-Level Game Approach
ISBN 978-3-8382-1247-0

198 Oksana Kim
The Development and Challenges of Russian Corporate Governance I
The Roles and Functions of Boards of Directors
With a foreword by Sheila M. Puffer
ISBN 978-3-8382-1287-6

199 Thomas D. Grant
International Law and the Post-Soviet Space I
Essays on Chechnya and the Baltic States
With a foreword by Stephen M. Schwebel
ISBN 978-3-8382-1279-1

200 Thomas D. Grant
International Law and the Post-Soviet Space II
Essays on Ukraine, Intervention, and Non-Proliferation
ISBN 978-3-8382-1280-7

201 Slavomír Michálek, Michal Štefanský
The Age of Fear
The Cold War and Its Influence on Czechoslovakia 1945–1968
ISBN 978-3-8382-1285-2

202 Iulia-Sabina Joja
Romania's Strategic Culture 1990–2014
Continuity and Change in a Post-Communist Country's Evolution of National Interests and Security Policies
With a foreword by Heiko Biehl
ISBN 978-3-8382-1286-9

203 Andrei Rogatchevski, Yngvar B. Steinholt, Arve Hansen, David-Emil Wickström
War of Songs
Popular Music and Recent Russia-Ukraine Relations
With a foreword by Artemy Troitsky
ISBN 978-3-8382-1173-2

204 Maria Lipman (ed.)
Russian Voices on Post-Crimea Russia
An Almanac of *Counterpoint* Essays from 2015–2018
ISBN 978-3-8382-1251-7

Contents

Maria Lipman
Introduction 7

Kirill Rogov
"Crimean Syndrome" 15

Nikolay Petrov
Crimea: Turning the Ukrainian Peninsula into a Russian Island 41

Ella Paneyakh
Evolution of the Russian Judicial System in 2014 65

Andrey Soldatov
The Taming of the Internet 87

Natalya Zubarevich
The Relationship Between the Center and the Regions: What Has Changed in Four Years? 107

Sergey Sergeyev
The Republic of Tatarstan: Reducing to the Lowest Common Denominator? 127

Tatyana Nefedova
Who Will Feed the Russian Population? 145

Alexander Verkhovsky
Nationalism as the Foundation for Mobilization 181

Andrei Desnitsky
The Russian Orthodox Church and Nationalism 193

Svetlana Solodovnik
Orthodox People Between the Social Church and "Strict Hierarchy" 215

Sergei Parkhomenko
Case of Dissernet: The Volunteer Network Community's Experience of Survival in an Aggressive Political Environment 237

Maria Eismont
Territory Free from the State 263

Alexander Gorbachev
Narrative Journalism in Russia: A Tentative History 285

Yulia Bederova
The Art of Complexity Surrenders to the Government of
Simplicity 299

Alexander Gorbachev
"Russia, Don't Tear Your Soul to Pieces: I'm the Same as You" 319

Introduction

Maria Lipman

This volume is a selection of articles by Russian authors that appeared in *Kontrapunkt/Counterpoint*, a Russian-language journal about Russian politics and society published by the Institute for European, Russian and Eurasian Studies at the George Washington University.

Counterpoint was a short-lived project, published for just three years, but the timing — 2015 to 2018 — was opportune for a journal covering Russian socio-political developments: the 2014 decision to cut off the Crimean peninsula from Ukraine and incorporate it into the Russian Federation is arguably the most radical move that has been made by Vladimir Putin during his two decades in power.

The annexation of Crimea became a turning point, and the changes that followed affected nearly all spheres of Russian life. In foreign policy, Russia shifted to a deepening confrontation with the West; the economy slowed down dramatically and entered what increasingly looked like a chronic stagnation; domestically, the Kremlin initiated a crackdown on rights and freedoms; and political rhetoric and television propaganda, especially in the early "post-Crimea" period, created in Russia the atmosphere of a fortress under siege, in which rallying around the commander was a matter not just of loyalty, but of national security and even national identity. The modernization rhetoric that had marked the period of "tandem" rule from 2008 to 2012, when Dmitry Medvedev held the office of Russian president and Putin that of prime minister, was abandoned and gave way to an anti-modernization course in politics and state-society relations in terms of the language, ideas, and symbols used by the state.

The post-Crimean evolution was somewhat paradoxical: the Kremlin was as anxious as ever to preserve the political status quo — that is, its unchallenged dominance over all political and societal forces — but in pursuit of this goal, the government initiated ongoing change in other spheres. The combination of the trend toward repression, the shift to conservatism, and the emphasis on "ideology" added up to an inexorable drift from the soft authoritarianism of the 2000s to a hardened and increasingly repressive authoritarianism in the 2010s.

The initial impact of the annexation of Crimea on the mindset of the Russian people was described by **Kirill Rogov** as "Crimean Syndrome" (his Counterpoint article of the same title opens this volume). That Crimea was now part of Russia was seen by the overwhelming majority of Russians as a triumph of historical justice. They felt victorious and proud — and this victory was not one of the glorious past, but one won by today's Russia. Moreover, it was a victory that came at no cost to the people, whether material or in terms of human lives; instead, it was seemingly a gift from Putin to his fellow countrymen. The general mood was upbeat: public concern about corruption went down, while approval of all branches and levels of state power went up; the economic situation in the country and even personal economic well-being were perceived as having improved, even though, in reality, individual incomes almost stopped growing.

The return of Crimea "to the Russian fold" thus helped Putin regain the legitimacy that had eroded when his announced return to the Kremlin caused mass street protests in Moscow and other large urban centers.

Meanwhile, the administrative and institutional (political) incorporation of Crimea in the Russian Federation (thoroughly tracked by **Nikolay Petrov** in the present volume) turned out to be a serious challenge and progressed far from smoothly. These developments, however, were barely covered by the state-controlled national mass media and were, in any case, hardly of interest to a Russian population overcome by "Crimea is ours" euphoria.

This powerful upsurge in positive popular sentiment enabled Putin to consolidate the overwhelming majority of Russians and pit them full force against the evil West, which condemned Russia for the very act that made Russians so joyful and proud. Another enemy was "the West's agents" in Russia — the minorities of excessively modernized and Westernized protesters, liberals, gays, and radical contemporary artists and their fans, as well as those who treated the Russian Orthodox Church without due respect or cast doubt on Russia's impeccable historical record.

The authoritarian shift intensified further when the annexation of Crimea was followed by the war in Donbas. The Duma passed one piece of anti-liberal legislation after another, imposing more and more constraints on civic and especially political activism; on public associations; and on various forms of public expression, including the media.

The judicial system and law-enforcement practices grew more repressive. "Even the few positive trends registered in the post-Soviet development of the Russian judicial system have been discontinued," wrote **Ella Paneyakh** in her *Counterpoint* chapter included in this volume.

Another avenue of government assault was the Internet. It was not until the 2010s that Putin grew seriously concerned about the Web and its potential for autonomous public organization. **Andrey Soldatov** documents the early stages of "taming the Web." The online space for free expression began to shrink in 2014, and the constraints grew increasingly tight in the years that followed.

The Russian regions have been a particular target of the post-Crimea crackdown. The regions' power had been substantially reduced almost as soon as Putin became president in 2000. In 2004 he cancelled gubernatorial elections and switched to appointing regional leaders. Gubernatorial elections were nominally reinstated in 2012, but in a way that enabled the Kremlin to hand-pick the winner. The Putin administration can easily replace a governor with somebody better suited to the Kremlin's interests; often, management of a region is entrusted to an "outsider" unencumbered by any local ties. This way, the Kremlin ensures that a formally elected governor does not depend on his constituents to keep him in power, but instead remains at the beck and call of the Kremlin.

Although Russia technically remains a federation, in recent years federalism has been radically curtailed, including by economic means, as detailed by **Natalia Zubarevich** and **Tatyana Nefedova**. "Regions serve as a source of income for the federal center," writes Zubarevich, "which not only reduces the economic assistance to the regions, but also appropriates their extra revenues." Nefedova draws a similar conclusion looking at predominantly rural regions: "The center's policy strips regions and municipal districts of their financial discretionary power." **Sergey Sergeyev** looks at Tatarstan, which used to enjoy a special status within Russia, but was stripped of its autonomy in the post-Crimea period.

Another consequence of the annexation of Crimea was the government's strengthened focus on nation-building that had not been among the Kremlin's major concerns until Putin was about to embark on his third presidential term. The reconsolidation of Putin's legitimacy after Crimea gave the nation-building effort a new boost. The Kremlin sought to respond to the unsatisfied public demand for a clearer sense of post-Soviet national identity—who are we, today's Russians; whither Russia; and what is Russia's stature in the world? The Kremlin's "supply" amounted to *derzhavny*, or great-state nationalism that included an emphasis on Russia's greatness and a demonstration of "sovereignty" as the right of the powerful, complete with quasi-traditionalism and an aggressively anti-Western and anti-liberal stance. For a few years, the public demand appeared to be satisfied. As **Alexander Verkhovsky** explains, the government's powerful emphasis on great-state nationalism superseded, as it were, the radical (ethnic) nationalist cause and helped marginalize radical nationalist groups that had been on the rise in previous years. **Andrei Desnitsky**, writing about the Russian Orthodox Church and nationalism, points out that the conflict around Crimea and Donbas became a hard trial for the Russian Orthodox Church, as its believers were sharply divided over the bloody armed conflict in Ukraine. Since Crimea's incorporation into Russia, Patriarch Kirill has been unable to travel to Ukraine, which has the second-highest concentration of Orthodox Christians behind Russia.

Probably encouraged by the state's strengthened interest in ideological issues, the Church has intensified its role as an ideological entrepreneur—in particular, in late 2014 it published a "Declaration of Russian Identity." Meanwhile, the state itself avoids clear-cut definitions of national identity, remains intentionally vague on potentially divisive issues such as national heroes or national holidays (on which the Russian communists, for instance, differ radically from the Russian Orthodox Church), and does not offer clearly articulated narratives of many crucial episodes of Russian history. The Kremlin celebrates the eternal sovereignty of the Russian state while remaining elusive on the question of the origins of current Russian statehood.

The turn toward quasi-traditionalism has inevitably led to state interference with art and culture. More or less direct censorship has become common, the formal constitutional ban on censorship notwithstanding. And since budgetary allocations remain a major source of funding for most kinds of arts, the state can use its economic influence to exercise discretion in the art sphere and decide what is or is not worth producing.

"The government is pointedly indifferent to complex art forms that are not intended for mass consumption," writes **Yulia Bederova** in her review of musical culture in today's Russia. The Ministry of Culture, which has greatly expanded its power in recent years, "proclaims that its goal is moral education by means of classical art forms," while contemporary artists are not infrequently seen as "alien" to Russian "traditional values." Artists may be forced to adjust their creative activities to the state's interests, but since, as was mentioned above, the government's "ideological" stance is blurred and a single ideational authority is absent, there is still space for diversity and free expression in arts and culture.

Alexander Gorbachev introduces the reader to Russian rap. "Traditional values" rhetoric does not seem to be posing an impediment to this genre, which was in full bloom in the mid-2010s, making it "practically the liveliest musical environment in Russia."

The post-Crimea hardening of the political course has changed the public atmosphere substantially. The government has increasingly demonstrated zero tolerance toward any form of autonomous political activism. Harder punishments and intimidation of activists, as well as assassination of their characters on state-controlled television, serve as a warning to anyone who might consider engaging in oppositionist activities. The government reminds the public — by various means, but increasingly by use of force — that such activism is not only dangerous, but also pointless. Quite a few niche liberal media that had historically gotten away with editorial independence fell under government pressure after the mass protests of 2011-12. The government crackdown was greatly facilitated by the fact that most media assets had already been redistributed to loyal owners, so the Kremlin could rely on them to replace the excessively audacious editors and temper the editorial line. This technique was deployed toward quite a number of publications, and by 2017, when *Counterpoint* covered this topic, the space for non-government media had visibly shrunk.

All the same, the experience with free expression (of various degrees) that citizens and organizations, including media ones, accumulated in the post-communist period and that grew especially visible at the turn of 2010s has not been wasted. Of course, the social climate has grown inauspicious, and activists, civic projects, and media outlets operate at the Kremlin's discretion, but the Kremlin still demonstrates relative permissiveness toward those, whose activism is not oppositionist and does not directly challenge the regime. The government remains reasonably soft on people at large, mostly leaving them to their own pursuits.

In this environment, civic initiatives — charitable, educational, self-help, environmental, human rights, and others — have become more numerous, as well as better organized, more skilled, and more determined. Some of the most important nongovernmental organizations, such as the Memorial Society and a few others, which have been under pressure since the early 2010s, have survived and continued their operations. And though many nongovernmental media outlets have come under pressure, high-quality reportage and even investigative reporting have not disappeared from the Russian media scene. **Sergey Parkhomenko** describes the inauspicious and often dicey environment in which nongovernmental organizations are operating in Russia and shares his own experience with Dissernet, an organization that has exposed, and waged a public campaign against an "industry of falsified dissertations" complete with its own large production centers and small artisanal workshops, as well as an elaborate infrastructure of market research and promotional services.

Svetlana Solodovnik writes about charitable projects in the Orthodox community that not only have a humanizing effect on society, but also help Orthodox citizens to gain self-confidence and defend their position even in unfavorable circumstances. **Maria Eismont's** contribution, "Territory Free from the State," is devoted to those local media that still care about editorial independence. One of them is 7x7, an online media project launched in Syktyvkar (Komi Republic) in 2010. The title of Eismont's chapter alludes to 7x7's motto, which is posted on its website. A recently established private media award, *Redkollegia* granted monthly to two or three journalists, aims to support those "who still pursue high professional standards in Russia at the time when free and high-quality journalism finds itself under government pressure." And as **Alexander Gorbachev** points out in his piece about the rise of narrative journalism in Russia, while independent media can hardly expect to have an effect on the government's policies, it can still bring significant information to the attention of the public—to "hook" its audience.

***

The last issue of *Counterpoint* was published in the summer of 2018. Putin had just started his fourth term after a very successful re-election. His power seemed unassailable, his support not only high, but also evenly distributed across Russia's vast expanse—even among the more critically-minded constituencies of the large urban centers.

In the fall, however, the picture began to look somewhat different. The pension reform, which raised the retirement age, left people strongly disaffected. Putin's approval rating dropped from an amazing level of over 80 percent to under 70. The regional elections, held in September that year, demonstrated that the government electoral machine, which had previously been effective in delivering victories to the Kremlin's hand-picked candidates, was not infallible, with non-government candidates claiming victory in several regions. The system began to look somewhat fragile and vulnerable.

Although the Kremlin and Putin remained dominant, this new vulnerability looked likely to push the government toward a still harder crackdown. Such a scenario was easy to imagine since Putin's repressive policies—against political activists, but also against elites (an increasing number of high-ranking office-holders, governors, mayors and others were prosecuted and found themselves behind bars)—tremendously empowered law-enforcement and security agencies.

On the other hand, grassroots social modernization, though slow and timid, is impossible to deny. The Russian people are developing social skills and demonstrating an ability to organize around a wide variety of nonpolitical causes. They not infrequently stand up for their socioeconomic rights, and occasionally even force the government to give in.

The interaction of these two trends—the increasingly repressive and somewhat insecure government and the somewhat more independent and disaffected people—will be one of the most important developments in the near future. Will the Kremlin be able to maintain the political status quo, and if so, at what cost? Will the fear of destabilization prevail in public perceptions? Or will disaffection and demands for social justice supersede habitual acquiescence? Another issue of paramount importance is how the political system would prepare for and navigate the transition that looms in 2024, when Putin's fourth term expires.

Unfortunately, *Counterpoint* is no longer around to cover these developments. But thanks to Ibidem Verlag, we have the opportunity to publish a collection of our authors' research and analysis. We hope this book will provide food for thought for those who are interested in Russian politics and society, and maybe shed some light on developments in our complicated and not infrequently impenetrable country.

We are very grateful to Ibidem Verlag for this opportunity and to IERES at GWU for sponsoring the production of *Counterpoint,* as well as the publication of this collection. Our very special thanks go to our IERES colleagues for their interest in and attention to our work—and simply for their friendship, which we value very highly.

"Crimean Syndrome"[1]

Kirill Rogov

The events of 2014—the annexation of Crimea, the sponsorship of the war in Eastern Ukraine, the radicalization of the Kremlin, and Russia's confrontation with the West—surprised most observers. No less shocking was the wave of popular support for the new radical politics. The phenomenon of patriotic mobilization (which in Russia received the name "krymnashism" [literally, "Crimea-is-ours-ism"—Trans.]) was all the more surprising since the beginning of the 2010s saw the weakening of support for the Putin regime, and a growing demand for democracy, which had been expressed in mass protests throughout 2012. During 2012-13, the efforts of the Putin administration to strengthen the institutions of authoritarian and repressive rule did not change the lack of support for the regime (Figure 1).[2]

---

1   K. Rogov's Counterpoint article: "Crimean Syndrome. Mechanisms of Authoritarian Mobilization" first appeared in English translation in Russian Politics and Law, Vol. 54, 2016, Issue 1. We thank Russian Politics and Law for the permission to reproduce their translation in this collection.
2   All the sociological data presented in this article are based on intervals between polls and conducted by the Levada Center (before 2008 by VTsIOM [All-Russia Public Opinion Research Center]). Data was obtained from the Levada Center Internet site (www.levada.ru), from the Levada Center archives, and from the Unified Sociological Data Archive (www.sophist.hse.ru). For technical reasons, both weighted and unweighted data were used – the difference does not exceed 1.5 percentage points. I express my deep gratitude to Arina Borodina, Lev Gudkov, and Karina Pipia for their invaluable assistance.

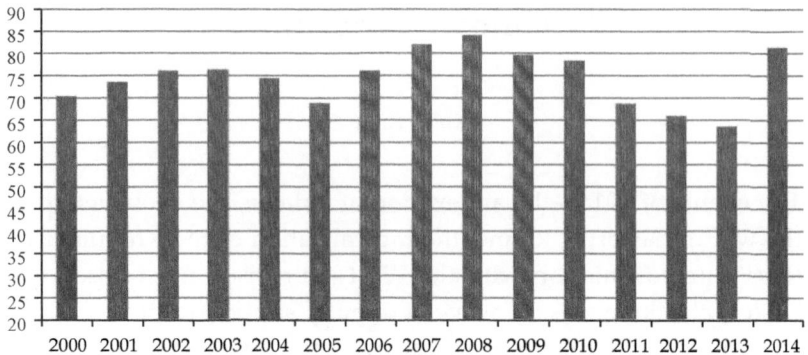

Figure 1. Average Approval of Putin as President and Prime Minister (%)

Thus, the about-face of public opinion after the annexation of Crimea seems all the more strange.

While the mechanisms of political mobilization under an authoritarian regime are the main focus of the present analysis, we are not suggesting that the "Crimean syndrome" can be easily explained by the influence of propaganda. On the contrary, the syndrome is a complex phenomenon that must be considered from a number of different viewpoints.

In very general terms, the Crimean–Ukrainian crisis as well as its precursor, the "small" 2011–12 crisis, can be seen in the context of Russia's transition from post-Soviet to post-Soviet legitimacy. After a painful transition and the formation of new governments, most post-Soviet countries (not including those under European influence) experienced in the 2000s a period of intensive recovery, accompanied by the consolidation of political regimes — between 2000 and 2008, the average annual growth rate for twelve post-Soviet countries was 8.3 percent. The quick economic growth legitimized these regimes, and allowed people to see past the systems' serious internal problems.

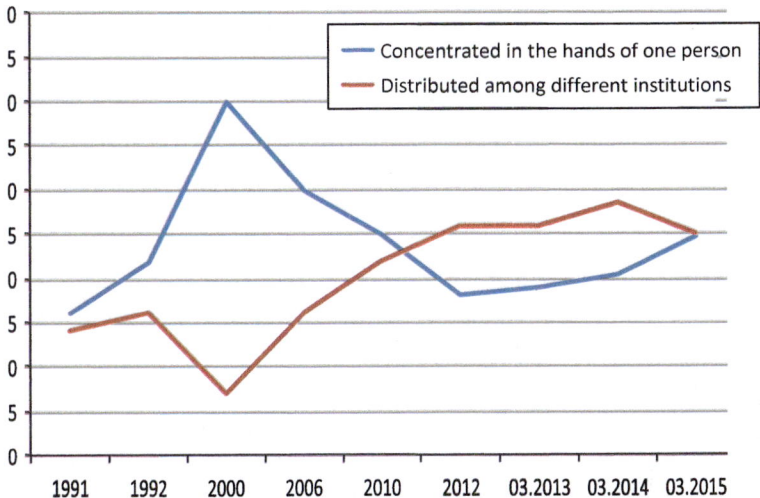

Figure 2. Distribution of Answers to the Question: "Should Power Be Concentrated in the Hands of One Person or Distributed Among Different Institutions That Would Check One Another?"

The 2008–9 crisis marked the end of this period, and raised the question of the future development of a number of post-Soviet states, where authoritarian regimes had up to that point for various reasons not become fully consolidated (e.g. Ukraine, Moldova, Russia, and Armenia).

Here we are principally interested in two aspects of public opinion and the direction of the national debate in the early 2010s.

First, the authoritarian consensus of the 2000s was eroding, that is, there was a significant decline in support for the centralized model of government, strongly associated with Vladimir Putin (see Figure 2).[3] The 2008–9 crisis undermined the positive association of centralized power and the economic prosperity of the 2000s. As a result, the long-term effectiveness of the regime was challenged and the demand for an alternative began to increase.

It should be noted that the available data do not indicate a dominant demand for democratization in the early 2010s, but rather

---

3 For more detail, see K.Y. Rogov, "Politicheskie tsikly postsovetskogo tranzita," Pro et Contra, 2012, no. 4–5, p. 56.

the collapse of the pro-authoritarian majority, which had been found in surveys since the beginning of the 2000s. Pro-Western support rose to 33–38 percent, while support for the centralized model fell from 45–60 percent in the mid-2000s to 30–40 percent, and the proportion of the model's opponents grew to 40–45 percent. The share of those who considered it necessary to strengthen the accountability of government, that is, to increase control from the bottom up, also increased from 40 percent to 60 percent.

The second major trend of this period is directly related to the search for a new, post–post-Soviet identity and the search for renewed legitimacy on the part of post–post-Soviet regimes. Thus, by the late 2000s and early 2010s, a kind of competition among "nationalisms" had emerged. The three main kinds of nationalism are the fundamentalist ethnic nationalism ("Russia for Russians") resulting from growing immigration problems and subsequent xenophobia in the period of rapid economic growth, the democratic nationalism of the new opposition (represented by Alexei Navalny), and finally the anti-Westernism and statist nationalism (often called imperial), which proved to be a powerful driver of the Crimean syndrome.

Despite the growing body of work regarding this subject, a systematic analysis of these trends as they relate to the Crimean-Ukrainian conflict is still needed.[4] First, the imperial (Crimea), ethnic (Russians in Ukraine), and anti-Western implications of Putin's new policy were his response to the democratic nationalism of the Maidan, as well as to the democratic nationalism of the 2011–12 protests in Russia. Meanwhile, the success of Putin and Russian propaganda in reframing the nationalism of Maidan as radically ethnic rather than democratic, created a discussion in the Russian opposition around Navalny's nationalism and the possibility of an

---

[4] See E.A. Pain, "Ksenofobia i natsionalizm v epokhu rossiiskogo bezvremen'ia," Pro et Contra, 2014, vol. 18, no. 1–2; B.V. Dubin, "'Chuzhie' natsionalizmy i 'svoi' ksenofobii vcherashnikh i segodiashnikh rossiyan," Pro et Contra, 2014, vol. 18, no. 1–2; M. Laruelle, "Alexei Navalny and Challenges in Reconciling 'Nationalism' and 'Liberalism,'" Post-Soviet Affairs, 2014, vol. 30, no. 4, pp. 276–97.

alliance of liberals and nationalists in the struggle for democratizing the regime.

The second crucial piece of the Crimean syndrome puzzle, which is sometimes neglected, is the economic factor. As already mentioned, the crisis of the authoritarian consensus was largely caused by doubts concerning the regime's ability to deliver lasting economic progress.[5] It should be said that these doubts had already been expressed by the elite circa 2010. Many argued that the prosperity of the 2000s had nothing to do with the particularities of the political system, but was the result of high oil prices. When then-president Dmitry Medvedev called for modernization, he had outlined the contours of an alternative political agenda, one that would compete with hierarchical control and concentration of power as preconditions for economic prosperity.

However, after oil prices dropped sharply in 2008–9, they began to rise in 2011 and the maximalist status quo was reestablished. As a result, Russia experienced its biggest oil boom in history. In general, from 2010 to 2014 export revenues amounted to $2.46 trillion, which exceeded the 2004–8 oil boom by a factor of 1.6.[6] However, the response of the economy to the inflow of petrodollars in the second phase of the oil boom was significantly different from its response in the first phase: capital outflows increased, investment activity decreased, and economic growth slowed. At the same time, against the backdrop of fading growth, government spending dramatically increased. Average consolidated budget expenditures increased from 31.7 percent in the first half of the oil boom to 37.6 percent during 2010–14. The flow of resources from the market sector to the nonmarket sector was reflected in income dynamics: social benefits grew by one and a half, while the share of market revenues declined sharply. In addition, as average wage growth slowed to an annual average of 5.7 percent, public sector wage growth (from 2011 to 2013) increased at an annual average of 10.3 percent.

---

5   D. Treisman, "Putin's Popularity: Why Did Support for the Kremlin Plunge, Then Stabilize?" Post-Soviet Affairs, 2014, vol. 30, no. 5.
6   Balance of payments data (www.cbr.ru/statistics).

Not only did the public sector expand, but so did the quasi-market sector, which included old government monopolies, government-owned banks, the newly created government corporations and oil companies, as well as large-scale infrastructure projects. During this period, redistributive networks — both formal (budgetary) and quasi-market and informal — played a larger role in the distribution of wealth than the stagnating market. The relationship between growth in public wellbeing and the market was weakened. The situation undermined the economic arguments of those who forecast the postcrisis wave of "retribution" for the rentier nature of Russia's economic growth; on the other hand, the situation normalized the idea of high capital inflows, and the key role of the government in the process of consolidation and redistribution of rents.

The new socioeconomic model created a new coalition of beneficiaries that were distributed across social strata (e.g., government employees, law enforcement, state corporation employees, the defense sector, holders of administrative rent, and other government-favored businesses). This diverse "rentier party," which consisted of those who beginning in the early 2010s began to reap significant rewards thanks to the expansion of redistribution, sympathized with Putin's doctrine of "resource sovereignty," which they understood as a specific form of public-oriented economic development, which also happened to have a pro-authoritarian and anti-West component. For this party, the annexation of Crimea marked a final break with the critics of the Russian economic model, and those who called for the modernization (Westernization) of the social order, for reduction of the government's role in the economy and its centralization of politics.[7]

Finally, the third focus of our analysis of Crimean syndrome is tied to the mechanisms of political mobilization under an authoritarian regime. Of course, the strengthening of the rentier and quasi-market socioeconomic system created the perfect conditions

---

7   K.Iu. Rogov, "Resursnyi natsionalizm: Politekonomiia reaktsii," Vedomosti, October 8, 2014 (www.vedomosti.ru/opinion/articles/2014/10/15/ resursnyj-nacionalizm-ot-yukosa-do-kryma).

for supporting "resource nationalism." However, the seeming universal extent of this support and the consolidation of the popular majority around a conservative, isolationist position would be impossible without specific institutional conditions that allowed the regime to falsify, if not the fact of support, then its scale.

March of the Loyalists: The Sociology of the Crimean Syndrome

Sociologically, the real peculiarity of Crimean syndrome lies not in the popular support of Putin and his policy toward Ukraine and the West, but in the abrupt shift of public opinion that occurred in March 2014. Russians not only stood behind Putin, but changed their thinking regarding a wide range of issues, including the best model of governance and its direction of development, perception of the West, and the problem of corruption. For instance, the proportion of people who thought the level of corruption in the country was increasing had held for several years at an average of 50 percent, but then quickly dropped to 30 percent. Conversely, all branches of the government saw their approval ratings significantly improve. Moreover, what is perhaps most striking, following the annexation of Crimea and the beginning of the war in eastern Ukraine, people dramatically increased not only their overall assessment of the situation in the country but also their assessment of the economy, and even their own personal financial situation. This is all the more striking since the first and second quarters of 2014 saw gross domestic product growth shrink, and income growth decline to near zero; for the economy, these were the two worst quarters of the past three years.

Most commonly, this shift is attributed to political mobilization, the "rally around the flag effect," or simply, the effect of propaganda. However, the runaway success of the propaganda machine seems surprising, given the relative openness of the Russian information sphere, and raises the question of society's willingness to accept the Kremlin's conservative and revanchist doctrine and to perceive it as organic and natural. In his detailed analysis of public sentiment in 2014, L. Gudkov describes the state of public opinion as "resentful nationalism," whose roots lie in the "paternalistic double think of post-totalitarian consciousness."[8] According to this perspective, the propaganda campaign merely consolidated the already latent conservatism that dominated social attitudes and structures.

Although sound, this position appeals to the deep structures of social consciousness, and implicitly ignores the medium-term trends observed in previous years by considering these trends as "ripples in the water." The approach seeks to understand the present through the prism of the past and glosses over current shifts in public opinion, which are likely indicative of future events. Thus, we propose, by contrast, to concentrate on the transition from the state of public opinion that was typical for the beginning of the 2010s to the new pro-authoritarian, conservative consensus. We will try to understand not only why today's public seems so conservative but also how a rather complex, multifaceted field of public opinion (observed in the early 2010s) transitioned into a nearly monolithic field of total unanimity in 2014–15.

On the one hand, our analysis is technical: we are interested in how an authoritarian regime with its distorted political menu implements the mechanisms of mobilization and what effect this has on public opinion, how a picture of overwhelming support emerges. On the other hand, our hypotheses raise the broader question of how we are to understand and interpret sociological data that are gathered within an authoritarian regime and under growing authoritarian pressure. Do surveys conducted within a democracy and an authoritarian regime represent the same object of inquiry? Should they be analyzed using the same interpretive tools?

Authoritarian Mobilization: The Role of Involvement

The rally 'round the flag effect was initially used to describe certain trends in U.S. political history. According to the general concept,

---

8   L.D. Gudkov, "Ressentimentnyi natsionalizm," *Vestnik obshestvennogo mneniia*, 2014, vol. 118, no. 3–4.

the effect usually occurs in the event of an external threat to the nation (international crisis) that is recognized as such by the majority of elite groups.[9] The condition of elite consensus is considered very important, but it is clear that under an authoritarian regime an elite consensus is fictitious: the formation of a unilateral flow of information is achieved through control of major media outlets and the reduction of discussion among the elite. Also, the model can be applied not only to foreign policy crises. Crises are marked by an increase in the flow of one-sided information accepted by the public, as well as a decrease in tolerance for alternative points of view and the repression of those who espouse such views.

Let us first consider the effect of an increased flow of one-sided information. There is no doubt that in 2014–15 Russian society faced a large-scale propaganda machine. Arina Borodina, an authority on Russian television, described the situation as follows:

> Beginning in February up to the present [July 2014 — K.R.] the vast majority of daily news programs and talk shows of the three main federal television channels were devoted exclusively to Ukraine. The domestic life of Russia and its citizens virtually disappeared from the television screens.... On average (for three months) the programs Vesti (airing at 8p.m.) and Vremya ran ten stories, each lasting from seven to ten minutes, and all devoted to the single topic of the "Kiev junta" and its "punitive operation."

Instead of the standard twenty- to thirty-minute slots, news programs began to run for an hour, and in some cases even longer. The weekly summary programs Vesti Nedeli (which airs on Russia 1) and Voskresnoe Vremya (Channel One) since March moved to a two-hour program.... For nearly two months, government channels, often without notice, changed their programming grid, shifted around the times of their main entertainment shows, and even excised their most popular TV series.[10]

---

9   W.D. Baker and J.R. O'Neal, "Patriotism or Opinion Leadership? The Nature and Origins of the 'Rally 'Round the Flag' Effect," Journal of Conflict Resolution, 2001, vol. 45, no. 5, pp. 661–87; and M.J. Hetherington and M. Nelson, "Anatomy of a Rally Effect: George W. Bush and the War on Terrorism," Political Science and Politics, 2003, vol. 36, no. 1, pp. 37–42.
10 A. Borodina, "Televizor Olimpiady i Ukrainy: rekordy propagandy," Forbes online, July 3, 2014 (www.forbes.ru/mneniya-opinion/konkurentsiya/261539-televizor-olimpiady-i-ukrainy-rekordy-propagandy).

Borodina concludes that although there was no official declaration of war against Ukraine, the intensity of the information flow was consistent with that of wartime. According to TNS Russia, the share of news audiences (who watched television) increased from 5.8 percent in September 2013– January 2014 to 6.5 percent in February 2014 and 8.4 percent in the period from March to August, that is, the share of people watching the news grew by an average 33 percent.[11]

The growing intensity of the information flow is demonstrated in a monthly survey conducted by the Levada Center about the most memorable events of the past four weeks. By summarizing the events most frequently mentioned by respondents, we can create an index of the main national agenda (the information mainstream). As can be seen in Figure 3, the index (the sum of the ten most mentioned events) significantly changes over time. In 2013, the monthly average was 187 points, while from January 2014 to August 2014 the average amounted to 275 points, that is, the number of reports of the month's ten most memorable events rose by a factor of 1.5. In essence, this means that it was one and a half times easier for respondents to remember and specify the mainstream topics that were fixed in their memory. After a lull in September–December 2014 (for which the monthly average was 225 points) the index again rose to 243 points in the first half of 2015. In general, from January 2014 to June 2015 the average monthly value of the index was 253 points, while in the previous eighteen months (from June 2012 to December 2013) the average was 184 points.

The index captures the efforts of the information machine by showing what impression it left in the minds of respondents.

---

11 S. Sobolev, "TNS zafiksirovala istoricheskii rekord interesa k telenovostiam," RBK, November 20, 2014 (http://top.rbc.ru/technology_and_media/20/11/2014/546dff7bcbb20f48e98df5fa).

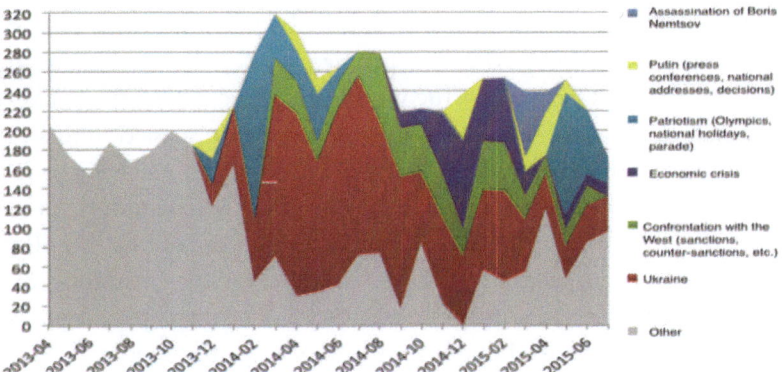

Figure 3. Index of Information Involvement, 2013–2015, and Its Content from December 2014 to July 2015

The list of memorable events was formed by media (primarily television), both before and after the Crimean–Ukrainian crisis, but in the post-Crimean period the degree of the penetration of the agenda is different.

The factor of involvement seems particularly important if, contrary to the standard view, we consider the change of public opinion from the standpoint of the "skeptical school," which assumes that the majority of citizens have a low level of certainty, consistency, and sustainability when it comes to political views and preferences.[12] In this case, change in the balance of preferences depends not only on the nature of elite discourse and debate but also on how accessible the arguments of that discourse are to the general audience. These issues are particularly evident in the context of hybrid and authoritarian regimes with their characteristic lack of multiparty systems and presence of a value dichotomy, which cultivates a culture of political apathy in the average voter.[13]

As shown by John Zaller, the probability and direction of change concerning the public's relationship with various promises

---

12 See P. Converse, "The Nature of Belief Systems in Mass Publics," in Ideology and Discontent, ed. D. Apter (New York: Free Press, 1964); J. Zaller. The Nature and Origins of Mass Opinion. (Cambridge: Cambridge University Press, 1992).
13 See Gudkov, "Ressentimentnyi nationalizm."13. J. Zaller, Nature and Origins of Mass Opinion.

and arguments from elite discourse are closely correlated with the respondents' levels of awareness. While the least-informed citizens are simply not interested in the political cycle, and as a result are indifferent to elite promises, the well-informed cohort is more likely to resist them; as a result, average and poorly informed voters are more willing to absorb the few arguments that do reach them (according to Zaller's "Receive–Accept–Sample" (RAS) model). As has been repeatedly emphasized, despite the focus of the skeptical school on the importance of elite discourse for the formation of a balance of preferences, it does not mean that citizens play a purely passive role in the exchange. In a democracy, the media reflect a diversity of views and arguments, and though the intensity of certain information flows will affect the distribution of preferences, the citizens (the recipients) also have their own active role in this process, and are capable of influencing the nature of elite discourse.[14]

In the context of an authoritarian regime, which controls the main sources of mass media and manipulates the agenda, the citizens do not receive a complete picture of elite discourse and must respond to a one-way information flow. But this does not mean that public opinion is completely manipulated. As we have seen, control of the mainstream media could not prevent a decline in support for the regime in the early 2010s. And even the sharp tightening of controls and the intensification of propaganda in 2013 did not lead to positive changes in ratings (see Figure 1 [above] and Figure 6 [later in the article]).

The Authoritarian Menu and the Right to Indifference

The dynamics of the information involvement index allows us to formulate a key hypothesis. In the context of an authoritarian regime, the reaction of the voters to the inadequate, one-sided information cycle is evident in their dissatisfaction, growing alienation, loss of interest in the information mainstream, and atrophy of political interests; and as a result, the level of indoctrination of the citizenry also diminishes.

---

14 Ibid.

It can be assumed that the decline of support for the regime in 2011–13 correlated with a decrease in median voter attention to the information mainstream, when the regime's reasoning and doctrines were promoted via television. The one-way flow of information did not reach an adequate number of recipients to form a sufficiently broad base of stable loyalists. The propaganda failed. In a competitive field, respondents (citizens) make a choice between competing interpretations A and B, and in a noncompetitive system, they make a choice between A and 0, where zero represents opting out of the information sphere and sociopolitical debate. At times, certain events that directly affect the interests of the citizens can bring them back to the mainstream agenda or get them to search for alternative interpretations outside mainstream sources. (The traditional, normative approach requires the layperson to be more conscious and aware of their preferences, but from the standpoint of skeptical realism, in a normal situation, the preferences of the average citizen are the reflection of elite discourse—alternative cycles and interpretations are possible only in a crisis situation, when for one reason or another trust in the mainstream agenda has been radically undermined.)

During 2012–13, Putin's mainstream expansion of the threats of pedophilia and homosexuality to traditional values and the church had a very limited effect, and could not stop the erosion of the television majority. But the new topics of Crimean annexation and the war waged by Ukrainian nationalists against the Russian population of eastern Ukraine brought a poorly informed contingent of citizens back into the political audience—people who had previously distanced themselves from politics and felt incapable of orienting themselves in the information cycle were again paying attention. These topics also brought back to television the average informed contingent of citizens, who had years ago lost interest in official news and had been under the influence of alternative information cycles, especially those of the Snow Revolution.[15]

In other words, the hypothesis is that in the context of a one-sided flow of information, the loyalty of citizens will be directly

---

15 This refers to the mass protests of 2011-12 (Editor's note).

linked to an authoritarian regime's ability to keep their attention on the menu items of the mainstream (the controlled information agenda) — to put it bluntly, its ability to keep the audience at the television screens. The weakening interest of the citizens in this menu will result in a decline of support for the regime. Conversely, a return to the screens will mean not only growing support for certain topical issues but also a resurgence of loyalty and an increase in the general level of indoctrination.

The sharp change in the political audience and growing number of people involved in the political agenda is demonstrated by the dynamics of the index of involvement. The return to television stimulated the level of overall loyalty: the influence of television on people's worldviews, which had declined in the previous period, rose again, which is reflected in the current aggregate of preferences. Incapable of making informed decisions concerning competing sides of the national agenda, the citizens of an authoritarian regime choose between paying attention to the official information flow and ignoring it.

Unfortunately, the Levada Center began asking the question regarding memorable events only in mid-2012. The available data suggest a correlation between growing loyalty and the index of involvement for 2014–15, but they do not allow us to test the hypothesis concerning the inverse effect, when declining interest in the information cycle should lead to a decline in the level of loyalty for the years 2011–12. The hypothesis could be corroborated by the measurement of changes in the level of interest in politics. The available data on this account do not contradict the hypothesis, but they are rather fragmented (Figure 4). However, what is interesting in these data is not so much growing political interest in the post-Crimean period, and that in previous years the level of interest in politics was gradually declining, especially among those who approved of Putin, but in 2014 those who approved of Putin became more interested in politics and increased the sample average (Figure 5).

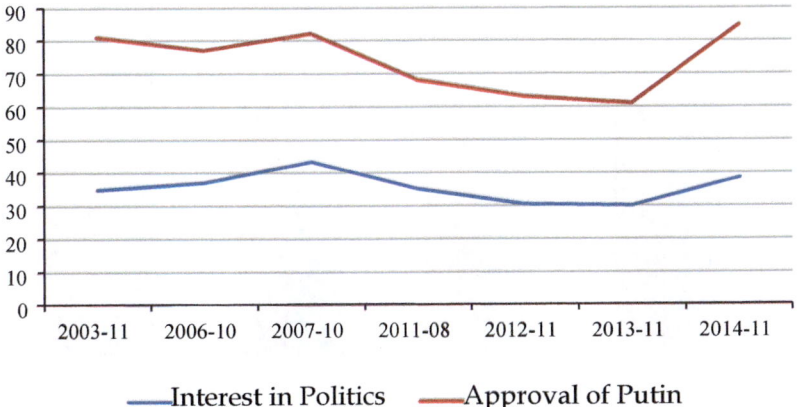

Figure 4. The Proportion of Respondents Who Reported an Interest in Politics, and the Proportion of Respondents Who Approved of Vladimir Putin As President and Prime Minister

A more reliable indicator of the relationship between awareness and loyalty is indicated by the prompt: "Name five to six politicians that you trust most of all." Figure 6 shows (1) the proportion of respondents who mentioned Putin in their answer, (2) the proportion of respondents who did not name a single politician (answers included: "There are none," "not interested in politics," and "difficult to answer"), and (3) the aggregate proportion of those who mentioned four politicians who follow Vladimir Putin in popularity. During 2010–13, the composition of the four remained unchanged: Dmitry Medvedev, Sergei Shoigu, Vladimir Zhirinovsky, and Gennady Zyuganov, but in 2014–15 the list included foreign minister Sergey Lavrov, who throughout the Crimean–Ukrainian crisis has been a vocally anti-western.

These numbers allow us to see the whole period, including both the phase of falling support for the regime (2011–13) and its recovery (2014–15). All three indicators are closely linked:

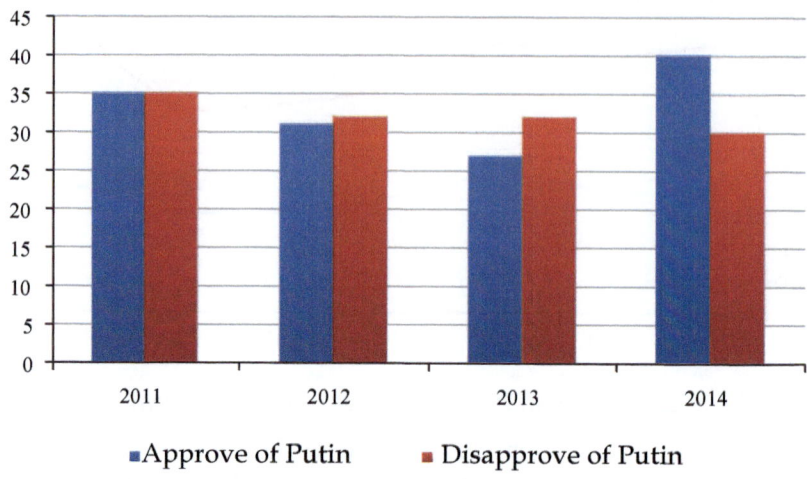

Figure 5. Cross-Test: Level of Interest in Politics Among Those Approving and Disapproving of Putin During 2011–2014

a decrease of confidence in Putin from 48 percent in 2010 to 40 percent in 2011–12 and 35 percent in 2013 correlates with an increase in the share of those who refused to provide any names (38 percent in 2010, 41 percent in 2011–12, and 45 percent in 013), and a decrease in the proportion of those who mention the next four politicians (from 74 percent in 2010 to 54 percent in 2013), and vice versa — an increase of confidence in Putin correlates with a decrease in the proportion of those who provide no names and growth in the proportion of those who mention the other four.

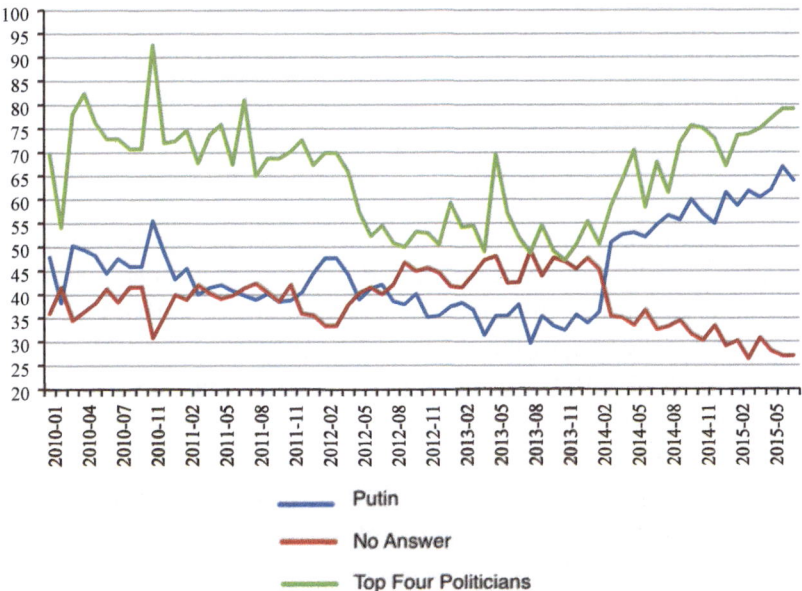

Figure 6. Dynamics of Trust in Politicians, 2010–2015

The latter relationship is not trivial. In a competitive environment, we would expect that the decline of one politician would be accompanied by growing interest in others. In a noncompetitive environment we see the opposite: reduction of confidence in the leader correlates with a general increase in indifference, manifested in the refusal to name any politicians and decreasing attention to other prominent individuals represented in the information cycle.

The Decisive Battle Between War and Neutrality

Thus, the skeptical view suggests that, aside from well-informed party groups, the majority of voters do not have stable well-defined, or consistent preferences; the main task of an authoritarian regime is to "hook" its citizens, or more precisely to keep them in front of the television in order to create and maintain a set of stereotypes and arguments that are amicable to the regime. The level of loyalty to official doctrine is more or less proportional to the amount of time spent in front of the television. However, this is difficult to achieve, which imposes limits on the omnipotence of propaganda. Also, propaganda is most effective when it manages to involve the least-informed and previously uninvolved citizens. According to the Zaller model, this is when the effect of indoctrination is highest.

In this case, war is generally an ideal occasion for using information capable of affecting the attitudes of the most apolitical groups. This situation echoes the observations of Barbara Geddes and John Zaller regarding strategies for providing support for different types of authoritarian regimes. Hard-line regimes (which are commonly referred to as totalitarian) create powerful propaganda machines, which aim to reach the least-educated classes, co-opting their support for the most conservative doctrines, while "soft regimes," existing in relatively favorable economic conditions, (e.g., the Brazilian regime of the 1970s) focus instead on gaining support among the medium-educated and middle-informed strata.[16]

In other words, war as a focus of mainstream information is a way to hook (and politically mobilize) those groups that are normally ambivalent about international events and political activity during peacetime. However, the relationship connecting loyalty, education, and involvement is nonlinear, and requires a more detailed analysis. We will confine ourselves here to the observation made above regarding growing political involvement in 2014. If in the pre-Crimean period, the level of interest in politics was positively correlated with the level of education, then in the post-Crimean period the difference in the level of interest in politics between the educated and less educated declined, that is, the effect of involvement was higher among the less educated (Table 1).

During his 2012–13 campaign, one of Alexei Navalny's slogans declared the present as time for "the decisive battle between justice and neutrality." This slogan pointed to the efforts of the opposition to galvanize people who, being presented with an inade-

---

16 B. Geddes and J. Zaller, "Sources of Popular Support for Authoritarian Regimes," American Journal of Political Science, 1989, vol. 33, no. 2, pp. 319–47.

quate and authoritarian menu, disassociated themselves from politics. In 2014, Vladimir Putin and his information machine countered this campaign with their call for a battle "between war and neutrality." The regime used this slogan deftly to win the argument in favor of war.

	Total	Highly educated	Vocational education	Secondary education	Primary Education
Interested in politics (November 2013)	29.3	35.5	28.7	26.7	23.8
Interested in politics (November 2014)	38.5	40.8	39.3	36.9	34.7
Difference	9.2	5.3	10.6	10.2	10.9

Table 1. The Dynamics of Political Engagement and Level of Education, 2013–2014

The Climate of Openness and Its Dynamics

The growth of the index of involvement in 2014–15 suggests that the poorly informed groups, which had previously felt alienated from politics, are now involved, as a result of sympathizing with the Russian separatists in Ukraine. Likewise, the medium-informed groups, which had previously lost interest in the official information of the mainstream have also returned to watching television news. These two circumstances have facilitated the growth of conservative trends and loyalty, which is reflected in the survey data. However, the mechanism of political mobilization is more complicated. When an authoritarian regime involves certain previously uninvolved groups it conversely displaces others.

War is not only the ideal occasion for involving depoliticized citizens but also an ideal occasion for justifying the repression of alternative views. It is particularly effective when formal and informal initiatives of repression are employed in tandem. Within this framework, it does not matter who killed Boris Nemtsov or for what reason. His death occupied a very important place in the information cycle (as shown in Figure 3). The main thing the average person knows about Nemtsov is that he was an opponent of Putin. A similar strategy is used for the promotion of repression: the trial of Svetlana Davydova (mother of seven children) for treason, received considerable media coverage (thanks in part to comments made by Press Secretary, Dmitry Peskov). In a survey of the main events, it was mentioned by 4.5 percent of respondents. The regime's authoritarianism and repression gained new legitimacy in the post-Crimean period. Further restrictions have been placed on the media, while the political opposition and various civil structures have been subjected to increasing pressure.

This phenomenon is often written about by sociologists. Elizabeth Noelle-Neumann described the processes of how aggregate preferences shift under the pressure of what she called the "climate of opinion."[17] Timur Kuran has argued that revolutions often seem like a surprise because of the "falsification of preferences" that are characteristic of most non-free regimes.[18] Some of the novelty of the subject is caused by the peculiarities of today's "nondemocratic continuum": hybrid semi-authoritarian regimes, soft competitive authoritarianism, harsh dictatorships, and so forth. Moreover, a regime's movement on this scale may occur gradually, while sociological data is being gathered. Thus, we tend to consider all the responses to the question "Do you approve of Vladimir Putin?" received between 2001 and 2015, as if they were comparable, ignoring the fact that the political and civil liberties situation, the level of pluralism in the media, and the level of repression have changed dramatically.

In essence, the question is how free are people to express their political preferences both at home and in the context of a sociological poll; in other words, how should we read data obtained from surveys concerning the most sensitive political topics? Significant changes in this area have been documented by sociologists themselves. If in 2003, roughly equal numbers of respondents (near 50 percent) declared that they were interested or not interested in the

---

[17] E. Noelle-Neumann, Obshchestvennoe mnenie: Otkrytie spirali molchaniia (Moscow: Progress-Akademia, Ves' Mir, 1996). [For English see: "The Spiral of Silence: A Theory of Public Opinion," Journal of Communication, vol. 24, no. 2, pp. 43–51.]

[18] T. Kuran, Private Truths, Public Lies (Cambridge, MA: Harvard University Press, 1995).

data of sociological surveys, in 2013–15 the ratio was 30 percent interested and 70 percent not interested.

However, for our purposes here, the most interesting data concern how comfortable people feel about publicly expressing their political preferences, and, in particular, with interviewers. Table 2 combines answers from a number of questions relating to the topic and gives us a glimpse of the climate of openness.

Do you think that people today speak truthfully about how they relate to authority and Vladimir Putin, or do they hide what they are really thinking				
	Feb. 2005	Jan. 2012	Aug. 2013	Jul. 2015
Truthfully	51	43	30	48
Half-truthfully	23	27	33	31
Not truthfully	22	24	31	17
Can you talk freely about the policies pursued by the government?				
	Aug. 2012	Jul. 2013	Aug. 2014	Feb. 201
1. Yes, always, everywhere	29.3	32.8	38.0	38
2. Yes, but with certain restrictions, and not everywhere	34.3	31	27.7	33
3. No, I cannot (I am afraid or feel awkward)	12.9	10.9	5.6	10
4. I do not have the need to express my political beliefs	19.2	21.4	26.1	17
5. It is difficult to answer the question	4.3	3.9	2.5	2
Do you think that people who are critical of the government during a sociological interview will later be persecuted by the authorities?				
	Jun. 2009		Aug. 2014	
Definitely, very likely	22.6		28	
Unlikely	45.7		44.4	
Impossible	20.9		16.8	
It is difficult to answer the question	10.8		10.9	

Table 2. Dynamics of Climate of Openness, 2005-2015

	2009		2015	
	Approve of Putin	Disapprove of Putin	Approve of Putin	Disapprove of Putin
Definitely, very likely	22	24	26	37
Unlikely	46	44	46	36
Impossible	21	22	18	13

Table 3. Cross-Test: Probability of Persecution because of Criticizing the Authorities in a Sociological interview and Approval of Putin

In the early 2010s, there was a dramatic decline in the share of those who believed that people could openly talk about their relationship with Putin and authority. Predictably, those who approved of Putin were also those who most believed in the truthfulness of the responses; however, in 2015 even among these the proportion was only 50 percent. Such a low level of trust in other people's answers indicates discomfort about being open and can be understood as a projection of the respondents' own feelings about the poll. In the 2010s, only 30–40 percent of respondents felt they could speak without restrictions concerning the policies pursued by the government. Finally, nearly a fourth of respondents felt it was very likely that expressing critical views during a sociological interview would lead to persecution by the government. In 2015, even a fourth of Putin supporters thought it was likely the government would persecute those who gave the wrong answers, and among anti-Putin respondents the share was 37 percent (Table 3).

Mobilization and Demobilization: The "Choice" of Public Opinion

These data problematize one of the basic presumptions of sociological research—namely, the assumption that the choice to participate in a survey is politically neutral. Sociological services do not regularly publish data on the response rate, but we know that today the number is quite low for most studies: of those approached by social scientists, no more than 30–35 percent agree to participate.[19] In a neutral environment, such a coefficient has low relevance. However, in the context of increasing authoritarian pressure, the decision to participate in a sociological survey may not be politically neutral and leads to selection bias. In Tables 2 and 3, the data reflect the views of those who agreed to speak with sociologists, and these data cannot disprove the hypothesis that some of the refusals were politically motivated.

Testing the existence and/or extent of politically motivated refusals requires special experiments that have yet to be conducted. (We do not even know how the response rate has changed in the post-Crimean period.) It is important to first formulate the framework of such an experiment, that is, to present the two possible scenarios on either end of the spectrum. Its arithmetic form, as shown in Table 4, is quite transparent. According to the standard model,

---

19 L.D. Gudkov, "Na zerkalo necha peniat', koli rozha kriva," Vestnik obshchestvennogo mnenia, 2012, vol. 11, no. 1.

political motivations do not affect the decision on participation in a public opinion poll. Here we assume that in the post-Crimean period the same proportion of people who agreed and disagreed to participate in the survey has changed their attitude toward Putin in the direction of greater loyalty. On the other hand, what if in the context of a massive information campaign, the denigration of dissent (accusations of being a "fifth column") and evidence of persecution has caused the distribution of participants to be politically selected. Eight out of a hundred people who had previously reported to sociologists their disapproval of Putin now refuse to speak with them. At the same time, eight people who had previously supported Putin, but did not participate in the information mainstream, now find themselves involved and/or suddenly realize the value of their opinions, and as a result, are more willing to respond to surveys. Between these two extremes lie intermediate scenarios in which some of the citizens sincerely change their political preferences, while others opt for silence or, on the contrary, opt to speak out in the context of the changing "climate of opinion."

	Reachability	Before Crimea Approve of Putin 63%	Disapprove of Putin 37%	After Crimea Approve of Putin 85%	Disapprove of Putin 15%	Changed opinion of Putin	Changed opinion regarding participation Among those who approve of Putin	Among those who disapprove of Putin
Politically neutral distribution								
Participated	35	22.05	12.95	29.75	5.25	8	0	0
Refused	65	40.95	24.05	55.25	9.75	14	0	0
Politically biased distribution								
Participated	35			29.75	5.25	0		−8
Refused	65			33.25	31.75	0	+8	

Table 4. Politically Neutral and Politically Biased Decisions to Participate in a Sociological Survey

If the hypothesis of the non-neutrality of the decision to participate in a sociological survey under authoritarian pressure is correct, it clarifies our understanding of the mechanisms of propaganda. The task of propaganda is not so much to convince the audience as to capture the attention and increase the tendency to express their preferences among some cohorts, while removing other cohorts from the political space and silencing other groups (by reducing their willingness to express their preferences). It is this effect that will lead to a rapid and significant shift in the balance of public preferences. And here we are not only talking of the decision to participate or not participate in a sociological survey, but a more general decision to publicly express one's predispositions and preferences, which, in turn, becomes the most important factor in the changing climate of opinion.

We do not want to say that separate from the picture we get from the aggregate preferences resulting from the surveys, there is some other more "real" picture. It is more a question of interpreting the picture presented to us by the surveys: to what extent it reflects the "deep structures" of mass public consciousness, and to what extent it reflects situational mobilization. All three of the above-mentioned concepts—Timur Kuran's falsification of preferences, Elisabeth Noelle-Neumann's spiral of silence, and John Zaller's RAS model—are similar in that they all emphasize the temporal aspect of an individual's response and those factors that act as a filter between a predisposition (Zaller's terminology) and actual answers (externalized preferences), such as the influence of authoritative judgment (elite discourse) or "desirability" (e.g., something understood as a dominant opinion in society, the acceptability of certain morals, and other concerns related to the "wrong answer"). These filters are not something external to public opinion, but on the contrary, as stressed by Noelle-Neumann, are the mechanisms of socialization and sociality, and therefore cannot be regarded as noise.

In this case, the slice of public opinion resembles the situation during elections. As is well-known, election results do not always mirror the picture of the balance of preferences received by sociologists. Voters will shift toward the candidate whose supporters are most mobilized (i.e., believe in the importance of voting). In the same way, public opinion will shift toward those groups that are more likely to externalize their current predispositions, are convinced of their social importance, and willing to express their views publicly, which includes answering the questions of sociologists.

Concluding Remarks: War and Crisis

The above approach does not give a complete understanding of public sentiment, but rather reveals the mechanisms of shifting aggregate preferences and the amplitude of these shifts. Just as the mobilization of the opposition in 2011–12 contributed to the crystallization of democratic demands and the protest movement, Putin's Crimean–Ukrainian campaign in 2014, supported by a substantial propaganda machine, contributed to the crystallization of conservative preferences — convincing certain groups that their predispositions are extremely important for society, while telling others that a specific set of preferences is currently the norm. Thus, the picture of aggregate preferences will depend not on the balance of fixed predispositions, but on which groups feel involved and competent enough to externalize their predispositions. Mobilization does not so much change preferences and predispositions, but rather the composition and "density" of involved citizens.

The conservative mobilization of 2014–15 was the product of a specific environment, particularly related to the dynamics of the socioeconomic process: the scaling up of non-market redistribution of resources and the growth of wellbeing, not related to economic growth. However, this contributed to the ideological consolidation of the "party of rent," the conservatism of which is different from the traditional "adaptive" conservatism of the paternalistic system, and is much more articulate when it comes to formulating its commitment to "limited access" and corporatist principles. This ideological consolidation created a group of "leaders of opinion," and finally formed the "party of Putin." However, this party was not only not a supermajority, it was not even a simple majority. To create the supermajority, it was necessary to create extreme social conditions, to essentially simulate a state of war.

Accordingly, it is possible that in the future a change in public opinion will be related to the process of demobilization of the mobilized groups, and the return of the demobilized. Currently, the Putin regime faces two major challenges: the return to the "peace agenda" and the continuing economic crisis. The return to the peace agenda is likely to show that the conservative wartime consensus was largely imaginary. Figure 2 shows that although supporters of Putin's model of centralization are again in the majority (50 percent vs. 35 percent), this majority is unstable. The manipulative effect of mobilization requires the imposition on the coalition of ever greater conditions (the effect of "resolution of the meeting"). And its presence in the post-Crimean consensus is easy to demonstrate. In this situation, the continuation of the "war" is the preferred solution, but a war needs victories, the price of which is increasingly costly for the regime.

As for the economy, the war and the economic crisis are in a sense antipodes and competitors in terms of their effect on the dynamics of public opinion. Although equally captivating, they generate opposite information flows: the war simplifies the agenda, giving poorly informed groups a sense of expertise and involvement; the economic crisis, on the contrary, makes the poorly educated experience a lack of competence, lowering their confidence in their preferences and predispositions, and making them fall silent. The stress weathered by society, especially its most informed members and a significant portion of its elite, looks very serious, which certainly gives the regime time to consolidate or even expand its current level of authoritarianism and repression. But to predict the dynamics of this stress is quite difficult, as it is difficult to predict the scale of the "hangover" that will affect the public as economic conditions continue to deteriorate. Paradoxically, the current economic crisis will likely be remembered by the majority as the result of Putin's decision to annex Crimea. In the medium term, this association does not promise anything good for Putin. Unless, of course, the price of oil returns to its previous high levels.

Crimea:
Turning the Ukrainian Peninsula into a Russian Island

Nikolay Petrov

A year and a half ago, the Russian Federation grew by two regions and three administrative entities: the Republic of Crimea, the federal city of Sevastopol, and the Crimean Federal District. The country's system of governance—already unwieldy and ineffective owing to its excessive centralization, on the one hand, and its insufficient coordination of the actions of various departments, on the other—faced a completely new and extremely difficult task. Crimea had to be integrated into Russia under unfavorable economic conditions, a problem compounded by the confrontation with Kiev and the imposition of Western sanctions.

The need to integrate the peninsula poses a huge array of diverse challenges for Crimea and Russia: infrastructural, tied to "breaking off" from Ukrainian territory and moving toward increasing self-reliance; economic; socio-cultural; and ethnic. For now—given that even the governance model has not been completely determined—we can only assess the approaches to solving and initial attempts to address these problems. Therefore, in this article we will focus primarily on the transformation of the socio-political space and administrative structures of Crimea in connection with its integration into the Russian Federation.

It appears that for the time being, the residents of Crimea are mostly satisfied with developments on the peninsula. According to an authoritative study by GfK Ukraine[1] conducted at the beginning of 2015, 82 percent of Crimeans fully supported the annexation of

---

1 "Socio-political attitudes of the residents of Crimea: A study conducted by GfK Ukraine for Berta Communications Company with support from the Canada Fund for Local Initiatives for the Free Crimea Project," GfK Ukraine, February 4, 2015, http://www.gfk.com/ua/documents/presentations/gfk_report_free crimea.pdf.

Crimea by Russia, 11 percent partially supported it, and only four percent opposed it. It is also important to note that among the tens of problems that most concerned the residents of Crimea, those connected with the structure of government came in last place: two percent of Crimeans expressed concern about the unsatisfactory work of law-enforcement authorities, three percent about a crisis of government administration and lack of law and order, and five percent about the government's indifference to the problems of ordinary citizens.

Nevertheless, scandals did periodically erupt in Crimea, tied to conflicts either between local elites (most often in Sevastopol) or between federal and local officials, as in Simferopol.

An analysis of Crimea's transformation from "post-Soviet" to "Russian" beginning March 21, 2014, is interesting for a whole host of reasons. First, just as an embryo goes through the fundamental evolutionary processes of its species in its initial development, the course of Crimea's accelerated integration allows us to more fully see and assess the specificities of the entire Russian landscape. Second, that landscape itself is continuing to transform, as the integration of Crimea is changing the Russian regime itself. Its history, as well as the history of the country as a whole, is divided into two periods: before and after Crimea. Third and finally, significant changes are taking place not only in Crimea itself and in "continental Russia," but also in the relationship between them. For Crimea, the essence of this relationship is a transition from the Ukrainian model—external administration in the context of a relatively decentralized government—to the Russian one, where external administration of the peninsula is carried out in the context of greater centralization.

Cadres for Crimea

Significant resources were mobilized for the integration of Crimea. Putin's best crisis manager, Deputy Prime Minister Dmitri Kozak, was picked to supervise the government, riding on the success of his last management project—the Sochi Olympics. The most important part of the work—personnel—was delegated to Oleg

Belaventsev, a Vice Admiral who at one time served in international intelligence and was a confidante of Sergei Shoigu. Having played an important role in the annexation of Crimea (in April 2014, he was awarded the title Hero of Russia by a "private" presidential decree), Belaventsev was appointed as a presidential envoy to the new Crimean Federal District. An FSB personnel officer, Andrei Yegorov, was sent to assist Belaventsev as Chief Federal Inspector for Crimea, and the Deputy Commander of the Black Sea fleet, Counter-Admiral Andrei Shishkin, as Chief Federal Inspector for Sevastopol. The development of the Crimean Federal District is being realized with the secrecy of a special forces operation: already integrated into Russia, and a year and a half after its founding, the district still lacks an official website. This is how the Belavenstev's first deputy and fellow former soldier, Nikolai Vodorezov, described the tasks of the Presidential envoy and delegation in Crimea:

> Oleg Yevgen'evich (Belaventsev) briefly formulated our goals to me like this: we answer for the organization of the whole life of the Republic of Crimea. We're not here as the "eyes of the state," we're not overseers, we're organizers. The president asks the envoy: what are you doing in the region, how are you establishing a Russian Crimea, what are you doing with the economy, with the public life of the peninsula?... Say we need the political parties to function on the peninsula—that means we need to organize the process of building the parties. It's not up to him to form the parties himself, but to organize—to help them legally register, so that public relationships develop. The same goes for the economy. The goal is to make Crimea a pearl... We want to lift the economy as quickly as possible, because Crimea is 23 years behind. That's why Savel'yev and Kozak and Belaventsev are here organizing the work and overseeing the implementation of the president's orders. Kozak identified the necessary activities and gave tasks to Oleg Savel'yev. Oleg Belaventsev is overseeing it all—that's how it's being executed.[2]

Oleg Savel'yev was put in charge of a specially formed federal ministry for Crimean affairs, which was supposed to address the

---

2 N. Gavrileva, Rossiya prishla v Krym nadolgo, navsegda… I An interview with the First Deputy of the Plenipotentiary Representative of the President in the Crimean Federal District, N. Vodorezrov, Millie Firka. Crimean Tatars. July 24, 2014, http://www.milli-firka.org/content/DBAGHHJB/language/russian#sthash.VwC3YTLz.dpuf.

economic development of the peninsula and its integration into Russia proper. Savel'yev, a political strategist and economist from the staff of Deputy Minister for Economic Development German Gref, was responsible for regional policy, state programs, and special economic zones at the Ministry for Economic Development. Viktor Palagin, the former head of the Administration of the Federal Security Service for Bashkortostan (2008–2013), who distinguished himself fighting Islamic radicalism and as a peacemaker among the various ethnic elites, was recalled from reserve and appointed to a key position heading the Administration of the Federal Security Service for the Republic of Crimea and Sevastopol. The year prior to his appointment to Crimea, Palagin served as vice-president of the United Shipbuilding Corporation, which is linked to Igor Sechin and Gennady Timchenko.

From this list, we can already see an "authoritarian," Chekist bent to the figures involved in the integration of Crimea, as well as a preponderance of St. Petersburgers. Both the former and the latter are characteristic of the current Russian regime: Evgeny Minchenko, an expert on Russian elites, included a significant share of the aforementioned individuals as "Crimea-makers" in what he calls "Putin's Politburo."[3]

Sponsors and Sponsorees

Essentially maintaining the federal center–region hierarchy, Moscow decreed the transfer of responsibility for the municipal level of Crimean government to sixteen powerful Russian regions, with which the rural districts of Crimea, as well as the cities of Sevastopol and Kerch, were paired as "sponsorees."[4] Simferopol was not

---

[3] «Politburo 2.0 i postkrymskaya Rossiya. Abridged version" Minchenko Consulting. October 22, 2014 http://www.minchenko.ru/netcat_files/File/Politburo%20October%202014.pdf.

[4] The list of "sponsor" regions and their Crimean charges includes: Tatarstan (Bakhchysarai District), Bashkortostan (Belogorsk District), Voronezh Oblast (Dzhankoy District), Belgorod Oblast (Kirovskoye District), Rostov Oblast (Krasnogvardeiskoye District), Kaluga Oblast (Krasnoperekopsk District), Krasnodar Region (Lenino District), Vladimir Oblast (Nizhnegorsk District),

on the list but is being assisted by St. Petersburg and Leningrad Oblast'. Another eighteen city councils, including resort areas, were not included on the list of sponsored entities.

There is a certain logic in the pairing of Crimean districts with one region or another. The sponsors of the two districts with the highest concentration of Crimean Tatars — Bakhchysarai and Belogorsk — were chosen based on ethnicity: Tatarstan and Bashkortostan are two of the largest Tatar Muslim regions. The oil-and-gas-producing Chernomorskoe District was placed in the care of Tyumen Oblast' on the principle of production specialization. According to the same principle, Tula Oblast' got the metallurgical-industrial region of Kerch. For its part, Moscow took sponsorship of Sevastopol, presumably due to historical ties and the latter's symbolic significance as the "City of Russian Glory." The scope of assistance from the "sponsors" is quite large, amounting to tens or even hundreds of millions of rubles per year for reconstruction and repair of educational, healthcare, socio-cultural, and transportation infrastructure, as well as special and medical equipment facilities.[5]

"Sewing" Crimea onto Russia after it was torn from Ukraine is comparable in difficulty to an organ transplant operation, where each vessel and nerve needs to be pulled out and attached anew. For each top official or office, an equivalent must be found at the regional level, and they do not always correspond to each other.

President Vladimir Putin gave the agency heads two weeks, beginning on March 29, to establish a law-enforcement system on the Russian model in Crimea. However, while several institutions — such as the Prosecutor's Office or the Ministry of Internal

---

Moscow Oblast (Pervomaiskoye District), Volgograd Oblast (Razdolnoye District), Samara Oblast (Saki District), Leningrad Oblast (Simferopol District), Lipetsk Oblast (Sovetskiy District), Tyumen Oblast (Chernomorskoe District), Tula Oblast (City of Kerch), Moscow (Sevastopol). By government decree, the highest officials of each of the entities were tasked with providing guidance and material assistance to ensure the proper functioning of public infrastructure and social services; monthly reports from the "sponsors" were envisaged.

5   See Oleg Belavetsev: "Trudnosti perekhoda nas ne pugayut" An interview with the Plenipotentiary Representative of the President of the Russian Federation in the Crimean Federal District, Federal Press, December 9, 2014, http://fedpress.ru/news/polit_vlast/reviews/1418141353-oleg-belaventsev-trudnosti-perekhoda-nas-ne-pugayut.

Affairs (MVD) — had Ukrainian predecessors, others, such as the Investigative Committee of Russia (SKR) or the Federal Drug Control Service of Russian (FSKN), needed to be established from scratch.

Each law enforcement institution took one of two approaches to forming a regional office in Crimea: the replace/introduce route or the adapt/coopt route. The latter was characteristic of the MVD — the largest agency on the peninsula, which was more or less maintained in its "Ukrainian" form — as well as of the Prosecutor's Office. The MVD in Crimea was headed by a local, Lieutenant Colonel Sergei Abisov, who was appointed on March 1, 2014, by the Supreme Rada in Kiev. By the end of March 2014, he had become an employee of the MVD of the Russian Federation — first as an acting, then, within a little more than a month, a full-fledged, minister for Crimea.

After all four of the deputies of the previous Ukrainian Prosecutor refused to take the position, Natalya Poklonskaya took up the post of Prosecutor for Crimea by a decision of the Council of Ministers of the Autonomous Republic of Crimea on March 11. By order of the Prosecutor General of the Russian Federation, she was appointed as acting prosecutor for Crimea on March 25, and by May 2 as full prosecutor. Two of Poklonskaya's deputies were also confirmed in March, one from Tomsk and another from Tula. Another two appeared in August: one local, another — Poklonskaya's chief deputy — the former deputy prosecutor for Yaroslavl Oblast. At the MVD, all the deputy ministers were locals from the beginning. It is hard to say, however, how long this pattern — "commissars" seconded by Moscow whose duties include hiring and overseeing the work of local staff working in the internal affairs agency — will continue.

Having received a position below her grade, Poklonskaya experienced rapid career progress: on March 27, two days after being appointed as acting prosecutor, she was given the rank of Senior Counselor of Justice, and a year later she became State Counselor Third Class (corresponding to the rank of Major General). Many believed that Poklonskaya was a temporary figure who would soon be replaced. Recently, as preparations were made for State Duma elections in Crimea, such rumors abounded in light of the fact that

Poklonskaya was being considered for a spot at the top of United Russia's candidate list either in Crimea or in a single-mandate district.

The Investigative Committee and the Federal Drug Control Service (FSKN) did not have direct predecessors under the Ukrainian administration and were established "from scratch." At the same time, the Crimean Administration of the Investigative Committee of the Russian Federation was hampered by its "scratch crew" of staff: among the hundreds of officials were representatives of different regions, including many St. Petersburgers. Meanwhile, the administration of the FSKN was formed with the frequent inclusion of local cadres.

The Investigative Committee (SKR) announced the start of its operations in Crimea on March 25. After that, investigators and criminalists from different regions were seconded to Crimea as "acting" officials, with final appointments coming in September. In September, the President appointed Mikhail Nazarov the head of the Central Investigative Bureau of the Investigative Committee of Russia in Crimea. Originally from Yaroslavl, he had served almost ten years as the head of the SKR in Mordovia. His chief deputy, Sergei Mikhailov, was the former Deputy Director of the SKR in Ulyanovsk Oblast, and another two deputies were also not locals: Andrey Anokhin from Kurgan came from the central administration of the SKR and Vladimir Arkhangelsky from the SKR of Penza Oblast.

Sergei Topilskii was sent from Shchelkovo, near Moscow, to be the director of the SKR in Yalta and arrived there with two of his subordinates. Due to a scandal (Topilsky attempted to cover up a fight that his staff had started at a restaurant), he was soon sent home. The Sevastopol Investigative Administration was headed by Yuri Moroz, formerly director of the SKR in Kamchatka Krai; one of his deputies came from the central administration of the SKR, the other from Krasnodar.

The Regional Authority of the FSKN for the Republic of Crimea and the Drug Enforcement Agency for Sevastopol have been operational since April 10, 2014. The division is headed by a local retired security officer, the former deputy director of the Authority for the Prosecution of Organized Crime (UBOP) of Crimea, Fakhruddin Gadzhiakhmedov. By some accounts, he is a Crimean Tatar born in Uzbekistan; by others, including the one on the Department's website, he is a native of Derbent in Dagestan. In 2010, the Ukrainian authorities had sent Gadzhiakhmedov, known as the "black colonel," into retirement as part of a routine change of leadership in the Crimean MVD. He was sent two specialists from the Russian regions to assist him with the division: Dmitri Kolozin from Kaluga, who became the Director of the Agency in Sevastopol, and Oleg Poskrebyshev from Pskov. In addition to them, the FSKN sent an entire legion to Crimea: 44 narcotics officers from Krasnodar Krai and 26 officers from the central administration of the Russian FSKN.

A little more than two months after it was formed, the Crimean division was almost half staffed. Six months later, in December 2014, the Inter-District Administration of the FSKN was operating in six Crimean cities: Yalta, Yevpatoria, Kerch, Dzhankoy, Krasnoperekopsk, and Feodosia.

Of particular importance is the FSB, where the above-mentioned "reservist" Viktor Palagin became the director for both Crimea and Sevastopol. (The structure of the FSB administration looks the same in the capital cities: a central office administers the FSB for Moscow and Moscow Oblast; another central office administers St. Petersburg and Leningrad Oblast.)

Reportedly, Palagin brought his former colleagues from the Bashkir Bureau of the FSB to Crimea, among them ethnic Tatars, as noted by the site "MediaKorSet."[6] One example is Colonel Rustem Ibragimov, who became Palagin's chief deputy. As early as the fall of 2014, at a meeting of the Council of Ministers of the Republic of Crimea, Palagin reported that the turnover of senior staff at the district and municipal bureaus of the FSB was complete.[7] Leadership

---

6 I. Petrov, "Krymskoe UFSB vozglavit chekist, zachistivshy Baskiriyu ot ekstremistov" RBC, April 9, 2014, https://www.rbc.ru/society/09/04/2014/57041ada9a794761c0ce8b9f.

7 "Federal'naya sluzhba bezopasnosti sdelala v Krymu kadrovye rotatsii" crimea.kz, September 2, 2014, http://crimea.kz/116476-Federal-naya-sluzhba-bezopasnosti-sdelala-v-Krymu-kadrovye-rotacii.html.

positions in a number of cities were filled with people from other regions of the Russian Federation: in Alushta someone from Krasnoyarsk, in Yevpatoria an individual from Volgograd, and in Yalta someone from Sochi.

The Judiciary

There are only about 500 judges in the general courts in Crimea, including the 83 judges of the Appeals Court, which was merged into the Supreme Court. The overwhelming majority of Crimean judges immediately applied for Russian citizenship and on that basis began hearing cases under Russian law. At the same time, Crimean judges took emergency retraining courses; a working group from the Supreme Court of the Russian Federation, led by its First Deputy Chairman, helped them to structure their work according to Russian practices. By May 1, 1,500 Crimean lawyers and notaries had received new status by passing qualifying examinations under a simplified procedure.

The highest post in the Crimean judicial system was occupied by Igor Radionov, a local who emphasized his Karaite roots. According to him, Sergei Aksenov, then fulfilling the duties of the Chairman of the Appellate Court of the Republic of Crimea, appointed him to his post on March 17, the day after the referendum.[8] Radionov's predecessor, Valery Chernobuk, who had worked as the Chief Justice in Crimea for three years, was from Dnipropetrovsk. He left Crimea and returned home when it became clear that the new authorities were not prepared to keep him in his position. Prior to that, however, he managed to apply for Russian citizenship, and then enlisted in a militia on the Ukrainian side. Three judges from his staff, including his deputy, left along with their former boss.

---

8   Radionov himself gives convoluted explanations as to how and why he became the acting head of the court: he says that Aksenov appointed him, but at the same time explains that his predecessor, Valery Chernobuk, disappeared for a week and half at a decisive moment, etc. See D Romanov. "Spravedlivost' - eto kompromiss, kotory sud'ya vyskazyvaet ot imeni gosudarstva," Interview with Acting Chairman of the Appellate Court of the Republic of Crimea, I. Radionov, pravo.ru. April 11, 2014, http://pravo.ru/review/view/104005/.

Ministry of Crimean Affairs

An order was signed on March 31, 2014, to establish a federal ministry for Crimean affairs, led by Oleg Savel'yev, "in order to increase the effectiveness of the work of the federal executive authorities in the integration of the Republic of Crimea and the city of Sevastopol into the economic, financial, credit, and judicial systems of the Russian Federation." Perhaps it would have been more logical to assign this task to the Ministry of Regional Development, but the latter's days were already numbered. Yet although the Ministry of Regional Development was liquidated in September 2014, it still managed to play a role in the integration of Crimea: it was this ministry that developed the aforementioned sponsorship scheme between the Russian regions and Crimea and Sevastopol, a scheme that was adopted by the Russian government.

The Ministry of Crimean Affairs was the third federal ministry established to address the problems of a specific region (behind the Ministry for the North Caucasus and the Ministry for the Far East), but the first to be dissolved. On July 15, 2015, just a year after it began operating, it was dissolved "as a result of the completion of Crimea's transitionary period and the integration of Crimea into the Russian Federation."[9] Some saw the numerous corruption scandals of the first half of 2015 as the reason for this. Others blamed the battle between various federal clans for money and power, a battle won by Envoy Belaventsev, who lobbied for the ministry's dissolution. In contrast to the other two "regional" ministries, the Minister for Crimea was not a lackey of the Envoy and Vice-Premier, which led to an unavoidable conflict of their interests in the territories entrusted to them.

The authorized staffing level of the Ministry of Crimean Affairs was 230 people, divided between Moscow, Simferopol, and Sevastopol. In reality, however, the number of ministry staff never reached this figure: prior to the dissolution of the ministry, there were 150 people working there.[10] The dissolution of the Ministry of

---

9 "Podpisan ukaz ob uprazdnenii ministerstva po delam Kryma, July 15, 2015, http://www.kremlin.ru/events/president/news/49998.

10 See "Korruptsiya schitaetsia uzhe neprilichnoi," An interview with the Minister

Crimean Affairs went practically unnoticed, as the ministry had failed to become a serious player and did not attract public attention.

The initial goals Savel'yev declared were quite ambitious. They included not only solving the first-order anti-crisis issues, but also the establishment of a streamlined and effective government administration from scratch—a system "far better than the one in Russia."[11] Yet it did not turn out better than in Russia, it turned out worse: the system of governance in Russia is multifaceted—formed over many years, it carries with it elements from various stages of the country's development—whereas Crimea ended up with a reproduction of Russian governance circa 2014.

Neither a significant inflow of investment nor a serious push to develop Crimea's economy (tied to the establishment of the special economic zone Savel'yev talked about) came to fruition. Indeed, it was impossible for it to be successful in just a year, in an

---

of Crimean Affairs, O. Savel'yev, Novosti. July 12, 2015, http://novosti-krim.ru/intervyu/13373-oleg-savelev-korrupciya-schitaetsya-uzhe-neprilich noy-intervyu.htm.

[11] From an interview with Savel'yev in May 2014: "The Ministry of Crimean Affairs was established as an instrument of the government to take on the unprecedented task of integrating Crimea and Sevastopol into the Russian Federation, noting that serious differences have developed between the two in terms of the legal system and the approach in the development of government as a whole. The task we've set before ourselves has many different aspects, is multi-leveled (multi-faceted) and will take a prolonged period to accomplish. Today, laws for the transition period are in effect, which allow us to deal with the gaps that appear at every turn; in infrastructure, finance, energy provision, insofar as the entire system of essential services was dependent for many years on our Ukrainian partners. <...> to create everything from scratch, not just like in Russia, but far better than in Russia. So that we could craft world-leading governing technologies (methodologies) here, and remove, or rather, not establish the same administrative barriers which we have spent many years trying to overcome in Russia. Over the last several years (in Russia) we have gained experience with deregulation of the economy, which has had a significant effect. However, we would like not to replicate, but to create, new governing approaches here. One of the proposed instruments of creating such a "model city" is the creation of a special legal and economic system. For now, it is tentatively called a "special economic zone." Oleg Savel'yev: "Krym prevratitsia v ekonomichesky gorod-sad blagodaria novym tekhnologiyam upravleniya," An interview with the Minister of Crimean Affairs, O. Savel'yev, Kryminform. May 11, 2014, http://www.c-inform.info/interviews/id/43.

environment of legal chaos, the redistribution of property, and Western sanctions. In disbanding the Ministry of Crimean Affairs, the Kremlin not only signed off on the failure of the governing experiment in Crimea, but also substantively changed the system of governance in Crimea, making it more transparent, more primitive, and fundamentally more oriented toward authoritarian means of control. After the liquidation of the ministry, whose functions were transferred to the Ministry of Economic Development, the Russian government decided to strengthen the government institutions in Crimea and Sevastopol with civil servants from the federal level, sending them to serve as first deputies to the ministers.

Until this time, the government of Crimea had been made up exclusively of local civil servants, either from "Aksenov's people" or, to a lesser degree, from among the cronies of State Council Speaker Konstantinov. The only outsider was Vice Premier Evgenia Bavykina, the supervisor of the economic bloc. A Muscovite, she, like Belaventsev, worked for Sergei Shoigu and was seen by local analysts as the "eye of the Kremlin" on Aksenov's staff.[12] To coordinate the actions of the regional authorities with the federal center, a State Commission on the Social and Economic Development of the Republic of Crimea and Sevastopol was established.

Political Parties

The political parties urgently needed to establish their offices in Crimea in order to be prepared for the State Council elections set for September. A little over 20 new party members were present at the founding assemblies of the Crimea and Sevastopol affiliates of United Russia that took place on April 7. United Russia did not deem it necessary to change its usual model, which it had used in several Russian regions: Konstantinov, the head of the regional parliament (State Council) and former leader of the local office of the Party of Regions, was appointed to a second role as leader of the party. Also included in the presidium of United Russia's policy

---

12 A. Sambros, "Kadry reshayut Krym: kak stroitsia kadrovaya politika na poluostrove" Carnegie.ru, June 30, 2015, https://carnegie.ru/commentary/60556.

council were two of Konstantinov's deputies in the State Council, Konstantin Bakharev and Andrey Kozenko; the head of the State Council Committee on Industry, Transportation and the Fuel and Energy Sectors, Pyotr Zaporozhets; and a senator and former head of the Supreme Council of Crimea, Sergei Tsekov.

The founding assembly of United Russia's Sevastopol affiliate took place on April 7. The first 23 citizens of Sevastopol received their membership cards from the hands of the Secretary of the party's General Council, Sergei Neverov, founding a new branch. Viktor Oganesyan, a deputy in the Legislative Assembly and high school principal, was elected First Secretary of United Russia's regional affiliate.

Three other parties from the Duma hurried to establish offices in Crimea led by State Duma deputies from other regions; after the elections, the Duma deputies were replaced by local functionaries.

On April 1, the United People's Front (UPF) became the first to establish an office in Crimea. Crimean Prime Minister Aksenov, Crimean State Council Chairman Konstantinov, and Olympian and Vice President of the Crimean Federation of Greco-Roman Wrestling Rustem Kazakov became its co-chairmen. Although Russian regions are familiar with having a famous athlete in a UPF leadership role, it was unique to have two "title leaders" from the region, one of whom would also soon lead "United Russia" in Crimea.

The Liberal Democratic Party (LDPR) established an office in Crimea at almost the same time as United Russia and chose as its leader Pavel Shpero, who had joined the LDPR of the USSR in March 1992, after the collapse of the Soviet Union, and had worked in the central administration of the LDPR in the mid-1990s. A mid-level entrepreneur, he had most recently been the leader of the "Tauric Cossack Legion" and deputy chairman of the Russian Society of Crimea.

In mid-April, A Just Russia held a general meeting of twenty of its members in Crimea and announced the creation of a regional affiliate and the formation of governing bodies there. As with the other "subcontractors," it was first led by a State Duma deputy, the head of A Just Russia's Altai Region affiliate, Alexander Terentyev; in November, he was replaced by the local Aleksandr Yuryev, who had been until 2012 a functionary of Yulia Timoshenko's "Batkivshchyna" ("Homeland") and was at the time a low-ranking civil servant. In Sevastopol, meanwhile, no one has yet replaced Mikhail Bryachak, a member of the A Just Russia faction in the State Duma and controversial businessman from Pskov with a reputation as the "king of the customs business."

The Communist Party (KPRF) approached the creation of its affiliates more responsibly: at the founding conference held at the end of May, Nikolay Kolomeytsev—a member of the Presidium of the Central Committee of the KPRF and First Secretary of the Rostov District Committee of the KPRF, who was in his fourth term in the State Duma—became the leader of the Crimean Communists. At the plenum of the newly-elected Crimean National Committee, a bureau was formed consisting of 14 people and elected secretaries. Oleg Solomakhin, a local cadre and former Secretary of the National Committee of the Communist Party of Ukraine, replaced Kolomeytsev in December.

The Crimean Tatar Problem

It was easy to "reformat" the political parties listed above from the Ukrainian party system to the Russian one, insofar as they had little real function. However, when it came to the Crimean Tatar Mejlis—the only real party native to Crimea—the authorities faced a serious problem and had to resort to different methods, up to and including hostile takeover.

The Crimean Tatars are more than just 10-15 percent of the population of Crimea. They are the most deeply rooted, well-organized and cohesive force in the peninsula, mobilized for integration and resistance in a hostile external environment. The representative of their interests has for many years been the People's Mejlis.

At first, the Kremlin attempted to enlist the support of the Mejlis' leadership, but these efforts were unsuccessful. Just days before the March referendum, the ex-leader of Tatarstan, Mintimer Shaimiev, had a substantive conversation with the leader of the Crimean Tatars, Mustafa Dzhemilev, in the course of the conversation connecting him by phone to Vladimir Putin. The leaders of the

Mejlis would not be co-opted, however, and they called for Crimean Tatars to boycott the referendum. As a result, a significant number of them did not participate in the referendum and the leaders of the Mejlis refused to recognize the results. After that, the Kremlin shifted to a strategy of isolating and pushing out disloyal Mejlis leaders while simultaneously creating loyalist "nuclei" both within the Mejlis and without. On April 22, while leaving Crimea, Mustafa Dzhemilev was presented with an order banning him from entering the territory of the Russian Federation until 2019. At the same time, Putin signed an order entitled "Regarding measures aimed at rehabilitating the Armenian, Bulgarian, Greek, Crimean Tatar and German peoples and government assistance for their revival and development." On the one hand, the order proclaimed the need to restore historical justice and eliminate the consequences of illegal deportations from the territory of Crimea. On the other hand, the order basically equated Crimean Tatars, for whom Crimea was not just home but their ancestral homeland, with the representatives of other repressed ethnic groups. Two months later, the head of the Mejlis, Refat Chubarov, also received a five-year ban on entering the territory of the Russian Federation. Between these two events, the authorities, citing "security concerns," forbade the Crimean Tatars from holding a May 18 memorial service in Simferopol's central square to commemorate the 70th anniversary of their deportation, and Putin held a meeting with Crimean Tatar representatives who were ready to cooperate with the new government.[13]

Toward the end of 2014, it became clear that the Kremlin had not successfully seized control of the disobedient Mejlis, and the authorities attempted to create an alternative with the "social movement" "Kyrym." Its leader became Remzi Iyasov, Vice Speaker of the State Council and one of the former leaders of the Mejlis, who was expelled for being a collaborator. In the words of Vasvi Abduraimov, the leader of the National People's Party, Milli Firka, established in 2006, Iyasov and several other Crimean Tatars

---

[13] See "Vstrecha s predstaviteliami krymskikh tatar." March 16, 2014, http://www.kremlin.ru/events/president/news/21028.

in positions of power represent "a 'servile class' of Crimean Tatars who try to cooperate with whomever is in power in Crimea."[14] When the independent Crimean Tatar television station ART was forced to stop broadcasting under pressure from the Crimean authorities in April 2015, the "Kyrym" movement pledged its support for the government-created public television channel "Millet" and radio station "Vetan."

The policy of sowing division among Crimean Tatars risks radicalizing some of them (note that in the last years of Ukrainian rule in Crimea the views of the radical Islamist organization Hizb ut-Tahrir, outlawed in Russia, had become more popular, and by various estimates it counted among its adherents between 3,000 and 10,000 Crimean Tatars who fled Crimea after its annexation by Russia) and increasing tensions within Crimean society. Moreover, it presents a potential risk to relations with Turkey.

Ukrainian politicians also continue to play political games with the Crimean Tatars. It is well to recall that it was not until 1999 that Kiev partially recognized the Mejlis formed in 1991, when President Leonid Kuchma ordered the formation of a Council of Representatives of the Crimean Tatar People. The Mejlis became the "Council of Representatives," which included 33 people elected by the Kurultay. Analogous councils were also formed at the local level with the participation of the municipal and district Mejlises. In 2010, Viktor Yanukovich attempted to bring the Mejlis under Kiev's control, reorganizing it and bringing presidential appointees into its membership, but was unsuccessful. In the 2012 Rada elections, the Mejlis participated as a partner of Yulia Timoshenko's opposition party "Batkyvshchina." It was not until March 2014, following Russia's annexation of Crimea, that the Supreme Rada officially recognized the Crimean Tatars as one of the "indigenous peoples of Ukraine" and the Mejlis as their representative body. The political games continue even now: in May 2015 the Supreme Rada decided to name the Simferopol airport in honor of pilot Amet-

---

14 "Mejlis gotovil krovavy konflikt v Krymu" An Interview with the leader of the People's Party Milli Firka, V. Abduraimov," Milli Firka. Crimean Tatars. March 22, 2014, http://www.milli-firka.org/c/DBAGGJKG#sthash.ZRpb52Oe.dpuf.

Khan Sultan and Poroshenko talked about a "roadmap" for giving Crimea national-territorial autonomy as part of the Ukrainian state.

In addition to political parties, during the first several months, a wide array of government and social entities began to develop representation in Crimea. By June, a branch of the Russian Military History Society appeared in Crimea, led by Aksenov. A regional affiliate of the Institute of Socioeconomic and Political Research (ISEPI) appeared in Crimea — the third branch after Volgograd and Kaliningrad. It was headed by Aleksandr Formanchuk, perhaps the most famous expert analyst in power in Crimea, who had begun his career years earlier in the Regional Committee of the Communist Party of the Soviet Union (CPSU). His deputy and director of the Sevastopol branch of ISEPI, Ivan Kusov, became the Deputy Director for Development of the Sevastopol affiliate of Lomonosov Moscow State University. The rush to open an ISEPI office was due to its status as one of the providers of government grants for civil society organizations; it would need to take the interests of Crimean organizations into account for the next budget cycle.

The People's Forum of Crimea was established very expeditiously and held its first meeting on June 30, 2014. It is composed of 40 people, half of whom are appointed by the State Council and the other half by the government. There are few actual community advocates in the Forum; most members are university professors, museum employees, veterans and other public-sector employees. The People's Forum of Crimea was headed by Grigori Yoffe, a famous politician who, at the time of the Forum's formation, was working as the First Deputy Chairman of the Supreme Council. The aforementioned Aleksandr Formanchuk became one of Yoffe's two deputies.

The process of establishing a People's Forum in Sevastopol went far less smoothly. The People's Front of Sevastopol made the relevant decision regarding the establishment of a "legitimate body for the implementation of popular authority" in mid-April 2014. Note that in Ukrainian Sevastopol the People's Forum had existed as a grassroots social organization since November 2011, yet it left no trace of itself behind. In early 2015, with a solid majority behind

Aleksey Chaly, the Legislative Assembly of Sevastopol took up debating legislation for a People's Forum, viewing the People's Forum as a possible bridgehead in the battle with Governor Sergei Menyailo. The relevant bill was passed in March, but the Governor vetoed it. He attempted to insert amendments into the bill, principally regarding removing the five-year residency requirement (unsuccessful) and forming the People's Forum from three, rather than two, sections, one of which the members of the Forum would determine by the formula 8 + 8 + 8 (successful). As a result, the governor signed the bill establishing a People's Forum in Sevastopol on June 15, 2015.[15] The Forum still has not been created, but according to Vladislav Grib, the Federal People's Forum official supervising Crimea, it is highly likely that Grigori Donets, a member of the Sevastopol branch of the All-Russia People's Front and head of the organization for historical preservation "Citizens of Chersonesus," will be appointed chairman of the Forum.[16] (By May 2015 only 325 non-governmental organizations were registered in the city.)

A Change in the Configuration of the Elites

As a result of the personnel decisions of the "Crimean Spring" and fundamental changes in the structure of the political and socioeconomic landscape of Crimea, the composition of the highest level of political leadership changed dramatically. A comparison of the Regional Institute for Political Communication's (RIPC) "influence ratings" for Crimean politicians from the "Ukrainian" year 2013

---

15 At a April 14, 2015 briefing, the head of the Legislative Assembly of Sevastopol, Aleksey Chaly, declared that in the city "there should be a normal, effective Social Forum, not some pseudo-community organizations run by outsiders who have no idea what's going on in Sevastopol, no understanding of its traditions." See A. Kononov, "Chaly mechtaet ob Obshchestvennoi palate Sevastopolia bez "prishel'tsev"," Politnavigator. April 14, 2015, http://www.politnavigator.net/po-mneniyu-chalogo-bylo-by-khorosho-esli-by-obshhestvennaya-palata-sevastopolya-sostoyala-iz-odnikh-mestnykh-a-eshhe-luchshe-esli-by-ta kaya-palata-voobshhe-byla.html

16 V. Raychenko, "V Obshchestvennuyu palatu Sevastopolia vojdut patrioty s piatiletnim tsenzom osedlosti". Politnavigator, July 30, 2015, http://www.polit-navigator.net/v-obshhestvennuyu-palatu-sevastopolya-vojjdut-patrioty-s-pya tiletnim-cenzom-osedlosti.html.

and the "Russian" year 2014 allow us to make a few observations about these changes.[17] The RIPC data suggest that in 2014 the "Mt. Olympus" of Crimean politics got higher, with steeper slopes: if in 2013 there were 37 politicians in the pantheon (those receiving 10 points or more from experts out of a possible 100), in 2014 there were just 31. There was near complete turnover in the ranks of influential politicians: only six of those present in 2013 maintained their positions in the new political pantheon (less than one-sixth of the total). Of those who remained, all rose from the lower half of the list, with the exceptions of Vladimir Konstantinov, who remained in the second spot, and Grigori Yoffe in the 8-9 spot. All six of the politicians who remained in the pantheon were current or former deputies in the State Council: the leader of the Republic, Sergei Aksenov, who leapt from the 20th to the first spot; Sergei Tsekov, who became a member of the Federation Council and vaulted from 27th to fourth; Grigori Yoffe, who exchanged a position as Deputy Chairman of the State Council for a post as Chairman of the Social Forum (from 9th place to 8th); Konstantin Bakharev, who became the First Deputy Chairman of the State Council (from 24th place to 9th); and Deputy Yefim Fiks, who led the Committee for Legislative, Government Building, and Local Self-Governance Issues in the State Council.

In contrast to most Russian regions, where members of the executive branch and federal civil servants represent a significant proportion of the most influential politicians, in Crimea 16 of the 31 most influential politicians are members of the legislative branch, including two at the federal level (members of the Federation Council of the Russian Federation Sergei Tsekov (No. 4) and Olga Kovitidi (No. 6)), one at the local level (Communist Stepan Kiskin (No. 25), a Deputy of the Simferopol City Council), and 13 at the republic level. The last group includes not only Speaker Konstantinov, but

---

17   According to information on the website RIPC http://ripc.at.ua, the influence rating of Crimean politicians is calculated based on an expert survey. In 2014 RIPC surveyed 31 experts from among Crimean politicians, journalists, sociologists, political analysts and political consultants. The criteria considered to measure influence were lobbying opportunities, professional activity, charisma, family connections, and financial resources.

also all three of his deputies—Konstantin Bakharev (No. 9), Remzi Ilyasov (No. 10) and Andrey Kozenko (No. 17)—and nine out of 12 committee chairmen.

Among politicians at the municipal level, the mayors of Simferopol (was 17th, moved to 29th), Yevpatoria (was 28th, moved to 30th), and Yalta (was 32nd, moved to 31st) maintained their positions in the pantheon; all three assumed office after March 2014.

There was complete turnover among representatives of the executive branch, municipal-level politicians, and Crimean Tatars. Among federal-level politicians, only Presidential Envoy Oleg Belaventsev (No. 3) and Minister Oleg Savel'yev (No. 7) were represented, while members of the security forces and businessmen were not represented at all, sharply distinguishing Crimea from all other Russian regions.

Conclusion

To conclude our review of the organizational and institutional "Russianization" of Crimea, we should, first and foremost, note its imported nature, as well as the fact that each of the actors involved took his or her own approach. The formation of the Crimean rung in the hierarchy began in March-April 2014 and was mostly completed by November, even in those places where a two-phase model was used—that is, where an acting official was first appointed from among the bureau employees seconded to Crimea and, upon proving himself, received permanent status several months later.

The haste with which cadres were selected notwithstanding, we can see a surprising level of staffing stability in the upper echelons of regional offices (over the past year, only the head of the Administration of the Federal Tax Service was removed, under mysterious circumstances in which he was accused of attempting to bribe an FSB officer). Apparent in the approach to Crimea are caution and consideration of the specific national context, which Moscow frequently demonstrates in the ethnic republics. In most cases, there was a reliance on local actors and cooptation took place. As a result, the local roots of regional leaders were much stronger than in the overwhelming majority of Russian regions, including even the republics.[18] Most likely, this means that the process of building the regional level of federal structures in Crimea is not yet complete and that we will become witnesses to their de-localization. If, like an embryo, Crimea's political development replicates on an individual level the stages of development of the species as whole, then the transition process to the standard model for the republics will likely not take long.

In the middle rung, including the sub-regional level of directors, the formation of Russian government institutions was mostly complete by the end of 2014. In almost all cases, with the exception (for now) of the MVD, a portion of the personnel was brought from the outside through the so-called "Crimean recruitment call," where employees were chosen from among those expressing an interest in filling (and successfully bidding to fill) the middle rung of leadership in a given institution. They were then seconded to Crimea, where after two or three months they received permanent positions. They also practiced the training of local cadres with the assistance of representatives of the central department apparatus, sent to the peninsula specifically for this purpose. The municipal level was in many ways left at the mercy of the Russian regions, which were tied as "sponsors" to every administrative district of Crimea, Kerch, and Sevastopol. Sponsorship included both financial and material assistance, as well as the transfer of experience.

In many respects, the new executive branch in Crimea was formed in a revolutionary way and without the noticeable participation of the center. Along with the regional government, there was also a radical turnover among the municipal authorities. Only after a year had gone by did the federal authorities, chiefly the FSB and Investigative Committee of Russia (SKR), begin to crack down as part of an anticorruption campaign, arresting prominent Crimean

---

18   On the Kremlin's personnel policy in the Russian regions, see N.V. Petrov, "Ot federatsii korporatsij k federatsii regionov ," Pro et Contra, 2012, Vol. 16, No. 4-5, https://carnegieendowment.org/files/ProEtContra_56_101-118.pdf.
N.V. Petrov, Who is running the Russian regions? Russia as a Network State. Ed. by Vadim Kononenko, Arkady Moshes, London: Palgrave-Macmillan, 2011, pp. 81-112.

civil servants. With the liquidation of the Ministry for Crimean Affairs in July 2015, the introduction of "commissars" — representatives of the ministries and departments sent to serve as deputy directors in Crimean government institutions — was announced. In that way, a transition was made from a model of external control over the actions of the Crimean government to a model of internal, integrated control.

The governing models for Crimea (Simferopol) and Sevastopol were different from the beginning. In the first instance, the legislative branch and its leadership — with some reorganization — was preserved, and the entire executive branch was changed, led by a local cadre from among the deputies. In the second instance, not only did both branches of government change, but a tandem was created: a non-local, Admiral Sergey Menyailo, wound up at the head of the executive branch, while businessman Aleksey Chaly became the "People's Mayor." As a result, the Sevastopol model turned out to be not only more public and prone to conflict, but also, in the end, more democratic. Additionally, in its compactness, the Sevastopol model has elements of direct democracy.

It is still difficult to assess how functional and effective the Crimean territorial institutions of the federal bureaus, which have been either newly formed or tailored to Russian blueprints, will be. Most visible are the activities of the FSB and Investigative Committee (SKR) under the auspices of the anti-corruption campaign. The Investigative Committee (SKR) reported that it solved a series of cold cases, however it is clear that large-scale actions, whether the distribution of Russian passports to Crimeans or the registration of small businesses, took far more time than initially planned. As Ekaterina Schulmann writes,[19] rather than integrating Crimea into the Russian political landscape, the authorities instead chose the path of carving out a special niche for Crimea in that landscape. We can also note that under the conditions of Crimea's integration into Russia, the vertical systems of control customary in the Russian regions

---

19 E. Schulmann, "Poluostrov isklyuchenij," Kommersant, March 17, 2015, http://www.kommersant.ru/doc/2688488.

work better than those requiring horizontal coordination and attempting to improve local conditions through the Ministry for Crimean Affairs.

Evolution of the Russian Judicial System in 2014

Ella Paneyakh

Following the mass protests of 2011-2012 and the annexation of Crimea, all the negative trends that existed in the Russian judicial system dramatically intensified, while several of the positive trends were broken.

The judicial system in Russia in the pre-Crimea era could not be considered an independent branch of government. Despite having received formal legal autonomy in the course of the reforms of the 1990s, it remained a part of the executive branch in terms of organization, values, and internal procedures (i.e., the established routine of managerial monitoring practices and accountability structures; it should be noted that the formal procedural rules, in contrast, changed significantly). All the trends characteristic of the current judicial system also have Soviet roots and, after a brief period of relative weakening in the 1990s, were easily resumed with the strengthening of the government "power vertical" in the 2000s. These trends include: subordination of courts to the law enforcement agencies; the federal hierarchy of judicial power—the subordination of judges to court chairmen in everyday matters, and a system in which court chairmen are, in practice, appointed by the higher courts; the de-facto inclusion of justices of peace in the system of general jurisdiction at the lower level; the automatic and "conveyer-belt" nature of legal proceedings and their orientation in favor of "state interests," which includes creating more convenient working conditions for law enforcement and budget savings (for example, in compensation for the exonerated); and bureaucratic accountability of judges. In the process of hearing criminal cases, judges were still at least somewhat interested in the quality of the prosecution's arguments, attempting to hand down more humane sentences to defendants whose guilt was proven more weakly than usual. However, in the course of investigations and inquiries, judges did not consider it possible to "interfere with the investigation": for example, in almost every case, judges approved the placement of citizens in pre-trial detention (that is, in conditions harsher than in a penal colony) with minimal justification. As such, judges routinely considered mere possession of a passport to be sufficient grounds for placing a defendant in custody, even if the passport had already been confiscated by investigators.

At the same time, in the post-Soviet period, some trends toward humanizing criminal proceedings began to take shape—wherever this did not conflict with the interests of the state's repressive apparatus. The first of these is the large percentage of sentences in which the defendant was freed by admitting guilt (reconciliation with the victim, or "active repentance"). Such trial outcomes are in the interest of all parties involved: the judge, who does not need to write a detailed text of ruling and worry about appeals to higher courts; the prosecution, which secures a guilty verdict (that is, confirmation of the legality of the criminal prosecution of the accused); the defendant, for whom this result is the most desirable of all possible outcomes, as acquittal is extremely unlikely (fewer than 1 in 1,000 in 2014); and the victim (if the case has one), who can receive formal and informal compensation for damages in return for agreeing to "reconciliation of the parties."

Another positive trend during the post-Soviet period has been a steady reduction in the proportion of defendants sentenced to prison terms. Under Yeltsin and Putin, there has been a broad consensus in society and government institutions that there should be fewer verdicts resulting in imprisonment (remember that in the post-Soviet period Russia became the world leader in terms of the number of people incarcerated relative to its population). Humanitarian considerations and recognition of the fact that incarceration is ineffective as a method of rehabilitation and as a policy for preventing crime, as well as the fact that prison culture negatively affects societal mores, the dissemination of accounts of torturous conditions in prisons, and concerns about the country's international image and budget all led to the conclusion that prison and penal colony populations had to be reduced. Public and human rights activists, expert groups, the ruling elite, financial interests, and the leadership of Federal Penitentiary Service were convinced of the need for this change; lawyers and, importantly, judges agreed. In opposition were some in law enforcement whose interests were directly tied to the criminal justice system remaining as repressive as possible.

The judicial system in Russia is practically incapable (and that incapacity is only increasing) of exonerating the innocent and of subjecting the work of law enforcement to judicial oversight. Standards for proving guilt are steadily, if slowly, being lowered; judges are completely servile to executive authority and do not oppose political orders. However, despite these issues, the judicial system of the 2000s tended to imprison fewer people, instead choosing more humane forms of punishment, primarily financial ones, such as fines or community service,[1] rather than imposing criminal penalties. A significant portion of defendants were spared criminal penalties, at least in those instances where the charges were less serious. Law enforcement was satisfied with these trial outcomes.

Two external shocks — the evolution of the regime to become more repressive after the public mobilization and protests in 2011-12 and its final authoritarian transformation in the post-Crimea era — intensified all the aforementioned negative trends and halted both positive ones. The proportion of sentences to prison time rose in 2012; in 2014, as will be shown below, the proportion of "financial" penalties (which prior to that had risen for several years) stopped increasing, while the proportion of cases that were dismissed noticeably dropped. Law enforcement agencies began to much more actively surveil citizens[2] — with the full knowledge of the courts. Accordingly, within three years, the number of petitions to the court to "limit citizens' constitutional right to privacy in written and telephone correspondence, mail, telegraph messages and

---

1   For employed individuals convicted of a crime, who are usually assessed this punishment, it is the withdrawal from his or her salary. That is, a fine drawn out over time.
2   We are talking about the "general" law enforcement activities of the Interior Ministry, FSKN, and Investigative Committee. Russian judicial statistics do not reflect political investigation, the use of SORM and the activities of intelligence agencies such as the FSB.

other communication transmitted either electronically or by post" in the course of investigations[3] rose one-and-a-half times, reaching over 500,000 annually, despite the number of criminal investigations remaining basically unchanged. However, as before, the courts granted such petitions in more than 99 percent of cases. In this article, the reader is first offered an overview of the substantive changes in the judicial system during the "post-Crimea" year of 2014, followed by an analysis of the judicial statistics compared to previous periods.[4] Figures from the Justice Department of the Russian Federation for 2008-2014[5] — that is, the official published statistics, which summarize information about all criminal cases moving through the courts over the course of the year, as well as other decisions made by the courts during court proceedings in criminal matters — were used for these calculations.

A Review of Changes in Legislation and the Practice of the Courts in 2014

In 2014, the Superior Court of Arbitration ceased functioning. The independent system of arbitration courts, which had been far superior in quality to the lower courts of general jurisdiction, was dismantled; in the regions, the "district" pyramids of arbitration (regional court — appellate court — district court of arbitration[6]) remained, allowing some experienced and qualified judicial personnel to be retained. However, hopes that a significant portion of the apparatus of the Supreme Court of Arbitration, having moved over to the apparatus of the Supreme Court of the Russian Federation, would take with it its workflow practices (including the practice of

---

3   Such decisions are a matter of state secrecy, classified and only issued only by judges with special clearance. However, open judicial statistics reflect general numbers of permissions granted by courts.
4   The author thanks Irina Chetverikova and Anastasia Skripkina for their help in processing the judicial outcomes statistics
5   Form 1. "Report on the work of the courts of general jurisdiction considering criminal cases in the first instance," Form 10.3. "Report on the types of punishment for the most serious crimes (without accounting for cumulative sentencing)."
6   "Mesto AS SZO v sudebnoi sisteme," Severo-Zapadny sudebny okrug, http://fasszo.arbitr.ru/welcome/showall/633200008.

keeping a publicly accessible register of cases on the internet) and comparatively high level of judicial qualification were not realized. The judges of the Supreme Court of Arbitration were largely put out of work, while the Supreme Court was filled from within the system by surrogates of the Chairman of the Supreme Court.

In May, Vyacheslav Lebedev was named Chairman of the reorganized Supreme Court; the interval between his application for extension of his term in office and the decision of the Federal Council was only eight days. The Federal Council granted his reappointment not only without open deliberation, but also without behind-the-scenes negotiations. The authority of the Supreme Court of Arbitration was transferred to the bench of the Higher Court for Economic Disputes, headed by Oleg Sviridenko, who, despite coming from the arbitration court system, had a poor relationship with the head of Higher Court of Arbitration, Anton Ivanov, and was the principal foe of progressive practices in the arbitration courts, as well as having a reputation as a person close to the power bloc surrounding the President.

The reappointment of the odious Olga Yegorova to lead the Moscow Municipal Court is also worth mentioning. Yegorova was the only candidate for the post, and the session of the Higher Qualification Board for Judges was pointedly short—no more than five minutes. Yegorova herself announced in the presence of journalists that she was invited to take up the post by the Chairman of the Supreme Court: "The decision to remain for a third term was not easy. I went to Vyacheslav Mikhailovich Lebedev, and he said that I was obligated to go and work, that he required my assistance," pravo.ru quoted her as saying.[7] The judiciary received an unambiguous message: appointments would be made on the principle of personal loyalty, a negative reputation in the eyes of the public would not cause even superficial problems for a judge, and a commanding style was encouraged in chairs of the court.

The relocation of the Supreme Court to St. Petersburg is planned. In light of the example of the Constitutional Court, which

---

7   V. Zhukov, "Naznacheniya, naprasnye nadezhdy i otstavki – 2014," pravo.ru, December 31, 2014, http://pravo.ru/review/view/114204/.

has already moved to St. Petersburg, one can predict with confidence a reduction in the Supreme Court's activity during the move and a decline in the overall importance of the Supreme Court in the structure of Russian state institutions thereafter. The move will see the authority of the judiciary continue to decline.

During a tumultuous 2014, the Constitutional Court did not assert itself, despite the fact that amendments to the Constitution were introduced during this period that changed the face of the judicial system (the takeover of the Higher Court of Arbitration by the Supreme Court was one such amendment, introduced February 5, 2014) and parliament (in an amendment from July 21, 2014, the rules for the formation of the Federal Council were changed: 10 percent of the members of the upper house were given lifetime appointments by the President). Additionally, during the same period the executive branch and parliament made decisions of questionable constitutionality. On March 19, the Constitutional Court unanimously upheld the constitutionality of an "agreement" on the annexation of the Republic of Crimea to Russia and the formation of two new federal districts (Crimea and Sevastopol). On April 8, the Constitutional Court upheld the constitutionality of legislation on "foreign agents"; on September 23, it left unchanged a law banning "propaganda of nontraditional sexual relationships," aka free speech on homosexuality. This list practically exhausts the participation of the high court in the political life of the country during this critical year: for the most part, the court took only routine cases.

Thus, of the three Higher Courts in Russia, the most progressive and professional—the Court of Arbitration—was liquidated; the second—the Constitutional Court—practically lost its importance; and the third—the Supreme Court—underwent a significant shake-up and is preparing for even greater uncertainty following its move from the center of power to the fringes.

Reform of the courts of general jurisdiction basically ceased, as did even discussions of reform. In place of the long-discussed reforms of the lower courts, the public was presented with the devastation of the Higher Court of Arbitration, while the practices of the lower courts remained unchanged. In part, the process of subsuming the nominally independent civil courts to the hierarchy of the courts of general jurisdiction continues. Within the judiciary, various projects of varying degrees of radicality are still being discussed: from the introduction of the post of "investigative judge" to a return to the Soviet institution of lay judges (people's assessors). However, the topic of the independence and objectivity of judges itself is forbidden to be raised among the judiciary and in the political arena—and if these goals cannot even be set, meaningful reform is impossible. Additionally, the necessity of reorganizing the absorbed judicial system of the annexed Crimea, with its significantly different legal foundation and completely different day-to-day operations, weighed heavily on the judicial system. It appears from the sporadic publications of online media that in Crimea's judicial system, there was somewhat more low-level corruption but far less servility and subordination to law enforcement agencies. The latter may become an even bigger problem for the Russian judicial hierarchy than the former.

The degradation of the judicial system and diminution of its role is happening in the context of increasingly repressive trends in legislation. More stringent laws have been passed regarding the treatment of "foreign" connections in every area: laws on dual citizenship, control of overseas accounts, and limiting the proportion of Russian media ownership by non-residents. Criminal liability was introduced for violating the procedures for holding demonstrations and meetings, and "anti-extremist" legislation was strengthened. The regulations for conditional early release were tightened, and while the significance of the courts decreased, they also received new powers, including the right to request that charges be revised to more serious ones (previously, judges had the right to reduce a sentence claimed by the prosecution but could not make it harsher).

In 2014, investigators regained the ability to open criminal cases for tax crimes without the submission of evidence from the taxation authorities. This means that in the conditions of an economic recession, businesses could be arbitrarily punished for making lower tax payments, and not only for tax evasion. The underlying notion of law enforcers is that tax evasion is easily identified by noticeably smaller sums than the "industry average" during the last fiscal period or compared to those paid by the same company in prior years. In the conditions of an economic crisis, that puts practically any company with average economic performance in jeopardy — under pressure, many go so far as to overpay, inflating economic results (there are precedents from the 1998 and 2008 crises). The Ministry of Internal Affairs proposed legislation for a simplified inquiry procedure: as though it were not enough that the evidentiary requirements for "obvious" cases are being reduced to a minimum, the head of the investigation authority can decide to apply this procedure without the agreement of the suspect or the complainant. Given existing judicial practice, the legislation would practically free the investigator of any responsibility for presenting actual evidence; it would be enough to maintain "the obviousness of the individual's involvement in the commission of a crime" and that "it would not be difficult to prove."[8] This removes the burden from investigators, who do not have to undertake difficult work in obvious cases (the existing practice requires them to complete a huge amount of paperwork and call unnecessary experts even in a self-evident matter), but also creates a wide opening for power abuse and fabrications. Imagine, for example, how easy it would now be to plant drugs or bullets and on that basis convict almost anyone.

In 2014, the Prosecutor's Office, which already had significant ability to pressure the courts, finally became part of the presidential hierarchy. Prior to that, there was some uncertainty as to whether the Prosecutor's Office belonged to the executive or judicial branch, but from February 5, 2014, amendments to the Constitution solidified its status as a part of the executive branch. The president gained the right to appoint not only the Prosecutor General, but also the Deputy Prosecutors General; the Prosecutor's Office, meanwhile, regained the right to general oversight of the Investigative Committee. That means that any "stalemate" between the Investigative

---

8   As of July 2015, the bill "O vnesenii izmenenij v ugolovno-protsessual'ny kodeks Rossijskoi Federatsii (v chasti vvedeniya osobogo poryadka dosudebnogo proizvodstva)" was still in the process of being prepared for submission to the State Duma, http://regulation.gov.ru/project/22294.html?point=view_project&stage=1&stage_id=7502.

Committee and the Prosecutor's Office will be decided in favor of the latter. Previously, the Investigative Committee could not remand a case to court without the approval of the Prosecutor's Office (see "prosecutors' gambling case"[9]), but nor could the Prosecutor investigate illegal actions by investigators on the Investigative Committee, as he did not have investigative powers or personnel. Now, representatives of the Prosecutor's Office can intervene in any action of the Investigative Committee under the auspices of oversight. To an even greater degree than before, any judicial conflict with the Prosecutor's Office will look like open defiance of "state interests" by judges.

It should be noted that, in general, the degradation of the judicial system has accelerated: evidentiary requirements have decreased, the subordination of judges to law enforcement authorities has increased, and the courts have become less important in the system of state power.

Design of Rulings in Criminal Cases: New Trends

The approach to judgments in criminal cases has become more repressive. The number of acquittals, which was already unusually low, continues to decline. Excluding cases of "private prosecution" (that is, cases in which the plaintiff is not necessarily represented by the Public Prosecutor's Office and there is no "state interest" involved in the conviction[10]), in 2014, fewer than one in 1,000 defendants were acquitted, or 0.09 percent. While this figure is negligible,

---

9   For example, "Igornoe delo: kak u kazino s'ekhala prokurorskaya krysha," RBC, August 15, 2011, http://top.rbc.ru/story/610618.shtml.
10 In 2014, cases of private prosecution (79,351 cases) accounted for 8.2 percent of all criminal cases tried by the courts and 79.6 percent of all acquittals. These cases usually end with much lighter sentences and only rarely with prison time (no cases in 2014). For differences in the outcomes and court procedures with and without the involvement of public prosecution, see Paneyakh, E., Prakticheskaya logika prinyatiya sudebnykh reshenij: diskretsiya pod davleniem i kompromissy za schet podsudimogo // Kak sud'yi prinimayut resheniya" empiricheskie issledovaniya prava; Edited by V. Volkov. Moscow: Statut, 2012. Pg. 107-127; Here it should also be noted that a portion of the cases of private prosecution come to the courts from the criminal justice system (law enforcement officers are not obligated to pursue cases on these articles, but they have the

it should be noted that from 2008, the proportion of acquittals in Russian courts fell threefold. During the entire year, only 800 "not guilty" verdicts were handed down in cases of public or semi-public prosecution (which account for 92 percent of all court cases) from a total of 880,155 cases. Thus, it is evident that Russian courts have practically ceased to acquit anyone. In 405 cases (less than 0.05 percent), charges were dropped based on exculpatory grounds.

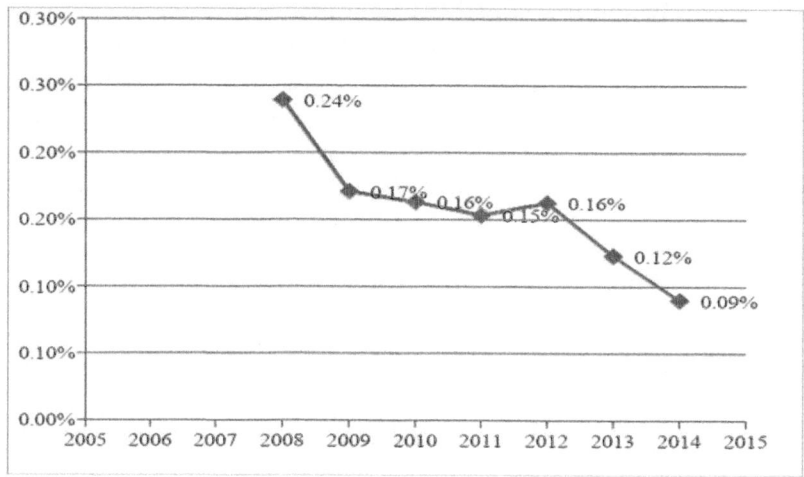

Figure 1. Change in the percentage of acquittals in public and semi-public prosecutions, 2004-2014

Not only did acquittals decline, but so too did other alternatives to a guilty verdict, such as the termination of court cases by reconciliation with the victim. Such an outcome often serves as an alternative to acquittal in cases where it is legally possible (namely those dealing with minor and less serious offenses where there is a victim). Conversely, from 2013, the proportion of prison sentences, which had been systematically declining for years, increased. Data

---

right to). It is possible, however, to exclude from the Judicial Department's detailed statistics only those cases of private prosecution which came to the court from private citizens. As M. Pozdnyakov demonstrated (2012, unpublished manuscript), the statistics on cases of private prosecution brought to the courts do not significantly differ from the statistics on comparable cases of public and semi-public prosecution; therefore, their exclusion should not have a meaningful impact on the conclusions.

for the first half of 2014 confirm this trend. However, in an analysis of the data from 2014, the effect of the broad amnesty declared in honor of the 20th anniversary of the Constitution that year should be considered.[11] To illustrate this effect, we can compare the data for 2013 and 2014. In 2013, the cases of 3,262 people were dismissed in court by amnesty and another 338 were exempted from punishment and pardoned by a court verdict[12] (of these, 1,937 were cases of semi-public prosecution and 152 were cases of public prosecution, respectively). These numbers are fairly typical. In 2014, the figures were 15,240 and 2,377 people. Of these, 13,293 were cases of semi-public prosecution and 2,377 were cases of public prosecution, for a total of 15,670 cases. This total figure is what we will amend further.[13] This figure constitutes a significant portion of all the cases of this type heard by the courts — around 2 percent. Considering that these figures do not change rapidly from year to year, such an unusually large number of pardons has a considerable impact on the direction of the trends being discussed (recall that we are talking about the entire body of court rulings, not just a sample, so any changes here are statistically significant).

Trends toward increasingly harsh — or, conversely, less repressive — outcomes to judicial proceedings depend on the judicial practice adopted in the court system, the balance of power between the various branches of government and the courts, and the level of public scrutiny. Additionally, the judicial system basically does not control the inflow of criminal cases, for all intents and purposes not exercising its power to refuse to hear cases. The judicial system

---

11 State Duma decree No. 3500-6 DG of December 18, 2013 "Ob ob'yavlenii amnistii v sviazi s 20-letiem prinyatiya Konstitutsii Rossijskoi Federatsii," Rossiiskaya gazeta, December 19, 2013, http://www.rg.ru/2013/12/18/amnistia-d ok.html.

12 The difference between the two situations is only a matter of formalities: In the first instance, the court doesn't bring the case to a close, while in the second instance, it wraps up the case, comes to a verdict and prescribes a specific punishment, but then exempts the convicted person from that punishment.

13 It seems that this does not take into account the already convicted persons release under the amnesty by court decisions. These are only those accused who amnestied during the trial. In other words, these are the people who would have been convicted, acquitted or whose cases would have been dismissed for some other reason if there had been no amnesty.

takes up whatever is presented to it by law enforcement authorities, who play by their own rules.[14]

In order to determine in which direction these systems are developing, we need to amend the data to take the effect of the amnesty into account. Therefore, in addition to the actual data for 2014, we will present data obtained by the following formula. If for each judicial outcome we take X_{actual} as the number of individuals for whom the trial actually ended in such an outcome, then

$$X_{\text{adjusted for amnesty}} = X_{actual} + \frac{X_{actual} * \text{number of pardons}}{(\text{total number of cases tried in 2014} - \text{the number of pardons})}$$

In other words, supposing that those receiving amnesty would have been distributed across the various judicial outcomes in the same way as those who did not receive amnesty, we can estimate what the data would have been without the 2014 amnesty. On the whole, such a rough estimate downplays the overall repressiveness of the system. For example, this figure underestimates the number of those convicted and overestimates the number of cases that were dismissed, since those who were convicted of more serious crimes had a lower chance of receiving amnesty as well as a lower chance that their cases would be dismissed on non-exculpatory grounds. (The most common reason for a case being dismissed on non-exculpatory grounds was reconciliation with the victim, which the law reserves for those accused of minor or less serious crimes.) Overall, those who committed less serious crimes, as well as those who would have received a sentence not associated with imprisonment, were less likely to receive amnesty. As such, the chosen method of estimation, although quite rough, works against the hypothesis that the judicial system is becoming more repressive. Most of the tables and charts below present both the actual data and the estimates adjusted for amnesty (with corresponding annotation). In order to further evaluate the trends for the year, in several places additional

---

14 M. Shklyaruk, "Traektoriya ugolovnogo dela v ofitsial'noj statistike: na primere obobshchennykh dannykh pravookhranitel'nykh organov," Saint Petersburg, IRL EUSPb, 2014.

data are presented for the first half of 2014, which was largely unaffected by the amnesty.

The total number of people sentenced to imprisonment, which had been falling during the whole post-Soviet period, would have risen if not for the 2014 amnesty.

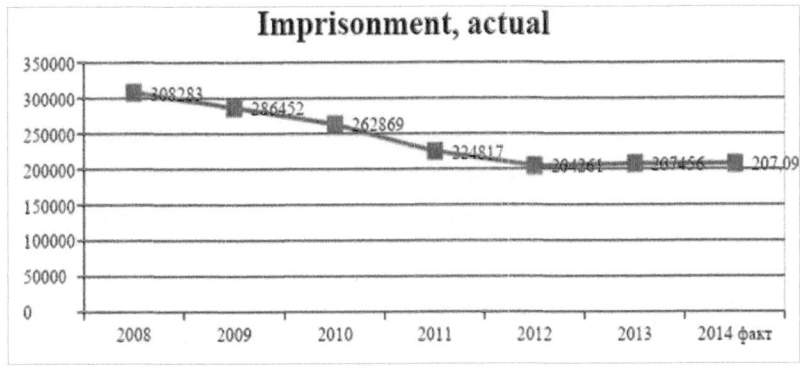

Figure 2. The number of prison sentences handed down, 2008-2014, actual
Basically, this line represents the proportion of various judicial outcomes among those who did not receive amnesty in 2014. The proportion of various judicial outcomes for all cases heard by the courts when those who received amnesty are included is represented by the line "2014 actual" (those receiving amnesty fall under "other outcomes" in the chart).

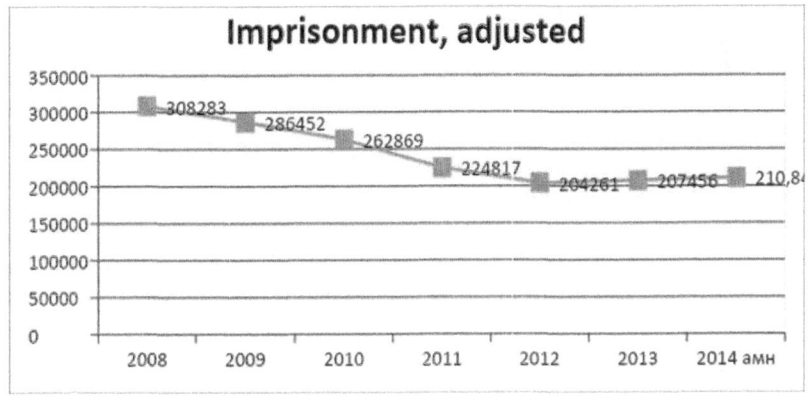

Figure 3. The number of prison sentences handed down, 2008-2014, estimated with adjustment for amnesty

The proportion of prison sentences as a share of all case outcomes also grew. The reduction, over the course of several years, in the number of prison sentences handed down had made it possible to talk about the humanization of sentencing, but that trend was reversed in 2012.

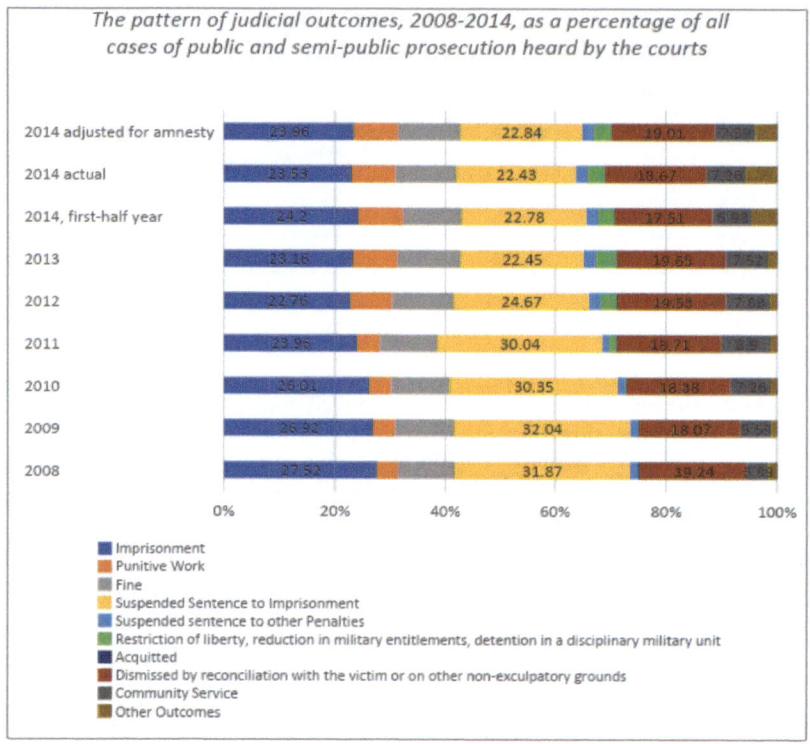

Table 1. The pattern of judicial outcomes, 2008-2014, as a percentage of all cases of public and semi-public prosecution heard by the courts

The chart shows the most common judicial outcomes. In real terms, the long-term rise in more humane forms of punishment as an alternative to imprisonment came to an end; when adjusted for amnesty, a small increase remained. At the same time, the proportion of suspended prison sentences (probations), which had been decreasing during the whole period, leveled off at a historic minimum. Fewer and fewer of those convicted can lead relatively normal lives after sentencing. The proportion of cases dismissed on non-exculpatory grounds fell from 19.65 percent in 2013 to 18.67 percent in 2014 (actual data; adjusting for amnesty has little impact on this trend)—see Figure 4.

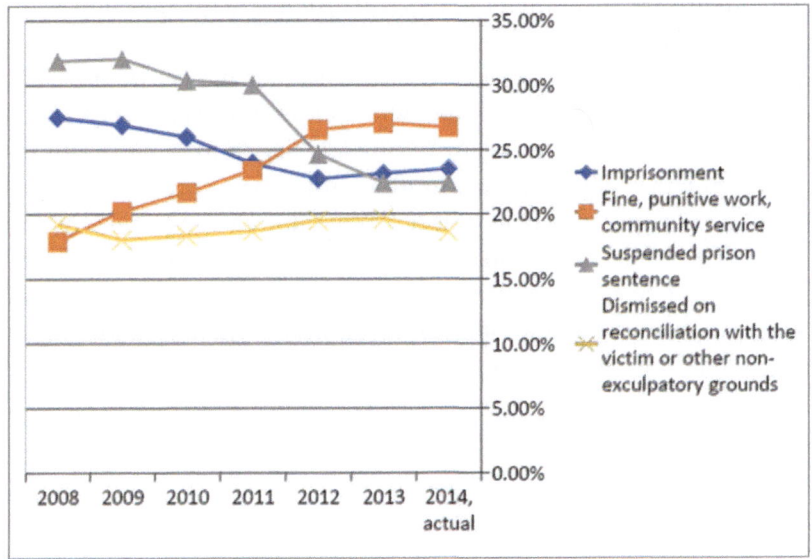

Figure 4. Pattern of judicial outcomes, 2008–2014, actual

Repressive trends do not appear only in sentencing. While in 2011 the courts returned 12,216 criminal cases to the prosecutor for gross errors (in exact legal language, "to correct deficiencies pursuant to article 237 of the Criminal Code"), in 2014 that number dropped to 9,817. That figure represents an approximately 25-percent decrease (the total number of cases of public and semi-public prosecution heard by the courts during this period fell only 6 percent, from 938,111 to 880,115—a much smaller decrease). Accordingly, the proportion of cases the courts returned to prosecutors decreased from 1.3 percent to 1.1 percent over a three-year period. This indicates a rapid decline in judicial oversight of the quality of law-enforcement work prosecutors presented to the courts.

If in 2011 the courts considered 190,822 petitions for parole and approved 56 percent of them, in 2014, they considered 132,358 (one-third fewer) such petitions and approved 41 percent of them.

The penitentiary system gives prisoners fewer and fewer opportunities to petition for parole, and the courts are less and less willing to approve those petitions.

It also became easier for security officials to get the court's approval for pre-trial "preventative measures" and for investigative and police search activities. It can be said that the courts basically never deny the requests of law enforcement in the course of an investigation. In addition, security officials began to request and receive from the courts far more authorization to restrict citizens' constitutional rights, such as select "preventative measures" in the form of detention and house arrest; extending the length of detention; conducting search and seizure of documents; monitoring and recording telephone and other conversations; and limiting the right to inviolability of the home.

Table 2 shows the comparative data on security agency petitions to the courts for 2011 and 2014.

		2011			2014		
		Considered	Approved	Approved (%)	Considered	Approved	Approved (%)
Pre-trial preventative measures	Detention (par. 1 sec. 2 pg. 29 Code of Criminal Procedure of the Russian Federation)	152,028	135,850	89%	147 428	133 755	91%
	House Arrest (par. 1 sec. 2 pg. 29 Code of Criminal Procedure of the Russian Federation)	1,539	1,346	87%	3,783	3,333	88%
	Lengthening the period of detention (par. 2 sec. 2 pg. 29 Code of Criminal Procedure of the Russian Federation)	180,315	176,840	98%	211,430	207,363	98%
Investigative actions	Search of a residence without the agreement of the occupants, search and/or seizure at the residence, seizure from pawnshop (par. 4,5, 5.1 sec. 2 pg. 29 Code of Criminal Procedure of the Russian Federation)	153,715	144,248	94%	180,157	173,118	96%
	Personal search (par. 6 sec. 2 pg. 29 Code of Criminal Procedure of the Russian Federation)	5,428	5,219	96%	7,564	7,311	97%
	Seizure of objects and documents containing information on deposits and accounts in banks and other lending institutions (par. 7 sec. 2 pg. 29 Code of Criminal Procedure of the Russian Federation)	61,283	59,641	97%	67,384	64,983	96%

		2011		2014	
	Authorization to seize, inspect and confiscate correspondence at post and telegraph offices (par. 8 sec. 2 pg. 29 Code of Criminal Procedure of the Russian Federation)	21,930	21,501 98%	25,949	25,055 97%
	Monitoring and recording of telephone and other conversations (par. 11 sec. 2 pg. 29 Code of Criminal Procedure of the Russian Federation)	144,762	140,047 97%	188,668	183,542 97%
	Seizure of property, including financial resources, of individuals and legal entities held in accounts, on deposit, or in custody of banks of other lending institutions (par. 9 sec. 2 pg. 29 Code of Criminal Procedure of the Russian Federation)	11,512	9,907 86%	22,748	19,726 87%
Operational-investigative activities (police work)	Restriction of citizens' Constitutional right to the confidentiality of correspondence, telephone conversations, telegraphic and other communications transmitted over telecommunications networks and by post	329,415	326,105 99%	513,278	509,022 99%
	Restriction of citizens' Constitutional right to the inviolability of the home	29,545	28,461 96%	32,239	31,667 98%

Table 2. Consideration by the courts of petitions from security agencies, 2011 and 2014

Especially striking is the growth in requests to carry out surveillance on citizens. In the space of three years, the number of court authorizations for wiretapping and intercepting electronic communications (see Andrey Soldatov's article in this volume) in the course of police investigations rose one-and-a-half times, to more than 500,000 per year. Moreover, courts gave such authorization 99 percent of the time. ("In the course of police investigations" means that surveillance is carried out in secret: operational actions are shielded by legislation on state secrets, and citizens do not have access to information about wiretapping even after the fact.) In 2014, the number of requests and authorizations for recording telephone and other conversations in the course of an investigation rose by one-third, approaching 200,000. Courts gave security agencies authorization to seize citizens' property twice as often, to conduct personal searches more than 30 percent more often, and to search residences 17 percent more often. Mind you, authorization from the courts for personal and home searches is something relatively rare in and of itself. As a rule, law enforcement gets by without it, disguising these actions as part of the arrest and body search in the first instance and notifying the court after the fact in the event of an "urgent" search in the middle of the night in the second case. Thus, growth in the number of petitions for court authorization for such actions could even be seen as a positive trend.

The fact that the use of house arrest as an alternative form of pre-trial detention more than doubled can be mentioned as another positive trend (although the ratio of the use of these preventative measures was 1:40 in 2014). It should also be noted that although law enforcement began to request authorization for pre-trial detention from the courts less often, the courts approved those requests even more frequently than before. Law enforcement filed petitions to extend the period of pre-trial detention more often, while the courts, as before, approved them 98 percent of the time.

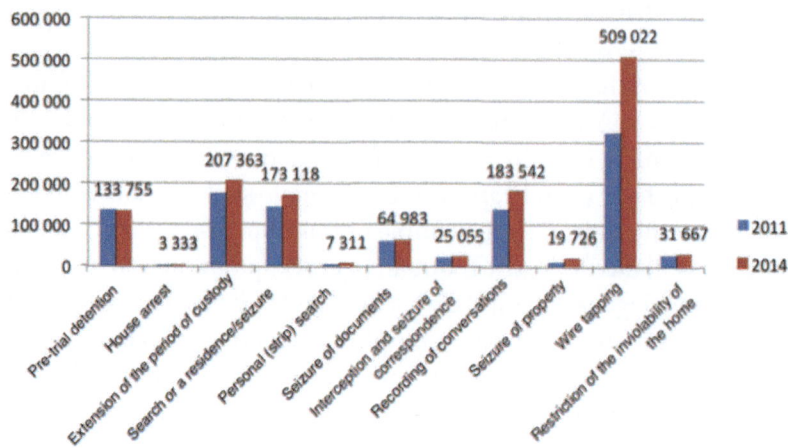

Figure 5. Law enforcement petitions approved by the court in the course of criminal proceedings, 2011 and 2014

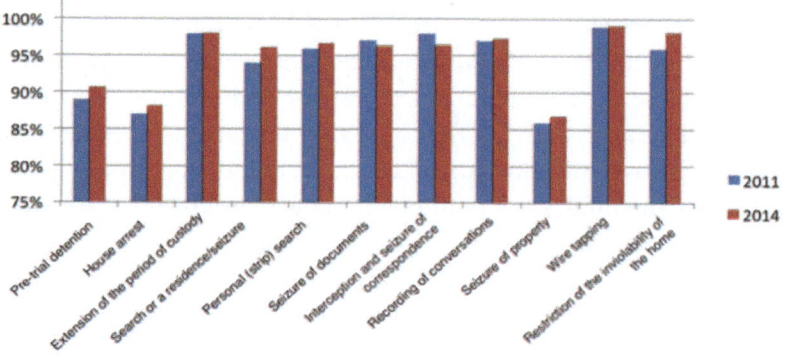

Figure 6. Proportion of law enforcement petitions approved by the court, 2011 and 2014

Conversely, complaints by citizens about the actions of officials carrying out criminal proceedings (pg. 125, Code of Criminal Procedure of the Russian Federation) were less frequently addressed: 11 percent of complaints were settled in 2011, while that proportion shrank to 7 percent in 2014. The same trend can be seen concerning petitions for compassionate release (par. 6 pg. 397, Code of Criminal Procedure of the Russian Federation) — in 2011 such petitions were approved 35 percent of the time, while that figure dropped to 22 percent in 2014.

The number of cases dealt with by special procedure, in which the prosecution's case is not disputed and later appeal of the court decision is basically impossible, also grew. In 2011, 56 percent of all cases heard by the courts were handled by special procedure, a figure that rose to 65 percent in 2014.[15] Repressive trends are intensifying: courts pay less and less attention to the legality of criminal prosecution and deal less and less strictly with investigators and prosecutors. Expert lawyers speak of sharply declining standards of evidence as courts lower demands for materials coming from law enforcement agencies. If earlier a formalistic approach was reflected in the fact that judges were less interested in the substance of the case being heard than in making sure that the documentation was correct and that the Code of Criminal Procedure was followed to the letter (at least on paper), they are now prepared to "forgive" carelessness in filing cases as well as clear procedural irregularities. In other words, federal courts are becoming an extension of the repressive institutions of the state to an even greater degree, unable to exert their own influence in deciding the outcome of even common-or-garden cases — to say nothing of "landmark" ones. The case of the Navalny brothers (the so-called "Yves Rocher Case"), in which the verdict was handed down in public before the judge had finished preparing the complete text, is a prime example of this trend: the formalities of the case limit judges less and less even when a case garners maximum public attention.

Conclusion

The continuing degradation of the courts, the reduction of their role in the overall system of government, their subordinate position in relation to law enforcement agencies in typical criminal proceedings, and their adherence to orders "from above" in cases of a political nature all affect the way that citizens themselves perceive the

---

15 Unlike other figures, this one includes cases of private prosecution the way the data is presented in the Judicial Department report doesn't allow them to be excluded from this category.

judiciary. Although the "ratings" of the Russian courts rose slightly on the post-Crimea wave, together with the ratings of other branches of government, citizens have an extremely low assessment of their influence.[16] In January 2014, in response to the question "What role do the various branches of government and public institutions play in the lives of Russians?", Russians put the courts lower than almost all the other official institutions (only the police were relegated to a lesser role). For comparison, ten years ago, although the courts scored fewer points in polling, in the eyes of respondents, they exceeded both the Duma and the Federation Council in importance.

In ratings of public trust in government institutions from September 2014,[17] the courts again occupied one of the lowest spots — only 26 percent of the population trusts them. A year earlier, 21 percent of people trusted the courts, representing one of the most insignificant increases on the list: practically all other government institutions gained far more "points" in polling from 2013 to 2014. Even against the backdrop of an increasingly loyal population and an overall positive perception of government institutions, the judicial system appears to be an outlier. 2014 failed to bring the Russian judicial system any victories or an improvement in operations; meanwhile, its prospects appear even more dismal.

---

[16] "Rol' sotsial'nykh institutov," Levada Center. February 12, 2015, http://www.levada.ru/12-02-2015/rol-sotsialnykh-institutov.

[17] "Doverie institutam vlasti," Levada Center, November 13, 2014, http://www.levada.ru/13-11-2014/doverie-institutam-vlasti.

The Taming of the Internet

Andrey Soldatov

Vladimir Putin gave the "Crimea speech" on March 18, 2014. After some words on the shared historical fate of Crimea and Russia, he shifted to the external threat:

> Some Western politicians are already threatening us, not only with sanctions, but with the prospect of aggravating our internal problems. I would like to know what they have in mind: the actions of some fifth column — a different kind of "national traitors" — or do they believe that they can worsen Russia's socioeconomic position and thereby provoke popular dissatisfaction? We consider such statements irresponsible and overtly aggressive and will react accordingly.[1]

Several days earlier, three independent online media outlets — grani.ru, ej.ru, and kasparov.ru — as well as Aleksey Navalny's blog were blocked by decision of the Federal Service for Supervision of Communications, Information Technology and Mass Media (Roskomnadzor) for "calls for unauthorized mass gatherings,"[2] while a new website, predatel.net (a list of "national traitors," in which the authors included Aleksey Navalny, Boris Nemtsov, Sergey Parkhomenko, Sergey Aleksashenko, Artem Troitsky, and other famous liberals), had already been online for 10 days. At that moment, the Russian approach to internet censorship took its final form: a combination of administrative measures to block undesirable information and intimidation backed by the very highest levels of government.

---

1. "Obrashchenie prezidenta Rossijskoi Federatsii," March 18, 2014, http://kremlin.ru/events/president/transcripts/20603.
2. "Ogranichen dostup k riadu internet-resursov, rasprostranyavshikh prizyvy k nesanktsionirovannym massovym meropriyatiyam," Rozkomnadzor, March 13, 2014, http://rkn.gov.ru/news/rsoc/news24447.htm?print=1.

Blacklists

Since November 2012, new legal standards have been in place that have effectively established censorship of the internet—specifically, the creation of the "Registry of Prohibited Information." The country currently has four "blacklists" of prohibited websites. The first consists of resources prohibited for extremism; sites accused of disseminating propaganda on child pornography, suicide, and drugs are on the second list; and piracy sites are on the third. The fourth list appeared in February 2014, on the initiative of Deputy Andrey Lugovoy, to block websites containing calls for unauthorized protests based on a prosecutor's demand (that is, without a court decision). It is precisely on this fourth list that ej.ru, kasparov.ru, grani.ru, and Aleksey Navalny's blog landed.

Elements of the system existed earlier: the blocking of websites began in 2007, although at that time it was by court order rather than systematic, such that websites blocked in one region might still have been accessible in another.[3] In November 2012, internet censorship became systematic: one agency—Roskomnadzor—is responsible for blocking blacklisted sites across the country, while frequent inspections by local prosecutors and Roskomnadzor have led to the installation of equipment for filtering "illegal content" everywhere, from schools to universities to libraries.

The Federal Financial Monitoring Service's (Rosfinmonitoring) system for blocking terrorists' bank accounts was used as a model. Rosfinmonitoring brings together data from the Prosecutor General's Office, the Ministry of Justice, the Investigative Committee, and the Ministry of Foreign Affairs to compile a list of organizations linked to terrorism. They then post the list on a special site, which all banks can access with a password, and the banks block the accounts of the blacklisted clients.

Roskomnadzor is now adding online media resources to a list of prohibited websites on the basis of court decisions; information

---

3   During this period, websites were blocked for publications of articles and books from the list of texts banned for extremism by the courts. See "Ekstremistskie resursy v Edinom reyestre zapreshchennykh sajtov"," Sova Center, http://www.sova-center.ru/misuse/docs/2014/08/d30056/.

received from the Ministry of Internal Affairs (MVD), the Federal Drug Control Service (FSKN), the Federal Consumer Protection Service (Rospotrebnadzor), the prosecutor's office; and sometimes even complaints from outraged citizens (for example, activists from Cyber-Army of the Safe Internet League). The registry, available at zapret-info.gov.ru, is updated regularly, and telecommunications service providers are required to familiarize themselves with its contents and block access to blacklisted websites or pages. Service providers can lose their licenses for neglecting to block content.

Intimidation or Technologies?

Experience gained from three years of the Russian system of internet filtering shows that it was technologically ineffective — users could access blocked websites at will, not only using tools such as Tor, but also by using Google Translate (when sending text to the translator, the source is accessed through Google's site and the blocking does not work, as it is targeted at access from the Russian Federation). However, the technical weakness of the filtration system never bothered Roskomnadzor. In spring 2013, the agency's deputy director, Maxim Ksenzov, presented the first results of the implementation of the internet-filtration program. He admitted that "in most cases, there remain ways for skilled users to bypass the blocking of websites,"[4] but immediately added that this was of little importance, as the "user base able to employ protected tunnels and/or special software to bypass website-blocking is currently insignificant."

Indeed, the number of users attempting to circumvent the censorship was low, and that was immediately felt by the journalists of the blocked websites, whose audience fell by almost half. Additionally, it turns out that in contrast to the big three political sites,[5] the

---

[4] Materials for Roskomnadzor Deputy Director Maxim Ksenzov's statement at Roskomnadzor's expanded session on May 14, 2013, in part regarding an analysis of existing methods of controlling access to online media resources and recommendations for their application, Roskomnadzor, May 15, 2013, http://rkn.gov.ru/press/developments/speech/news19960.htm.

[5] "Zablokirovannye za osveshchenie "Bolotnogo dela" internet-izdaniya schitayut, chto blokirovka ravnotsenna ikh zakrytiyu ," Vedomosti, March 10, 2015,

owners of other blocked sites (which even by official figures numbered in the thousands) were not prepared to fight for their rights. That same day, Ksenzov's boss, Roskomnadzor Director Alexander Zharov, spoke about this fact with visible satisfaction: "Among the thousands of owners of these outlets, only a few publicly disagreed, and there is only one documented case of someone going to court."[6] He added that 82 percent of Russian citizens expressed support for the law on the Registry of Prohibited Information.

At the same time, unlike, for example, China, which has created an army of thousands of censors to implement its political censorship of the internet, Roskomnadzor remains a relatively small agency in which only tens of people deal with the internet. Roskomnadzor has "volunteer assistants" who search for expressions of disloyalty. That work is carried out by two organizations — the Safe Internet League and MediaGuard (Mediagvardia) (a project of United Russia's "Young Guard") — but the work of these activists is not very effective. According to the Safe Internet League's annual report for 2014, the League has 20,000 "cyber warriors" in Russia, the CIS, and Eastern and Western Europe (this figure is impossible to verify using independent sources), but they generally look for sites offering sexual services, etc.[7]

Of the two organizations, MediaGuard probably puts more emphasis on political searches. By its own count, MediaGuard has 3,926 activists who have managed to take down 2,475 sites since the start of the project — a small number considering that the project was launched in February 2013. For comparison, by the summer of 2015, Roskomnadzor had blocked 500 mirrors of grani.ru alone, where each mirror is considered an independent resource. According to data from Roskomsvoboda (a project of the Pirate Party, which advocates for total freedom of the internet), at the time of

---

    http://www.vedomosti.ru/newspaper/articles/2015/03/10/blokirovka-bez-granits

6 "Roskomnadzor director, A.A. Zharov's, statement at Roskomnadzor's expanded session," Roskomnadzor, May 14, 2013, http://rkn.gov.ru/press/developments/speech/news19962.htm

7 "Liga bezopasnogo interneta". Annual Report for 2014, Liga Internet, 2014, http://www.ligainternet.ru/upload/docs/2014-LigaInternet.pdf.

writing, 677,693 sites have been blocked since the Registry of Prohibited Sites' inception.[8]

Despite the technical imperfections, the primary goal of government censorship has been achieved: the space for free speech on the internet is steadily being reduced. The fact is that informal methods, such as intimidation and direct (but not transparent) negotiations with the largest internet companies, are more effective than formal legal actions, administrative blocking, or blacklists. The internet giants themselves were the first to suggest this idea to the Kremlin: in fall 2012, frightened by how crudely, from a technological perspective, the procedure for blocking sites was defined in the law on the Registry of Prohibited Information, the large internet companies turned not to the public nor to the courts to protect their interests, but directly to the highest authorities, where all important decisions in Russia are made.

The law was supposed to block sites by IP address, but since tens or hundreds of different sites can share the same IP address, this could result in the blocking of entire internet services. This is precisely what happened with YouTube when a scandal erupted about the film "The Innocence of Muslims," which many considered offensive to believers. Roskomnadzor reacted quickly and prosecutors in many regions demanded that internet service providers block access to the film. The three largest telecom operators—MTS, Vimpelkom and Megafon—restricted access to the offending video. In so doing, Vimpelkom entirely blocked access to YouTube, where the video was posted, in Chechnya, Dagestan, Karachay-Cherkessia, North Ossetia, and Stavropol Krai. MTS and Megafon showed more flexibility and only blocked access to the video itself. The scandal prompted the leaders of the largest internet companies to appeal to the president's administration.

At the very first meeting, Deputy Chief of Staff Vyacheslav Volodin made it clear that the policy of internet censorship itself was not up for debate and instead offered to discuss the technology used for blocking sites. The companies agreed to this approach.

---

8   Statistika blokirovok, Raspredelenie blokirovok sajtov po vedomstvam. Ru-blacklist.net by Roskomsvoboda, http://reestr.rublacklist.net/visual.

Thus, with stunning ease, the line between free and censored internet was crossed, making future assaults easier for the Kremlin. As a result, the authorities managed to shift onto businesses not only the costs of developing the technological solution, but also the costs of filtering content (Russian telecom operators must purchase the blocking equipment at their own expense).

The leaders of internet companies—both Russian companies and international corporations (Google and Twitter)—took a weak position from the very beginning. Therefore, it is not surprising that, beginning in the fall of 2012, in the course of meetings with government agencies—from the working group of the presidential administration to meetings in the Ministry of Communications and Roskomnadzor—they constantly retreated under the pressure of new legal initiatives to restrict Runet freedom, including the constant addition of reasons for which sites could be blocked.

The constant flow of new control measures in and of itself creates a feeling of constant threat on Runet: the existence of a regime that is frenetically churning out new laws forces internet companies to tread carefully, practice self-censorship, and continually run to consult with the Kremlin. It is unclear how long the government can keep up the current pace of legislation—the range of possible initiatives is limited, after all.

Putin's Role in Taming Runet

The pros and cons of the opaque process of negotiations between the authorities and the internet companies became clear on June 10, 2014, when the sector's business leaders met with Vladimir Putin. This was the second meeting between Putin and internet business leaders in 15 years. He had last met with Runet's business leaders in 1999; in the intervening years, the internet had grown immensely, transforming into a sector employing 1.3 million IT professionals. Runet represents 8.5 percent of GDP, and the markets are engaged in the internet business in various ways—the internet business generates more than five trillion rubles, while online commerce is already more than 2.5 percent of all commerce.⁹

During this period, Russia was one of only a few countries in which the domestic IT sector was able to lead the market, not give up the field to global platforms, and operate without needing any form of government protectionism.

That success was achieved in large part thanks to the establishment of "rules of the game," the most important of which was the Kremlin's recognition of the role of Runet's non-governmental organizations. At the aforementioned meeting in late December 1999 in the Government House, they were granted, with Putin's consent, the right to conduct a preliminary review of all legislation regarding the internet. In the 2000s, this rule was followed and those in the IT sector could discuss lawmakers' ideas on their own sites, including ROCIT (the Regional Public Center for Internet Technologies), founded in 1996 to protect the rights of web users. That meeting with Vladimir Putin, then still prime minister, was the only discussion of that format between Runet's leaders and Putin, and they anxiously awaited a new meeting.

Putin did not show an interest in the internet for many years, but in spring 2014 he made several key statements about the World Wide Web — calling the internet an invention of the CIA and attacking Yandex.¹⁰ The result was a drop in Yandex, Mail.ru, and Qiwi stock prices on the NASDAQ exchange. These statements, made in the context of an unrelenting stream of repressive legislative initiatives, caused panic in the internet community. American portfolio investors began coming to Moscow, concerned about the prospects of the Russian internet sector. After that, the country's largest internet companies received invitations to a meeting with the president, this time in a Moscow business center rather than a government building.

---

9   "Internet Entrepreneurship in Russia Forum," President of Russia. June 10, 2014, http://en.kremlin.ru/events/president/news/45886.
10 "Mediaforum nezavisimykh i mestnykh SMI," April 24, 2014, http://kremlin.ru/events/president/transcripts/20858.

Before Putin's arrival, the companies' leaders met in an open session, discussing the future of the Russian internet. However, Arkady Volozh (Yandex), Dmitry Grishin (Mail.ru Group), Andrey Cheglakov (Rostelekom), German Klimenko (Liveinternet), Nikolay Molibog (RBK), Sergey Fage (Ostrovok.ru), Mael Gave (Ozon), Alexander Mamut (Rambler & Co), Oskar Khartmann (KupiVIP.ru), and Boris Dobrodeev (vKontakte) avoided talking about the harmful effects of government regulation of Runet in its current form. The "blogger" law, which requires the registration of bloggers with more than 3,000 followers, was mentioned only once, by Mr. Dobrodeev's son, new to vKontakte, who found a point of pride for the industry in it: on vK, he said, there are about 80,000 groups with more than 3,000 followers, which is almost more than the number of online media outlets in the country. None of the participants mentioned Vladimir Putin and his harsh words about the internet.

When Vladimir Putin finally arrived at the business center, it became clear that he had agreed to the meeting with no intention of having a serious conversation with the sector's leaders. The meeting was organized by the Internet Initiatives Development Fund, which was established by the Agency for Strategic Initiatives (the Agency itself was established by Putin during his time as prime minister in order to become Skolkovo's innovation rival) and the fund used the presence of recognized industry leaders, including Yandex and Mail.ru, to lend legitimacy to their own startups and present them to the president. Apparently, this was the principal tactical aim of the meeting. Incidentally, it was successful: the fund's director, Kirill Varlamov, a former Uralmash engineer, nominee of the All-Russian People's Front and Putin confidant during the 2012 elections, sat to Putin's right at the meeting, while Yandex's Arkady Volozh got the seat to his left. These government-financed replicas gained legitimacy from the presence of industry leaders.

Dmitry Grishin was the only person who raised the issue of the regulation of Runet, although the tone of his remarks clearly reflected the altered relationship between the Kremlin and the industry by summer of 2014:

We are not cold-hearted; we actually love our country. We want it to be comfortable to live and work here and for it to also be comfortable to exist online. We understand that the internet has become large, that it has grown and become an inextricable part of our society. Therefore, in principle, regulation is necessary. And if we look at the ideas that are set out in the regulatory measures, they are quite correct. Unfortunately, however, it sometimes happens that the realization of this regulation intimidates people. It would really be desirable to develop, perhaps, a systematic process, allowing us not only to listen, but also to hear, so that we could see that there is feedback that can be implemented. That would be very, very important.[11]

Despite having the opportunity to speak to Putin directly, leading industry representatives decided not to defend themselves. No matter what might be rumored, Varlamov's Internet Initiatives Development Fund was the only beneficiary of direct talks with the president—Putin made it clear that for him, the face of Runet would not be independent players establishing modern, competitive companies, but the state-sponsored projects of the Internet Initiatives Development Fund.

A year later, in spring 2015, Putin again hosted internet entrepreneurs, this time at the presidential residence in Novo-Ogarevo. The room was filled exclusively with representatives of startups supported by Varlamov's Internet Initiatives Development Fund.[12] At this meeting, the establishment of a new platform for dialog between the Kremlin and the internet industry was announced: the Internet Development Institute would be tasked with replacing the social networks established by the real internet business leaders in the 1990s.

These civil society organizations, which served as platforms to discuss legislative initiatives within the framework of the agreement reached with Putin in December 1999, had by then already been placed under government control. In December 2014, ROCIT, which had visibly been in crisis for several years, was hurriedly resuscitated; Leonid Levin, head of the State Duma Committee on Information Policy, Information Technology and Communications,

---

11 Quote from the Internet Entrepreneurship in Russia Forum cited above.
12 "Vstrecha s internet-predprinimateliami,", March 27, 2015, http://kremlin.ru/events/president/transcripts/49019.

and a PR professional with no direct experience in the internet industry, became chairman of the board.

Varlamov, as well as ROCIT Director Sergey Grebennikov, joined the institute's board, and it is explicitly stated on the institute's website that its creation was "supported by the Administration of the President of the Russian Federation, represented by V.V. Volodin."[13]

The Interests of the Intelligence Agencies

Many legislative initiatives put forward under the pretense of battling illegal content and protecting the personal information of Russian citizens were actually determined by the interests of the intelligence agencies. What makes Russian internet censorship unique is that it is directly tied to electronic surveillance. This connection between internet censorship and surveillance was already noticeable in the summer of 2012, when the Registry of Prohibited Information law was being discussed.

The internet companies then rushed to the Kremlin to discuss exactly what blocking mechanisms the government would use and took a united front against blocking by IP address, because, as mentioned earlier, this method would put entire services at risk over one video or post. The only alternative to this crude method was DPI technology (deep packet inspection), which is capable of blocking individual pages on any internet service—from YouTube to social media. Although DPI is not mentioned in the legislation on internet censorship, the Ministry of Communications and Mass Media, as well as representatives of the largest internet companies, decided that it was the technology that was most suitable for internet censorship.

According to State Duma Deputy Ilya Ponomarev,[14] at the end of August a working group presided over by Minister of Communications Nikolay Nikiforov convened, with participants from Google and other leading players in the online market. Using the

---

13 Institut razvitiya Interneta (IRI), http://xn--h1aax.xn--p1ai/about/.
14 Personal conversation with author in 2012.

case of YouTube as an example, they discussed how to create a mechanism to block individual videos rather than YouTube as a whole. "They agreed on a mechanism that satisfied everyone," claimed Ponomarev, a proponent of the amendments and the registry, clarifying that he was talking specifically about DPI.

Most technologies that analyze internet traffic can see only the headers of information packets being transmitted over a network, as well as their point of origin and final destination. DPI technology allows an internet provider to look into the packets, giving them the ability to not only monitor traffic, but filter it, clamping down on a particular service or blocking content.

As Eric King, head of the research arm at Privacy International, noted during a conversation with the author, DPI allows the government to dig into everyone's internet traffic and read, copy, or even modify his or her messages and viewed pages. "We now know," said King, "that these technologies were used in Tunis before the revolution."

By September 2012, it had become clear that DPI's identification capabilities could easily be combined with SORM, the national surveillance system.

SORM (System for Operational Investigative Activities) was developed in the bowels of the KGB at the end of the 1980s and has been constantly updated since. As a result, today SORM-1 is responsible for wiretapping, including mobile networks; SORM-2 intercepts internet traffic; and SORM-3 is supposed to provide for the collection of information from all types of communications networks, long-term storage of this information, and access to the personal details of subscribers. The system's primary distinguishing feature is the absence of any type of controls, which has remained in all versions of SORM. This is explained by a technical difference between the Russian SORM standard and the European ETSI and American CALEA systems.

In the United States and Europe, a law enforcement agency gets a court order to surveil a specific individual and passes it on to the telecom operator, which retrieves the information and sends it to the intelligence agency. In Russia, an FSB officer also must get permission from a judge, but he is not required to show it to anyone but his supervisors. Telecom operators do not have the right to know whose conversations or correspondence the intelligence agency is intercepting. Therefore, the system is technically designed differently: the FSB has at its disposal SORM's control points (PUs), which are located in the local FSB administration's building. This system is copied throughout the country, and in each regional center of the local FSB administration the cables from all the regional telecom operators are combined. The system is designed this way because it was developed by the USSR's KGB, and presumably in those days no one thought about any kind of controls on government surveillance. After the fall of the Soviet Union, the requirement to get a court order was added, but they did not bother to change the system from a technical perspective, with the result that it is not necessary to show the court order to anyone outside the ranks of the intelligence agencies.

In the fall of 2012 in Moscow, at the largest information security conference, InfoSecurity, there was a discussion of "SORM in a Convergence Environment." Normally, only professionals participate in such events, and the room was filled with SORM division chiefs, telecommunications bosses, and representatives of specialized technical equipment manufacturing companies. DPI immediately became one of the most important topics in the discussion. Many people were convinced that DPI was the only way to ensure that SORM functioned in the new "convergence" conditions, in an era of cloud computing and diverse telecommunications services. The idea of pairing SORM with the DPI technology at the disposal of the telecommunications operators did not seem to make anyone uncomfortable, although professionals must have known that combining the two was illegal at the time.

The two technologies, SORM and DPI, finally came together in April 2015, when Russia launched a new, updated SORM system on the internet. This new version of SORM was introduced by the Ministry of Communications Order No. 63, signed in April 2014, despite protests from the telecommunications operators.[15] The order requires the installation of equipment capable of intercepting information on services such as "webmail email services, including mail.ru, Yandex.ru, rambler.ru, gmail.com, yahoo.com, aport.ru, rupochta.ru, hotbox.ru."[16]

With the help of the combined functions of SORM and DPI, Russian intelligence agencies were able, for the first time, to not only surveil specific individuals, but also detect and identify, in the general stream of data, anyone discussing certain topics online or visiting certain pages on websites or social media platforms. This change brings the Russian system much closer to the concept of mass surveillance than it was a year ago.

However, new surveillance technologies are not only being introduced together with content filtering. Besides the registration of bloggers, the anti-blogger law of 2014 requires companies providing platforms for bloggers (the law calls them "organizers of the dissemination of information on the internet") to "store within the territory of the Russian Federation information on the reception, transmission, delivery, and/or processing of voice information, written text, images, sounds, or other electronic communications of internet users, and information about these users, for a period of six months from the end of their engagement in such activities, and to provide specified information to authorized government authorities carrying out investigative activities or ensuring the security of the Russian Federation..."[17]

---

15 Prikaz Minkomsvyazi Rossii "Ob utverzhdenii Pravil primeneniya oborudovaniya system kommutatsii, vklyuchaya programmnoe obespechenie, obespechivayushevo bipolnenie ustanovlennikh deystvii pri provedenii operativno-po-zusknikh meropriyatii. Chast III. Pravila primeneniya oborudovaniya kommutatsii I marushrutizatsii paketov informatsii setey peredachi dannikh, bklyuchaya programmnoe obespechenie, obespechivayuschevo bypolnenie ustanovlennikh deystvii pri provedenii operativno-rozisknikh meropriyatii," Minkomsvyaz Rossii, April 16, 2014. http://www.minsvyaz.ru/ru/documents/4249/#tdocumentcontent.

16 Ibid.

17 Federal law of the Russian Federation from May 5, 2014. No. 97-F3 "O vnesenii izmenenij v Federal'ny zakon "Ob informatsii, informatsionnykh tekhnologiyakh i o zashchite informatsii" i otdel'nye zakonodatel'nye akty Rossijskoi Federatsii po voprosam uporyadocheniya obmena informatsiej s

That means that blogging services and social networks must provide Russian intelligence agencies with round-the-clock access to their users' metadata. While the security agencies were getting new powers, other government agencies were buying social media monitoring systems en masse. The author of one of the most high-profile projects of this kind was another parastate entity masquerading as an NGO: the Foundation for the Development of Civil Society, led by Konstantin Kostin, the former head of the presidential administration's Office of Internal Policy. The foundation plans to research new media with technology from the American company Crimson Hexagon. Announcing the project in July 2013, Kostin said, "We have created a system that will analyze what is happening on Russian social media, and not just politics."[18]

Although surveillance opportunities for the intelligence agencies have increased significantly in recent years, the Russian approach to internet censorship—at least for now—does without mass arrests of bloggers or journalists for their published posts. The situation in Russia seems considerably less harsh than, for example, in Turkey, where dozens of journalists are behind bars for their work. (Interestingly, despite this fact, the level of freedom of speech in Turkey is rated higher than in Russia.[19]) It seems that the Russian system of internet censorship does not need mass repression of bloggers and journalists to be effective.

---

ispol'zovaniem informatsionno-telekommunikatsionnykh setej," Rossijskaya Gazeta, May 6, 2014, http://www.rg.ru/2014/05/07/informtech-dok.html.

18 "Former head of the Kremlin's Internal Policy Office, Konstantin Kostin: Naval'nomu opasno idti na vybory. Kar'yera Nemtsova zakonchilas' na vyborakh mera Sochi," TV Channel Dozhd, July 1, 2013, http://tvrain.ru/teleshow/govorite_s_yuliey_taratutoy/eks_glava_upravlenija_vnutrennej_politiki_kremlja_konstantin_kostin_navalnomu_opasno_idti_na_vybory_karera_nemtsova_zakonchilas_na_vyborah_mera_sochi-346962/.

19 For example, Freedom House rates press freedom in Turkey as "partially free" and press freedom in Russian as "not free." See 2015. "Freedom in the World," Freedom House, https://freedomhouse.org/report-types/freedom-world#.Vda9hCztmkp.

The Next Step

There are now three courses of action, the effectiveness of which will determine the plan of attack on Runet's freedom going forward.

The first is putting pressure on global platforms such as Google, Facebook, and Twitter to move servers storing Russians' personal data to Russia. The first attempts of this kind were made not long before Edward Snowden's arrival in Moscow, and Russian lawmakers specifically referred to Snowden's revelations when promoting the server transfer law approved in the summer of 2014.[20] The law set September 2015 as the deadline for transferring the servers. This story is a typical example of the Russian approach to taming Runet; pressure on companies and intimidation are combined with expanded technical and administrative capabilities for the intelligence agencies. Negotiations on the transfer of servers are being held behind closed doors in the Kremlin; over the past year, all major global platforms have sent their representatives to Moscow for talks. The pressure appears to have been effective. PayPal moved its servers to Russia in February 2015.[21] In April, at a meeting in the Ministry of Communications, Rostelecom employees reported that Google had moved servers to their facilities.[22] Samsung began moving their servers to Russia in June.[23] Undoubtedly, all parties involved in these negotiations are well aware that moving

---

20   Law No. 242-F3 "O vnesenii izmenenij v otdel'nye zakonodatel'nye akty RF v chasti utochneniya poryadka obrabotki personal'nykh dannykh v informatsionno-telekommunikatsionnykh setyakh," (known as the "law on personal data") adopted in July 2014 requires the personal data of Russians to be stored in Russia. It set September 2015 as the deadline to transfer the servers with the data.

21   "PayPal perenes servery v Rossiyu, chtoby khranit' personal'nye dannye " ITReviewer.ru, February 13, 2015, http://itreviewer.ru/news/26703/paypal-perenes-servery-v-rossiyu-chtoby-hranit-personalnye-dannye/.

22   "Google nachala perenosit' servera v rossijskie data-tsentry ," RBC, April 10, 2015, http://top.rbc.ru/technology_and_media/10/04/2015/5522a9f69a794752a5f478fa

23   "Samsung perenosit dannye rossiyan na rossijskie servera," Business info, June 11, 2015, http://b-online.ru/infobusiness/3299-samsung-perenosit-dannye-rossiyan-na-rossiyskie-servera.html.

the servers makes the information on them available to the Russian intelligence agencies.

The second course of action is to combat tools for circumventing internet censorship, such as virtual private networks (VPNs) and Tor. The number of Tor users in Russia has exploded since the fall of 2013, and the authorities are aware of this fact. Government officials, legislators, and activists loyal to the administration have repeatedly called for a ban on these types of tools, and it seems this could be yet another avenue for introducing additional legal restrictions and another front in Roskomnadzor's offensive. The problem, however, is that a legal prohibition will do little in this case. A highly effective technological solution is needed. Additionally, pressure on companies, an integral element of Russia's approach to internet censorship, does not work here: there are no Tor offices in Russia, and because it is a non-profit product specially created to work in countries with repressive regimes, it is impossible to blackmail Tor's creators by closing the Russian market. At the same time, putting pressure on Russian internet service providers to block Tor at their own expense does not look like a promising solution either—technologies to block Tor are not available on the market, so internet service providers simply do not have them.

The third course of action is changes to the infrastructure. The Russian internet, despite its 25-year history, is still highly centralized and geographically vulnerable. Russia is connected to the global network in the West by fiber-optic cables, mainly laid through St. Petersburg to Helsinki and Stockholm (a line to Frankfurt was only recently added), with the lion's share of the cables belonging to Rostelecom, a national telecommunications company operating under state control. Moreover, Russia, on the scale of its vast territory, has relatively few Internet exchange points—only around a dozen (for comparison, the United States has 85). The oldest and largest of these, MSK-9, is in Moscow on the premises of the M9 international telephone station, which also belongs to Rostelecom. These issues periodically prompt Russian officials to think about creating a closed internet infrastructure in Russia, which, at the zero hour, could be disconnected from the outside world while keeping the system functioning within the country. In September 2014, the issue was discussed at a meeting of the Security Council.[24]

In the spring of 2015, the issue was raised again—according to *Kommersant*, the Ministry of Communications is ready to propose a plan to the government to improve the resilience of Runet's infrastructure by creating a domestic IP-address registry, as well as a network traffic route monitoring system, necessary for the network to operate autonomously.[25] This course of action also involves de facto nationalization of the management of the Russian segment of the Internet: officials are insisting on transferring the management functions of the Russian domain .ru from the Coordination Center for Top-Level Domain RU (this center—a non-governmental organization—was established as part of the agreements reached at the meeting with Putin in December 1999) to some government department. If that happens, management of Runet's most important functions will be permanently transferred to the government.

However, even in a worst-case scenario, where global platforms transfer their servers to Russia, mail services and social networks such as Gmail, Facebook and Twitter become transparent to Russian intelligence agencies, content is instantly blocked by Roskomnadzor, and the Russian government gets a "switch" to disconnect Runet from the outside world, it is unlikely that these measures will help the authorities prevent disaffected people from mobilizing via the Internet, should the need arise in society due to some kind of crisis situation.

Russian intelligence agencies, like their predecessor, the KGB, developed their methods of protecting the regime with the expectation of dealing with a handful of dissidents and malcontents. Today, they can block content created by activists and journalists, but they cannot stop the flow of information created by thousands of users—witnesses to a disaster, for example. As the 2011-2012 Moscow protests showed, this kind of content is created in cascades,

---

[24] "Sovet bezopasnosti obsudit otklyuchenie Rossii ot global'nogo interneta," Vedomosti, September 19, 2014, http://www.vedomosti.ru/politics/articles/2014/09/19/suverennyj-internet.

[25] "Runet gotovyat k avtonomii," Kommersant, March 27, 2015, http://www.kommersant.ru/doc/2694953.

completely independent of the "Western devils" or interference from other foreign powers.

Moreover, the Kremlin constantly makes the mistake of trying to interact with social networks the same way as it does with traditional media. An example is the campaign to replace the owner of the vKontakte network. As if repeating the scenario in which the Media-Most company was wrested from Vladimir Gusinsky in the early 2000s, vKontakte's founder, Pavel Durov, was pushed first out of the company's leadership and then out of the country, to be replaced by Boris Dobrodeev, the son of the director of the All-Russia State Television and Radio Broadcasting Company (VGTRK). The Kremlin mistakenly believed that if the company was under state control, then the network would be as well. However, when the conflict began in Ukraine, information on Russian soldiers in the conflict zone became available through vKontakte, as servicemen reported on their whereabouts, posting photos on social networks. In this case, it was irrelevant whether Durov or Dobrodeev was leading the company: no one in the company had control over the content generated by users. Blackout, a complete shutdown of the Internet, remains the only solution available to the Kremlin in the event of a large-scale crisis, and this is unlikely to be seriously considered even by the most radical Kremlin officials.

***

Unlike in China and the Central Asian countries, during the first 20 years of its existence, the internet in Russia developed as a free space. Attacks on internet freedom began only in the summer of 2012, by which time the Runet had already taken on its key features. Its infrastructure was built on Western technologies, and filtration and content-blocking functions were not built in from the beginning. Additionally, Runet did not grow up inside a "Great Firewall," and an army of government censors did not track local Internet users' every move.

The nature of Runet became a major challenge for the Kremlin when Russian authorities began to establish control over this digital space in the summer of 2012. These differences explain why the control strategies chosen by the Kremlin were quite different from those used in, say, China.

The key element of Russia's approach is a continuous deluge of repressive, broadly worded initiatives, which forces companies to run to the Kremlin and other relevant government agencies for clarification. Technologies (both content filtering and electronic surveillance) play a subordinate role in this scheme—they are meant to intimidate, ensuring the loyalty of both internet companies and ordinary Runet users.

Paradoxically, the content filtering systems' imperfections only increase the effects of their implementation: fearing that their services would be blocked completely, internet companies agreed to a dialogue with the Kremlin, offering their own technical solutions and bearing the costs of their development and use.

In the three years since active attacks on Internet freedoms began, large companies have publicly protested only once. Intimidation is at the heart of this approach. It has proven partially effective—by focusing on the technical aspects of this new reality, both Russian internet companies and global corporations have moved surprisingly well from operating on an open internet to working within a censored space. In the three years since active attacks on Internet freedoms began, large companies have publicly protested only once: in October 2013, Vimpelcom, one of the country's largest telecommunications operators, sent a letter to the Ministry of Communications criticizing a draft order that would establish new requirements for systems to legally intercept internet traffic. In the letter, Vimpelcom argued that in addition to imposing additional costs on operators by requiring them to purchase expensive equipment, some provisions of the order were in conflict with the Constitution, which protects the right of citizens to private correspondence.[26] Several other companies supported Vimpelcom's protest,

---

26 "Federal'ny Server Bezopasnosti," Kommersant, October 21, 2014, http://kommersant.ru/doc/2324684.

but the order was signed in April 2014 despite the companies' outrage. The order took effect in April 2015, finally combining the functions of two surveillance technologies—SORM and DPI.[27]

Intimidation works best, however, when it is targeted at specific individuals, and the Kremlin has made far more progress in taming internet companies' leadership than in taming users. The story of soldiers' "Ukrainian" posts on vKontakte proved that the Russian approach to internet censorship was ineffective when content depended on users' actions in a crisis situation.

---

27 See Prikaz Minkomsvyazi Rossii "Ob utverzhdenii Pravil primeneniya…"

The Relationship Between the Center and the Regions:
What Has Changed in Four Years?

Natalya Zubarevich

The crisis has been going on for four years and has become a difficult challenge for the system of governance as a whole as well as for the relationship between the center and the regions. All levels of government have been forced to adapt to the financial contraction. Adaptation requires an adequate assessment of the crisis' duration and the risks associated with it, as well as the most likely trajectory of the recovery—whether stagnation, slow growth, or fast growth. With fewer financial resources, it is necessary to reexamine priorities and the scale of aid to the regions. It is also necessary to find new sources of income and to stimulate the drivers of growth. The system of governance must be changed in order to make it more effective. So how will these challenges be met?

A Resolution to the Crisis: Growth or Stagnation?

The Russian economy's stagnation began in 2013, before the fall in the oil price. It was caused by a worsening investment climate and the rise of institutional barriers to growth. The external shocks of 2014 (the fall in the oil price and, to a lesser degree, the imposition of sanctions) led to an economic recession, but it was moderate compared with the previous crises that Russia had weathered. The most severe declines were in investments, household income, and consumption (see Figure 1).

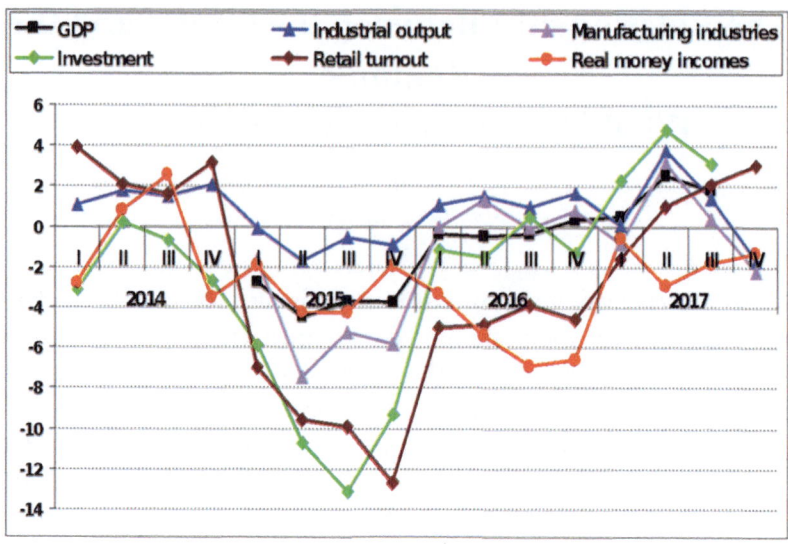

Figure 1. Dynamics of key socio-economic indicators compared with the same quarter of the previous year (percent). Source: Rosstat data.

Beginning in 2016, the Russian government claimed several times that the crisis had ended and that the economy had begun to grow, although judging from the statistical data, this growth was so weak and unstable that it was nearly indistinguishable from stagnation. In late 2017, industrial output began to fall again, and the annual data showed almost no growth in the manufacturing sector (0.2 percent).

The economy's most pressing problem is the decline in investment. For the period from 2014 to 2016, investment shrank by 12 percent, with a decline occurring in the overwhelming majority of regions. It is unlikely that the modest (4.4 percent) growth in investments during 2017 will improve the situation. Investments were concentrated in the regions with the clearest competitive advantages in terms of resources and agglomerations. The important oil-and-gas-producing region of Tyumen Oblast, along with its autonomous okrugs, received nearly 17 percent of the country's investment, while more than 11 percent went to Moscow. In more than half the regions, the decline continued.

The public's most pressing problem is that real incomes have fallen for four years in a row: they shrank 12 percent between 2014 and 2017. People have "tightened their belts," reducing consumption, but it is becoming more and more difficult to economize. Beginning in the spring of 2017, retail trade turnover began to rise due to the growth of consumer credit. Studies show that consumer credit expanded more vigorously in those regions with lower household incomes,[1] even though it is precisely there that the risk of defaulting on credit is highest due to low earnings and unstable employment. It is likely that the individual bankruptcy law Russia has adopted will need to be applied more vigorously, which might increase social unrest. In general, household incomes in the country will rise in 2018 thanks to the indexation of pensions[2] and public-sector wages[3] (the decision on 4 percent indexation was made prior to the presidential elections). It is estimated that these measures will bring about small wage growth in 2018 (about 2 percent), and while this is unlikely to be felt by households, statistically speaking the negative trend will turn to a positive one.

The likelihood of significant economic growth is extremely small. Russia will be on the spectrum between stagnation and weak growth, without noticeable wage growth or rising standards of living. Judging by official statements, the federal government continues to delude itself with hopes of a brighter future. However, the actual policies are far more adequate than the public rhetoric; the government is employing a whole host of measures to adapt to the new realities.

---

1   E. Grishina, Dokhody i uroven' bednosti v pervom polugodii 2017 g.," Russian Economic Development, No. 8, (2017): 48-52.
2   "Indeksatsiya na 4.1 protsenta: glava Mintruda rasskazal o roste sotsial'nykh mensij" RIA Novosti, November 18, 2017. URL: https://ria.ru/society/20170918/1505020259.html
3   M. Gusenko, Dobavyat vsem, Rossiiskaya gazeta, October 5, 2017. URL: https://rg.ru/2017/10/05/biudzhetnikam-povysiatzarplatu-v-2018-godu.html

Budgetary Policy: Fiscal Priorities

Understanding the essence of the policies being carried out helps us analyze budgets. Beginning in the 2000s, a hyper-centralized system of government formed in Russia. Its economic foundation was the concentration of huge oil rents at the federal level and the subsequent redistribution of a portion of those rents to the regions. Two taxes flow exclusively to the federal level: a resource rent tax on the extraction of oil and gas resources, which depends on the price of oil, and the more stable VAT. Another large revenue source for the federal budget—export duties on oil, petroleum products, and natural gas—is also tied to commodity prices.

The fall in the oil price in 2014 primarily impacted the federal budget, where rents were concentrated. The rapid growth of expenditures on national defense—by 28 percent in 2015 and 19 percent in 2016—was another destabilizing factor. Additionally, transfers to the Pension Fund, necessary to cover the deficit, grew. As a result, the federal budget deficit reached 2 trillion rubles in 2015 and nearly 3 trillion rubles in 2016. A rise in the oil price in 2017 reduced the problem slightly—the annual deficit now stands at 1.3 trillion rubles—but that figure is somewhat deceptive: a portion of the transfers to the Pension Fund in 2017 were made not from the federal budget, but from the National Wealth Fund. If all the money had come from the federal budget, as it did in previous years, the deficit would have been 2 trillion rubles. Shrinking oil rents forced the federal government to find other revenue sources, and the primary source became the people. In 2015-2016, public-sector workers' salaries, pensions, and welfare payments were not indexed, while public utility rates, property taxes, public transportation fares, and excise taxes on gasoline and other types of fuel rose, leading to rising utility bills, higher expenditures for automobile owners, more expensive plane tickets, etc. Indirect taxes and payments for small businesses increased as well.

The regions became yet another revenue source for the federal government, not only through reduced aid to the various constituent entities of the Russian Federation, but also by extracting additional revenues from them. We will start with ways in which aid was reduced. First was the reduction of transfers payments for 2014-2016 from 1.73 trillion rubles in 2014 to 1.63 trillion rubles in 2016 (see Table 1). If transfer payments to Crimea are excluded, the reduction was less significant—from 1.60 to 1.54 trillion rubles. The reduction of transfer payments occurred in the context of a budget crisis in the regions. It began in December 2012, before the federal budget crisis, because of additional expenditures connected to the execution of the President's 2012 "May decrees," which raised wages for those employed in healthcare and education, among other measures. The regions were not able to handle the increased expenditures, with the result that the overwhelming majority ran budget deficits and the aggregate debt of the regions and municipalities reached 2.6 trillion rubles in 2016. The situation improved in 2017: owing to increased federal budget revenues from higher oil prices, transfer payments to the regions rose 8 percent, with the exception of those to Crimea, which rose 6 percent.

	2014	2015	2016	2017
Revenues, billions of rubles	8746	9308	9924	10758
Transfer payments, billions of rubles	1728	1683	1635	1771
Transfer payments as a share of revenue (percent)	19.8	18.1	16.5	16.5

Table 1. Consolidated budget revenues of the regions and transfer payments. Source: Federal Treasury data.

While reducing grant aid to the regions, in 2015-2016 the Ministry of Finance began to allocate twice as much in government loans to address the problem of mounting regional debt. Loans were issued at ultra-low rates (0.1 percent), but are still not equivalent to grant aid, as the money needs to be repaid. By November 2017, the amount of debt had declined by 8 percent compared with the beginning of the year, and its structure had improved: low-interest government loans accounted for almost half (44 percent), while high-interest bank loans accounted for less than a third. Government loans, however, are a temporary means of easing serious debt issues; the plan is to drastically reduce the quantity of them beginning in 2018 and then to eliminate them entirely. The federal government will restructure previously-issued loans and extend their repayment periods by 7 or even 12 years for those regions that increase budget revenues faster than the rate of inflation and ensure a balanced budget by optimizing expenditures. Reducing government lending is the second cost-saving measure, but it is being phased in over time and serves as both a "stick" and the "carrot," by way of extending the loans' repayment periods. The risks are clear: 15-20 of the regions with the highest debt burdens and significant deficits are not capable of meeting the Ministry of Finance's demands. In two of them (the Republic of Khakassia and Kostroma Oblast), the "stick" has been used since January 2018: treasury tracking of expenditures was introduced, meaning that all of the region's budget expenditures will be monitored by the federal Ministry of Finance.

The third cost-saving measure is federal pressure on the regions to optimize their budget expenditures on social welfare programs. This is the only area in which the regions maintain relative independence, so the federal authorities can influence them only indirectly; all other social sectors are already tightly regulated from the top. The federal Ministry of Labor and Social Welfare developed a uniform methodology for assessing the neediness of households, on the basis of which welfare payments would be allocated. The idea is a good one—social assistance should focus to a greater extent on helping the poor—but in light of the falling incomes of the entire population and the political risks, it will not be straightforward to implement. Generally, regional budget expenditures on welfare payments did not grow in 2017, and in almost 40 percent of regions, they decreased. Fiscal priorities outweighed political risks.

There is yet another method (the harshest) aimed at cost optimization, which is still being discussed. The Ministry of Finance developed a so-called "model budget" for each region, in which budgetary spending needs are calculated by a uniform standard with adjustments for regional differences. The methodology takes the country's diversity into account to some degree, but fiscal priorities are paramount. According to the Ministry of Finance's calculations, budget expenditures exceed the standard in 67 regions, meaning that the regions need to spend less. This is an attempt at equalization by "lowering the bar." If a model budget is introduced, the budgetary hierarchy will become even more rigid, the center will dictate to the regions how much they should spend, and the federal budget will save substantially on transfer payments. However, overly rigid systems are unstable, and the political risks will inevitably grow. In the meantime, the Ministry of Finance is solving its own cost optimization tasks and is apparently confident that it can solve the regions' problems by "hands-on management" and "plugging the holes." The regions resist as much as they can, as this is their last bastion of control.

In addition to economizing on aid to the regions, the federal government also seized a portion of the regions' budgets. The proportional division of corporate taxes changed: the federal government began receiving 3 percent of the total 20 percent rate, with the regions receiving 17 percent (previously the ratio was 2 percent to 18 percent). This decision was motivated by the need to equalize the budgetary capacity of various regions of the Russian Federation, as corporate taxes are extremely unequally distributed across the regions: revenues are largely concentrated in the more developed regions and a quarter of all corporate taxes go to Moscow. The leaders of the most developed regions initially tried to protest the reduction in their share of corporate tax revenues, but with the exception of the authorities in Tatarstan, the protests stopped after the president approved the measures (and even Tatarstan eventually had to accept the change). As a result, the federal budget received in excess of 72 billion rubles, of which only half was redistributed as aid to less developed regions under a highly disputed algorithm.[4] The proportional distribution of excise taxes on fuel was also changed in favor of the federal government in 2017, a reduction that occurred in 70 regions and caused them to receive 7 percent less in excise duties.

---

4 K. Nikitin, Chto ne tak s nalogovoi amnistiej, Vedomosti, January 23, 2018, https://www.vedomosti.ru/opinion/articles/2018/01/23/748623-nalogovoi-amnistiei.

Furthermore, the federal government used legal loopholes in order to extract a portion of Sakhalin's corporate tax revenues. Sakhalin's government was receiving 75 percent of corporate tax revenues from the "Sakhalin-2" project that was being developed as part of a production-sharing arrangement, but in late 2017, the proportional distribution of these revenues was changed in favor of the federal government. The idea of "dekulakization" emerged after the sharp increase in Sakhalin's budget revenues in 2015 (230 billion rubles), however over the last few years they decreased by nearly half (130 billion rubles in 2017) — which did not prevent the federal government from taking a share of the corporate tax revenue. The authorities in Sakhalin Oblast tried to resist and even threatened public protests due to reduced social spending. To the best of this author's knowledge, they were only able to influence the redistribution of tax revenue, getting a 50:50 split rather than the 75:25 in favor of the federal government that the Ministry of Finance had wanted. The initiator of "dekulakization" was Yuri Trutnev, plenipotentiary representative for the Far East Federal District.

The risks of "dekulakization" were also great for Moscow because of several years of rapid growth in its budget revenues (from 1.55 trillion rubles in 2014 to 2.1 trillion rubles in 2017) owing to the growth of corporate tax revenues as well as revenues from the capital's assets. A fifth of all budget revenues from the regions go to Moscow, and the advantages of the capital's status only became more apparent during the crisis. Moscow's government officials justifiably saw political risks in this situation, and in February 2017 they announced the start of an expensive, large-scale renovation program (relocating residents from old buildings), which President Putin approved. The program was supposed to "kill two birds with one stone" — to prevent the federal government from taking a portion of the revenues from the capital's huge budget at all costs, and to boost the ratings of Mayor Sobyanin, who faces reelection in September 2018. The renovation program violated property ownership rights and was the cause of mass public protests, but it accomplished the goal of protecting the capital's budget revenues.

Generally, during the years of crisis, the federal government's budgetary policies toward the regions became harsher and three current policy trends formed:

- Economizing on aid to the regions, or even taking a portion of their budget revenues to replenish the federal budget;
- Ensuring the regions spend less and balance their budgets, while demanding that they carry out orders from the federal government, i.e., bear additional costs;
- Providing "hands-on" assistance in cases where budgets are in a state of crisis in order to avoid socio-political instability — often with the use of loans that need to be repaid — and simultaneously controlling the region's budget expenditures.

As a result, the federal center's fiscal control over the regional authorities was strengthened regardless of the state of any given region's budget.

Drivers of Growth and Geopolitical Priorities: Conflicts of Interest

Cleary, Russia must accelerate its economic development. Urban agglomerations, import-substitution, and large industrial projects have been declared the primary drivers of growth supported by the government. This fact is talked about so much that it is difficult to see the actual processes behind the rhetoric. We will try to dissect them here.

Interest in the development of agglomerations increased after the fall in the oil price, and not by chance. Russia has two competitive advantages: the high availability of raw materials and the "agglomeration effect." Twenty-one percent of Russians live in cities with populations of more than one million people, and human capital is concentrated. The agglomeration advantage acts in two ways: the effect of scale (cost savings from concentrated populations and economic activity) and the effect of having a large variety of businesses, workers, and consumers. Variety promotes development, even if the Russian government does not understand this fact.

Oil rents can be collected even with bad institutions in place, while the development of agglomerations requires institutional modernization, including the creation of effective local government and significant investments in infrastructure and the urban environment. In Russia, they are trying to form agglomerations administratively by carving out adjacent municipalities and attaching them to large cities. More often still, they develop plans on paper that are sometimes completely disconnected from reality. It is enough to look at a map to see the absurdity of the Ekaterinburg—Chelyabinsk—Perm agglomeration proposed in one of these plans.[5]

The biggest obstacles to the development of cities with populations larger than one million and their agglomerations are institutional—that is, they are connected to the status of municipalities. The so-called "reforms" in local government carried out in the last decade led to a sharp decline in the authority and budget resources of municipalities, including the largest cities (those over one million in population). Money and power are concentrated at the regional level, and it is generally the regional authorities that are responsible for healthcare, education, social welfare, and the development of infrastructure. In order to finance the growing power of the regions, increasing shares of municipal budget revenues were siphoned off to regional budgets. The most important source of tax revenues for large cities is individual income taxes, and the share of individual income taxes going to municipal budgets was reduced over the period from 2012-2016 from 30 percent to 15 percent, with the remainder going to the regional budget. Real estate taxes in Russia are low and cannot form a revenue base for municipalities: for comparison, total personal property (car) tax revenues, which go to the regional budget, are three times larger than real estate tax revenues. Corporate income and real estate taxes also go to the regions.

As a result, even the municipal budgets of large cities (urban districts or city okrugs) are highly subsidized and depend on transfer payments from the regional budget. From 2015 to 2017, transfer payments comprised 57-59 percent of the budget revenues of city

---

5   A. Kudrin, Goroda vmesto nefti, Vedomosti, July 20, 2017, https://www.vedomosti.ru/opinion/articles/2017/07/20/724744-goroda-nefti.

okrugs. Meanwhile, two-thirds of transfer payments are subventions — that is, funds transmitted for the implementation of regional responsibilities and merely distributed by the city. Another quarter of transfer payments are subsidies that are distributed for purposes specified by the regional authorities, which the city must co-finance. In such a system, the local government is completely dependent on the policies of the regional authorities, which have little regard for the city's interests, and does not have enough funds to do anything itself.

The many proposals for the development of agglomerations rarely consider the necessity of reestablishing the financial independence and authority of the cities and directly electing local government leaders.[6] The hope is generally that the federal government will add funds for the development of infrastructure if the city (population larger than 1 million) can land on the list of "specified" agglomerations. The chances are slim, and so far, large sums have only been allocated for politically important projects (the Olympics, Universiade, APEC summit). Cities that will hold 2018 World Cup matches received significantly less due to the crisis. As a result, these cities are falling further and further behind Moscow and St. Petersburg, which are regions of the Russian Federation and have far more power and resources. Agglomerations can become drivers of development only with modernization of the institutional environment, but that is difficult to envisage.

Import-substitution was declared a priority in 2014, after the annexation of Crimea and the Western sanctions and Russian counter-sanctions that followed. In agriculture and the food industry, import-substitution is considered to have been successful. Indeed, the rate of growth of agricultural production was good — 3-5 percent — and only began to decrease in 2017 (see Table 2). However, in 2012 and 2013, before the imposition of sanctions, it was higher — between 6.2 percent and 5.8 percent. The production of foodstuffs grew more slowly than the agricultural sector due to decreased effective demand from the public, whose incomes had fallen for four

---

6   In 75 regions the heads of the large cities are not elected by the people, but by the deputies of local government bodies.

consecutive years. Nevertheless, specialization in food production helped regions during the crisis, and the trajectory of their industrial production was better than the national average during the period from 2014 to 2016. Moreover, the agro-industrial complex received significant assistance from the government; 2-3 percent of all regional budget expenditures were directed toward supporting it. In other manufacturing sectors, import-substitution is going extremely poorly, as shown by the trend in production: in 2015 it was negative (-5 percent), while in 2016-2017 it was close to zero (see Figure 1).

	2014	2015	2016	2017
Change in agricultural production compared to the previous year (percent)	3.7	3.0	4.8	2.4
Change in production of foodstuffs compared to the previous year (percent)	2.5	2.0	2.4	5.6*
Amount assistance to the agro-industrial complex from regional governments (billions of rubles)	276	312	276	271

Table 2. Change in agricultural and food production and the amount of regional government assistance to the agro-industrial complex.
Source: Rosstat and the Federal Treasury
*Data do not include alcohol and tobacco, the production of which steadily declined during the period.

Large industrial projects are still not numerous and are being implemented by leading companies in the fuel and energy sectors. The government actively supports large businesses, which leads to the loss of budget revenues. Projects are exempted from paying basic taxes and export fees for several years, or even receive direct subsidies from the government.[7] Numerous benefits were offered to Sibur for its new gas liquefication plant on the Yamal peninsula and the export of its production; to Gazprom for its gas processing plant being built in Amur Oblast for export to China; and to Rosneft for the reconstruction of its Zvezda shipbuilding factory in Primorsky Krai for building ice-class tankers. The Russian government hopes that these projects will create demand for domestic technologies and highly qualified personnel. Government-supported industrialization is the typical Keynesian model, which is becoming more popular in Russia, however the experience of other countries has shown the vulnerability of this model, especially under conditions of rapid technological growth, as there may not be enough demand for the products of the new businesses in which the government has invested significant resources.

In addition to attempts to accelerate the country's development, the federal government also has other policy priorities — geopolitical ones. Here, the goal is entirely different: to hold territory, regardless of the economic costs. The author has already addressed this issue, identifying three geopolitical priorities on the basis of an analysis of budget statistics, namely Crimea, the Far East, and the North Caucasus.[8] So what changed at the end of 2017?

First, Crimea became the most important of the geopolitical priorities. In 2017, the amount of transfer payments to the Republic of Crimea rose by 55 percent, while transfer payments to Sevastopol rose by 45 percent. In total, Crimea and Sevastopol's share is nearly 6 percent of all transfer payments to the regions, and they are the largest single recipients of federal aid. Moreover, investments in Crimea rose 4.2 times and investments in Sevastopol 2.4 times from January to September of 2017. Between 80 and 85 percent of the in-

---

7 K. Simonov, "Kogda ekonomika neekonomna," Vedomosti, January 16, 2018. https://www.vedomosti.ru/opinion/columns/2018/01/16/747879-ekonomika-neekonomna.

8 N. Zubarevich, "Geopoliticheskie prioritety v regional'noi politike Rossii: vozmozhnosti i riski," Counterpoint, no. 1, September 2015, https://publications.hse.ru/en/articles/167964852.

vestments are government investments, primarily for the construction of the Crimean Bridge, roads, and energy infrastructure. Russian businesses rarely invest in Crimea, fearing sanctions.

Second, the geopolitical significance of the Far East markedly declined. There is not enough government money for the huge territory, and with the exception of the state-controlled Rosneft and Gazprom, businesses are reluctant to invest there. From 2013 to 2016, investment in the Far East Federal District declined by 11 percent in real terms, which is comparable with the average trend for Russia (-12 percent). For the period from 2014 to 2017, investments in the Far East as a proportion of all investments in Russia grew only marginally—from 6 percent to 7 percent. That percentage is very small for a region (okrug) that occupies one-third of the country's territory. Assistance from the federal government is also modest: the Far East receives less than 12 percent of all transfer payments to the regions, the same percentage allocated to the republics of the North Caucasus.

Third, among the regions of the North Caucasus, the prioritization of Chechnya became even more noticeable, not only in terms of spending, but also symbolically. In 2017, the Ministry of Finance allocated Chechnya a "personal" grant of 17 billion rubles in addition to equalization grants and other transfer payments, yet again showing the region's special relationship with the federal government. Chechnya ranked third in terms of transfer payments received in 2017 (62 billion rubles), behind Crimea and Sevastopol (119 billion rubles) and Dagestan (75 billion rubles). Transfer payments as a share of Chechnya's budget revenues consistently exceed 80 percent. It can also be expected that Dagestan will receive a higher priority status, since Vladimir Vasilyev, who formerly served in the police and the State Duma, was appointed its leader in 2017.

Fourth, the exclave of Kaliningrad Oblast was included among the priorities, although that is a special case. Following Russia's accession to the WTO, it was necessary to revise the special economic zone system in Kaliningrad Oblast, as it did not comply with WTO rules. Thus, in 2016-2017 the federal government increased transfer payments in order to preserve the incentives for companies operating there. In 2017, transfer payments rose by 52 percent, most of which went to compensate companies operating in the special economic zone.

The conflict of interests between stimulating drivers of growth and geopolitical priorities is obvious, and for now it is largely being resolved in favor of geopolitical priorities that are extremely expensive for the federal budget and are not capable of accelerating the country's development. However, for the federal government, territorial ties are more important.

Stricter Control and Harsher Punishments: The Rotation of Governors

Changes in the system of administering the regions reflect tighter control from top in several areas. In 2017, a new methodology was adopted to evaluate governors' effectiveness. The previous methodology had proved inadequate from a scientific perspective: the included indicators did not reflect the effectiveness of governance. As a result, Chechnya and Dagestan, which can hardly be considered effectively governed, were consistently among the leaders. The new methodology increased the number of indicators reflecting social and economic trends; there were also more benchmarks characterizing the state of the regions' budgets as well as allowing for the evaluation of the people's attitudes toward various aspects of regional governments' policies. However, no statistical, budgetary, or sociological measurements can replace the most important way that the people can evaluate the actions of the regional leaders: free and fair elections. The federal authorities are not prepared to do that and prefer to use formalized integrated assessments with various indicators in an attempt to raise their quality. These assessments only weakly influence political decision-making, although none of the governors want to be at the bottom. Small ("prize") bonuses are distributed to the governments of the best regions according to the assessments.

Another trend is increased repression of governors, vice-governors, and mayors by bringing criminal cases against them and punishing them with imprisonment. This trend is the norm across the entire country: the repressive machine is working more intensively in order to secure the loyalty of the elites. Russia is having difficulty emerging from the crisis and needs to place blame on someone. Governors have become the scapegoats, blamed for corruption, the long economic recession, and the people's declining standard of living. Political loyalty to Putin no longer helps. Political scientists and the media are actively discussing why criminal cases were brought against the dismissed leaders of the Mari-El Republic and Udmurtia in 2017, and in previous years against the governors of Sakhalin Oblast, Kirov Oblast, and the Komi Republic. However, there is a sense in which it is irrelevant who was imprisoned for what: the deterrent effect is important for the stability of the regime, ensuring the complete loyalty of regional elites to the federal authorities.

The next trend is the replacement of officials and influx of younger officials into the regional leadership as directed from the top. In 2017, there were two series of gubernatorial replacements, but this is not the first time that such large-scale changes have taken place. In the late 2000s, during Dmitry Medvedev's presidency, new governors were appointed in more than 30 regions. The next series of resignations happened in 2012-2013 in connection with the return of gubernatorial elections: roughly a year before the elections, the Kremlin replaced those appointees who had low approval ratings in their regions.

Governors are turning into scapegoats, being held responsible for problems created in large part by the decisions of the federal government. The scheme repeated itself in 2017. Governors with low approval ratings were dismissed, as were those whose regions had experienced elite conflicts, as both constituted a risk ahead of the presidential elections. A new face at the head of the region's leadership can decrease people's dissatisfaction and inspire hopes of a better life, thus increasing turnout for presidential elections and support for the head of state, who made the correct personnel decision. Gubernatorial elections are successful under the conditions of electoral authoritarianism and the candidates the Kremlin sends to the regions win handily. Electoral techniques are well-established:

the municipal filtering system removes strong rivals and low election turnout guarantees the necessary result.

2017 is distinguished by the strategy of making the gubernatorial corps more youthful. Young technocrats who had management experience at the federal level but were unfamiliar with their new regions (Novgorod, Nizhny Novgorod, Kaliningrad, Ivanovo, and Pskov Oblasts; the Republics of Udmurtia and Buryatia; and Nenets Autonomous Okrug) were sent to the regions. Only the head of Perm Krai, Maxim Reshetnikov, who previously worked in the Ministry of Regional Development and Moscow city government, and the former mayor of Samara, Dmitry Azarov, appointed Acting Governor of Samara Oblast after three years serving as a senator in the Federation Council, have had success in their native regions.

The governor of Karelia, Artur Parfenchikov, is also a native of his region but spent a long time in the federal government. The sole exception to this trend of young governors is the governor of Krasnoyarsk Krai, Alexander Uss, who headed the Legislative Assembly before his current appointment. The Kremlin did not risk experimentation in this vast and complex region, where the assets of many of Russia's largest companies are concentrated.

Aside from the young technocrats, representatives of the security services (*siloviki*), generally from the Federal Security Service, also became governors. In the early 2000s, members of the military and security services were also chosen to lead the regions but proved unable to govern due to a lack of economic and political experience. In 2017, four representatives of the security services were appointed; three of them were elected as governors (in Tula, Yaroslavl, and Tver Oblasts), while the acting governor of Kaliningrad Oblast asked to resign before the elections. The appointment of an older general from the Ministry of the Interior, Vladimir Vasilyev, as head of the Republic of Dagestan is a different case, a reprise of the imperial strategy of governor-generalship in "alien" territories. The risks of such a decision are high.

The new governors gauged the situation in the regions and, as their first order of business, began requesting additional funds from the federal budget to carry out the president's orders. While this is permissible for the "newbies," hard times await them in the future: the powers of the regional authorities are increasingly limited, while control by the federal authorities, including the security services, is growing. Governors are turning into scapegoats, being held responsible for problems created in large part by decisions of the federal government. The risk is lower for former representatives of the security services, who have more protected "flanks" and connections with federal security service officials. However, it is unlikely that those advantages will aid the regions' development.

Conclusion

In conclusion, let us highlight the most important trends in regional development and the relationship between the center and the regions over the past few years.

An ever-stricter hierarchy of power is forming in Russia. The power of the regions is decreasing and control and punishment are becoming harsher. Rigid systems are less stable in the event of political and economic turmoil.

Budget resources are growing quickly only in Moscow, which can afford major expenditures on improvements and renovations, a reality that increasingly distances it from other regions of the country.

The drivers of economic growth either exist only on paper due to institutional barriers (agglomerations); are weak (import-substitution); or are limited, expensive, and dependent on financial support from the government (export projects of large energy-sector companies).

The role of geopolitical priorities in regional policy is growing, but the priorities are becoming fewer. The chief one is Crimea, with Chechnya also retaining special privileges.

The reaction of regional authorities to these trends has been increased opportunism, and the quality of governance has decreased as a result. The system is adapting to changing conditions, and while the wheels will not come off the bus, tensions are growing. Several years ago, while presenting at the Davos Forum, Aleksey Kudrin said that the regions would be the drivers of modernization in Russia. Today, that statement can only be treated as gallows humor.

The Republic of Tatarstan: Reducing to the Lowest Common Denominator?

Sergey Sergeyev

Over the course of the quarter-century from 1992, Tatarstan held a special place among Russian regions. However, at the end of 2016, the republic's fortunes changed. This began with a series of bankruptcies of the republic's banks. One of the first to implode, in December 2016, was "Tatfondbank," the second largest bank in the republic, headed by the Prime Minister of Tatarstan, Ildar Khalikov. The second most important event in the political life of the republic was the expiration of the power-sharing agreement with the federal government. The agreement was adopted in 2007 for a period of 10 years. In the summer of 2017, that period expired; the ruling elites of Tatarstan hoped that the agreement could be extended, but those hopes were not realized. In the summer and fall of 2017, after Vladimir Putin spoke about the impermissibility of forcing the study of non-native languages, a "linguistic crisis" developed in the republic. Perhaps at first the regional authorities did not believe that the federal government seriously intended to force them to change the parity in the teaching of the Tatar and Russian languages. But after the Prosecutor's Office began demonstrative inspections of schools, even the most stubborn had to relent: most secondary schools now teach Tatar language just two hours a week (with a further hour sometimes added for the study of Tatar literature) and only with the written permission of parents. The Minister of Education and Science of Tatarstan, Engel Fattakhov, resigned.

The online newspaper "Business Online" (closely tied, it appears, with one of Tatarstan's sub-elite groups) announced an "undeclared hybrid war" waged by "federal clans" against Tatarstan with the goal of "plundering the republic."[1] Officials rushed to distance themselves from these statements: "I don't see any kind of politically orchestrated pressure on the republic," said the Chairman of the State Council of Tatarstan, Farid Mukhametshin, at a meeting with the editors of media outlets in the republic.[2]

Nevertheless, it is clear that over the course of 2017, Tatarstan suffered significant blows to its finances and its image. The regional myth about it being the best, most advanced, most innovative republic, carefully created and nurtured over a period of more than 20 years, was extinguished. What happened was what we can describe as the "former straight-A student effect": a student who constantly received only As (sometimes deserved, sometimes not) suddenly got a C, and then another, and then a D… and consequently experienced a certain shock.

However, it is surely premature to talk about the final destruction of the regional myth. The tensions that arose in the relationship between the republic and the federal center touched off another regional myth or version of the myth—the notion of a hard-working and proud republic bravely resisting the greedy and aggressive federal center (or some dark forces within it). It is not difficult to see that such a narrative attempts to frame the private interests of the regional elites as the general interests of the whole region (representing a population of diverse groups with equally diverse, and at times conflicting, interests).

A Time of Sovereignty

In analyzing the events of 2017 in Tatarstan, it should be taken into consideration that the motives of the primary actors were, in large part, dictated by the history of Tatarstan's relationship with the federal center dating back to the 1990s.

---

1 "Gibridnaya vojna protiv Tatarstana: pora gotovit'sia k sleduyushchemu raundu? Pyat' vyvodov iz proigrysha v "yazykovom konflikte,'" Biznes Online, December 1, 2017. https:// www.business-gazeta.ru/article/365561.

2 N. Goloburdova, Farid Mukhametshin: "Politicheski splanirovannogo nazhima na respubliku ya ne vizhu," Biznes Online, December 28, 2017. https://www.business-gazeta.ru/ article/368429.

It would be superficial and naïve to present the matter as if the proclamation of Tatarstan's national sovereignty in August 1990 were the realization of the age-old aspirations of the Tatar people. In reality, the proclamation of sovereignty was the result of a complex game between three centers of power: the weakening but still quite strong Soviet center; the then-coalescing Russian center; and the regional center, which was then clearly in line with the Soviet center and in opposition to the Russian one. Soon after the elections of the national deputies of the RSFSR (and TASSR) in April 1990, the Supreme Council of the USSR passed a law "On Power-Sharing between the Soviet Central Government and the Constituent Entities of the Federation," which allowed the leaderships of formerly autonomous entities to elevate the status of their republics. Consequently, a peculiar "second front" opened against the Russian government, then headed by Boris Yeltsin. It is notable that in the Declaration of National Sovereignty adopted on August 30, 1990, it was not indicated to whom Tatarstan was subject—was the republic simultaneously a subject of the RSFSR and the USSR or was it directly part of the USSR?

The then-leader of the Tatar ASSR, Mintimer Shaimiev, was loyal to the Soviet central government and worked against the Russian leadership however he could. The referendum on the question of whether to introduce the position of President of Russia, held in March 1991, was not conducted in the republic, while the Russian presidential elections held on June 12, 1991, occurred in the context of a partial boycott by the republic's leadership: officially, only elections for the President of Tatarstan were held, with a ballot for the Russian presidential election provided only at the request (sometimes even written request) of the voter.[3] During the attempted coup of August 1991, the leadership of Tatarstan supported the State Committee on the State of Emergency (SCSE) and, fearing arrest, fabricated the threat of ethnic conflict, playing, as they said, the "national card." After the situation normalized somewhat, the

---

3 See, for example: irek_murtazin (Murtazin, I). June 12, 1991, Live journal irek_murtazin, June 12, 2014.

decision was made to hold a referendum in Tatarstan on the republic's status.

The referendum of March 21, 1992 had a complex formulation that included, among other things, a reference to the international independent legal identity of the sovereign republic. (The Supreme Court of Tatarstan issued a clarification that the question did not imply secession from Russia.) Sixty-one percent of those who took part in the referendum agreed with the question as it was formulated; with 82 percent turnout, this amounted to a little more than half (50.2 percent) of all eligible voters in Tatarstan. At the same time, more than one-third of those who voted expressed their lack of confidence in Shaimiev's policies. The situation could be described as a stalemate: the federal government could not regain control of the republic without the use of force, but the regional elites faced significant opposition to their plans.

The first Duma elections and a referendum on the Constitution of the Russian Federation in Tatarstan were not held (voter turnout was 13.9 percent). However, Yeltsin was able to consolidate power, and the regional authorities in Tatarstan, preferring not to tempt fate any longer, agreed to a compromise: in February 1994, they ratified a "Treaty on the Delimitation of Jurisdiction and the Mutual Delegation of Powers between the Government Authorities of the Russian Federation and the Republic of Tatarstan." The compromise was based on the de-facto division of spheres of influence: the leadership of Tatarstan agreed that Tatarstan was part of the Russian Federation, only under special conditions. Both the Constitution of the Russian Federation and the Constitution of the Republic of Tatarstan were formally recognized (although they conflicted with each other). Tatarstan paid taxes to the federal government (in smaller proportions than other regions), held federal elections on its territory, and generally recognized the primacy of the federal authorities on federation-wide issues. For its part, the federal government practically withdrew from interfering in the internal affairs of the republic. Kazan University professor Midkhat Farukshin characterized the situation as follows: "One involuntarily got the impression that entire regions were being left at the mercy or complete disposal of regional barons."[4] In particular, local government in Tatarstan at the city and district level was only fully implemented in 2005; before that, it existed only at the village level, and local authorities of the federal government operated at the city and district level.

Beginning in the summer of 2000, when the Constitutional Court of the Russian Federation recognized the position of sovereign republics within Russia as unconstitutional,[5] the situation began to change. However, the process was not instantaneous and the reaction of regional elites to the decision of the Constitutional Court was far from friendly. The opening of a branch of the State Treasury in Tatarstan was also met with resistance, as was the issuance of Russian passports; a revised version of the Constitution of Tatarstan was ratified only in 2002. It must be mentioned that from the end of the 1980s through the beginning of the 2000s, political innovations—competitive elections, elements of proportionality in the electoral system, and local government bodies in place of Councils' authority—came from the center, while the regional elites in Tatarstan met the changes with considerable reluctance and annoyance and implemented them belatedly and in "watered-down" versions. In contrast to the period from 1994 to 1999, the republican authorities allowed federal interference, but only to a limited degree and on an ad hoc basis.

A Time of Spectacles and Innovations

The policy of sovereignty was left in the past. In its place, Tatarstan installed the policy of spectacle. Its chief characteristics were a non-

---

4 Farukshin, M.Kh. Izbiratel'noe zakonodatel'stvo i vybory v Tatarstane: opyt regional'nogo pravovogo separatizma / Osobaya zona: vybory v Tatarstane. Edited by Mikhailov, V.V., Bazhanov, V.A., Farushkin, M.Kh. Ulyanovsk, 2000. pp. 10-24.

5 "Ruling of the Constitutional Court of the Russian Federation from June 27, 2000, No. 92-O, examining the consistency of several provisions of the constitutions of the Republic of Adygea, the Republic of Bashkortostan, the Republic of Ingushetia, the Komi Republic, the Republic of North Ossetia, Alania and the Republic of Tatarstan with the Constitution of the Russian Federation, as requested by a group of deputies of the State Duma,"Rossiiskaya Gazeta, July 25, 2000.

ideological stance, entertainment, and consumerism. "Enjoy yourselves and forget about politics" was the message that the regional elites sent to the masses, and the masses readily agreed. Indeed, the policy of spectacle helped to address several problems at once. The "sovereign republic" slogan implied political mobilization—by supporters as well as opponents (as observed in the period from 1991 to 1993). As far as the regional elites were concerned, there was no need for political activism: the authorities in Tatarstan convinced the federal government that the situation in the republic was entirely under control. Any political activism represents a potential threat to electoral authoritarianism, which allows only elections that will produce unchanging outcomes in favor of the party in power. In addition, perhaps as a result of inertia, the authoritarian post-communist regime in Tatarstan felt the need to give society certain ideological and philosophical guidance and dictate a development path. The "sovereignty" slogan needed to be replaced with something, otherwise it would create an ideological vacuum. It is also significant that the policy of spectacle allows for renewed requests for subsidies from the federal government. Finally, if holidays and competitions are of an international nature, such a policy allows the republic to remind the world of its existence, increase recognition of the region, and improve its reputation.

The first major milestone in realizing the policy of spectacle was the celebration of the 1,000th anniversary of Kazan in summer 2005. This included a number of events that took place over the course of nearly two and a half months: the opening of the Kul Sharif Mosque in the Kazan Kremlin; the return of a copy of the icon of Our Lady of Kazan; a summit of the leaders of the CIS and the State Council of the Russian Federation; the opening of a completely revamped version of one of the central streets in Kazan, called the "Petersburg" street (at the beginning of the street was installed a bust of Lev Gumilyov bearing the inscription "I defended the Tatars from slander my entire life"); and the commissioning of the new Kazan metro. At the time (August 2005), it was both one of the shortest in the world (at only five stations) and one of the most expensive (about $60 million was spent on its construction).

On the whole, the Kazan millennial celebration can be considered a success for its organizers, despite the fact that one of the side-effects of the celebrations was that Kazan accrued municipal debt (the amount, according to various accounts, was between 6.9 and 12.3 billion rubles as of the end of 2005), while total expenditures reached around 90 billion rubles, including 12 billion rubles from the federal budget and 38.6 billion rubles from the regional budget.[6] Additionally, the hurried reconstruction of central Kazan led to the destruction of a significant portion of the city's historical structures.

The new Mayor of Kazan's team, which came to power in late 2005 and early 2006, set an ambitious goal: to hold the Universiade. Of course, it was impossible to achieve this goal without the support of the republic's leadership and the federal authorities.

Besides considerations of prestige, the continuation of the policy of spectacle had an entirely pragmatic motive: the city needed funds for development. After the International Federation of Student Sport decided to hold the 2013 Summer Universiade in Kazan, 228 billion rubles were invested in the city's infrastructure and building athletic facilities.[7] Unsurprisingly given its high debt load, Tatarstan's credit rating began to drop. According to the Audit Court's data, the republic's debts reached 85.9 billion rubles, which ranked the region third in Russia on this indicator, behind Moscow (188.4 billion rubles) and Moscow Oblast (97.9 billion rubles). However, President Minnikhanov declared that he did not see anything terrible for the republic in this fact: "I am not worried about that at all. Which rating should we look at? The people's approval rating is more important to me than a credit rating."[8] Minnikhanov also noted that Kazan had been transformed during the period it was

---

[6] I. Veletminskiy, "Detektor lzhi dlia mera," Rossiiskaya Gazeta, July 9, 2008 https://rg.ru/2008/07/09/metshin.html; Ilsur Metshin, "Kazan' – tret'ya stolitsa.I tochka," Official page of Ilsur Metshin : http://metshin.ru/ru/blogs/30; "Kazan' gotovitsia k zaplyvu na 2015 god," Tatcenter, August 5, 2013. http://tatcenter.ru/news/kazan-gotovitsya-k-quotzaplyvu-quot-na-2015-god/.

[7] "So studencheskim razmakhom," Kommersant-Vlast No. 26, July 8, 2013, https://www.kommersant.ru/doc/2225428.

[8] V. Sitnina, "My zhe ne proeli eti den'gi," An interview with the President of Tatarstan, R. Minnikhanov, Kommersant-Vlast No. 26, July 8, 2013. https://www.kommersant.ru/doc/2224772.

preparing for the Games: without the support of the federal government, such a large-scale modernization of the entire city would have taken at least 15 years.[9] In any case, as soon as the active phase of construction ended, the credit ratings went up. Apparently, the Russian leadership was also satisfied — both by the impressive opening ceremonies and by the outcome of the competitions. The policy of spectacle continued even after the Universiade: in the summer of 2015, Kazan held the World Aquatics Championships, in the summer of 2017 it hosted Confederations Cup matches (sponsored by FIFA), and in the summer of 2018 it will host World Cup matches.

Even during preparation for the Universiade, the republic's leadership had probably already realized the limitations of betting solely on sporting events. After Minnikhanov became President of Tatarstan in early 2010, the republic's authorities attempted to position Tatarstan as a region not only for sport, but also for innovation (here "innovation" is understood in the strictly technological sense). In 2010, they began studying the creation of "IT villages" in Tatarstan — their very own versions of Skolkovo where Russian and foreign IT specialists could live, work, and relax. A location outside Kazan was selected for the first IT village. At the end of 2011, the IT village was given the name "Innopolis," and on June 9, 2012, Prime Minister Dmitri Medvedev launched the project, participating in the laying of a time capsule with a message for its future residents. Three years later, on June 9, 2015, the new city officially opened. It was initially intended that "Tatar Skolkovo" would house 150,000 people by 2030: IT specialists and their families, students and professors at the IT university, and the staff of the shopping mall and service sector. Of course, there is still some time until 2030, but for now the successes of Innopolis are unimpressive: at the beginning of 2017, it had a permanent population of a little more than 100 people, and only 2,500 rented housing there.

All in all, if in the 1990s the policy of Tatarstan's elites could summed up as the "policy of sovereignty," then in the 2000s and

---

9   "Dmitri Medvedev i Rustam Minnikhanov podveli itogi Universiady," Biznes Online, July 17, 2013, www. business-gazeta.ru/article/84196.

the first half of the 2010s it could be summarized as the "policy of spectacle and innovation."

The Collapse of Tatfondbank

When the country was awash in petrodollars, the differences between the interests of the federal elites and Tatarstan's regional elites were not particularly salient to the outside observer. However, the federal government remembered the confrontation with Tatarstan's elites in the period from 1991 to 1993, as well as the delays they faced when Tatarstan's law was brought into line with Russia's in the early 2000s. If Tatarstan's regional elites considered Tatarstan's special status, its "differentness," as a resource—in the informal organizational culture of the Russian post-nomenklatura, those who were "different" could expect to be dealt with more cautiously—the federal elites perceived Tatarstan's pretensions to a special status as an inconvenience, if not a potential threat. Moreover, the regional elites in Tatarstan always viewed themselves as representatives of the republic, while the federal elites treated the regional authorities like managers that they had placed at the head of the regions.

That potential contradiction became noticeable in the conditions of the post-Crimean era, when regional revenues, especially those of the donor regions, began to be viewed as a source for replenishing the federal budget. Minnikhanov, considered the informal doyen of the governors' corps, reacted with distress to the federal authorities' "unfriendly" intergovernmental financial policies. After the decision to "expropriate" a portion of the income tax revenues to the federal government (prior to 2017 income tax revenues were divided between the regions and federal government in the ratio of 18 percent to 2 percent, and from 2017 in the ratio of 17 percent to 3 percent), which represented a loss of 3.5 billion rubles for Tatarstan, Minnikhanov gave an angry speech at a session of the State Council of Tatarstan that compared the policies of the federal government to dekulakization.[10] In reality, Tatarstan's budget lost

---

10   Rustam Minnikhanov, "Raskulachivanie bylo uzhe, my posledstviya videli...,"

even more: revenues declined by 2.8 billion rubles due to a change in the allocation of the excise tax on petroleum products. (Previously, the republic had received 88 percent and the federal government 12 percent, but in 2017 the ratio changed to 66 percent to 34 percent.) Tatarstan's budget lost a further 1.9 billion rubles due to an increase in the tax rate on mineral extraction.

Minnikhanov's critical statements about the withdrawal of funds from donor regions to support subsidized entities landed in third place on the St. Petersburg Politics Foundation's list of the top 30 events in December 2016.[11] A number of media outlets immediately called Minnikhanov's speech "blackmail" and a "Tatar revolt"; they interpreted the President of Tatarstan's words almost as a refusal to pay taxes to the Russian government, and there were calls to punish the leader of the republic as a warning to other would-be regional "khans."[12] At the same time, among governors of the donor regions (notably the governor of Kaluga Oblast, Anatoly Artamonov), Minnikhanov's speech was met with understanding, if not support.[13]

Meanwhile, it just so happened that in December 2016, not long after Minnikhanov accused the federal government of "dekulakization" of the regions, the second largest and most important bank in Tatarstan, Tatfondbank (TFB), suffered a collapse. Its owners primarily lent to their own or affiliated entities, which had ceased to be profitable, and as a result the difference between the

---

Biznes Online, December 26, 2016. RL: www.business-gazeta.ru/video/333026

11 "Rating of the Foundation 'Saint Petersburg Politics,'" Peterburgskaya Politika, December 2016, http://www.fpp.spb.ru/fpp-rating-2016-12.

12 See for example: Orlov, D. Shantazh Minikhanova ne zastavit Kreml' izmenit' finansovuyu politiku, Regionalnyye kommentarii http://www.regcomment.ru/opinions/shantazh-minnikhanova-ne-zastavit-kreml-izmenit-finansovuyupolitiku/.

13 Kolebakina, E., Goloburdova, N., Gavrilenko, A. "Vy zhivyote svoimi illuziyami!": kak Minnikhanov dal boi "raskulachivaniyu v Moskv, Biznes Online. January 13, 2017, https://www.business-gazeta.ru/article/334251; Kolebakina, E. Anatoly Artamonov: "Ya zhe ne patsan! Prezhde chem pojti na eto, ya obshchalsia na vsekh urovnyakh". Biznes Online, January 14, 2017, https://www.businessgazeta.ru/article/334363.

bank's obligations and the actual value of its assets reached 118 billion rubles.[14] The bank was not formally state-owned, but its board was headed by Prime Minister Ildar Khalikov. As the scandal caused by the bank's failure continued to grow, Khalikov was forced to resign in April 2017.

The effect of Tatfondbank's collapse was significant. TFB held the accounts of more than 30,000 legal entities (6,000 of which held accounts exclusively at TFB) and more than 350,000 individuals (about 30 percent of whom had deposits in excess of the 1.4 million rubles that the Deposit Insurance Agency is required to compensate). The worst affected were a group of about 2,000 investors who had put their money into funds managed by a TFB subsidiary, TFB Finance. Their money was invested in TFB bonds that did not fall under the deposit insurance system and thus became worthless after the bank failed.

At the end of 2016 and beginning of 2017, measures could probably still have been taken to save TFB. However, the republic did not have enough money for a bailout and the federal authorities were unable or unwilling to come to the rescue.

The authorities in Tatarstan managed to prevent a social upheaval. Rather than tens of thousands of protesters, only a few hundred people took to the streets. On March 3, 2017, about 300 angry depositors of the failed banks (TFB's collapse had set off a chain of bankruptcies of smaller banks) marched through the center of Kazan to deliver their petition to Prime Minister Khalikov (the media called the protest the "storming of the Cabinet of Ministers," but that was typical journalistic exaggeration[15]). Another result of TFB's failure was reduced confidence of both businesses and individuals in the regional banks and of investors in the republic more generally. In order to restore confidence, the region's leaders took the un-

---

14 E. Ivanova, "Kak 144 zaemshchika "s'eli TFB: yurlitsam ostanetsia nol' bez palochki?" Biznes Online. April 12, 2017, https://www.business-gazeta.ru/article/342672.

15 A. Grigoryeva, "Shturm kabmina – slishkom sil'no skazano," Interview with S. Sergeyev, Idel. Realities, March 10, 2017, http://www.idelreal.org/a/28359219.html.

usual step of creating an assistance fund for the affected TFB depositors, headed by Minnikhanov's assistant, Airat Nurutdinov (the management company Tatenergo and JSC Grid Company allocated the funds from their net profits). Depositors actually began to receive the appropriate payments.[16] However, in late January 2018, during Putin's working visit to Tatarstan (January 24-25, 2018), police removed the few isolated depositors who were protesting TFB in hopes of drawing the Russian president's attention to their plight.

The Loss of Special Status

In 2017, Tatarstan awaited the conclusion of a new treaty on the delimitation of jurisdiction and the mutual delegation of powers between the government authorities of the Russian Federation and the Republic of Tatarstan. The fact that the treaty was never signed became an important "non-event" in the life of the republic.

The 2007 treaty, which replaced the treaty of 1994, expired on July 24, 2017. Tatarstan timidly but regularly reminded the federal government of its desire to renew the treaty. In May 2017, at a congress of the peoples of Tatarstan, Tatarstan State Counselor Mintimer Shaimiev announced that the treaty could be extended without any changes to its contents. On July 11, 2017, deputies of the State Council of Tatarstan adopted an appeal to Putin in which they noted that the practice of implementing a treaty between Moscow and Kazan "convincingly proved the vitality of Russian federalism," but they did not directly request to extend the treaty and only proposed the formation of a special commission on legal issues. After it became clear that the efforts of the treaty's supporters were useless, Minnikhanov stated in a routine message to deputies of the State Council of the Republic that the treaty was merely a means of governing the relationship between the republic and the federal government that had played a role in the past; now, the

---

16 E. Ivanova, Ayrat Nurutdinov: "S 1 fevralia prinimaem zayavleniya ot yurlits do 500,000 rublej i invalidov." Biznes Online, December 29, 2017, https://www.businessgazeta.ru/article/368516.

key factor is not so much the form of the arrangements between the republic and the federal government itself, as it is their essence: the ability to find mutually acceptable solutions to problems in the common interest of both parties.[17]

The 2007 treaty, which the republic's ruling elites wanted to extend (at least by and large), was to a large extent a symbolic document that emphasized Tatarstan's special status among other subjects of the federation. Only a very few issues governed by the document were of a real-world, as opposed to declaratory, nature, specifically the maintenance and development of Tatar culture in other regions of the Russian Federation. The fact that those who were advocating for the extension of the treaty could not clearly articulate why it was needed also played a role in the federal government's refusal to renegotiate the treaty. In reality, the treaty was necessary to preserve symbolic capital—that is, to maintain the "otherness" of Tatarstan's regional elites. However, it was precisely this recognition that the federal government now refused.

The "Language Crisis"

If the failure to extend the treaty was a painful blow to the ego of Tatarstan's regional elites, then the refusal to maintain parity in the teaching of the Tatar and Russian languages in Tatarstan's schools had wide public resonance.

According to data from the 1989 census, 48.5 percent of the population of the republic were Tatars and 43.3 percent were Russians. According to data from the 2002 and 2010 censuses, the percentage of Tatars grew 4–4.5 percent and the percentage of Russians fell accordingly. Between the 1960s and the 1980s, Tatar language was studied as an elective in most schools of the TASSR. Beginning in the 1991–1992 school year, the situation changed: the Tatar language was introduced as a mandatory subject in all secondary schools of the republic, regardless of ethnicity or the desires of stu-

---

[17] Poslanie Prezidenta Respubliki Tatarstan R.N.Minnikhanova Gosudarstvennomu Sovetu Respubliki Tatarstan. President of the Republic of Tatarstan, September 21, 2017.URL: http://president.tatarstan.ru/news/view/1015109

dents and their parents. In 1992, the Supreme Council of the republic adopted a "Law on the Languages of the Peoples of the Republic of Tatarstan" that legislated the equal study of the Tatar and Russian languages. (In 2004, a revision of that law was passed that maintained the principle of parity.) Equal teaching time was achieved by reducing the number of hours devoted to teaching Russian. According to the calculations of Lyudmila Luchsheva, the number of hours dedicated to the study of the Russian language was reduced by nearly half compared to other regions of the Russian Federation.[18] In order to do this, from the mid-1990s, all schools in Tatarstan used a curriculum developed by the Ministry of Education and Science of Russia for students who were non-native speakers of Russian. Among the Russian-speaking population, the percentage of parents who wanted to teach their children the Tatar language was relatively high, at about 60 percent.[19]

Later, however, in the 2000s, that desire faded due to both dissatisfaction with the quality of Tatar language instruction and the fact that knowledge of the Tatar language, in and of itself, is not professionally advantageous in Tatarstan; hometown and family connections are more important for successful advancement.[20]

Because some parents were unhappy with the reduction of Russian language instruction, protests ensued. In 2004, Kazan lawyer Sergey Khapugin filed suit against the Ministry of Education of Tatarstan, demanding that his son be protected from forced study of the Tatar language. The case reached the Constitutional Court of Russia, which held that the principle of parity in language instruction was not in conflict with the Russian Constitution, but also that the study of the Tatar language should not take place at the expense of the study of Russian.

In 2011, a series of rallies and protests were held in defense of the right to study Russian at the same level as it was taught in most

---

18 A.L. Salagaev, S.A. Sergeev, L.V. Luchsheva, Novye problemy i protivorechiya sotsiokul'turnogo razvitiya Respubliki Tatarstan (Kazan: KNRTU Press, 2011) 182.
19 A.D. Korostelev, "Yazyk – istochnik soglasij i protivorechij," Sotsial'naya i kul turnaya distantsii. Opyt mnogonatsional'noj Rossii, Moscow, 1998. 192.
20 Salagaev, A.L. et al, op. cit. 182.

other subjects of the Russian Federation.[21] The effect of these rallies and protests was, in essence, zero. Moreover, in 2014, unified republic-wide testing (URT) in the Tatar language was introduced for ninth-graders in Tatarstan, sparking a new wave of protests to Moscow. Although officially students and parents were assured that the testing was merely a formality and the grades from it would not end up on report cards, some schools sought to motivate students to study Tatar by scaring them into believing that a poor result on the URT would prevent them from receiving a certificate of completion for the ninth grade.

At a July 2017 session of the Council on Inter-Ethnic Relations in Yoshkar-Ola, Vladimir Putin stated that "forcing a person to study a non-native language is as impermissible as reducing the level and time devoted to the instruction of Russian."[22] In Tatarstan, that statement had far-reaching effects.

The first reaction of the republic's authorities to Putin's statement on languages was a statement from the Minister of Education and Science of Tatarstan, Fattakhov, who said that Putin's words did not apply to Tatarstan. The Russian president's administration thought otherwise. On August 29, a list of orders from the Russian president was published in which the Prosecutor General and the Federal Education and Science Supervisory Service were ordered to verify compliance, in the various subjects of the Russian Federation, with citizens' right to the voluntary study of the ethnic languages of Russia and the state languages of the republics of Russia, and to report their findings by November 30. That order inspired the opponents of Tatar language study; they renewed their campaign to ban mandatory study of the Tatar language, as well as to allow those schools where most parents supported it to transition to the curriculum used for schools with a (native) Russian language of instruction. In September, the government of Tatarstan decided that beginning on January 1, 2018, the amount of Russian-language instruction should be increased to the levels recommended by federal

---

21 Ibid. Pg. 192.
22 Zasedanie Soveta po mezhnatsional'nym otnosheniyam, President of Russia, July 20, 2017, http://kremlin.ru/events/ president/news/55109.

standards, but it was already too late. Students' parents began writing letters rejecting the study of the Tatar language and prosecutorial inspections of schools were initiated in order to establish whether any requirements of the laws on education were being violated. In turn, the Tatar intelligentsia spoke in defense of the Tatar language: 60 writers from Tatarstan sent letters to the Russian president asking him to preserve the mandatory study of the Tatar language in schools.[23]

It would be a gross oversimplification, and simply false, to say that Tatars supported, and continue to support, the study of the Tatar language at the previous level while Russians are against it. First, most Russians in Tatarstan are not against the study of Tatar in principle—they only wanted it taught to a lesser degree than it was prior to 2017. Second, many Russian-speaking Tatars are in solidarity with them on this point (some of them do not even speak Tatar themselves). A rough estimate suggests that the proportion of such Tatars is no less than 10 percent of the population of the republic (and maybe higher).[24] In any case, in public opinion polls, that is the percentage of respondents identifying themselves as Tatar who answer "sensitive" questions concerning ethnic relations in the same way as those who identify themselves as Russian. Moreover, as shown by public opinion polls conducted at the end of 2017, a significant percentage of the population[25] was not interested in the "language crisis" whatsoever. The regional elites' relentless pursuit of the status quo in language instruction is tied to the fact that parity in the study of the Russian and Tatar languages symbolized a balance in the relationship between Moscow and Kazan that was one of the cornerstones of the regional "ideology"—or, if you

---

23 K. Antonov, "Vladimira Putina prosyat zashchitit' tatarsky yazyk," Kommersant, September 25, 2017. https://www.kommersant.ru/doc/3420927.

24 Judgement based on the result of polls in which the author participated in 2001–2003 and 2007–2009.

25 N. Goloburdova, VTsIOM (Russian Public Opinion Research Center): My vidim, chto yazykovuyu temu kto-to iskusstvenno perekachivaet, Biznes Online, December 12, 2017, https://www.business-gazeta.ru/article/366645.

will, the regional myth—of the 1990s. For the regional elites, to reject this principle would be to openly admit their provincial, second-class status in relation to the federal center.

The language crisis ended in late November 2017. The federal government and the regional elites of Tatarstan reached an asymmetrical compromise: Tatar language instruction in schools would be preserved, but only with written permission from parents and, in most cases, only for two hours per week. Minister of Education and Science Fattakhov, who lost the opportunity to come to a compromise in the summer before the prosecutorial inspections of schools, returned to his previous post as head of the Aktanysh District.

One of the consequences of resolving the "language crisis" in that way was acute discontent among the part of Tatarstan's elite and society that had insisted on maintaining the status quo and now felt that they were the losers. Publications in the newspaper "Business Online," mentioned at the beginning of this chapter, became their manifesto: conflict with the federal government was called the "hybrid war" against the republic and new "blows" to Tatarstan were predicted. The public, however, was divided, and only a minority were inclined to associate themselves with the losing regional elites and the Tatar intelligentsia: only 7 percent of Tatarstan residents polled in late 2017 named the study and use of the Tatar language as among the most important issues they faced (for comparison, 23 percent of respondents named low salaries and 13 percent the high price of housing and public utilities).[26] The more prevalent view is that the economic and political problems of Tatarstan are tied to internal factors: recruiting elites predominantly on the principle of personal loyalty or based on family or hometown connections led to a gradual accumulation of errors in various arenas, which in the context of a generally worsening socioeconomic situation gave rise to a systemic crisis.

So what awaits Tatarstan? Most likely, over the next five to seven years, slow movement will be made down the same path that was set over the past 10-15 years. Tatarstan will come to look more

---

26   Ibid.

and more like other regions of Russia, and its special status, about which the regional ideologues talked and wrote so much in the 1990s and 2000s, will persist only in the memories of their contemporaries.

Who Will Feed the Russian Population?[1]

Tatyana Nefedova

Labor: Who Is Involved in Agriculture?

The rural areas constitute the vast territories outside cities in which, according to the definitions of encyclopedias and the suppositions of city-dwellers, the majority of the population able to work should be involved in agriculture. But this is not the present reality. Of the 37 million rural residents, 21 million are of working age, but only 4.9 million are employed in agriculture, according to official data.[2] The remainder work in the public sector, trade, or forestry management, or are unemployed and live off their mothers' pensions.[3] There are no indicators that make it possible to precisely determine the level of unemployment in rural areas: for one thing, the majority of those who are truly unemployed are not registered with the employment service, and for another, seasonal work and informal employment, including on private farms[4], are widespread, as is temporary work in other places and industries (displacement).[5] Those employed by agricultural enterprises number even fewer, at just 2.3 million people, with the remainder of those officially employed in

---

1 The Chapter has been prepared as part of the Russian Academy of Sciences' Institute of Geography Project No. 0148-2019-008: "Problems and Prospects of Russia's Territorial Development given its non-uniformity and global instability."
2 Ekonomicheskaya aktivnost' naseleniya Rossii. Moscow: Federal Statistics Service, 2014.
3 In spite of the increase in life expectancy in Russia, the difference between that of men and women remains large. In 2000, the difference was 13 years (59 for men, which is the same as that for several central African countries, and 72 for women); in 2012, it was 11 years (65 and 76, respectively). "Moscow: Federal Statistics Service," 2014, http://www.gks.ru/bgd/regl/B13_16/Main.htm.
4 T.G. Nefedova, "Otkhodnichestvo v sisteme migratsij v sovremennoi Rossii. Predposylki. Geografiya.," Demoscope-Weekly № 641–642 and 643–644, 2015, May 4–17 & May 18-31, http://demoscope.ru/weekly/2015/0641/tema01.ph p;http://demoscope.ru/weekly/2015/0643/tema01.php.
5 Yu. M. Plyusnin, Ya. D. Zausayeva, N.N. Zhidkevich, A.A. Pozanenko, Otkhodniki (Moscow: Novy khronograf, 2013).

agriculture (2.6 million) either business owners or supported by trade from private farms.

Official employment in agribusiness in the post-Soviet years decreased significantly more rapidly than the total number of workers in agriculture—and, of course, than in the economy as a whole (see Figure 1). Only in the mid-2000s, riding the wave of agricultural expansion and modernization (see Figure 2), did agricultural holding companies begin to gain strength, although this growth was somewhat curtailed by a shortage of agribusiness workers.

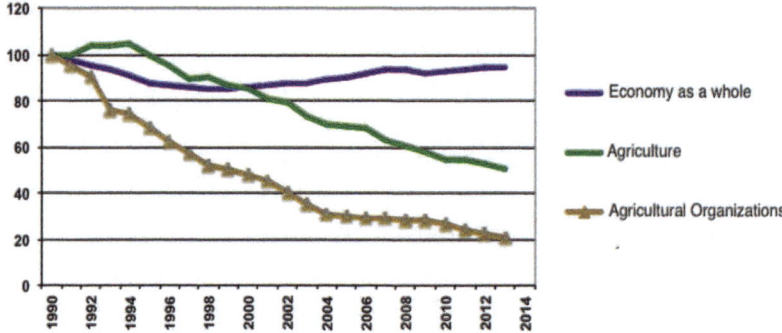

Figure 1. Employment dynamics in the economy and in agriculture as a percentage of the 1990 figure
Sources: Trud i zanyatost' v Rossii. Moscow: Federal Statistics Service, 2010; Ekonomicheskaya aktivnost' naselenya Rossii. Moscow: Federal Statistics Service, 2002, 2007, 2011, 2015.

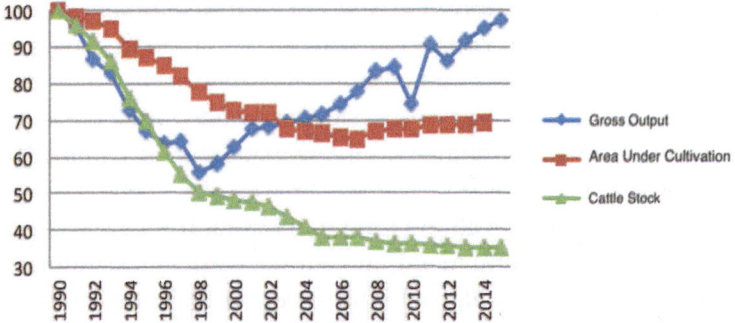

Figure 2. Dynamics of agricultural production, area under cultivation, and cattle stock as a percentage of the 1990 figure
Sources: Regiony Rossii. Moscow: Federal Statistics Service, 1998, 2005, 2010, 2014. Informatsiya o sotsial'no-ekonomicheskom polozhenii Rossii. Moscow: Federal Statistics Service, 2015.

Agricultural labor's loss of prestige in the post-Soviet period was exacerbated by—and reflected in—the sharp decline in agricultural salaries. Whereas during the Soviet period agricultural salaries were around the median across Russia and even exceeded incomes in education and several areas of industry, they fell 15-20% below the median Russian income in the 1990s and by the 2000s were just barely half the median: as of 2014, the average agricultural salary was 17,000 rubles, compared to an all-Russian average of 32,000. And this is for relatively successful working businesses; real payments, especially outside the agricultural season, could be several times less.

Figure 2 shows the dynamics of economic production, area under cultivation, and numbers of cattle stock. The multiple directions of the curves speak to the fact that in the 2000s, agriculture was not reestablished everywhere in the same way. Relative success was noted in individual regions, areas, and farms that achieved production increases while generally cutting back on the area under cultivation and numbers of cattle stock. Due to the fact that the way out of the crisis looked different in different regions, there was increased polarization along the poles of "north-south" and "suburb-periphery."[6] This is connected with the variation in geographical conditions across the vast country, the uneven distribution of the population, and the regions' varied reactions to the crisis and reforms of the 1990s. Variation was intensified by weak connections between Russia's territories.

Long-term out-migration of the population from villages was no less important in influencing the current agricultural situation and the labor sources available to the sector. In 1959, the rural population accounted for 48% of the entire population of Russia; by 2015, that figure had fallen by 19 million people, for a total of 26% of the population. Since the birth rate was exceeding the death rate in many regions up until the 1990s, the primary reason for the decline was therefore out-migration. In the late Soviet period, rural residents in the European portion of Russia mainly left the regions surrounding the Moscow District and those in between Moscow and St. Petersburg. Only the southern republics and districts, as well as the suburbs of large population centers, managed to keep young people in rural locations (and continue to do so).[7] In the non-black earth regions, over the decades after the Second World War, the rural population declined by half; in the periphery of the non-black earth regions, this figure reached as much as 80%. In areas of low population density, the departure of young and more active residents inevitably led to the degradation of the social environment, in turn driving out the remaining young people. This flight was aggravated by the specialization of Soviet collective farms in one kind of agriculture (decreasing knowledge diversity) and the neglect of infrastructural and social conditions in the villages.

---

6   T.G. Nefedova, Desyat' aktualnykh voprosov o sel'skoi Rossiii. Otvety geografa, (Moscow: URSS, 2013)
7   N.V. Mkrtchyan, I.S. Kashnitsky, "Styagivanie naseleniya s periferii v regional'nye tsentry: Rossiya i evropejsky sever," N. Ye. Pokrovsky, T. G. Nefedova, eds. Potentsial blizhnego severa: ekonomika, ekologiya, sel'skie poseleniya. K 15-letiyu Ugorskogo proektat (Moscow: Logos, 2014); Nefedova, T. G. ibid.

In the early 1990s, Russians from other former republics of the USSR began to move to rural locations; however, outward migration to the cities soon resumed (see Figure 3). This exacerbated the natural decline in the village population and resulted in the aging of the population, which in turn resulted in a general decrease in labor resources for rural territories.

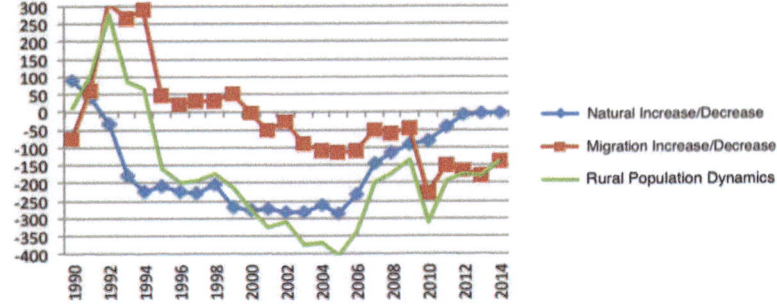

Figure 3. **Rural population dynamics from 1990 through 2014 and its main components**
Sources: Demograficheskу Ezhegodnik. Moscow: Federal Statistics Service, 2014; Chislennost' naseleniya Rossijskoi Federatsii po gorodam, posyolkam gorodskogo tipa i rayonam. Moscow: Federal Statistics Service, 2015.

In non-black earth areas, the difference in population density between suburban and peripheral regions reached 8-10 times long before 1990 (see Figures 4.1 and 4.2).

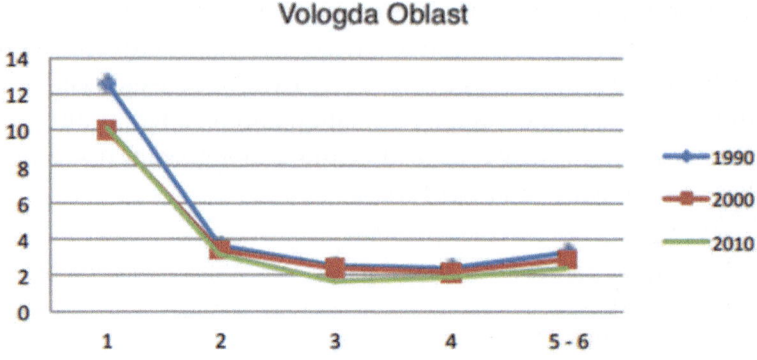

Figure 4.1. Change in population density in Kostroma Oblast by distance from the center, people per square kilometer

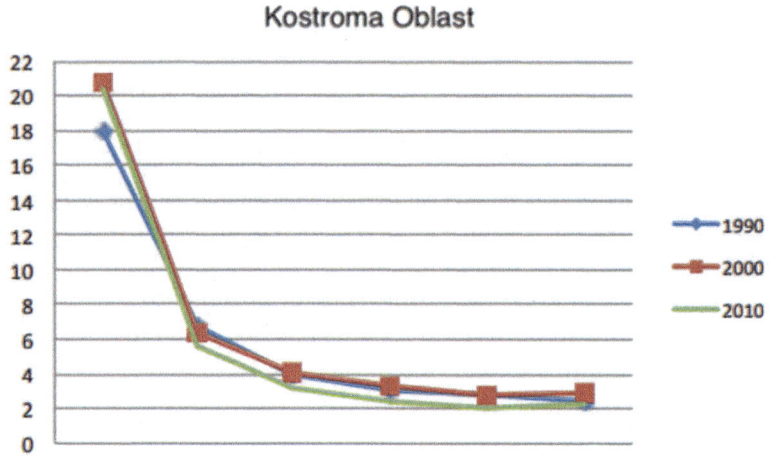

Figure 4.2. Change in population density in Vologda Oblast by distance from the center, people per square kilometer
Sources: Chislennost' naseleniya Rossijskoi Federatsii po gorodam, posyolkam gorodskogo tipa i rayonam. Moscow: Federal Statistics Service, 1990, 2000, 2010.[8]

So are there enough people in rural areas to provide foodstuffs for the cities? An important aspect of modern agriculture is its move away from the Soviet labor-intensive model toward the post-Soviet model of labor economy. In Soviet times, many spheres, including agriculture, found themselves with surplus workers and low levels of labor productivity. In spite of the significant numbers of workers, it was not possible to bring in the harvest without help from city residents. Losses from the irrational organization of peasant labor, transport, and product storage amounted to almost half of labor costs.[9] In the post-Soviet period, many farms closed, while others modernized and adapted to new conditions. In many regions, these changes produced labor force "excesses" — people who could not find work in rural areas.

Local populations responded to the agricultural crisis and the polarization of space by leaving rural areas to find work in cities and suburbs. According to our surveys of the non-black earth regions, the share of itinerant workers ranged from 5 to 30% of the able-bodied population.[10] In the case of workers from the Kostroma District, the main areas they were drawn to were Moscow and its environs (half of all those who departed), though they also went to neighboring Yaroslavl and to St. Petersburg. In addition to departing for far-off population centers, there also was movement to nearby ones — itinerant workers lived in dormitories or rented apartments and returned home to their families on the weekends — or to local cities for day work. In regions adjacent to the Moscow District, for example the northern parts of the Tula District, one in three workers found employment in the capital region; buses would come to the villages for workers. In the regions between Moscow and St. Petersburg, between 10 and 30% of the economically active population traveled to work in one of the two metropolises.[11] The population of Novgorod District tended toward the

---

8   In Figures 4.1 and 4.2, 1 represents the areas immediately adjacent to the regional center, 2 represents the neighboring areas at two degrees of separation from the center, 3 represents those three degrees removed, etc., up to the outlying areas (sixth and seventh degree removed) of the region.
9   V.G. Kostakov, "Trudovye resursy sela," Znanie – sila No. 2, 1983.
10 T.G. Nefedova, "Otkhodnichestvo v sisteme migratsij sovremennoi Rossii."
11 T.G. Nefedova, A.I. Treivish, eds, Puteshstvie iz Peterburga v Moskvu: 222 goda spustya. Kniga 1: Dva stoletiya rossijskoi istoriii mezhdu Moskvoi i Sankt-Peterburgom T.G. Nefedova, K.V. Averkieva, eds, Kniga 2: Puteshestvie iz Peterburga v Moskvu v 21 veke (Moscow: URSS-LENAND, 2015).

northern capital and its suburbs, while the population of the Tver District was oriented primarily to the Moscow capital region.

The migration of peasants to find work, especially during the winter months, is not a new phenomenon. It was widespread in the 19th and early 20th centuries. In Soviet times, migration was practiced by oil crews. However, the post-Soviet period saw a significant increase in the variety of occupations in which itinerant migrants engaged, as well as in their destinations, in part because of the rise of rural itinerants from the southern and Volga basin regions, which had previously been able to retain their populations.[12]

The urge of residents of villages and small towns to move to large population centers is connected not only with low incomes and lack of infrastructure at home, but also with the advantages of city life — the social environment, education, careers, etc. For many, itinerant work was a stepping stone to moving to the big city. The very fact of mass exodus from rural areas in the late Soviet period, when businesses were still working and salaries were still being paid, speaks to the incomplete status of urbanization in Soviet Russia.[13] Evidence of this can be seen in the fact that in the 2000s, during a period of economic growth, departure from rural areas began again (see Figure 3). However, for those seeking to move to the city, city housing remained unaffordable; it was this "poverty trap"[14] or "housing serfdom,"[15] that caused mass labor migration. Workers could not buy or rent family housing and were forced to live in two houses, of which the one near place of employment was rarely fully functional. According to polls, half of itinerants do not intend to move to large population centers,[16] a decision that reflects not only

---

12 T.G. Nefedova, "Otkhodnichestvo v sisteme migratsij sovremennoi Rossii."
13 T.G. Nefedova, A.I. Treivish, "Teoria 'differentsial'noi urbanizatsii' i ierarkhiya gorodov v Rossii na rubezhe 21 veka," A.G. Makhrova, ed, Problemy urbanizatii na rubezhe vekov (Smolensk: Oikumena, 2002) 71–86.
14 S. Guriev, Mify ekonomiki: zabluzhdeniya i stereotipy, kotorye rasprostranyayut SMI i politiki (3rd ed., revised) (Moscow: OOO "United Press" 2010)
15 A.G. Makhrova, P.L. Kirillov, "Rossijskaya urbanizatsiya i zhil'ye gorozhan," Demoscope Weekly No. 645-646, June 1-14, 2015, http://demoscope.ru/weekly/2015/0645/tema01.php.
16 M.B. Denisenko, L.B. Karachurina, N.V. Mkrtchyan, "Migratsionny potentsial lits, ishchushchikh rabotu, i bezrabotnykh (po resul'tatam sotsiologicheskogo obsledovaniya)," Demoscope Weekly No. 397-398, November 2009, http://de

the problems with housing, but also the psychological barriers connected with moving, leaving behind a customary way of life, a farm, etc.[17]

The modern period of rural itinerancy is characterized by a clear contradiction: in search of wages, the population often leaves the very regions where there are vacant jobs. Therefore, itinerancy is often accompanied by a deficit of workers in those places, not only in agriculture but also in the public sector. Nevertheless, since jobs with higher wages are concentrated in large cities and their environs, they become a powerful pole of attraction. This "drains" the remaining able-bodied population and blocks the development of rural areas, especially in non-black earth regions. During research in village settlements and small cities located between Moscow and St. Petersburg,[18] we heard many complaints about job vacancies in the local police, schools, medical clinics, and hospitals, not to mention agribusiness. For example, a new hospital in the small town of Likhoslavl in Tver Oblast could not be opened because all qualified personnel were working in the Moscow metropolitan area.

It is also important that even as employment opportunities in large companies (including agricultural ones) have declined massively, the majority of the rural population is not prepared to engage in small business. One reason for this is the institutional barriers facing small business in Russia (taxes, bureaucracy, corruption, lack of infrastructure for product distribution), but even more important is the fact that in areas that have experienced depopulation over the course of generations, negative social selection has disrupted commercial and any other farming activities in those locations. Due to demographic aging and the loss of social support that villages and small cities used to receive from collective farms, even part-time private farming is deteriorating.[19] Moreover, many of the farmers in non-black earth areas are new arrivals. An additional

---

moscope.ru/weekly/2009/0397/analit03.php.
17   Yu. M. Plyusnin et al, Op. cit.
18   Puteshestvie iz Peterburga v Moskvu: 222 goda spustya.
19   Nefedova, Desyat' aktual'nykh voprosov o selskoi Rossiii, 183–233.

barrier to the development of small business outside the metropolises is low consumer demand among the population.

In Russia to date, centripetal tendencies dominate over centrifugal ones: the population is gravitating toward large cities instead of "scattering" to small towns and villages. Moreover, there is a definite bifurcation in the consciousness of modern city-dwellers: it is necessary to live in large cities, and though people want to live in small towns or villages, it does not work out. With the huge expanses and continuing depopulation of Russian villages, there has arisen a specific form of suburbanization and de-urbanization: a significant number of city residents own a second, seasonal home, or *dacha*, in the suburbs or in more distant areas. Moreover, the distance of the second home from large population centers is growing, which cannot help but affect rural areas as well.[20] During the summer in some of the more scenic regions of non-black earth areas, city residents increase the population numbers by 2-4 times. The consumer demands of seasonal residents provide work for part of the permanent local population. But most importantly, these seasonal residents, mostly city dwellers with median incomes and higher education, create a different social atmosphere and activate the local community. The main impediments are infrastructure and the service sector, which lag far behind.

The southern regions have done a much better job of maintaining their rural labor forces. Here, there are large agricultural companies; there are also separate enterprises that are the heirs of the collective farm system. Most striking is the varied structure of modern agriculture, with active competition between private and commercial farms. In the southern rural areas, as in the suburbs, there is higher population density, the population is younger, and the villages are larger. The cities have invested in these areas to support the food production facilities that supply their foodstuffs.

Itinerancy has also become characteristic of the southern regions. Here, however, it has been connected not so much with the

---

20 T.G. Nefedova, "Rossijskie dachi v raznom prostranstve masshtaba i vremeni," Demoscope Weekly No. 657-658, 5-18 October 5-18, 2015, http://demoscope.ru/weekly/2015/0657/index.php.

various crises in agriculture as with the transition to less labor-intensive crop production and the modernization of facilities. All of this has led to the significant overpopulation of Russia's rural south[21], activating urbanization processes there. Many of the south's problems are connected with the fight for land resources.

Land: Does Russia Have Too Little or Not Enough?

The phrase "agricultural lands are our strategic resource" has become commonplace of late. It usually refers to the fact that Russia accounts for 12% of the world's arable land (a questionable figure, if you consider that part of this land is located in areas poorly suited to crop production and is actively being overgrown by forest) or to the unique quality of Russian black earth lands. Farmland makes up only 13% of Russia's enormous territory, though to the south of Oryol, Tula, Kazan, and Orenburg — where the black earth lands are located — it can reach upwards of 60% of the total. In the majority of the remaining territory, the percentage of cultivated land is not large; the fields between the forests are not extensive, which makes them more difficult to reach and cultivate; and soils are poor and often acidic. The increase in the area of land under cultivation in non-black earth areas in the second half of the 20th century coincided with a strong outflow of the population from rural areas. However, in many places with difficult climatic conditions, facilities were forced to plow huge areas that they could then neither properly care for nor harvest the crops from. In the 1990s, in conjunction with the economic crisis and the cessation of subsidies to unprofitable farms, there was a sharp decline in the area of cultivated land (see Figure 5). The net losses over the past 24 years comprise 37 million hectares, or about one-third of the 119 million hectares under cultivation in 1990. Part of the formerly cultivated lands has long been overgrown by forest; since 1990, the area covered in forest has increased by 32 million hectares.[22]

---

21 Nefedova, Otkhodnichestvo v sisteme migratsij v sovremennoi Rossii.
22 "Informatsiya o sotsial'no-ekonomicheskom polozhenii Rossii v 2014 g. Moscow: Federal Statistics Service, 2015," http://www.gks.ru/wps/wcm/connect/ross tat_main/rosstat/ru/statistics/publications/catalog/doc_1140087276688.

That being said, the way in which the remaining cultivated areas are used has noticeably changed. The sowing of wheat, which has become one of Russia's main exports, has not declined, and has even exceeded the sharp decline in area cultivated for feed crops, which has in many ways affected livestock numbers (see Figures 5 and 2).

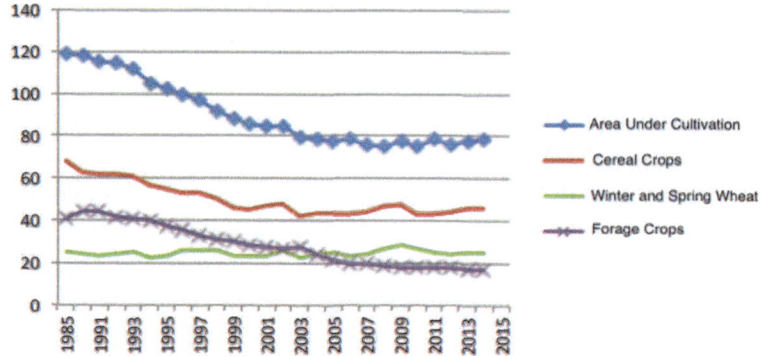

Figure 5. The dynamics of sown areas from 1985-2014, million hectares
Source: Razvitie agropromyshlennogo RSFSR by kompleksa. M: Goskomstat RSFSR, 1990; Narodnoe khozyaistva RSFSR. M.: Goskomstat RSFSR, 1991; Regiony Rossii. M.: Federal'naya sluzhba gosudarstvennoi statistiki, 2002, 2008, 2014; Osnovnye pokazateli sel'skogo khozyaistva v Rossii. M: Federal'naya sluzhba gosudarstvennoi statistiki, 2015.

The reduction of the area under cultivation is causing the authorities some concern. In his yearly message in 2015, the president suggested searching out unprincipled owners of agricultural land and impounding land in order to later bring it to auction.[23] The Minister of Agriculture, deputies, several governors, and simple "well-wishers" began to call for a return to working the abandoned lands. However, the resolution of this problem has several aspects.

---

23 "Putin postavil vopros ob iz'yatii neispolzuemykh zemel' selkhoz naznacheniya," Agropages.Ru, December 29, 2015, http://www.agropages.ru/page/11767.shtml.

The first of these is geographic. The areas of farmland and crop acreage under cultivation are in fact changing, but at different tempos in different regions of the country. The largest reductions in crop acreage—some 13 million hectares (see Figure 6)—are in non-black earth areas and are much more precipitous than the reductions in arable land.[24] In these regions, there have been significant losses of human capital in rural areas. Considering the social constraints, no more than one-third of formerly cultivated lands can be returned to active production, mainly in the suburbs and "half-suburbs"—that is, in areas not too distant from large cities. But in these places as well, housing and dacha construction is consuming agricultural land. And it is hardly feasible or rational to return to production those lands that are on the outer edges of these regions. An exception to this is the existence of large agricultural holding companies (see below) that are capable of supporting their affiliated sites with minimal employment needs even in the peripheral areas of the regions.

---

24 Agricultural acreage includes hayfields, pasture, and crop lands, where the planted area is not equal to the tillable total as part of that total is "resting" and fallow. In addition, crop rotation must be observed, the structure of which depends on the natural conditions and specialization of the farms. Inventory of farmable land happens every several years; the data on planted area comes from companies' annual reports and is therefore more current. In Soviet times, the difference between the area of available farmland and what was actually planted (including the planting of annual or perennial grasses) in Russia was 10-11% and mostly in the south. Now, it is around 40% and mostly in black earth areas. This means that part of the farmable land there has long been abandoned and grown over in forest, not to mention the natural grazing areas due to the lack of grazing cattle.

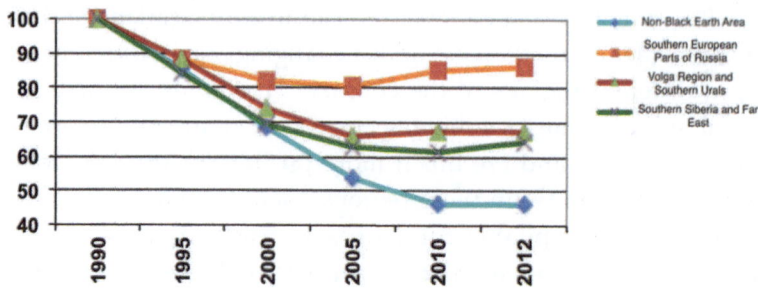

Figure 6. Area of land under cultivation from 1985 to 2014, in millions of hectares
Sources: Razvitie agropromyshlennogo kompleksa, RSFSR. M: Goskomstat RSFSR, 1990; Narodnoe khozyaistva RSFSR. M.: Goskomstat RSFSR, 1991; Regiony Rossii. M.: Federal'naya sluzhba gosudarstvennoi statistiki, 2002, 2008, 2014;.Osnovnye pokazateli sel'skogo khozyaistva v Rossii. M: Federal'naya sluzhba gosudarstvennoi statistiki, 2015.

No less significant are the losses of crop acreage that have taken place in the steppe regions of the Volga basin and the Urals (almost 12 million hectares). Partial revival of these lands is made easier by the fact that they are non-forested areas, along with the potential of the local population and the appearance of newcomers. The main thing is to find a balance between cultivation and pasture uses for lands, taking into consideration ecological issues connected with an increase in grain as a share of crop production and the necessity of developing pasture for beef cattle production.

In the south of the European part of Russia, losses are relatively small (2.5 million hectares) and there are active efforts underway to restore crop acreage, with a sharp increase in the share of grain production up to 70-90%, albeit with failures to rotate crops, which have caused soil depletion.

Meanwhile, the eastern regions, which have lost 10 million hectares of crop acreage—a figure on a par with the non-black earth areas—continue to lose population as well. Restoring agriculture in these areas is possible only in part, and only by attracting Chinese, Koreans, Vietnamese, etc., to serve as a labor force. Thus, Russia will simply have to be reconciled to the loss of more than 20 million hectares of former cropland; the remainder of the lands can be returned to production.

From the legal and financial point of view, reclaiming abandoned lands is fraught with difficulties. Of the 12 million owners who received tracts of land in the early 1990s, the majority rented them to enterprises or sold them outright to companies that are in part holding lands in the hopes of selling them for a profit. In addition, there are many ownerless lands whose previous owners died without heirs or with heirs who live in cities. A law has been passed that stipulates that owners forfeit their agricultural land if it is not used as intended for more than three years, but it is extremely rarely implemented, particularly because the criteria for use or non-use of the land are formulated in an extremely vague way, leaving ample room for corruption. But the most important aspect is that lands declared unused must be put up to auction, and if there is no buyer (as is often the case in peripheral areas), they must be purchased by the municipal authorities, which have no money for even the most critical needs. Nor is the cost of restoring agricultural land to production small. In non-black earth areas, if the land has not been in use for more than 5 years, restoring it to agricultural use can cost up to 15,000 rubles per hectare; if more than ten years, 30,000 rubles. Not infrequently, therefore, lands are seized due on the basis not of whether they are used or not, but of whether they are in demand: in the south and the suburbs, there is an ongoing battle for land.[25]

No less important is the informational aspect: in order to seize abandoned lands or to increase fines for their non-use, a minimum of accessible data is needed on all plots of land. The cadastral maps of the Russian Registry Department are insufficient, as many plots are not registered and there are no data about their use in the registry — even though modern technology would allow for the nature of land use to be displayed about any location and to any degree of detail if there were a desire for such information.

But the main problem is not the amount of land in use, nor even the number of employees, but the organization of production

---

25 Nefedova, *Desyat' aktuakl'nykh voprosov o sel'skoi Rossii*, 262–312.

and labor productivity. A comparison of Russia with European countries shows that with comparable areas under cultivation (108 million hectares in all countries of the EU) and a comparable density of employees in agriculture per hectare of cultivated land (4-5 people), European countries produce three times as much grain, four times as many vegetables, six times as much meat, and five times as much milk.[26]

In order to understand what has happened to Russian agriculture in recent decades, it is useful to look at where production has shifted and how regional leaders have changed. From Table 1, it is clear that the southern regions and the republics of Tatarstan and Bashkortostan have grown stronger. Of the non-black earth districts, the most agricultural is, paradoxically, the Moscow District. But since 2012, agricultural enterprises have clearly begun to lose ground due to the spread of construction.

---

26 "Rossiya i strany mira. Moscow: Federal Statistics Service, 2012, 2014," http://www.gks.ru/wps/wcm/connect/rosstat_main/rosstat/ru/statistics/publications/catalog/doc_1139821848594.

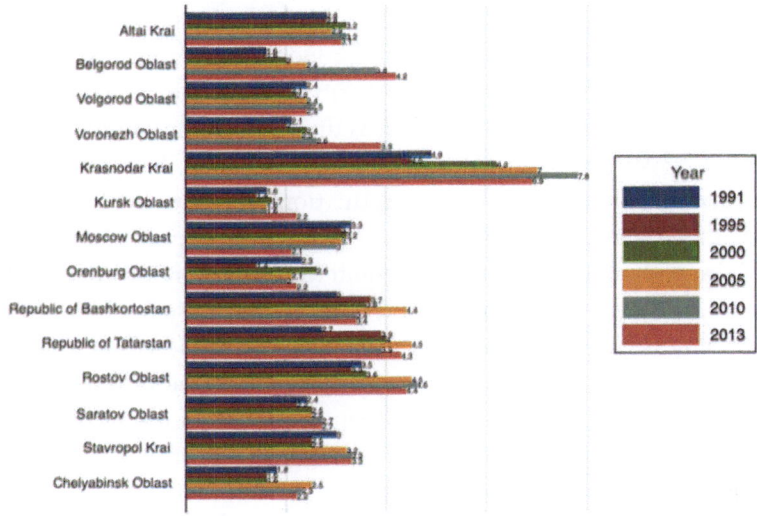

Figure 7. Area of land under cultivation by microregion of Russia, in thousands of hectares
Source: Regions of Russia. Moscow: Federal Statistics Service, 2006, 2010, 2014.

The general "shift" of agriculture to the southern regions of Russia reflected a normal territorial division of labor under market conditions: production moves to regions that provide natural and labor resources; as a result, capital is also drawn there.

Capital: The Price of Concentration

Agriculture is one of several economic sectors where real structural reforms have taken place. The main trend of the last decade has been the consolidation of property and the strengthening of agricultural holding companies. The principle of these holding companies is vertical integration of food production enterprises and agricultural producers, including trade, finance and service structures. In the 1990s, great hopes were pinned on peasant farms, but these were not justified, simply because over the decades of Soviet rule, the peasant psychology and relationship to the land had been lost.

In the West, the processes allowing the cooperation of farmers "from below" lasted for decades if not centuries. In Russia, there was no time for any such ramp-up. With the sudden breakdown of the government system of supplying foodstuffs, neither the collective farm managers nor the vast majority of collective farm workers could adjust to the new conditions, as they lacked the skills for commercial private farming, which entailed great risks. The most flexible turned out to be the food production facilities, which had a guaranteed market even in spite of burgeoning imports. But it was these imported goods that forced them to adapt more rapidly to the new competitive environment and to modernize. By the end of the 1990s, a new class of highly qualified executives had come into being in the big cities. The problem, however, was the raw materials base: it was too risky to depend on the crisis-ridden collective farms, but there were few private farmers. It was at that point that leading agricultural manufacturers began not only to invest in agricultural facilities, but also to introduce their own management to them.

A striking example of this are the agricultural holding companies of Moscow, which depends much more heavily on imported goods than other regions do.[27] Nevertheless, the zone for the harvest of foodstuffs is large in Russia, since modern production and transport technologies allow products to be supplied over a sizable geographic area. When they became private enterprises, such giants as the Cherkizovsky, Ostankinsky, and Mikoyanovsky meat-packing plants at first tried to sign contracts with area collective farms, but deliverables and quality were irregular. Around that time, the city facilities began buying up shares in village farms and renting their lands; the Moscow city government joined the process of vertical integration of agribusiness in the framework of a special program. By 2010, the number of Moscow food manufacturing facilities included in this program had risen to 25, and village farms to 140.

These agricultural holding companies, although receiving insignificant support from the Moscow government, provided approximately 20% of the capital's foodstuffs. In recent years, a number of agricultural holding companies have lost financial support

---

27 Nefedova, Ibid. 96–106.

from the government, but supplies provided to Moscow have not changed significantly as a result. The majority of the agricultural holding companies that came together in the 2000s remain independent enterprises (or joint ones with foreign partners) and continue to actively work in various regions of Russia. Agricultural holding companies specializing in meat production have obtained agricultural facilities for raising cattle and growing feed not only in the area around Moscow, but also in regions to the south and southwest of Moscow District, at the intersection of the black earth and non-black earth zones. In addition, Moscow holding companies produce pork and poultry in facilities in several southern regions, where larger quantities of grain are grown. Moscow dairy holding companies prefer to work with the facilities in Moscow and surrounding districts. An exception was "Wimm-Bill-Dann," founded by young men who raised their initial capital by trading technical equipment and then investing that in the production of packaged juices from concentrates shipped in from elsewhere. When they rented a small factory workshop on the territory of the Lianozovsky dairy plant, "Wimm-Bill-Dann" became one of the first to occupy the niche of producing yogurt, a new product for Russia in the 1990s. Subsequently, "Wimm-Bill-Dann" bought up several Moscow dairy facilities and the Ramensky dairy plant in the Moscow suburbs and undertook an extensive expansion into other regions of Russia and even into other countries of the CIS, since the company's strategy was to bring production as close as possible to the consumer. The company signed contracts with village farms according to which it invested in purchasing equipment and livestock, introduced its own management, provided veterinary services, and administered quality control in return for regular deliveries of milk.

Investment in agriculture began to grow especially rapidly after the default of 1998, when imports fell sharply; this brought a temporary halt to the trend of falling production (see Figure 2). Various different kinds of investors discovered that for relatively small investments, agriculture—especially cultivating crops, pork, and poultry—was an advantageous sector with a relatively fast return on investment.[28] It is this path of the formation of agricultural holding companies "from above" that turned out to be most suitable for contemporary conditions in Russia.

By the end of the 1990s, leading agricultural manufacturers had begun not only to invest in agricultural enterprises, but to introduce their own management there as well. Agricultural holding companies exert significant influence over rural localities: even in the difficult years of the 1990s, the larger ones were able to "sew together" the Russian expanses, operating branches in various regions of Russia and overcoming regional barriers.[29] Vertical structures of regional and even municipal scope played an important role in healing the economy of regional centers and small and medium-sized cities.

Thanks to large holding companies and their better equipment, there has been an increase in labor productivity, a partial return to use of abandoned territory, and an increase in cattle productivity. It is precisely the large holding companies that began to rehabilitate disrupted breed stock and seed farming. Such holding companies create jobs for the local population, offering comparatively good salaries for rural areas, but at the same time they need many fewer workers than the collective farms.

Agricultural holding companies choose to invest in more viable farms in the south or located nearer to large cities, thus intensifying the polarization of the rural space. There are, however, individual examples of holding companies or their affiliates coming to remote areas, especially in the field of beef production, as in the example of "Miratorg" in Bryansk and neighboring districts, where the cattle are kept "cowboy style" out to pasture.

In the ideal situation, holding companies are a step toward industrial agricultural production that shatters Russian and Soviet ideas of agriculture. For example, in dairy holdings, cows are not put out to pasture, but stroll about enclosed, bright, well-ventilated

---

28   A. Nikulin, "Noveishaya gigantomaniya," Politichesky zhurnal No. 12, (April 2005) 63.
29   Nefedova, "Agropromyshlennaya kontsentratsiya v rossijskikh regionakh," EKO – vserossiisky ekonomichesky zhurnal 478, No. 4, (2014) 64–83.

megafarms that have automatic manure removal. Calving, like the milking of cows, takes place in separate halls with full mechanization and control of the quality of milk, which helps to immediately determine the composition needed for feed. Each agricultural holding company has its own equipment and produces its own feed (often in southern regions, where the cost of grain is lower); at the same time, the system control area and processing sites can be located hundreds of kilometers away. Therefore, the impression of a complete absence of agricultural production in the regions between Moscow and St. Petersburg is deceiving: a traveler sees fields overgrown with hogweed and no grazing cattle, even when back from the highway there are large agricultural holding companies at work in places like Konakovsky and Kalininsky regions in Tver Oblast, Krestetsky region in Novgorod Oblast, and also within Moscow and Leningrad Oblast. These facilities belong to capital from Moscow, St. Petersburg, and even Belgorod ("Belgrankorm—Veliky Novgorod"), grow grain for feed in their southern affiliates, and are oriented toward the powerful consumer markets of the capitals. Total meat production in these regions outpaces Soviet-era volumes.[30] In addition to guaranteed sales in trade networks, large holding companies often create chains of their own stores.

However, over-concentration creates new problems. The process of consolidation, as a rule, is difficult to stop. An increasing number of fully functional independent farms have become attached to (swallowed up by) the larger enterprises, which in a number of regions has already led to severe constriction of mid-level enterprises. Cumbersome structures whose divisions are often located in different regions are difficult to manage. In the subjects of the Russian Federation, where agricultural holding companies occupy a significant share of the agricultural production complex (Tatarstan, Belgorod, Moscow, Leningrad Oblasts), entire regions find themselves dependent on one or two companies.[31] The largest agri-

---

30   Puteshestvie iz Peterburga v Moskvu: 222 goda spustya.
31   Nefedova, Ibid.

cultural production companies have ultimately merged with foreign global giants, as with the examples of "Wimm-Bill-Dann" (PepsiCo) and "Yunimilk" (Danone).

Though agricultural holding companies are private enterprises, there is great pressure from regional authorities in certain places. The most striking example of this is in Belgorod Oblast, which one official aimed to transform into the "meat capital" of Russia. In many ways, he managed to accomplish this (see Figures 11-12): sixteen large agricultural holding companies use more than 2/3 of all agricultural lands of the district. At the same time, by buying 40% of cultivable land and owning a controlling interest in land shares in territories earmarked for the holding companies, the regional authorities control their activity to a significant degree.[32]

The example of agricultural holding companies in Tatarstan shows where super-concentration of production can lead, especially with regional self-sufficiency.[33] In the 2000s, twenty large agricultural holding companies used about 70% of agricultural acreage in the republic, and about one-third was used by the three largest: "VAMIN Tatarstan," "Ak Bars-Agro," and "Krasny Vostok-Agro." The majority of previous collective farms of the republic were bought up by large holding companies that in a number of municipal regions produced from 70 to 90% of the milk, meat, and grain. With their arrival, milk obtained per cow and the profitability of production grew in the early stages, but employment in the village farms was reduced by 2-3 times. Loans taken to build megafarms were supposed to have paid for themselves within 8-10 years. However, by 2011-2012, the profitability of many holding companies in Tatarstan had begun to fall. The financial crisis of 2008-2010, a spate of drought in 2009-2010, regulation of the tax base, and—most importantly—unclear prospects for support from the republic (previously, up to 10% of the budget expenses of Ta-

---

32 O.P. Fadeyeva, "Sotsial'no-ekonomicheskij potentsial sel'skoi mnogoukladnosti (na primere Belgorodskoj oblasti)" Region: ekonomika i sotsiologia No. 4, 2012.
33 Nefedova, Ibid

tarstan went to supporting the agricultural-industrial complex) revealed an extremely high debt ratio for the agricultural holding companies of the republic. With insufficient working assets, holding companies increased the sale of grain. But because they then did not have sufficient feed, milk production levels began to fall along with quality. They began to slaughter "extra" cattle, but they encountered a powerful opposing administrative resource—the republic maintained strict control over livestock populations. The most serious problems began for the holding company "VAMIN" in 2010, although the regional authorities managed to regulate the situation with federal bank creditors; by 2012, its debt had risen to 20 billion rubles, and in 2013, an arbitration court introduced competitive production procedures to the enterprise. The bankruptcy of a company of that size was an ordeal for the republic, but they were nevertheless able to save the skeleton of production with the help of the regional government. The former owner, who had been given the company at the beginning of the 2000s by the president of the republic, was replaced by new ownership, and a new brand called "Simply Milk" appeared on the shelves to replace the old brand, which had been named according to the first letters of the first and last names of the previous owner.

Holding companies in Tatarstan and Belgorod Oblast were examples of regional autarky under strong leadership of the regions. However, more typical was the relative independence of large international holding companies from regional authorities. Having gained a foothold in the regions, managers of agricultural holding companies can dictate their terms, including sale prices on milk, feed, etc., overwhelming producers who do not work with them. At the same time, holding companies rarely work with individual farms and small enterprises because the deliverables are often unreliable and it is difficult to control the quality of small volumes of different types of production.

On the whole, throughout Russia, agricultural organizations (whose number includes agricultural holding companies and other enterprises of a wide variety of sizes) produce half of all production, including 74% of grain, 70% of sunflowers, and 69% of beef cattle and poultry.[34] The share of private farms is shrinking, but it nevertheless remains high for a country where 74% of the population lives in cities: according to statistics, such farms produce 41% of all agricultural production and lead the production of potatoes (80%) and vegetables (69%); their milk production is on a par with companies (47%).[35] If we consider that not only agricultural holding companies but also independent retail chains and large processing plants are unprepared to work with small farms, and that the structure of distribution of their products, in particular wholesale markets, is undeveloped, then what we have is a disconnect: rural residents have nowhere to sell their products except for natural use, supplying city-dwelling relatives and seasonal home-owners, and private sales in small markets. For their part, city residents wind up being dependent on agricultural holding companies or imported foods. In many southern regions of both European and eastern Russia, the human potential for small business exists, but small rural producers are afraid to come out of the shadows. As a result, jobs are not being created in rural areas. Farmers, a new phenomenon in post-Soviet Russia, have hired workers, but there are fewer farmers in reality than are listed in official data (a total of 250-260,000 across Russia).[36] They are rarely involved in animal husbandry, which remains as unprofitable as before, except in the southern and eastern republics, where this sector of traditional life has a somewhat shadowy nature. Nevertheless, they produce a quarter of

---

34 "Osnovnye pokazateli sel'skogo khoziajstva Rossii," Moscow: Federal Statistics Service, 2014-2015, http://www.gks.ru/wps/wcm/connect/rosstat_main/rosstat/ru/statistics/publications/catalog/doc_1140096652250.
35 Ibid.
36 Usually, when we came to a municipal region, we asked the key questions "How many farmers are listed in your area?" and "How many farmers make an accounting of their production?" The second group was on average five times fewer. Investigation of individual farms showed that these 20% were the real producers, even to the extent that some of these farms, especially the grain ones, compared in size with collective farms both in terms of area of utilized land and production volume. The remaining farmers either rented land to the others or conducted non-trade or low-trade operations, and their role was not great, with the exception of the production of vegetables on open soil, which is labor-intensive.

grain and 30% of sunflowers, mainly in the southern regions, and 14% of vegetables in the south and in suburbs.

The government is trying to stimulate animal husbandry on small farms, but there has been a response only from those regions where labor potential remains. For example, in rural areas of Tatarstan, the livestock numbers for large horned cattle, sheep, and goats on private farms (especially in Tatar and Chuvash regions) are significantly higher than in other agricultural territories. A program to develop family animal husbandry farms (those with 24+ head of cattle) began to take effect in Tatarstan in 2010; they intend to bring the number of such farms up to 1,000. This program is equally popular in Belgorod Oblast, which continues to be very attractive to migrant workers. But in non-black earth areas, such farms are few: the local population does not express interest, especially with the gradual end of the Soviet generation, and support from regional authorities is insufficient. Mini-farms focused on the production of cheese are sometimes created by city residents who want to try their hand at farming.

In the near future, it will likely continue to fall to large producers to supply large Russian cities with the majority of their foodstuffs. Small farms' niche is in supplying rural areas and small cities, as well as in producing unique and expensive products for the well-off populations of large cities.

Food Security and Import-Substitution

The question of whether agriculture can adapt to the new conditions of sanctions, anti-sanctions, and the fall in the oil price often boils down to problems of food security and import-substitution. But these problems are not so simple. The "thinning" of the Russian budget due to sanctions and the fall in the oil price, and consequently the limited possibilities for government support of agriculture, falling volume of goods, and inflation—all of these things have placed the population of the country and its agricultural-industrial complex in a new situation. By the end of 2014, the total debt of the agriculture sector in Russia to banks had reached more than 2 trillion rubles, exceeding the annual gross product of the sector. This "cash gap" demanded new loans. Sanctions, though they did not apply directly to agriculture, affected large Russian banks that gave loans to agribusiness. The share of unprofitable companies increased. The rise in prices of imported goods led, in 2015, to the raising of prices on the most necessary resources, including equipment and parts, fertilizer, breeding stock, and seeds.[37]

From 2006 to 2013, agriculture received government support through a national project for the development of the agricultural-industrial complex and a series of general and sector-specific programs. The recipients of these programs were mainly the relatively successful companies that could renew livestock numbers, purchase equipment, modernize production through preferential rate loans and the expansion of leasing, etc. But among just such companies, many turned out to be refinanced, and therefore in 2015 they struggled more due to the introduction of sanctions. They could only be saved by restructuring the debt, which the difficult situation of the banks themselves and the public budget made problematic.

On the other hand, the devaluation of the ruble made it too expensive to import foodstuffs, which could theoretically have stimulated local production even without anti-sanctions, as happened after the devaluation in 1998. At the end of the 1990s, the equipment was not in such bad shape as today, and there was capacity available. Unfortunately, the majority of the companies outside agricultural holdings (with the exception of more successful southern grain farms and several suburban farms) now use such old equipment that it prevents any rapid reorientation without investment loans.

---

[37] Breedstock and seed farms were destroyed in the 1990s and only began to be revived in the second half of the 2000s in individual enterprises. As far as fertilizer goes, the price of importing it rose 30% in 2015, even as fertilizers produced in Russia were being sent abroad, allowing the chemical companies to profit from the devaluation of the ruble. (See "Novy glava Minsel'khoza, u vas problemy! 5 grafikov," Vesti. Ekonomika, April 24, 2015, http://www.vestifinance.ru/articles/56389.

So, are Russian farms capable of replacing imported products and providing food security, and how can we understand this? In recent years, such calls to arms are often heard as "at any price, as in war, save and restore food security as a synonym of the prosperity of the Russian village," as the only reliable guarantor that is seen as "reliance on our own strength, robust use of the huge underutilized potential, including both cultivatable and abandoned agricultural land."[38] We have already addressed the issue of abandoned lands, but the idea of food security is also far from clear-cut.

A country can be described as food-secure under economic conditions where the population of the country on the whole and every one of its citizens is provided with access to food products in the quality, assortment, and volume necessary for the development of the individual, health, and functioning. On a national scale, this means:

- reliable physical access to foodstuffs;
- economic access to foodstuffs for various levels of the population;
- food independence of the state in terms of staple food items; and
- development of agriculture and broadening production of food items.

Since the Soviet authorities strove for self-sufficiency over the course of decades, the idea of food security has become implanted in the minds of Russian citizens in terms of the last two points (3 and 4) — that is, as security for the state and not for the population, including because Russia depended for too long in the Soviet years on imported products, including grain and meat.[39]

Grain imports are practically a thing of the past. The export potential of Russian grain was valued at 25-30 million tons in 2014-2015. Non-grain cultivation is still trying to find its place in the

---

38 O prodovol'stvennoi bezopasnosti Rossii. Doklad gruppy ekspertov Izborskogo kluba pod rukovodstvom akademika RAN S.Yu Glazieva.ttp://www.izborsk-club.ru/content/articles/1725/.

39 L.P. Arskaya, "Prodovol'stvie i sotsial'nye otnosheniya. Moscow: Moskovsky obshchestvenny nauchny fond," Institut Sotsiologii RAN, 2007.

global market. It is worth noting that the volume of grain produced is practically the same as during the Soviet period (see Figure 8), so the historical grain deficit was in part connected with irrational grain rations for feed. But the main factor driving the grain surplus is the sharp decline in the number of cattle livestock.[40] (see Figure 2).

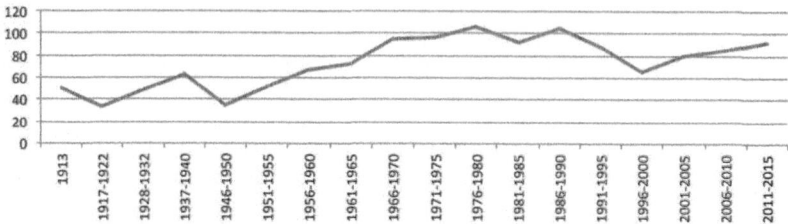

Figure 8. Production of grain on Russian territory in the 20th and 21st centuries, in millions of tons
Source: Sel'skoe khozyaistvo, okhota i okhotnich'e khozyaistvo lesovodstvo v Rossii, 2015. Statistichesky sbornik. Moscow: Federal Statistics Service, 2015

Animal husbandry remains the main task that lies ahead for import-substitution, especially regarding beef. The percentage of imported meat gradually came down in the 2000s (Figure 9) due to the production of poultry—and, to a lesser extent, pork—within agricultural holding companies. Today, imported meat amounts to 18% of personal consumption, although half of all beef is imported. Agricultural holding companies could only partially compensate for the decline in dairy cattle numbers, which, with the growth of consumption and competition from Belarus in the milk market under the Customs Union, led to increasing importation of milk and milk products (Figure 10).

---

40 It takes 7 kilograms of grain to produce 1 kilogram of meat, and 20 kilograms of grain to produce 1 kilogram of butter and cheese. Considering the reduction in livestock number and the production of animal husbandry products, and the resulting protein deficiency in the diet of Russians, it would take 20-30 million tons of grain to revive the industry, which is the current export potential.

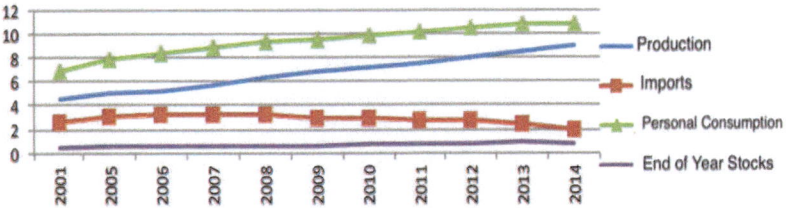

Figure 9. Balance of production and consumption of meat products from 2001 through 2014, in millions of tons

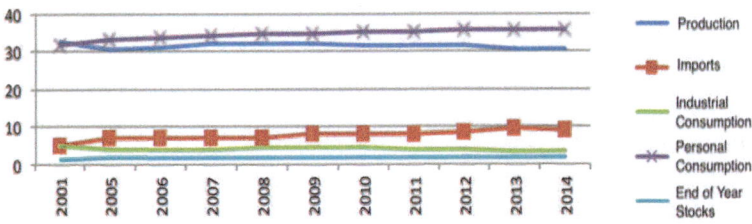

Figure 10. Balance of production and consumption of milk and dairy products from 2001 through 2014, in millions of tons
Sources (Figures 9-10): Balansy osnovnykh produktov zhivotnovodstva (s uchetom itogov VSKhP 2006 g.), Moscow: Federal Statistics Service, 2010; Osnovnye pokazateli sel'skogo khozyaistva v Rossii. Moscow: Federal Statistics Service, 2014; Potreblenie osnovnykh produktov pitaniya naseleniem Rossijskoi Federatsii. Moscow: GMTs Rosstat, 2015.

The main producers of meat are the southern regions and those surrounding large cities. Of those providing meat to other regions of Russia, we note in particular the Oblasts of Belgorod (by far the leader due to its poultry and pork production), Kursk, Tambov, Lipetsk, Bryansk, and also Leningrad Oblast (see Figures 11 and 12). In addition to these, Tatarstan and Bashkortostan are leaders in the production of milk and dairy products, as are several Siberian regions. In the majority of regions, production barely covers — or does not cover — consumption within that region (including not only feeding the human population, but also food supplements for calves).

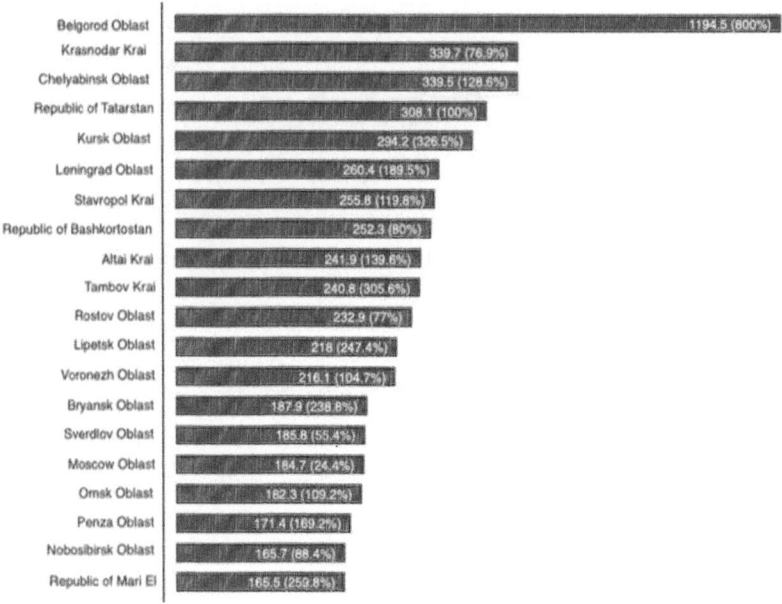

Figure 11. Production of meat products and availability of them to consumers in leading regions in 2014
Source: Consumption of staple foodstuffs by the population of the Russian Federation. Moscow: Main Inter-regional Center of Rosstat, 2015.

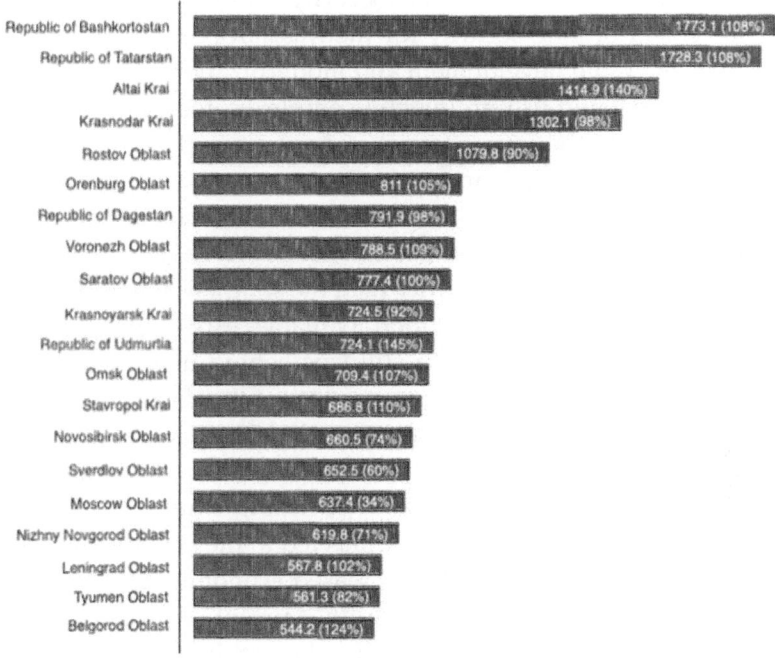

Figure 12. Production of milk and availability of it to consumers in leading regions in 2014
Source: Consumption of staple foodstuffs by the population of the Russian Federation. Moscow: Main Inter-regional Center of Rosstat, 2015.

At the very end of December 2015, a new National Security Strategy for the Russian Federation was passed.[41] And though national security on the whole is defined therein as "the condition of protection for the individual, society and the state from internal and external threats, under which the realization of constitutional rights and freedoms of the citizens of the Russian Federation is provided for, who deserve a quality of living standard, sovereignty, independence, governmental and territorial integrity, and stable socio-economic development of the Russian Federation," in the section

---

41 Ukaz Prezidenta Rossijskoi Federatsii ot 31 dekabrya 2015 goda, No. 683 "O strategii natsional'noj bezopasnosti Rossijskoi Federatsii," Rossiiskaya gazeta, http://www.rg.ru/2015/12/31/nac-bezopasnost-site-dok.html.

entitled "Provisions for Food Security" priority is given to "achievement of food security for the Russian Federation." Later, the goals of "rapid development and modernization of the agricultural industrial and fish production complexes, food industry and infrastructure of the internal market, increased efficiency of state support for agricultural goods producers, etc.," are highlighted. There is no mention of elementary access to staple foods.

The Russian population has turned out to be much more severely affected by food insecurity than the state as a whole. In spite of the fact that there is more food available, especially meat, per person than in the past, Russia still lags behind many developed countries. In the 2000s, an average of 80% of the dietary guideline amounts for meat and dairy products were consumed, and just over half of the guideline for vegetables and fish. At the same time, up to 40-50% of the population's food spending went on meat and dairy products. Increased prices connected to the embargo on food imports have already led to the increased economic inaccessibility of staple products. Moreover, given the current cost of living, the increase of prices for these items will put more than 20 million people on the edge not only of poverty, but of physical survival. In 2015, a decrease in the consumption of several meat products was already observed. There was even talk of their overproduction[42], but exporting this excess production is not straightforward due to the complexities of entering the global market, where Russian products meet with competition from other meat producers.

Conclusion: What's Next?

Against the backdrop of the decline of many sectors, the current agricultural complex in Russia is a developing and modernizing sector trying to realize its export potential. However, to speak of the agricultural-industrial complex in Russia as a whole is inaccurate, since there are significant differences between and even within regions.

---

42 "Sel'skoe khozyaistvo Rossii vybiraet vektor razvitiya," Vse Dela, 24 aprelya, 2015, http://www.vsedela.ru/index.php?topic=2699.0.

In southern regions, not only are there better natural conditions, but there is also a higher rural population density with greater labor capability. The southern regions receive investment, and export zones have been formed there, as well as bases for supplying production to city-based processing facilities. The same has taken place in the suburbs of large cities, where even housing and dacha expansion have not been able to drive out agricultural enterprises and divisions of agricultural holding companies. Instead, these enterprises have only been pushed to the edges of the metropolitan areas, since in the remote rural regions of non-black earth areas and the eastern part of the country, there are not adequate human and infrastructure resources for the agricultural holding companies to develop, even with the abundance of abandoned land.

Nevertheless, if we use the advantages of interregional division of labor, the agricultural territories being developed are more than enough to provide foodstuffs to the population of the country; there is enough even for export. In spite of the crisis, dozens of companies announced in 2015 that they were expanding business. The government selected 23 companies with investments of more than 5 billion rubles[43], including in the sectors of animal husbandry and vegetable production, promising to include them in a state program to subsidize loans for a period of no more than eight years (for animal husbandry and greenhouses, that is insufficient considering construction time; there will not be time for the expenses to be repaid). In spite of the fact that individual agricultural producers have been awarded subsidies, they themselves recognize the investment climate in Russia as being extremely difficult, with high-interest loans, and even more because in connection with the growth in the dollar exchange rate, the interest rate will be driven up.

---

43 T. Kulistikova, "Big Money dlia agroproma: investory gotovy vlozhit' v krupnye proekty $5.8 mlrd," Agroinvestor, Dekabr' 2015, URL: http://www.agroinvestor.ru/investments/article/22645-big-money-dlya-agroproma/full/#cut.

It is easier for large companies with varied types of business—such as "Miratorg" (an investment leader) or "Rusagro"—that can invest in certain production based on income received from others. Banks willingly give loans to companies that are firmly on their feet. But for those who need the loans most of all, it is harder—and often impossible—to get them. Upon non-payment of loans, the banks take possession of the assets and land of the enterprises, which they often do not know what to do with. In the end, they are purchased by large agricultural holding companies, as when "Rusagro" bought up 20% of the debt of the company "Razgulyai." All of this leads to further consolidation. But the government relies on the giants. For example, "Rusagro" was first a Belgorod company producing sugar, sunflower oil, margarine, and pork that embarked on an active territorial expansion and invested in the creation of a large pork production facility and in the production of soy and corn in the Primorsky krai. The main consideration was not so much providing for the local population (outside of the regional capitals, the population is quite sparse and delivery of cold meats is quite a complex matter) as taking their products to first the Japanese and then the Chinese markets. This was a clear attempt to take advantage of the economic-geographic situation of the Primorsky krai, however the project was complicated by bad infrastructure and an unfavorable institutional environment. Labor resources could also become a problem, but the holding company is looking at it optimistically, hoping to use foreign labor as well. For this project, the Ministry of Agriculture is offering subsidies at a rate of 8.25% annually, and the commission on the project's financing, a loan at approximately 11.5%, should ideally make the project profitable.[44]

Nevertheless, "oxygen" is needed not only for individual "close" agricultural holding companies, but also for businesses that are massive and varied, large, mid-sized, and small. A sensible combination of importation, domestic production, and export of

---

44 "'Nakormim vsekh': Gendirektor Rusagro Maksim Basov – o perspektivakh ekspansii v Primorye," PrimaMedia.ru, 20 aprelya, 2015, http://primamedia.ru/news/433353/.

goods is needed, one that would not lead to the impoverishment of the population due to rising prices. The experience of recent decades shows that with the reduction of deliverables to the domestic market or the prohibition of certain imported goods, the prices on the products of Russian producers always go up, no matter what the government promises.

In 2015, the government tried to help the crop-growing sector by giving the regions 1.4 billion rubles, including 1 billion rubles for financing regional programs. Krasnodar krai and Rostov Oblast received 17% and 12%, respectively, and Amur Oblast 16%.[45] The focus on supporting breakthrough projects that allow for broadening domestic markets is clear. The majority of the remaining regions will struggle against the crisis however they can.

The government's statements about rapid import-substitution serve, most likely, as a calming mantra. It is unclear what will happen with sanctions, the oil price, or the exchange rate of the ruble, nor how deep the crisis will be and what level inflation will reach. The situation is changing rapidly. Prohibiting the import of food from the EU and the US is not stimulating domestic producers to actively invest, since the ban could be lifted at any moment. At the same time, a prohibition has been introduced on inbound products from Turkey and Ukraine, and the winner from this move is again most likely Belarus and to a lesser extent Kazakhstan, through which the prohibited goods will move.

For now, the planning horizon for the majority of producers is limited to 2016. In such a situation, stable, favorable conditions need to be created for all producers, from the largest to the smallest, including sharp reduction of taxes and administrative pressure. This is especially important for the smallest producers, since people have already demonstrated remarkable adaptability in difficult conditions and the ability to provide products for themselves and their local areas. It is all the more important because part of the ru-

---

45 "Pravitel'stvo vydelilo 1.4 mlrd rublei regionam na sel'skoe khoziajstvo v 2015 godu," DP.Ru, 20 oktyabrya , 2015, http://www.dp.ru/a/2015/10/20/Pravi telstvo_videlilo_1/.

ral population working away from home in cities may find it necessary to return and look for work in the village due to the crisis and associated layoffs. It is important to stimulate the infrastructure for delivering the production of all producers to consumers. However, laws on taxes and duties[46] for small businesses, coupled with the squeezing out of mid-size and small producers and sellers of foodstuffs from large cities under pressure from lobbyists of retail chains and agricultural holding companies, are more likely to produce the opposite result.

---

46 The widely advertised new measures on tax amnesty: two years free from one or more taxes for new enterprises in the social, production or technical spheres; simplification of filing for patents; simplification of the administration of taxes; moratorium on audits; individual approach to the determination of fines for enterprises; and others. Yet at the same time, a whole host of new rules have been introduced that increase the tax burden for small businesses: increase in insurance payments, property tax based on cadastral values of property used for commercial purposes, and trade tax according to trade area (this last so far only in Moscow). But a new system is being introduced to make businesses legally responsible for tax violations on the basis of a simple statement from law enforcement bodies (see "Dejstvuyut li l'goty na nalogooblozheniye malogo biznesa v 2015 godu," IP inform.ru, http://ipinform.ru/razvitie-biznesa/malyj-biznes/nalogi-malogo-biznesa.html). The most important thing is that the number of audits has not decreased. Wherever we went, the first complaint was always, "They don't let us work!" And most often auditors come to good farms, that have something to take, and nit-pick over the smallest details.

Nationalism as the Foundation for Mobilization

Alexander Verkhovsky

Marlene Laruelle undoubtedly deserves to be called one of the finest scholars of modern Russian nationalism.[1] So if she poses the question of whether nationalism can become a force for change in Russia, we can anticipate that her answer will not be banal and that her train of thought deserves careful attention. Furthermore, it is worth listening to such an expert now, at a time when some observers are talking about the rise of Russian nationalism in the "post-Crimea" era and others are talking about its decline in light of the sharp drop in attendance at the "Russian marches."

One hypothesis is that *imperial* nationalism is on the rise while *ethnic* nationalism is in decline.[2] However, the author of the article "Is Nationalism a Force for Change in Russia?" rightly points out that classifying Russian nationalists by such binary criteria is neither accurate nor productive.[3] First, because even in theory such criteria do not define a clear distinction between the two, and second, because in practice groups may have convoluted ideological trajectories and, more importantly, the most bizarre mixture of views.

Nevertheless, I would say that completely rejecting these criteria is clearly premature: first, the objects of classification actively use those criteria themselves, and second (and more importantly), the priority that they choose — whether the "Russian people" or the

---

1 See, for example: M. Laruelle, In the Name of the Nation (New York: Palgrave Macmillan, 2009).
2 For an example of such analysis see: E. Ponarin & M. Komin M, "Dilemma russkogo natsionalizma. 'Impersky' i etnichesky natsionalizm v postsovetskoi Rossii," Politia No. 4 (2016): 82-93.
3 M. Laruelle, "Is Nationalism a Force for Change in Russia?" Daedalus Vol. 146, Issue 2 (Spring 2017): 89-100, http://www.mitpressjournals.org/doi/abs/10.1162/DAED_a_00437?journalCode=daed.

"State"/ "empire" / "civilization" — noticeably correlates with other substantive characteristics.

Ethnonationalists predominantly dream about an ethnically defined Russian nation-state that would, in their view, be a guarantee of equality with others (preferably the world's most powerful nations). They define "Russianness" by culture or simply by blood, and more often advocate for democracy (if not always liberal democracy) than dictatorship. Those in the second group, who are usually labelled "imperialists" or "statists," focus on the global and unique mission of Russia. In the context of this belief system, Russia is conceived through a statist ideocratic lens; "Russianness" is understood through its connection with this ideocracy and, in part, through culture, while an authoritarian model most often lies at the foundation of the State.

That being said, both types of nationalists can be in fierce opposition to the current regime, consider themselves "fellow travelers" with it, or even be among its supporters. Here again it is impossible not to agree with Laruelle that a group's relationship to the regime is no less important for classification of political groups in a country run by an authoritarian government than in a democratic one. Guided by that criterion, she divides nationalists into three categories: the political leadership itself (including the President and his administration), members of the opposition, and everyone between the two. She also very accurately describes the last group as "parastate" actors, rather than "pro-Kremlin" actors, as other authors often do, underscoring the fact that this third category is always playing its own game or, at least in most cases, not simply doing the administration's bidding.

Laruelle begins her review with the opposition groups and identifies three: the National Bolsheviks (Limonov's party), the "skinheads" (and their progeny, the Movement Against Illegal Immigration, DPNI), and the National Democrats — that is, a colorful variety of groups attempting to somehow combine nationalist attitudes and at least some degree of liberal-democratic values. These three groups are probably the most visible, but the list leaves out entire movements, such as the nationalist-oriented Orthodox parties or the Communists, who are clearly not fewer in number than the National Bolsheviks or the National Democrats. Perhaps the author is implying that those groups are part of the parastate set, but that is not clearly stated, so they are absent from Laruelle's classification. Moreover, the term "skinhead" is an anachronism: the part of Russian nationalism that grew out of Nazi-skinhead ideas has already evolved significantly, giving birth to an entire spectrum of different movements.

Perhaps these criticisms are no longer significant insofar as we are talking about a dying breed: there was a precipitous decline in members of the nationalist camp beginning in 2012, and this trend only intensified from 2014.[4] The decline affected everyone: Eduard Limonov's National Bolsheviks, "pure neo-Nazis" (such as Maxim Martsinkevich of "Restrukt," who has long been behind bars and will not be released any time soon), and practically all respectable democratic nationalists (for example, Konstantin Krylov's National Democratic party).

All of these groups experienced pressure from the authorities, pressure that markedly and steadily increased from the fall of 2014, just not to equal degrees. Naturally, those who opposed the "Russian Spring" — which was about half of all groups, especially the more radical segment — found themselves under the most pressure.[5] (Laruelle assesses a group's support for one side or the other in the Donbass war based on the number of people who left to fight for a given side, but that assessment is incomplete. There were more combatants fighting on the side of the Donetsk People's Republic (DPR)/Luhansk People's Republic (LPR) and more notable authors

---

4   A. Verkhovsky, "Natsional-radikaly ot prezidentstva Medvedeva do vojny v Donbasse," Counterpoint No. 2 (2015), http://www.ponarseurasia.org/sites/default/files/documents/verkhovsky_counterpoint2.pdf.
5   You can familiarize yourself with the dynamics of the Russian nationalist movement's development in summary form in the corresponding (relevant) sections of SOVA Center's annual reports, written by Vera Alperovich. This article relies on these sources to a significant degree. All the reports are available on the Center's website. Latest: V. Alperovich, "Ultrapravye v proteste. Zima-vesna 2017 goda," SOVA Center, 2017, http://www.sova-center.ru/racism-xenophobia/publications/2017/08/d37611/.

whose publications actively provided them with ideological support; on the ground, however, the ratio was closer to 50:50, while "pure neo-Nazis" were more likely to side with Kiev.)

Of course, this does not mean that the nationalist movement is not capable of overcoming its current decline. However, it seems likely that a new rise, whatever form it may take, will happen with different leadership in a different configuration and, most likely of all, around a new set of ideas. "Parastate" nationalists are not experiencing such a precipitous decline. On the contrary, the ideological strengthening of the State from 2012, and especially from 2014, creates demand for such activism, and "parastate" actors are attempting to engage with the regime as partners. That tactic has not been particularly successful, since the would-be "partners" are not strong enough in comparison with the State. Even large and ideologically active players such as the Russian Orthodox Church cannot be equal partners with the Kremlin, and much less can an association of publicists such as the Izborskii Club lay claim to such a status, even though they enjoy the support of several oligarchs.

This balance of power means that parastate actors, with their ideological projects, are more likely to be vying for attention from "state" nationalists—in the classification system proposed by Laruelle, this groups is the President's administration. Competition implies both conscious adaptation to a potential customer and attracting the attention of society with radical utopian projects. Such projects might shock the liberal establishment, whose members sometimes call this group fascists, but Laruelle evenhandedly writes that they are not fascist projects because they lack the key element of a fascist movement: a revolutionary aim. (I will add that fascism in this sense is less and less prevalent among nationalists in the opposition camp as well.)

"Parastate" nationalist actors are not organized by parties or movements. Clearly, this is because such organization would be counterproductive for their relationship with the administration, not to mention that they do not have the numbers for it. In order to somehow structure this field, Laruelle uses the term "ecosystem." An "ecosystem" is how she describes the diverse conglomerate of groups and actors—civil servants, businessmen, publicists, activists, PR specialists—connected by the experience of client relationships with the State, as well as, in some cases, a very loose ideological affinity, but without a formal party affiliation.

However, painting everyone in their own ecosystem is not so simple. The author identifies at least two large ecosystems. The first is tied to the military-industrial complex: the Izborsky Club acts as its intellectual representative, while in the official political arena it is represented by the Rodina party. The second ecosystem is tied to the "Orthodox businessmen" Yakunin and Malofeev and is more visible on the international stage (an example is Yakunin's "Dialog of Civilizations" project[6]) despite enjoying less support domestically. In Laruelle's terminology, the first ecosystem is "red" and the second is "white"—that is, in terms of historical orientation they prefer the USSR or the Romanov Empire, respectively. The division is not sharp, however, and is rather a matter of what is emphasized. Both groups were involved in the war in Donbass, just in different ways; both actively lobbied for the war, but by all accounts, any direct organizational efforts were tied to Malofeev personally.

Laruelle also rightly considers the Russian Orthodox Church a "parastate" ecosystem. The fourth ecosystem she defines basically by process of elimination, including in it a diverse group of politicians, among them Sergey Baburin, Gennady Zyuganov, Natalya Narochnitskaya, and even Sergey Naryshkin (but for some reason leaving out Vladimir Zhirinovsky). All of these people play on the nationalist theme or played on it earlier (especially when it comes to the issue of "fellow countrymen"), yet this does not justify grouping them into an ecosystem in the same way as the previous three groups. It can be tentatively suggested that some of these politicians are predisposed to align themselves with one of the three previous

---

6 "Dialog of Civilizations" is a series of international conferences and publications called to bring together "civilizations," as understood in a basically Huntingtonian conceptualization. These civilizations are explicitly called to unite against the dominating influence of the secular and liberal West, although within the context of the projects a wholly western rhetoric of tolerance and multiculturalism is cultivated, albeit more likely understood in the geopolitical sense. See, the Foundation "Dialog Tsivilizatziy" website, http://dofc-foundation.org/ru/.

ecosystems, while it is entirely possible that others are forming their own smaller groups.

Although they try to present themselves as independent social movements, these groups' prospects depend entirely on the course and practical decisions of the presidential administration. The presidential administration can use their policy formulations and connections to Western partners to bring the groups in as propagandists, and perhaps even give them wider local powers—as was the case in 2014 in Donbass, when Aleksandr Borodai and Igor Girkin (Strelkov) became close to Malofeev and ended up as key figures in the war beginning there.[7] However, the presidential administration, as the central decision maker, does not see them as partners—as stated earlier, that status cannot be bestowed on anyone in Russia, and they do not see any means of action other than through the administration. Even open opposition to the policies of the regime, it seems, is for the most part a means of bargaining and influence, rather than of forming an opposing and alternative course. And presumably it will remain that way as long as the political regime maintains stability.

Laruelle also correctly notes that the regime itself does not put forward a unified nationalist ideology, but rather a collection of "signals." That deliberate ambiguity remained even after two waves of clear ideologization in 2012 and 2014. The primary aim of these efforts was not purely ideological, but rather for propaganda purposes—not so much to rally the majority around some idea as to rally them around the regime, even as those in that majority represent a wide variety of ideological inclinations. At the same time, the regime relatively clearly identifies the dissenting pro-Western minority, emphasizing its opposition to the "patriotic" majority.

One thing can be said for sure about this collection of "signals": it is not ethnic Russian nationalism. Of course, nor is it "civic" nationalism, insofar as civic nationalism implies political engagement and a certain degree of political freedom for citizens. To what extent is it "imperial" nationalism? Laruelle is skeptical, and there

---

7   N. Mitrokhin, "Nashestvie farsian," Grani.ru. May 19, 2014, http://graniru.org/opinion/mitrokhin/m.229356.html.

are certainly arguments to be made for and against, but her interpretation of Putin's nationalism as "state-controlled" — that is, anti-Western and statist — is undoubtedly correct. Putin's public pronouncements regarding the national issue correlate perfectly with the general principles of "imperial" or "civilizational" nationalism discussed earlier. Moreover, official nationalism is not inclined to identify itself in any terms, including those. The Kremlin does not even openly declare its fundamental statism in order to preserve its own freedom of maneuver, which is the key value of the highest officials. For now, there are no apparent reasons that would compel the Kremlin to modify its version of nationalism, although some variations in its course are certainly possible — to enliven Putin's reelection campaign, for example.

Nevertheless, sooner or later both the regime and the dominant quasi-ideology will inevitably change, if only because nothing is forever (the nature of the changes, however, will depend on a whole range of factors), so today we can attempt to imagine which of the nationalist actors described earlier could play a substantive role in this change. In her article, Laruelle examines the possible role of the opposition. In her opinion, they can present two alternatives to the official nationalism that would have prospects in Russia, although both are still relatively weak.

The first is the Islamic movement. Formation of an informal collective identity within the framework of that movement goes against the informal hierarchy of ethno-cultures (in which Russian civilization is identified with a certain ethnic-Russian and Orthodox "core"[8]); Islamism, however, is a completely different topic.

The second alternative is a European-style national populism — that is, a movement defending social benefits from "aliens" combined with cultural isolationism. Such movements are usually related to the traditional neo-Nazi far right groups but develop separately from them. Laruelle sees potential for the development of a

---

8   The concept of the ethnic Russian, Orthodox "core" is formulated quite clearly in "O strategii gosudarstvennoi natsional'noi politiki Rossijskoi Federatsii na period do 2025 goda," approved by presidential decree on December 19, 2012, http://base.garant.ru/70284810/.

similar national populism in Russia, likewise on the basis of democratic nationalist, rather than neo-Nazi, groups.[9] But herein lies the problem: Laruelle, like many other researchers, exaggerates the importance of these groups.

This kind of exaggeration is understandable.[10] First, the members and sympathizers of these groups include many active and prominent authors, so they are more visible online. Second, they were political news a decade ago, which brought an unjustifiably large amount of attention to them, including for their attempts to partially lean toward the liberal democratic opposition (incidentally, it should be noted that from late 2010 the DPNI tried to do the same thing). Third (or perhaps it should be first), Aleksey Navalny can be classified as a democratic nationalist, and his political significance is far greater than that of other nationalist leaders.

We also need to remember that all the democratic nationalists' organizations are relatively small in numbers. At the Moscow protest marches, as at the "Russian marches," their overall numbers never reached more than a few hundred people. Contrary to Laruelle's opinion, they played a very insignificant role, despite their efforts. As Emil Pain[11] has demonstrated, as early as 2012, Navalny himself chose to forget about his "enough feeding the Caucasus" line and noticeably distanced himself from the nationalist agenda. Although it is true that he returned to that agenda at the height of the anti-immigrant hysteria of 2013 while campaigning for Moscow mayor, he was no different in that respect from other candidates (with the possible exception of Sergey Mitrokhin) and he promptly forgot about migrants again afterwards.

---

9   This distinguished the National Democrats from the "Russkie" movement, which also laid claim to the role of a Russian version of the French National Front or the Austrian Freedom Party, but remained in coalition with current and former neo-Nazis, who appealed to the themes of freedom and democracy only when the authorities put too much pressure on them.

10 Domestic scholars are also prone to exaggerating the importance of these groups; Emil Pain is an example. Pain later revisited his assessments, but maintains his belief that the National Democrats still play a substantive role in Russia: E. Pain, "Evolutsiya nationalizma v Rossii," Politicheskaya kontseptologiya No. 3. (2016): 231-251.

11 E. Pain, Sovremenny russky natsionalizm v zerkale runeta // Rossiya - ne Ukraina: sovremennye aktsenty natsionalizma, SOVA Center, 2014: 8-31.

The nationalist movement's crisis of 2014-2015 nearly killed the democratic nationalists. The "New Strength" Party simply shut down, the National Democratic Party almost ceased to operate, and the already small National Democratic Alliance became even less visible. The new groups with a democratic nationalist orientation that formed from the ashes of the "Russians" movement are still quite weak.

A new variant, for now still a series of experiments, appeared in place of the democratic nationalists as a specific branch of the nationalist movement—a systematic union of the far right and National Populists with the liberals. The first harbinger was when Vyacheslav Maltsev—famous for his scandalous xenophobic statements—appeared in the second spot on the candidate list for the liberal party Parnas during a parliamentary campaign. Liberal politicians appeared not just near people like the neo-Nazi Dmitri Demushkin at a rally, but under the same roof with them. Another example is the "New Opposition," a small and ephemeral coalition uniting diverse groups, from liberal democrats to recent radical far-right figures, with practically no shared ideological foundation.

Perhaps the most salient example of the rise of national populism is Maltsev's movement, Artpodgotovka, only thinly veiled under the banner of the democratic nationalists. In terms of notable supporters (the word "activists" is not entirely appropriate here), this movement began to surpass all the other nationalist groups, which continued to break up and divide. However, the participation of the Artpodgotovka caucus and Demushkin's Nationalist Party in the demonstrations organized by Navalny on March 26 and June 12, 2017, provided some grounds for talking about a possible national-populist revival that would include Navalny himself (during the debates with Strelkov on July 20, 2017,[12] Navalny considered it necessary to remind everyone that he was indeed a nationalist).

Does that mean that the scenario Laruelle describes, assuming nationalism's rise from below, could become a reality? I think that

---

12   A complete recording of the debates is available on the YouTube channel Navalny LIVE, https://www.youtube.com/watch?v=cjbQdbJUibc.

for now that is extremely unlikely: national populism is modest in scale even in the context of a generally weak Russian opposition (at least until Navalny even episodically positions himself as a nationalist), and it is still impossible to compare it with corresponding European movements. Additionally, the authorities, extremely sensitive to any potential threat, have already reacted by sharply increasing pressure on the nationalist segment, which proved to be as vulnerable as before: in July 2017, several nationalist leaders, including Maltsev, left Russia; by all appearances these are difficult times for Artpodgotovka.

The current situation does not allow us to speculate about a future in which Russia's development will be determined by political movements and parties. Accordingly, it is impossible to say whether the nationalists will be dominant among these political movements, and if so, who among the nationalists will come out on top. It depends on a number of circumstances that are impossible to know now, including how a transition to real contests between political movements can occur in Russian politics, as well as the dynamics of waves of migration, economic processes, the development of relations with other countries, the situation in the North Caucasus, etc. For now, it is only possible to conclude that nationalism is not able to become a driving force in the mobilization of the opposition.

A more intriguing option discussed by Laruelle is a nationalist turn within the small ruling circle. If we rule out the extremely unlikely course of events in which that entire ruling circle would suddenly disappear, then we can expect that sooner or later there will be an internal reorganization. It is entirely possible that after such an event, members of one of the openly nationalist "ecosystems" would end up at the top. To what extent would these people change the face of official nationalism? Laruelle believes that radical change should not be expected: the new version of the official quasi-ideology will not be ethnonationalism or more aggressive imperial nationalism because the parameters are limited by the regime's instinct for self-preservation. The core of this ideology will remain statism. However, the relationship between different approaches to the formation of a future official agenda might still vary significantly depending on subjective factors including the aforementioned objective circumstances.

We can assume with some confidence that a meaningful reorganization at the top will result in widespread ideological mobilization, as the reorganized regime will need to expand its base of support as well as discredit and partially repress opponents. We saw how that would look in the ideological mobilization of 2012, although then the mobilization was necessary not because of a reorganization at the top but because of protest from below. It is difficult to imagine what the ideological basis of this future mobilization could be, other than some version of nationalism or another.

The Russian Orthodox Church and Nationalism

Andrei Desnitsky

The Russian Orthodox Church, as a rule, occupies an elusive position regarding those events that lie outside the strictly ecclesiastical sphere. Official documents are usually extremely restrained and not concrete, and any colorful display by a representative of the ROC can be considered the opinion of the speaker.

If we try to clarify the position of Russian Orthodoxy by relying on the assertions of those who identify themselves with it, the picture becomes still more out of focus. The majority of those who call themselves Russian list themselves, according to any evaluation, as Orthodox, but at the same time—again, according to any evaluation—it is a clear minority who regularly attend services and defer to the judgment of the bishop. It is not hard to gather examples and quotations in support of one position or another and, on that basis, affirm that it is also representative of the ROC.

For example, here is what Archpriest Alexander Shumsky writes regarding rocket strikes in Syria:

> we Russians have contemplated the firestorm that has risen from the wide open spaces of the Caspian with pounding hearts, with great joy, feeling in this firestorm the Scourge of God mercilessly crushing the Sodom degenerates... Out sails a small boat from the reeds of the Volga delta, hammers calibrated rockets out to a kilometer and a half away, and then goes right back into the reeds. The crew of the Russian boat continues to pull up the little pike and perch, to drink a little vodka with their fish soup, and the crew of the American aircraft carrier goes to the bottom, to feed the fish. It's a pleasant feeling, reader, isn't it?[1]

At first glance, this is the opinion of the fringe, since official statements sound much less aggressive.[2] But Fr. Alexander is a

---

1 A. Shumsky, "Liberaly! Poluchajte Russky 'Kalibr'!" Russkaya Narodnaya Liniya, October 10, 2015, http://ruskline.ru/news_rl/2015/10/10/liberaly_poluchajte_russkij_kalibr/.
2 See, for example, V.R. Legoyda, "Tserkov' molilas' i molitsya o mire na

member of the Union of Writers and the Missionary Commission of the Moscow Diocese. That is, such opinions from the mouth of a priest of the ROC are today entirely tolerable (as opposed to any equally articulate praise of liberalism, for example).

In this article, we attempt to understand, looking at official statements and documents, exactly how the leadership of church structures (or, in church language, the hierarchy) relates to Russian nationalism, how that relationship has changed in recent years, and how all of this relates to the current direction of the government.

As far as the situation in the 1990s is concerned, it has been examined in a fair amount of detail in Alexander Verkhovsky's monograph *Political Orthodoxy: Russian Orthodox Nationalists and Fundamentalists, 1995-2001*.[3] On the whole, the events and tendencies described in this text have continued in the 2000s and 2010s.[4] Here, it is worth focusing on what has happened in very recent times, especially in connection with the conflict in Ukraine and with the current political direction of the Russian government.

We note right away that in the most recent period, it is not so much the events themselves that have changed as their gravity, not so much the trends as the speed of their development. For example, any conversation on nationalism in Orthodoxy twenty years ago would have inevitably led to a discussion of the problem of antisemitism. Today, antisemitism has not gone away, but it has retreated to the background: they berate not so much the Jews as the Western liberals, and the fact that some of them are also Jews is just another brushstroke in the portrait.

Blizhnem Vostoke," Russkaya Pravoslavnaya Tzserkov': Official website of the Moscow Patriarchate, October 10, 2015, http://www.patriarchia.ru/db/text/4242159.html.

[3] A.M. Verkhovsky, "Politicheskoe pravoslavie: russkie pravoslavnye natsionalisty i fundamentalisty, 1995-2001," Moscow: Sova, 2003.

[4] More recent works from the same author: A.M. Verkhovsky, A. Malashenko, "Natsionalizm rukovodstva RPTs v pervom desyatiletii XXI veka," A. V., Filatov, S. B. Eds. Pravoslavnaya tserkov' pri novom patriarkhe. Moscow: ROSSPEN, 2012 Pp. 141-170; Verkhovsky, A. M. Russkaya pravoslavnaya tserkov' kak tserkov' bol'shinstva, Pro et Contra. 2013, № 5. C. 17–30, http://carnegieendowment.org/files/PeC_60_all.pdf.

To What Extent is Orthodoxy Russian?

By nature, Christianity does not belong to a tribe, but is a universal religion. Its main tenet is the possibility for anyone from any nation to enter the church by personal choice, rather than by right of birth, belonging to a particular culture, speaking a certain language, etc. At the same time, Orthodox Christianity is deeply rooted in the history and culture of Byzantium and several other countries and peoples, primarily of the southern and eastern Slavs; it is above the national, but it is impossible to call it non-national, and therefore its historical relationship with various versions of nationalism has evolved in various ways.

Before the revolution, the church in Russia did not have a single, official name, with the most widespread name being the "Orthodox Catholic Greek-Russian Church." We draw attention to the fact that the first characteristics here are those of faith: orthodox, catholic in the sense of universal, and not at all national. Even the form of the word "Russian" used here is *rossiiskaya*, which relates to the state of Russia and not the ethnic group, while the prefix *greko-* indicates continuity with the Byzantine Greek tradition, leaving no space for particularly Russian orthodoxy in the ethnic sense.

Not coincidentally, the Russian emperors did not limit their interests to Russian lands: the necessity of defending Orthodox brothers in the Balkans and the dream of a cross on the Hagia Sofia in Constantinople, for which imperial Russia entered into war more than once, including the First World War, are part of the global project of a single Orthodox empire combining both Byzantine and Russian roots. This project was first put forward as a goal no later than the rule of Tsar Aleksei Mikhailovich, and returned to the forefront in one version or another under very different governments with very different ideologies.

During the fall of 1943, church structures that had been destroyed by the Bolsheviks in the USSR were renovated, but they received an entirely new name: the Russian Orthodox Church [*russkaya* and not *rossiyskaya*, of ethnicity and not of the state]. Under conditions of war, the Soviet government moved slogans of international solidarity of workers to the background and actively spread patriotic, Russian nationalist propaganda, for which they needed the help of the church. Evidently, it is for this reason that it was first called *russkaya* and not *rossiyskaya* (in contrast to almost any other official institution of the RSFSR), and only after that "Orthodox." From that time, not once has there been a discussion of returning to the previous, pre-revolutionary name, though the idea of returning to the "state of affairs of January 1917" remains a very popular one among Orthodox believers.

There is perhaps no person among contemporary Orthodox believers in Russia who has put more energy into the formulation of an official opinion on the question of the relationship between church, state, and society than Patriarch Kirill. Under his leadership, the "Foundations of Social Concept" were decreed at the council in 2000, almost without discussion, as a directive document of the ROC.[5] The document states in part (point 2.1):

> The Church by its very nature has a universal and consequently supra-national character. In the Church, 'there is no difference between the Jews and the Gentiles' (Rom. 10.12). As God is not God of the Jews alone, but also of those who descend from pagan peoples (Rom. 3.29), so too does the Church not divide people either by nationality or by class.

This is followed by some general words about national culture, etc., but this question is not examined in any more detail. In private speeches, Metropolitan — and later Patriarch — Kirill was much more concrete.

> The fundamental contradiction of our age and simultaneously the main challenge to human society in the 20th century is the confrontation of liberal, civilized standards on the one hand, and values of national and cultural-religious identity on the other.[6]

---

5   "Osnovy sotsial'noj kontseptsii Russkoi Pravoslavnoj tserkvi," *Russkaya pravoslavnaya Tserkov'*. Official website of the Moscow Patriarchate, September 12, 2005, http://www.patriarchia.ru/db/text/141422.html.

6   "Kirill, Metropolitan of Smolensk and Kaliningrad. Norma very kak norma zhizni," *Tserkov' i vremya*, No. 2, 2000, http://www.wco.ru/biblio/books/kirill3/main.html.

This assertion begins a policy article he published in 2000. Here, everything is stated in the clearest terms: on one side is liberalism and on the other is national identity, and the church is on the latter side.

How is this linked to the general principle put forth in "Foundations"? Here, the concepts of the "Russian world" or "Holy Rus'" help to understand. Most recently, this discussion appeared and took shape in the mid-nineties; during that period, the idea of a "Russian world" was connected with the name of Petr Schedrovitsky.[7] The "Russian world" was raised to the level of a state ideologeme by President Putin: "The Russian world can and must unite all who value the Russian world and Russian culture, wherever they may live, whether in Russia or beyond its borders."[8] These words became one of his policy statements.

The tenor of Patriarch Kirill's speeches is somewhat different:

> Holy Rus' is not an ethnic concept, not a political one or one of language; it is a spiritual concept... a commonality of values, a common spiritual orientation — and it forms our spiritual unity that is higher than any political border.[9]

This is how the Patriarch formulated it when speaking in Moldova, an Orthodox country but one that does not share Russian culture. However, the use of the word *Rus'* and *russkii* underscores the ties to the key ethnic group, a position that is characteristic not only of Patriarch Kirill.

"Russian Orthodoxy is deeply international. But at the same time, it gives cosmic dimension to people's lives... Never to remain closed within itself, but to enlighten the world with the light of

---

7   T.V. Poloskova, V.M. Skrinnik. Russky mir: Mify i realii," Moscow: Moskovsky fond "Rossiyane," 2003.
8   Cited in L.A. Sycheva, "Russky yazyk, russkaya kul'tura, russky mir," Rossijskaya Federatsiya segodnia No. 14, 2007, http://russia-today.ru/old/archive/2007/no_14/14_look.html.
9   "Svyatejshy Patriarkh Kirill: Moldova - neot'emlemaya chast' svyatoi Rusi,'"Russkaya Pravoslavnaya Tserkov'. Offitsial'ny sajt Moskovskogo patriarkhata August 21, 2010, http://www.patriarchia.ru/db/text/1254808.html.

Christ—that is the mission of our Church."[10] With these words, Patriarch Aleksiy II addressed the participants of the 6th World Russian People's Council in 2001, which included President Putin, who was present at the gathering for the first time. It is worth noting that this gathering, conducted since 1993 under the leadership of Metropolitan and later Patriarch Kirill, has become the main forum in which ideas regarding the role of the church in Russian society and the structure of that society are put forward and discussed.

After the above-mentioned words in Patriarch Aleksiy's speech, there followed policy statements, which in 2001 sounded like rhetorical flourish: "Russia and all of Orthodox civilization should become one of the centers of decision-making in the world and should favorably impact its present and its future."

At the end of 2014, the Chair of the Synod Department for the Interaction of Church and Society, Archpriest Vsevolod Chaplin, formulated it briefly, and, as usual, provocatively in the following way: "Russia is a center, and maybe the only center of the world."[11] Fr. Vsevolod not infrequently polemically sharpens the position of the current church leadership, and sometimes seems to send up "trial balloons."[12] At times, his statements sound entirely extravagant, but he continues to be responsible for the church-society relationship and has not been reprimanded over the course of his many years in that post.

From Nation to Empire—or Vice Versa

Speaking of nationalism in the ROC, it is important to understand that deeply ethnic nationalism concentrated on the interests of only

---

10 "Slovo Svyatejshego Patriarkha Moskovskogo i vseya Rusi Aleksiya II na otkrytii VI Vsemirnogo Russkogo Sobora," Russkaya Pravoslavnaya Tserkov'. Archive of the Official website of the Moscow Patriarchate 1997-2009, https://mospat.ru/archive/page/church-and-society/30407.html.
11 "Rossiya ostanovit amerikanskij proekt, kak eto sdelala s Gitlerom, schitaet protoierej Vsevolod Chaplin," Interfax. Religion, December 24, 2010, http://www.interfax-religion.ru/?act=news&div=57397.
12 On the role of Fr. V. Chaplin in the relationship between the church and society, see in particular: A.V. Makarkin, "Vsevolod Chaplin: konfliktny protoierej," Politcom.Ru. October 20, 2015, http://www.politcom.ru/19223.html.

one ethnic group is not characteristic of its representatives. This refers to the whole empire, the center of which is the Russian people. However, the word "empire" is not usually spoken, and much more often people speak of "civilization," "the world," or even "the people," which are not determined by ethnic categories alone. But in essence it is precisely an imperial idea: a strong, multi-ethnic state controlled from a single center, and the church that corresponds to it.

According to the definition of Archpriest Artemiy Vladimirov, we are "a single Orthodox people consisting of many languages and tribes."[13] Of the many others beyond the eastern Slavs, like the Tatars, Buryats or Chechens, there is an open question as to whether they are included in the "single people," and that question remains unexamined. In their silence, these ethnic groups are accepted as allies, something along the lines of the Roman *foederati* (barbarian tribes who voluntarily served the empire), and moreover, no one demands that they convert to Orthodoxy. It would also be possible to ask the question of whether the Orthodox Greeks or Romanians are included in this single people, but that is never even raised.

Patriotism is declared to be the absolute priority for believers. Metropolitan of Krasnodar Panteleimon formulated it in the following way during a press conference on February 10, 2014: "For the Church, the most important thing remains the question of preservation of absolute patriotism in the souls and hearts of our citizens, that is to say, one hundred percent loyalty to their native land."[14] At the height of the conflict in Ukraine, he outlined a thought about the singularity of faith and national identity:

---

13 "V Novogodnem pozdravlenii 2014 goda: S Novym godom! Pozdravleniya svyashchennikov," Pravoslavie.Ru. January 1, 2014, URL http://www.pravoslavie.ru/jurnal/67205.html.

14 "Metropolitan of Krasnoyarsk Panteleimon: Moshchi sv. Valentina my privozim ne radi "shou", a radi istseleniya dush i tel," Pravmir.ru., February 10, 2014, http://www.pravmir.ru/mitropolit-krasnoyarskij-panteleimon-moshhi-sv-valentina-my-privozim-ne-radi-shou-a-dlya-isceleniya-dush-i-tel.

> To this day, the Russian people are great, beautiful, and their children are blessed... As on the Kulikovo field, when through the prayers of the venerable Sergiy a small number of troops from the great prince destroyed the horrible, devilish power of the Horde that had so cruelly oppressed the peoples of Russia and, in particular, the Russians.[15]

Thus, the ROC is called to be not only the national church—like that of the Georgians or the Romanians—but the church of the empire (usually called the "Russian world"), which is, in the absence of Byzantium, the only Orthodox empire in the world with authentic Orthodox values.

Speaking before the participants of the 6th International Festival of Orthodox Media "Faith and Word" in 2014, Patriarch Kirill spoke about the power of the Moscow patriarchate over all the "northern countries." This rejoinder was obviously directed at the Constantinople Patriarchate: Moscow rules over not only its own "canonical territory," but over a whole part of the world—that is, over everything that is located to the north of the ancient borders of Byzantium (just as Antioch rules over the East and Alexandria over the South). From the strictly canonical point of view, serious objections are possible, but for Moscow this is a principled position.[16] It is, of course, more of an ideal, and in reality the current church jurisdictions are not appointed according to parts of the world.

In his aforementioned work, Verkhovsky defines the ROC's "ideological project" as "a church variant of Russian civilized nationalism."[17] It is possible to say that the imperial idea (a great state that includes various people with varying creeds) acts here in contradiction to a deeply national-confessional approach, but this contradiction in religious circles is hardly ever recognized and is not

---

15 "Metropolitan of Krasnoyarsk and Achinsk Panteleimon: Spastis' ot vojny mozhno tol'ko v svetloi vere Khristovoj, kotoruyu propovedoval Sergyi Radonezhsky," Pramvir.ru. July 18, 2014, http://www.pravmir.ru/mitropolit-krasnoyarskiy-i-achinskiy-panteleimon-spastis-ot-voynyi-mozhno-tolko-v-svetloy-vere-hristovoy-kotoruyu-propovedoval-sergiy-radonezhskiy.

16 A number of objections can be found on the blog of Deacon Andrey Kuraev, " Patriarkh Moskovsky na meste Papy Rimskogo," Live Journal dyak_kuraev, September 24, 2014, http://diak-kuraev.livejournal.com/688407.html.

17 Verkhovsky, Politicheskoe pravoslavie, p 21. For theoretical basis of such an approach, see M. Laruelle, In the Name of the Nation (NY.: Palgrave Macmillan, 2009)

spoken of, and the project of "Orthodox empire" remains more an ideal than reality. Everything that brings reality closer to that idea is accepted as good, but the sphere of influence of that empire, or the "Russian world," is thought of as greatly transcending the state borders of Russia or even the former USSR. It is not difficult to note that the same approach was accepted by the Russian regime in 2014 as the ideological underpinning of the state's political direction. We will discuss the consequences that this had for the church below.

But thoughts on the special place of Russia in the world and its contraposition to the soulless West have been a trend among Orthodox people since long before the 2014 conflict. "Desert of Civilized Alienation" was the name of Kirill Benediktov's article published in the fairly moderate journal *Foma* back in 2013.[18] The author continually underscores that he is not hostile to the West, but he bitterly asks the question, "So why do we need such a West, one that considers Russia an unfortunate misunderstanding veering from the mainstream of history?"

Other such projections are very characteristic: the West does not love or value us, does not consider us its equal, we would be better off without it. This, it goes without saying, is the very softest of the possible positions, where so often over recent years one had to hear of open war of the West against Orthodoxy. Such a view of the West is not a reaction to the conflict surrounding Ukraine, but rather one of the main catalysts of that conflict from the Russian side.

However, in the 2000s a discussion began that continued into the 2010s about the so-called *uranopolitism* — the idea that Christians' true homeland is the Heavenly Kingdom. This teaching is connected most notably with the name of Fr. Daniil Sysoev, who was killed in a church in 2009, purportedly for preaching Christianity among Muslims, which puts him into the category of a martyr. Rejection of the ideals of the "Russian world" is seen by radical nationalists as a concession to the liberals and virtual heresy. Thus, in 2010, Alexander Zhuchkovsky wrote:

---

[18] K. Benediktov, "Pustynya tsivilizovannogo otchuzhdeniya," Foma, July 18, 2013, http://foma.ru/pustyinya-czivilizaczionnogo-otchuzhdeniya.html.

> The anti-Russian ideas 'forgivable' to the Podrabineks (in the sense that no one asks them) are unforgivable for a person vested in priestly robes and speaking out about his ideas not in the context of a suspicious 'liberal discourse,' but in the trustworthy manner of religious sermons... The Cold War has not ended for Russia, and is continuing on today, changing only in instrumentation and execution. Unfortunately, Fr. Daniil and other such 'Podrabineks in robes' have taken the side of our detractors in this war.[19]

Connected with this is a sympathetic relationship with Islam: because of its silence, traditional peaceful Islam is understood as a potential or even an actual ally in confronting the West, while criticism is directed at the Wahabis, terrorists, etc. "Orthodoxy and traditional Islam are together against a common godless enemy," was the title of one of Kirill Frolov's speeches in March 2015.[20] This, of course, leads to a contradiction with the thesis of Fr. Daniil, according to which Islam is a false religion that can only be argued with.

Treatment of non-Orthodox Christians, meanwhile, is often less tolerant. "Muslims are closer to us than Protestants," opined a Russian priest living in Kyrgyzstan, an opinion that can be considered typical.[21] We note that such statements can be heard from the mouth of Vladimir Putin, who usually refrains from theological declarations.[22]

Symphony for the 21st Century?

At the end of 2012, when there was some question about the stability of the existing government regime, Patriarch Kirill said:

> The Church does not seek to obtain the status of the state. Bitter experience of the past century has shown that any link to the state machine is fraught with the fact that with any change in the political landscape, the Church will

---

19 A. Zhuchkovsky, "Lozh' "uranopatriotizma"," Agentstvo Politicheskikh Novostey, August 4, 2010, http://www.apn.ru/publications/article22585.html.
20 K. Frolov, "Pravoslavie i traditsionny islam - vmeste protiv obshchego bezbozhnogo vraga," Religare, March 29, 2015, http://www.religare.ru/2_106368.html.
21 I. Dronov, "Nam blizhe musul'mane, chem protestanty," Russkaya Narodnaya Liniya, January 17, 2011, http://ruskline.ru/news_rl/2011/01/17/protoierej_igor_dronov_nam_blizhe_musulmane_chem_protestanty/.
22 In "Priamaya Liniya" on Channel One 16 December 2010.

invariably be equated in the minds of the people with the previous course and regime.[23]

Regime change, however, did not take place, and in the following few years the tone of the patriarch's speeches noticeably changed. In January 2015, he spoke before the State Duma for the first time in history.[24] In his speech, he defined the composition of the main values for our country: "faith, statehood, justice, solidarity, and dignity." Essentially this very formula was put forth by the patriarch as a national idea not long before the World Russian People's Council in November 2014 (we will return to this speech again).

The patriarch underscored that all these values have in one way or another been developed throughout Russian history, which, while it may not be without conflict, is of a piece and without contradiction: faith in ancient Rus', statehood in Imperial Russia, justice in the revolutionary years, solidarity in the USSR, and dignity of the new times all harmoniously complement one another. The only era not on board is the nineties with its liberal values—that is, values foreign to our people.

This is not just a theory—the patriarch clearly specified the church's readiness to take this ideology to the masses. In particular, he offered to teach a course in school on the principles of traditional religion over the course of more than a year (as it is currently) and in each grade from second to ninth. A corresponding proposal was soon received by the Ministry of Education. The course was first announced as culturological, but the patriarch has since shifted the accent, proposing to educate children through the lens of national ideology, on the scale of the entire country and at the government's expense:

---

23 "Eparkhial'ny doklad 2012 goda," Russkaya Pravoslavnaya Tserkov'. Official website of the Moscow Patriarchate December 28, 2012, http://www.patriarchia.ru/data/2013/09/05/1235679205/ES2012.doc.

24 "Vystuplenie svyatejshego Patriarkha Kirilla na otkrytii III Rozhdestvenskikh parlamentskikh vstrech," Russkaya Pravoslavnaya Tserkov'. Official website of the Moscow Patriarchate, January 22, 2015, http://www.patriarchia.ru/db/text/3960558.html.

> This course has been designed for the education not only of the moral consciousness of the children, but also of their national consciousness... in order to stand against, to the extent that it is possible, the dangerous and destructive external influence on human development.

(Thus far, the program is far from implementation.)

In essence, this is a modernized version of the Byzantine "symphony of powers," under which church and state work closely together to achieve common goals.[25] And here the question can be posed: to what degree are church figures providing support for state policy, and to what degree are they trying to turn that policy to their own advantage?

In less formal speeches, the conviction is often expressed that a turn to traditional values and getting rid of the liberal past have only begun and there is a long road left to travel in that direction. Archpriest Artemiy Vladimirov, for example, calls on Orthodox people to join the ranks of the National Liberation Movement (NLM), which stands for the liberation of the country from its Constitution.[26] Fr. Artemiy has spoken more than once in support of this nationalist organization, although video clips and text of his speeches have recently been removed from their site. In such speeches, the priest is markedly loyal to the president, whom he prefers to call "commander," evidently in the hope that it is Putin who will lead the next crusade against liberalism. As in the case of Fr. A. Shumsky, the radical statements of Fr. Artemiy are evidently fully acceptable for a priest of the ROC, and by all appearances he has a fairly large number of supporters.

Priests often take active part in the public ideological fight. "Russia has proven to be very steadfast and effective against outside aggression, that has been shown by history, but absolutely

---

25 On how this ideology came together in the 1990s, see A.S. Desnitsky, "Svyashchenstvo i tsarstvo v rossijskom obshchestvennom soznanii (is istorii odnogo arkhetipa)" Continent No. 104, 2000, 248–278.

26 According to a Sova center report: "Izvestny svyashchennik prizval vstupat' v ryady NOD dlia zashchity suvereniteta Rossii,'" Sova. Center for information and analytics, November 25, 2014, http://www.sova-center.ru/religion/news/authorities/elections/2014/11/d30725/. The news was deleted from the NOD Website itself: http://rusnod.ru/news/theme6416.html.

helpless against aggression from within." This phrase from the beginning of the film "The Biochemistry of Betrayal" is spoken by Archimandrite (now Bishop) Tikhon Shevkunov, abbot of the Moscow Sretensky Monastery, who is by education a film screenwriter.[27] In this film, the church as represented by him is the very sound strength that stands against the onslaught of the liberal betrayers of the nation.

In fact, first in a line of historical documentaries on the fate of the Fatherland is a film by Fr. Tikhon himself called "Death of Empire: A Byzantine Lesson." It came out at the beginning of 2008 and differs greatly in style from the propaganda of 2014, as it narrates medieval history in a soft, academic manner. But it is this film that with great clarity defined the still-forming state-Orthodox ideology. The film was, of course, not about Byzantium, but about modern Russia; its short contents fully adhere to a formula: salvation — through statehood and Orthodoxy — from the West, from their own oligarchs, and from those who dissent.

Sretensky Monastery, of which Fr. Tikhon is the abbot, was restored in the nineties and houses a seminary and publishing house that has become perhaps the largest and most successful of all the Orthodox publishing houses in the country. The current reconstruction of the monastery complex is removing the historical structures. Some years ago, Fr. Tikhon was unofficially called Putin's spiritual father. In recent years, especially since Putin's divorce, these conversations have ceased, but it is difficult to find a person in Russia today whose statements in the 2000s correspond to the same degree with the policies of the Russian president in 2014-2015.

At the end of October 2015, Fr. Tikhon was made bishop, and this happened rather rapidly: he was chosen on the 22nd, named on the 23rd, and ordained on the 24th. Yet heretofore he had remained in the role of archimandrite (essentially "on the way" to bishop) for an unusually long period of 17 years. Evidently, this development

---

27 "Biokhimiya predatel'stva," film by Konstantin Semin and Oleg Sergeev. Television Channel Rossiya 1, February 17, 2014, http://russia.tv/brand/show/brand_id/57584/.

has to do with some sort of staffing intrigues which are still unclear to us, but there is reason to believe that Bishop Tikhon is the Kremlin's main candidate for the patriarch's throne after Kirill.

Fr. Tikhon's book, *Unsaintly Saints and Other Stories*, released in 2011, sold out in million-copy runs, was translated into various languages, and has essentially become a brand. There is a cafe of the same name on the territory of the monastery. The author describes the book's main idea in the following words:

> Disciplined obedience to the abbot of the monastery was for all of us unconditional and went without saying. I underscore this word unconditional, so that it not seem strange or foolish or awkward to lay people... They just do not understand that in the monastery there is a different life that answers to certain rules. It is not possible for just anyone to feel the goal and the sense of these laws.

The path of the true believer is presented in the book as a chain of everyday miracles: the Lord intervenes directly in their lives, saves, punishes, and, under conditions of full obedience to one's spiritual father, protects against all earthly considerations.

In the lives of the characters in the book, there is nothing specifically Orthodox or generally Christian except for external details and most rituals. They could be Buddhists if they were from Kalmykia, or Muslims if they were Tatars or Dagestanis. But they are Russian, and their spiritual tradition is Orthodoxy. In precisely this may lie the key thesis for the variation of Orthodox Russian nationalism that has become a trend in recent years: Orthodoxy is the main indication of Russian national identity, and this identity, in turn, is the main component of the project of the great anti-Western empire. We are Orthodox not because we believe in Christ, but because we are Russian. Judgments on the special Russian and Orthodox civilization that is fighting for a rightful place under the sun occupy more and more space in the speeches of official representatives of the ROC, and Christ and the Gospels occupy less and less.

In this there is neither any atheism nor disdain for faith; rather, it is just that questions that are specifically religious are considered decided once and for all, whereas this geopolitical and ideological battle is relevant and important today.

What is this, a state initiative or nostalgia for the USSR? But roughly the same line is held by Orthodox writer Irina Ratushinskaya, whom it is difficult to suspect of boot-licking or, equally, Sovietism: in Soviet times, she was tried for preaching Christianity, later lived in England, and belonged to the fellowship of Metropolitan Anthony of Sourozh (Bloom). She writes:

> Who are these defenders of New Russia that is being bombed now, where have they come from, these brave, wonderful people who try (in spite of the fact that, in my opinion, they are uncomfortable for both the current Russian and current Ukrainian regimes) to stand against evil? Look how they are supported by the people! ...in Russia it will be difficult, but it is nevertheless the center which should be sought out, from whence it is closer to God!"[28]

The last words are her conclusion from the words of Bishop Anthony, though she herself admits that it is her rendering.

Obviously, such ideas are widespread among Orthodox people with various worldviews and biographies. For many, ideas of Orthodoxy are intimately connected to the necessity of empire, the role of which can be played by some idealized image of the USSR in which Orthodoxy would not be persecuted, but become a state religion and even ideology.

The "Russian World" after Donbass

The conflict around Crimea and Donbass became a serious test for the idea of the "Russian world" or Orthodox empire. In this conflict, the patriarch's official position is strictly neutral. Nevertheless, in August 2014, Patriarch Kirill wrote an open letter to the heads of all local Orthodox churches. In this letter, the armed conflict in Donbass was characterized in the following way: "Uniates and others who have split off to join them are trying to prevail over canonical Orthodoxy in Ukraine."[29] Facts of violence against Orthodox priests

---

28   N. Bul'chuk, "Konechno, blagoslovlyayu! Konecho, v Rossiyu!," interview with poet I. Ratushinskaya, Pravoslavie.Ru. March 11, 2015, http://www.pravoslavie.ru/put/77803.htm.

29   "Patriarkh Kirill obratilsya k Predstoyatelyam Pravoslavnykh Tservkvej s pros'boj vozvysit' golos v zashchitu pravoslavnykh na vostoke Ukrainy," Pravmir.ru, August 14, 2014, http://www.pravmir.ru/patriarh-kirill-obratilsya-k-predstoyatelyam-pravoslavnyih-tserkvey-s-prosboy-vozvyisit-golos-v-

of the ROC MP are given, but evidence of violence against clergy of other confessions is not mentioned, even though such information has been received from the conflict region.

In the course of the conflict, it has turned out that the majority of residents of Ukraine—the second largest country in the "Orthodox Russian world"—do not want to see their country as a province of a great empire. It is difficult for us to evaluate now what portion of Ukrainian congregants or parishes have left the ROC or, more importantly, what part of them will remain in the structures of the ROC purely because it is the only local church in Ukraine whose canonical status raises no questions with anyone; undoubtedly, however, a large part of Orthodox Ukrainians do not identify themselves with the "Russian world."

In 2014, however, it also became clear that the project of "civilized nationalism" was thoroughly desirable both for the Russian regime and for a significant part of Russian society. The Kremlin broadly used the slogans of the "Russian world," but translated them into practical triviality ("Crimea is Russian land"), used for its own political interests, although the church hierarchy was in many cases forced to pay the bill, by which we refer to its colossal loss of reputation among the Ukrainian flock.

In May 2014, Bishop Ilarion, who arrived on an official visit for the 75th birthday of Bishop of Dnepropetrovsk and Pavlograd Iriney, was not allowed onto the territory of Ukraine, and was forced to give his birthday present of a congratulatory certificate and church medal to the celebrant in the airport—neutral territory. Currently, Patriarch Kirill cannot make a pastoral visit to the country where an enormous number of priests and congregants of the church that he leads live; the priests and congregants themselves have often ceased to pray for him during services or have transferred to other jurisdictions altogether. Thus, in June 2015, the patriarch stated:

> In spite of the fact that one mention of the Russian World in Ukraine in terms of current political doctrine has become almost a crime, we will continue— quietly, calmly, but insistently—to witness this truth, the truth of the Kievan

zashhitu-pravoslavnyih-na-vostoke-ukrainyi/.

baptismal font, the creation by our forefathers of a single Eastern Slavic civilization that we have agreed to call the Russian World.[30]

This statement is already far in tone from the earlier, triumphant ones. The project of resurrecting the great Orthodox empire is becoming increasingly transparent, and nationalistic discourse all the more politicized. To use Verkhovsky's terms, it is possible to speak of a slow but palpable drift of the ROC leadership from "civilized nationalism" toward "pure ethno-nationalism," where a representative of the ROC can even scold the Kremlin for not being nationalist enough.[31]

Thus, Fr. V. Chaplin, on not receiving an invitation to a scheduled meeting of the Council for Coordination with Religious Organizations under the auspices of the President of the Russian Federation in October 2015, announced on Ekho Moskvy that this was an attempt to silence criticism of failed national policy of the 1990s and disregard the religious and ethnic identity in an effort to create a "secular nation" according to Western recipes.[32]

This provocative manner is typical of Fr. Vsevolod: he blames the Kremlin for a pro-Western position using media that has for a quarter-century had a reputation for being undoubtedly pro-Western (independent of whether that actually corresponds to the editorial politics of the radio station). But he is far from alone in his accusations.

In November 2014, the above-mentioned 18th World Russian People's Council chaired by the patriarch passed the "Declaration of Russian Identity."[33] The concept of a "single Orthodox people consisting of a multitude of tribes" turned out to be far from

---

30 Svyatejshy Patriarkh Kirill: "Net nichego bolee dalekogo ot istiny, chem otozhdestvlyat' russky mir isklyuchitel'no s Rossijskoi Federatsii," Russkaya Pravoslavnaya Tserkov'. Official website of the Moscow Patriarchate, July 20, 2015, http://www.patriarchia.ru/db/text/4164499.html.
31 Verkhovsky, A. M. Natsionalizm rukovodstva RPTs... P. 158.
32 " Zayavlenie chlena soveta po vzaimodejstviyu s religioznymi ob'edineniyami pri prezidente RF protoiereya Vsevoloda Chaplina," Echo Moskvy, October 3, 2015, http://echo.msk.ru/blog/echomsk/1637440-echo/.
33 Deklaratsiya russkoi identichnosti. Russkaya Pravoslavnaya Tserkov'. Official website of the Moscow Patriarchate, November 12, 2014, http://www.patriarchia.ru/db/text/508347.html.

enough. Five points were outlined in the declaration according to which it was possible to determine who was Russian—and, presumably, to what extent they were Russian, considering that a positive answer to each point was 20%. Thus, "a Russian is a person who considers himself or herself Russian; one that has no other ethnic preferences; one that speaks and thinks in Russian; one that accepts Orthodox Christianity to be the foundation of national spiritual culture; and one who feels a sense of solidarity with the fate of the Russian people."

One might ask why this declaration was necessary and how the previous seventeen World Russian Councils had managed without a definition of who exactly was a Russian, anyway? How was this declaration to serve a country in which ethnicity is not indicated in personal identification documents and where any discrimination according to ethnic principles is directly forbidden by the Constitution? Who and how will it help to have the knowledge that an individual is Russian on three and a half out of five indicators, particularly if the ideal that is being put forward is building an empire that consists of various peoples?

It must be assumed that the declaration was passed in order to state that it is church structures and societal organizations connected with them (the likes of the World Russian Councils) that play the key role in the determination of Russianness. If you want to be a Russian patriot, you must "accept Orthodox Christianity as the foundation of national spiritual culture" and, correspondingly, the church hierarchy as the highest authority in this area. It is not strictly necessary to personally believe in Christ for this.

This claim looks especially relevant after the events in Donbass, where Russian nationalism turned out to be tightly fused with Soviet ressentiment. Earlier, far from all the nationalists were respectful of Orthodoxy, as many among them were supporters of paganism. But it is completely understood that in Russia, paganism cannot be a mass movement and for the most part remains the purview of historical reenactors. At the same time, nostalgia for the USSR is a phenomenon that is truly massive, and Orthodoxy, of course, would not want to cede its superiority to agents of communist ideology.

Then again, the ideological conflict between Orthodoxy and communism that seemed completely relevant in the nineties ended in reconciliation on the official level. The awarding of a church medal (for the first time in history) to the leader of the Communist Party, Gennadiy Zyuganov, in June 2014 was symbolic. On this occasion, the patriarch addressed him with the following words: "You seek to care for the prosperity of the people and defend traditional moral values. I hope that in the future, your fruitful activity will allow for progress of socially significant initiatives and an ethical transformation of society."[34] And in fact, the Communist Party of the Russian Federation has today been incorporated into the government system and promotes vague "traditional values," speaking against "Western liberalism." Roughly the same can be said of the leadership of the ROC.

At the same time, it is possible to note that the relationship of the ROC to current and past Russian regimes has at last been fully settled: Yeltsin, his government, and all liberals are essentially of a piece with Satan and his army, while Putin is the long-awaited liberation from that nightmare. Recent criticism of Putin by the Orthodox nationalists can be reduced to the fact that his policies are too soft and that efforts to restore the empire have not been brought to fruition. Orthodox nationalists describe "the existing rule in Russia today" as "authoritarian, masked by Western democracy...," although they see Putin's role as positive on the whole and approve of him for overcoming liberalism and reestablishing the ideal form of government, the monarchy, of which so many elders have prophesied:

> Putin's regime is gradually becoming the people's regime — a non-liberal democracy opposing the virtual power of 'offshore aristocrats' and their managers inside the Garden Ring. If such a transformation occurs gradually, then in the future it will be possible to consider a lawful monarchy. Of course, if that pleases God.[35]

---

34 "Pozdravlenie Svyatejshego Patriarkha Kirilla G. A. Zyuganovu s 70-letiem so dnya rozhdeniya," *Russkaya Pravoslavnaya Tserkov'*. Official website of the Moscow Patriarchate, http://www.patriarchia.ru/db/text/3679826.html.

35 A. Kazin, "Putin-minimum and Putin-maksmum," *Russkaya narodnaya liniya*,

At the same time, the economic views of Russian Orthodox nationalists remain just as clouded as before. Usually, any thoughts on the economy present a mixture of slogans that fit poorly together and dreams that are more fantasy. "Russian computers should be created in Russian monasteries: smart prayers, smart deeds, smart monasticism," said Kirill Frolov at the Medvedev Modernization in 2010.[36]

Strictly religious questions are given less and less attention in official speeches. In the 1990s and part of the 2000s, an apocalyptic mood was characteristic of many Orthodox people: the world was gradually submitting to the Antichrist, Federal Tax Identification or new passports were signs of his visible power, and true Christians could do nothing but suffer through all these temporary vicissitudes or even tortures in expectation of the final victory of Christ over the powers of evil.

Today, it is acceptable to believe that Russia is awaiting a shining earthly future, and therefore the mood has paradoxically shifted: Christians are not so much anticipating with fear or with hope the end of the current world and the arrival of Christ as they are believing that the existence of a strong, stately Russia will stave off or at least postpone this event. There exists an intellectual club named "Katekhon", whose very name cites a quote from Apostle Paul (2 Thessalonians 2:7): Russia, like Rome and Byzantium before it, is playing the role of the last barrier on the road of the Antichrist.[37]

So Orthodox Russian nationalism in its imperial variant has become in recent years a component part of new state ideology and "traditional values" that are preached by the ROC leadership. In essence, the return to them is the singular project of the future, which the regime now offers to society, but in it, as before, there are far more general slogans than concrete proposals. At the same time,

---

May 26, 2014, http://ruskline.ru/analitika/2014/05/26/putinminimum_i_putinmaksimum/.
36 V Skolkove predlagayut sozdat' pravoslavny innovatsionny tsentr," RSN, July 23, 2010, http://rusnovosti.ru/posts/100726.
37 Katekhon, "Intellektual'ny Klub," http://www.katehon.ru/.

a slow drift is noticeable in the ROC, from imperial "civilized nationalism" toward ethnic nationalism.

The church leadership seeks to use for its own purposes both government structures and the wave of patriotic-nationalistic feelings in society. But so far it is unclear whether it might itself be used for other purposes under its own slogans, which are now taking on another meaning. The recent reputational losses of the church are fairly palpable not only among the Ukrainian flock, and any improvements on that score are doubtful.

The relationship between the patriarch and the Kremlin vacillates between cautious cooperation and mild competition, and the main subject of disagreement is this national question: who better and more fully represents the interests of the Russian people, and to what extent is Orthodox church membership a significant sign of "Russianness"? The church leadership is drawn into ideological arguments that do not bear a direct relation to the life of the church per se, and it is increasingly actively identifying itself with the proverbial "majority" who are pro-Kremlin and oriented toward nationalism and imperial-Soviet resentment, all while losing trust in the eyes of the "minority" and narrowing its own field of maneuveur.

Orthodox People Between the Social Church and "Strict Hierarchy"

Svetlana Solodovnik

By the end of the 2000s,[1] several areas of social action by parish communities and independent Orthodox organizations had emerged, among which charitable foundations play the most prominent role. First and foremost, this is targeted financial assistance to the sick and the poor; help for the homeless and orphans, including efforts to socialize them — which have been unsuccessful in most cases; help for lonely seniors (making repairs, transportation to the clinic) and prisoners (food parcels, supplies, medicines, and spiritual literature); volunteer work in hospitals and orphanages; and the creation of sisterhoods and (much less frequently) brotherhoods at monasteries and parishes, which mostly engaged in the same type of work.

All these initiatives are ongoing and are continuing to develop, but an impressive list of other initiatives has been added to them. A new practice is the organization of psychological and legal consultations at churches. In Moscow, legal advice (by appointment) is available at the church of the Intercession of the Theotokos in Pokrovskoye-Streshnevo, the church of the All-Merciful Savior in Mitino, and the church of St. Tatiana the Martyr at Moscow State University. Legal aid is also available at the Synodal Department for Charity, which now employs 21 volunteer lawyers.

Psychological consultations began on the initiative of one of the chief members of Moscow's priesthood, Protoiereus Georgy Breev, and are now available in many parishes. Some take another

---

1 The author published a detailed review of Orthodox civil initiatives in 2008 (see S. Solodovnik, "Pravoslavnye grazhdane," Pro et Contra No. 2-3, 2008, http://uisrussia.msu.ru/docs/nov/pec/2008/2-3/ProEtContra_2008_12_2-3_04.pdf. This article is dedicated to the changes that have taken place over the past eight years.

approach: the clerics of the church in Brattsev, for example, cooperate with the Moscow City Psychological Assistance Service. Lectures by Orthodox psychologists have become commonplace in parishes. In some churches, certified doctors (therapists, cardiologists, homeopaths) give medical consultations.

Nearly every autumn, the church now collects money for firewood for village pensioners. The project began with the idea of helping the inhabitants of remote villages, which go almost completely without heating, but over time it became clear that many elderly people, not just those who live in dying villages, have to economize on heating. The Orthodox Miloserdie Relief Service, which initiated many charitable projects, even launched a special website, "Give Firewood,"[2] where people can choose which district they want to help. In 2012, the project covered needy people in Smolensk Oblast (22 districts, 472 homes), while in 2013 it covered Ivanovskaya Oblast (10 districts, 159 homes). Last fall, about 650,000 rubles were collected in record time — just two weeks — to purchase firewood for Sverdlovsk Oblast (the Kamen Diocese took charge of the project, providing firewood to 79 homes).[3]

Sociologists on Volunteering and Charity

It is still not easy to obtain reliable data on what proportion of the Russian population participates in charitable and volunteer activities (even less concrete information is available on what form of charity people are involved in, how regularly, etc.); it is especially impossible to determine what part of this charitable activity is by the Orthodox community. Perhaps the most detailed information on this issue is contained in the monitoring report of the Center for Civil Society and Commercial Sector Research at National Research University Higher School of Economics.[4] The report showed that

---

2   "Podari drova!" http://podari-drova.miloserdie.ru/podari-drova_2015/.
3   "Rodnaya zemlya: Russkoe geograficheskoe obshchestvo otmechaet svoe 170-letie," Tsargrad-TV (YouTube), August 18, 2015, https://www.youtube.com/watch?v=ztPF8mEgysM&feature=youtu.be&t=71.
4   The public survey was conducted by FOM (a representative sample of 33,200 respondents over the age of 18 in 83 subjects of the Russian Federation and 2,259

46% of Russians gave money to the poor (including beggars); of those, 11% gave many times, while 31% gave several times. 51% of the country's residents did not make monetary donations. People with higher education, those with an income of more than 20,000 rubles (38% of whom gave several times), Muslims (23% gave many times), and residents of the North Caucasus and Central districts (Muscovites lead in the Central district) responded more frequently to requests for donations than others.

It has also been revealed that Russians who believe that the country should follow Soviet models of economic and political development or who found it difficult to answer the question about what kind of future they preferred for the country were less likely than others to make monetary donations.

According to the survey, 25% of Russians (6% "many times," 16% "several times," and 3% "once") engaged in voluntary activities benefiting others (not family members or close relatives). However, most often this is not charity work, but participation in trade union, street/house committee, and parent association activities. 72% of respondents did not engage in any volunteer work.

A study by the Russian branch of the British Foundation for the Support and Development of Philanthropy (CAF) contains newer data on the volume of private donations in Russia, but it practically does not address volunteerism.[5] In 2015, 50% of the population made charitable donations (in 2014, it was 41%). In absolute terms, this corresponds to 44.5 million people (up from 33 million in 2014). The proportion of people and families donating directly increased (30% vs. 24% in 2014). At the same time, apparently due to the crisis, the average value of donations decreased, which led to a decrease in the amount of funds transferred to NGOs—146 billion

---

settlements). However, it was quite a long time ago, in 2011. See I.V. Mersianova, I.E. Korneeva, "Blagotvoritel'nost' i uchastie rossiyan v praktikakh grazhdanskogo obshchestva: regional'noe izmerenie," Moscow: National Research University Higher School of Economics Press, 2013.

5   "Sostradanie i spontannost': chastnye pozhertvovania v Rossii," Fond podderzhki i razvitiya filantropii, http://www.cafrussia.ru/page/sostradanie_i_spontannost_chastnie_pozhertvovaniya_v_rossii. The study was conducted among adult population of 15 Russian cities (total population 500,000+, sample size – 1,200 people), excluding the territory of the Far East.

rubles, compared to 160 billion in 2014. Meanwhile, the number of volunteers (the only question on the survey devoted to the topic of volunteerism) is not growing: it remained at 2%, as it was in 2014.

HeadHunter's online survey, conducted last year among 606 undergraduate and graduate students and 204 representatives of Russian companies that had hired young professionals with no work experience during the previous six months, addresses the issue of volunteerism in detail. Unfortunately, the survey cannot be considered representative, as it was conducted among an active segment of the population (and the sample size is small). According to HeadHunter, 40% of Russian undergraduate and graduate students take part in volunteer and charitable projects. Half of them (51%) organize university activities, 28% donate blood, and 27% help in orphanages. Some students help homeless animals, take part in city projects (such as tree planting), and help veterans. Roughly half of employers (52%) said that their company was involved in volunteer or charitable work. Companies predominantly help orphanages (52%).[6]

The head of the "Danilovtsy" Volunteer Movement, Yuri Belanovsky, is skeptical about the information on Russians' mass participation in volunteer projects. He has previously stated:

> My colleagues and I know almost everyone who is even somewhat serious about volunteering in Moscow. For us, it is not a one-off action that is important — you came, gave a flower and never showed up again — but regularity: that a person gave a few hours of their time for these activities at least once a month — and for a year or two, so that it's a long-term deal. All of us involved in this know that the segment of people who volunteer this way is quite narrow. So, if we make a simple estimate, in Moscow it is a maximum of 20,000, say, 25,000 people — these are people who will do at least five good things this year before summer. And in my opinion, we are not talking about tens of percent of the population. Although, of course, if you consider that person who plants a tree under his office window once a year and therefore considers himself a volunteer, then maybe...

---

6   "Volontyorstvo i trudoustrojstvo," Career.ru, November 24, 2015, http://career.ru/article/17929.

Miloserdie

Miloserdie is the most powerful and effective of the Church's charities. In many ways, it sets the tone and points out possible courses of action to everyone else. Miloserdie is carrying out 24 projects;[7] in recent years, much has been done in cooperation with the Marfo-Mariinsky Convent, where, for example, a rehabilitation center for children with motor system impairments has been opened. Sick children aged three to ten attend the center twice a week, and specialists (psychologists, speech therapists, massage therapists, and instructors) work with them until the children master some basic skills (sitting, walking, eating). About 30 children pass through the center every month, with more than 300 passing through the center in a year. The small capacity is due to a lack of space—the center was designed for six children per day. The Moscow government has provided a new building, which will double the number of wards, but it requires redevelopment and repair.

Also at the Marfo-Mariinsky Convent is a Children's Field Hospice program run jointly with Miloserdie Service. Palliative care is a relatively new medical sector for Russia; it includes home care for people with rare diseases such as Duchene syndrome, mucopolysaccharidosis, spinal muscular atrophy, etc. About 25 families with terminally ill members visit the center every day; two people are constantly on phone duty, ready to answer any question, as patients need a lot of information to regulate the course of their disease. For example, there are about 600 patients in Moscow with ALS (atrophic lateral sclerosis—a disease in which motor neurons degenerate and respiratory muscles gradually atrophy). Since 2012, Miloserdie has been running a new program called "Dykhanie,"[8] which provides ALS patients with breathing devices. The device costs 180,000 rubles for an adult and 320,000 rubles for a child and state benefits do not cover the cost. This, however, is only the basic equipment; a device with all the accessories costs around a million

---

7   "Proekty pravoslavnoj sluzhby 'Miloserdie'," Miloserdie, https://www.miloserdie.ru/friends/.
8   Programma "Dykhanie" http://www.air4help.ru.

rubles. Once a month, ALS patients come with their families to the Marfo-Mariinsky Convent to ask questions and just chat.

The development of palliative care in Russia is largely the work of the Orthodox. Thanks to the years-long perseverance of priest Alexander Tkachenko, the country's first children's hospice, a "joint venture" of the state (the hospital receives funding from the city) and three NGOs that rely on private donations, opened in St. Petersburg in 2010. In Moscow, a children's hospice with 17 beds, "House with a Beacon," is just being built (it is a project of the Vera Foundation for Assistance to Hospices); the opening is planned for 2018.

In 2012, another Miloserdie project—the crisis center "House for Mom"—was launched. Up to ten women (with or without children) in difficult life situations can live in the house at a time: for example, a pregnant unmarried woman whose parents kicked her out of the house, or an orphaned mother who does not have a home, or a non-resident married woman with a small child whose husband suddenly lost his job and cannot continue to rent an apartment until he finds a new one. The center provides assistance to women regardless of age, citizenship, ethnicity or religion. Those who have been helped include not only Russians, but also citizens of Ukraine, Moldova, Tajikistan, Venezuela, and Congo. Expectant mothers can prepare for childbirth with free courses for pregnant women at the Marfo-Mariinsky Convent. During the three months that a woman can live fully supported at the "House for Mom" (the term can be extended, if necessary—the longest stay at the center to date is nine months), lawyers, social workers, and psychologists help her to replace important documents, find a job, find housing, and reconnect with relatives. In three years, 105 women and 113 children have been sheltered at the crisis center.

"House for Mom" is a rather popular project in the church, and Miloserdie is not a pioneer in this arena. The Diocese of Vladivostok, for example, has been involved in a similar project, called "Cradle," since 2008. In total, there are 27 shelters for pregnant women and young mothers in Russia established with the involvement of the Russian Orthodox Church (ROC).[9] Moreover, the impetus for the spread of this practice was a grant competition organized by the Synodal Department for Charity and Social Services (of which Miloserdie is also a part) called "Protecting Family, Motherhood and Childhood," which resulted in shelters being established in Voronezh, Neftekamsk, Primorsky Krai, and other places.

In March 2015, one of Miloserdie's long-standing projects, St. Sophia Children's Home (first for girls and then for boys), was repurposed and became one of the first non-state orphanages in Russia for children with special needs. The service's sisters had visited State Orphanage No. 15 for Mentally Retarded Children (now called Kuntsevsky State Center for Family Education) for the last eight years, and it was they who first came up with the idea of taking some children from the boarding school to the Center for Therapeutic Education. Children studied in the center for a year and made progress, but in the orphanage all their progress was lost because it was impossible to spend time working with every child. The primary treatment for such children is personal attention, but with two adults caring for 25 children, they barely have time to feed and bathe them.

At St. Sophia Children's Home, where 22 children were transferred from the orphanage, children live as a family—almost everyone is assigned a personal adult, and they play and take walks with the children, and take them to classes at the same Center for Therapeutic Education; those who are capable attend regular or specialized schools. And what is also extremely important is that no one is planning to send these children to a psychiatric residential institution when they reach adulthood (as is the usual practice), where a semi-vegetative existence or early death awaits them. The Children's Home and the Marfo-Mariinsky Convent have taken it upon themselves to guide these children in adulthood, helping them in any way possible.

---

9   "Statistika," Russkaya Pravoslavnaya Tserkov'. Otdel po tserkjovnoj blagotvoritel'nosti i sotsial'nomu sluzheniyu, http://www.diaconia.ru/statistic .

The project is funded by the Moscow Department of Social Protection and Rusfond.[10] The department provides half of the funds needed for the orphanage—about 60,000 rubles per month per child. Rusfond provides the other half—another 60,000 rubles per child per month—from collected donations. According to the agreement between St. Sophia Children's Home and Rusfond, total donations for the first year were to be more than 17 million rubles.

In addition to supporting permanent projects, Miloserdie periodically publishes articles on its website that help people solve a variety of everyday problems: what to do if there is not enough money to pay for utilities,[11] how non-residents can get free medical treatment in Moscow,[12] how to protect your child from bullying at school,[13] etc.

In recent years, the Orthodox Miloserdie Service has subsisted mainly on donations from private benefactors. In 2013, it collected 75% of the necessary funds from private donations, whereas now they collect just 60%. The "Friends of Miloserdie" program,[14] whose members (more than 6,000 people) regularly contribute a portion of their income, allowed the service to collect about 3 million rubles per month in 2012. That sum has grown in recent years despite the crisis: in 2015, Friends of Miloserdie's donations for the service's projects amounted to more than 64 million rubles. There are, of course, grants and contributions from the Patriarchy's budget (the Synodal Department for Charity is, after all, a type of church ministry, and Miloserdie is a division of the Synodal Department), but the bulk of funds come from people who want to help.

---

10   Rusfond, http://rusfond.ru/.
11   N. Volkova, "Bednost' i uslugi ZhKKh: kak oblegchit' finansovoe bremya," Miloserdie.ru. January 19, 2016, https://www.miloserdie.ru/article/bednost-i-uslugi-zhkh-kak-oblegchit-finansovoe-bremya/.
12   N. Volkova, "Kak priezzhemu besplatno lechit'sya v Moskve," Miloserdie.ru. January 20, 2016, https://www.miloserdie.ru/article/kak-priezzhemu-besplatno-lechitsya-v-moskve/.
13   S. Galaninskaya, "Kak zashchitit' rebenka ot travli?" Miloserdie.ru, January 20, 2016, https://www.miloserdie.ru/article/kak-zashhitit-rebenka-ot-travli-v-shkole/.
14   "Obshchestvo druzej Miloserdiya," https://www.miloserdie.ru/friends/join/

Around 40,000 people per year (approximately 100 people per day) receive Miloserdie's various social assistance services. Miloserdie's charity work is carried out by 500 employees and approximately 1,500 volunteers.

In the fall of 2015, the service opened a new platform for Friends of Miloserdie: the Monarch Business Center in Moscow. The Center now regularly hosts free concerts where anyone can donate to support the beneficiaries of Miloserdie's assistance services on the spot.

The Biblical Hour

In contrast to the "guardian" activists at war with "immoral art," another part of the Orthodox community is trying to build a dialogue with secular culture. Recently, a joint project of the web portal "Orthodoxy and the World" and the All-Union State Library of Foreign Literature launched "Pravmir on the Important Things," a series of meetings with a variety of people who talk about important things not related to current events. At the first meeting,[15] which took place on November 20, 2015, they discussed the topic "Why live if there is death?"

Established in 2011 at the same library, the Bible Institute Educational Center continues its "Bible Hour" lectures devoted to the study of biblical texts in the context of modern culture. In December 2015, biblical and religious scholar Anna Shmayina-Velikanova delivered a presentation entitled "The Biblical Backgrounds of Boris Pasternak's Poems."

The Transfiguration Fellowship of Minor Orthodox Brotherhoods (Transfiguration Brotherhood), together with the St. Philaret Orthodox Christian Institute, regularly organize exhibitions[16] and

---

15 "Zachem zhit', esli est' smert' - Protoierei Aleksei Uminsky, Lyudmila Ulitskaya and Nyuta Federmesser," Pravmir.ru, November 20, 2015, http://www.pravmir.ru/zachem-zhit-esli-est-smert-protoierey-aleksiy-uminskiy-lyudmila-ulitskaya-i-nyuta-federmesser/

16 "V Podmoskov'ye otkrylas' vystavka, posvyashchennaya 90-letiyu kampanii po iz'yatiyu tserkovnykh tsennostej," Newsru.com, April 28, 2012, http://o53xo.nzsxo43souxgg33n.cmle.ru/religy/28apr2012/ausstellung.html.

conferences[17] that attract people not only from across Russia, but from around the world at the Transfiguration Center in Krasnoye village outside of Moscow, which they restored with their own resources (and, to a large extent, their own hands). The circle of participants is continually expanding to include not only Orthodox volunteers and other active believers, but also people from a variety of different backgrounds: museum workers; scholars; sociologists; and employees of secular NGOs, particularly Memorial, with whose regional branches the brotherhood is increasingly carrying out joint projects.

In the summer of 2015, the program "Russian Opera in a Russian Monastery" began at the Belopesotsky Holy Trinity Convent (Stupino). The E.V. Kolobova New Opera's production of "Boris Godunov" was shown outdoors. Other directors also expressed their willingness to participate in the project. This is not an initiative of the Orthodox community, however, but of the Moscow Region's Gubernatorial Administration, whose staff is seeking to prove that contemporary art can "be churched, be spiritual."[18] However, the Mother Superior's consent to provide a platform for the project is a rather bold step, indicating that the church's mentality is gradually changing, which certainly will not delight supporters of "traditional church life."

Church Ministry of Social Protection

The most tangible changes in the realm of Orthodox charity concern how church leaders relate to social activism. Until the late 2000s, Orthodox social activism grew mainly from the bottom up. Church leadership did little to support grassroots endeavors; the only evidence of any attention being directed to this topic was the "Orthodox Initiative" grant competition, organized with the Patriarch's blessing.

---

17   S. Solodovnik, "Deistvovat' bez nadezhdy na skory uspekh," Ezhednevny Zhurnal, October 10, 2014, http://ej.ru/?a=note&id=26227.

18   "V podmoskovnykh monastyryakh budut pokazyvat' opery," Interfax. Religion, December 2, 2015, http://www.interfax-religion.ru/?act=news&div=61168.

After taking the helm of the church in 2009, Patriarch Kirill almost immediately called for the addition of three mandatory, full-time, fully-salaried employees in each parish: a social worker in charge of charity, a catechist, and a youth leader. This practice is gradually beginning to take root. The idea of turning the church into a powerful civic force through community development and social activism is apparently attractive to the patriarch. "By supporting Orthodox initiatives, we solve the problem of developing civic consciousness, social responsibility, and genuine solidarity in society," he said at a meeting of the Coordinating Committee of the "Orthodox Initiative" competition in the spring of 2011.[19]

The Synodal Department for Charity and Social Service is in close contact with dioceses, helping them to develop volunteer movements and social programs throughout Russia. Specifically, it was this department that acted as the coordinator of church assistance to victims of the fires in 2010, collecting about 100 million rubles (about 8,000 volunteers took part in the collection and distribution of aid), during the flood in Crimea in 2012 (50 million rubles were collected, which went to targeted assistance for more than 3,500 families), and for refugees from Ukraine in 2014 and 2015 (more than 56 million rubles were collected, which were primarily distributed among large families; single women with children; and sick, disabled, and elderly people without support).

A distance learning course for church social work, organized by the department in conjunction with the Orthodox St. Tikhon Humanities University, is available on the department's website.[20] Each lesson draws 200-300 people from different regions. Specialists assembled by the Synodal Department travel to the dioceses to give seminars on various topics: for example, they explain to parents and parish social workers how to work with children with cerebral palsy, Down Syndrome, or sensory and behavioral issues,

---

19 Patriarkh Kirill (Gundyaev), "Vystuplenie na zasedanii koordinatsionnogo komiteta po podderzhke sotsial'nykh, obrazovatel'nykh, informatsionnykh, kul'turnykh i inykh initsiativ ," Vremya i vera, March 1, 2011, http://www.vcrav.ru/common/mpublic.php?num=864.

20 "Otdel po tserkovnoj blagotvoritel'nosti i sotsial'nomu sluzheniyu," http://www.diaconia.ru

teaching them how to deal with behavioral problems and develop communication skills. In his introduction to the distance course, Bishop Panteleimon stresses that "social service is not only for professionals, but for every member of the Russian Orthodox Church, every person who calls himself an Orthodox Christian."[21]

"On the Principles of Social Work Organization in the Russian Orthodox Church," a document adopted by the Inter-Council Presence in 2011, lays out the principles of social service at all levels: church-wide, diocesan, parochial, and monastic. In 2013, the Inter-Council Presence set out to further detail the way the Church cares for the poor, disabled and others in need of assistance — in particular, to identify who is considered poor and who is not. However, the relevant documents[22] have not yet been adopted; it is possible that the process has stalled due to economic instability.

The "Orthodox Initiative" grant competition, held since 2005, has become more professional.[23] Since 2013, it has been organized by the Collaboration Foundation to Support Humanitarian and Education Initiatives, which is closely tied to Business Russia and the Ministry of Economic Development. Patriarch Kirill clearly managed to attract new sponsors. The number of participants is growing every year, and the Serafim Sarovskiy Foundation, which provided funds for the competition from the beginning, was apparently no longer able to provide all the funding to support it. While in 2008 the competition winners consisted of 48 projects from 13 regions, and the grant fund amounted to a little more than 12 million rubles, in the 2012 competition the grant fund increased to 115 million rubles and the winners consisted of more than 350 projects

---

21 "V Moskve startoval novy kurs distantsionnogo obucheniya dlia sotsial'nykh rabotnikov," Russkaya Pravoslavnaya Tserkov'. Otdel po tserkovnoj blagotvoritel'nosti i sotsial'nomu sluzheniyu, October 6, 2014, http://www.diaconia.ru/v-moskve-startoval-novyj-kurs-distancionnogo-obucheniya-dlya-socialny kh-rabotnikov.

22 "Mezhsobornoe prisutstvie razrabatyvaet dokumenty o pomoshchi maloimushchim i invalidam," Foma. July 8, 2013, http://foma.ru/mezhsobornoe-prisutstvie-razrabatyvaet-dokumentyi-o-pomoshhi-maloimushhim-i-invalidam.html.

23 "Pravoslavnaya initsiativa. Mezhdunarodny otkryty grantovy konkurs," http://pravkonkurs.ru/.

from 78 regions of the Russian Federation and 39 countries. In most Russian regions and neighboring countries, Competition Coordination Centers have been established to provide information and assistance with drafting applications. Since 2015, they have been working in cooperation with the Association of Program and Policy Evaluation Specialists in Russia, which organizes training seminars in the regions.

The winners of the 2014-2015 competition were, among others, the Tomsk Regional Orthodox Community Foundation "Favor" — to provide social support for children with disabilities, in particular organizing a summer camp for them; the Lithuanian weekly newspaper "Review" — to publish 14 Orthodox inserts to the newspaper; the Moscow Interregional Charitable Fund for Prisoners — to prevent recidivism in women released from prison; and the Krasnodar branch of the Brotherhood of Orthodox Rangers (Scouts) — "to build a robust system of cultural and spiritual connections between children and young people of the Orthodox parishes of Crimea with members of the Brotherhood of Orthodox Rangers." Each received 500,000 rubles. The 2015-2016 competition received 1,370 applications from 77 Russian entities and 9 countries (the pronounced decline in applications from abroad may be due to the sharp depreciation of the ruble). The results of the contest will be tallied and published no later than March 31, 2016.

State Charity

The problem is that the patriarchy is not ready to finance Church endeavors out of pocket. The Church's financial system has become even more opaque than it was before (Patriarch Alexy II periodically announced some figures of the ROC's income at diocesan assemblies and the Bishops' Council, but Patriarch Kirill did away with this practice) and the Patriarchate's representatives, who regularly complain about the lack of funds, beg the government for money for even the most status-oriented of their social projects. And the state is increasingly responding to these requests. As it does in the larger economy, the government gives preference to those organizations that support it and takes from those that do not.

After the 2011-2012 protests, the regime staked itself to a conservative and anti-Western agenda; the "foreign agent" stigma loomed over disloyal non-governmental organizations. Meanwhile, the Church, which did much to quell the protests through the mouths of its representatives, has become an even greater ally and even a pillar of state power, and can therefore count on state grants and other forms of assistance.

The volume of state infusions of funds into church infrastructure is constantly growing. According to RBC's calculations, in 2012-2015 the ROC and related institutions received at least 14 billion rubles from the state and government organizations. Meanwhile, the new version of the budget for 2016 allocates 2.6 billion rubles[24] for church infrastructure, despite the crisis and lack of money for necessities such as medicine.

It should be noted that this consists of not only funds for the restoration, but also for construction of churches and monasteries. In 2013, for the first time, the State Duma allocated nearly two billion rubles to "finance diocesan management facilities" — that is, to construct administrative buildings for the new dioceses and archdioceses that emerged as a result of Kirill's reforms. Obviously, the expansion of a loyal clerical bureaucracy that can be counted on to instill loyalty in citizens is in the regime's interests.

At the end of 2014, the government allocated 1.1 billion rubles from the federal budget to create ROC spiritual and educational centers as part of the special federal program "Strengthening the Unity of the Russian Nation." According to RBC,[25] all the grant recipients were registered shortly before the competition in December 2013–February 2014, which leads one to suspect that they were created for the money. However, the government is in no rush to verify how the money was spent. On the contrary, the ROC is being released from the financial oversight of the Ministry of Justice.

---

[24] S. Reiter, A. Napalkova A, I. Golunov, "Rassledovanie RBC: na chto zhivet tserkov'," RBC, February 24, 2016, http://www.rbc.ru/investigation/society/24/02/2016/56c84fd49a7947ecbff1473d.

[25] S. Bocharova, F. Rustamova, "RPTs vydelili dva milliarda rublej na dukhovnye tsentry," RBC, November 28, 2014, http://www.rbc.ru/politics/28/11/2014/54774e8acbb20ffbe61293aa.

Amendments to the law have recently been adopted that deny the Ministry of Justice the right to request any financial documents from religious organizations that do not have foreign funding (the ROC is considered *a priori* to not have such funding) and deny judicial authorities the right to request information about the financial activities of parishes in credit and financial institutions.

Other amendments to Article 222 of the Russian Civil Code exempt religious organizations from the rules on extrajudicial demolition of unauthorized buildings. Moreover, this applies not only to some chapel or cross, but also to structures "designed to service religious property." That is, a monastery garage, say, even if it has been cited three times, cannot be recognized as an unauthorized construction and demolished without a court decision, unlike a market stall.

According to a report from the Center for Economic and Political Reforms,[26] in 2013–2015 the ROC became one of the largest recipients of presidential grants, receiving 63 grants totaling more than 256 million rubles. Funds were received by entities of the Moscow Patriarchate and organizations closely associated with it, including, among others, the Department of Religious Education and Catechism (29.5 million), dioceses (23.6 million), the "Orthodox Youth" Interregional Community Organization (16.9 million), the Trinity Lavra of St. Sergius Monastery (9.5 million), the Sreten Theological Seminary headed by Bishop Tikhon Shevkunov (9.7 million), and the St. John of Kronstadt Charitable Foundation (7 million rubles).

At the moment, the organization of a unified network of church drug rehab centers, which would allow them to be integrated into the national drug rehabilitation system, is among the priority projects. In addition to a presidential grant, The John Kronstadt Foundation (created specifically to support the ROC's anti-drug activities) also received a grant of more than 4 million rubles

---

26 "Issledovanie CEPR: kto poluchaet prezidentskie granty NKO," Tsentr ekonomicheskikh i politicheskikh reform, December 21, 2015, http://cepr.su/2015/12/21/issledovanie-cepr-kto-poluchaet-prezidentskie-granty-nko/.

from the City of Moscow Public Relations Committee.[27] The patriarchate is not hiding the fact that integration into the state system will allow it to make the Church a major grant recipient,[28] and, if it is very lucky, be awarded a line in the budget in the long term. It was precisely from the federal budget that funds to finance "diocesan management facilities" and spiritual education NGOs were allocated to the ROC—while it is true that funds were allocated within the framework of a special federal program, which appeared in the budget as a result of amendments made by the State Duma, one thing leads to another...

Another tempting idea is to create socially oriented NGOs in parishes. After the state expressed its readiness to provide priority support to these NGOs[29] with the intention of shifting some of its social obligations onto them, this possibility was widely discussed in the church.[30] "It is important to realize that religious organizations *are* the very same socially oriented NGOs that can and should claim government support," said the Bishop of Smolensk and Vyaz'ma Panteleimon back in 2012.[31]

Why should the state not invest in religious NGOs if they bring tangible benefits to society? There are, I think, three possible objections. First, the church has a steady income from parishes, which deduct funds for "general church needs," and parishioners have a right to a share of those funds. Secular NGOs, meanwhile, do not have the Patriarchate behind them, and they can rely only

---

27 "Nashelsia. Tserkovnaya pomoshch' narkozavisimym lyudyam i ikh blizkim v gorode Moskve," http://protivnarko-msk.ru/.
28 A. Reutsky, "V Tserkvi ob'yedinyat prikhody i tserkvi, zanimayushchiesya reabilitatsiej narko- i alkozavisimykh v edinuyu set' ," Tserkovny Vestnik, April 9, 2014, http://e-vestnik.ru/news/zerkjv_reabilitaziya_narkozavisimih_7866/.
29 I. Nagornykh, "Sotsial'no orientirovannye NKO pomogut gosudarstvu "tyanut' gruz problem", Kommersant, August 10, 2015, http://www.kommersant.ru/Doc/2785657.
30 Seminar "Kak i dlia chego sozdavat' obshchestvennuyu organizatsiyu pri prikhode?" proshel v Sankt-Peterburge // Sankt-Peterburgskaya Mitropoliya Russkoj Pravoslavnoj Tserkvi, July 2, 2015, http://mitropolia.spb.ru/news/otdeli/?id=80696#ad-image-0
31 "Zavershilas' III mezhregional'naya konferentsiya po tserkovnomy sotsial'nomu sluzheniyu," Deaconia.ru. December 24, 2012, http://old.diaconia.ru/news/zavershilas-iii-mezhregionalnaja-konferentsija-po-tserkovnomu-sotsialnomu-sluzheniju/.

on grants or crowdfunding. Second, in extending a helping hand, the State will certainly expect to dictate its priorities—and the church, having become addicted to the inflow of grant money, will no longer be able to independently determine what types of social action it develops. The third objection is that, on the whole, the work of Orthodox organizations remains ineffective.

Miloserdie, the standard-bearer of Orthodox charitable initiatives for which no effort is spared, is to a certain extent the lone exception. For the St. Philaret Institute, reviled until quite recently, constant activity was the key to survival. Non-denominational but with a large share of Orthodox, the "Faith and Light" Movement, which brings together families of people with intellectual disabilities, organizes annual Christmas fairs, which have become very popular in Moscow and brought fame to the movement itself. The "Danilovtsy" Volunteer Movement was made famous by the scandal surrounding the group Pussy Riot, one of whose members was once a volunteer for the organization. The Ark School, closely tied to Orthodox groups, is well known simply because children with disabilities need to study somewhere!

Have we heard much about other Orthodox social organizations? Periodically, information emerges about the homeless assistance group "People of the Rail Stations" and the Orthodox people's movement "Kursk Station. Homeless Children"; the charities "Legend" and "Russian Birch" are in the news—and that is pretty much it. All these organizations are based in Moscow, but they are merely a drop in the bucket, given Moscow's size and the city's need for social work. Meanwhile, across Russia, 17,108 Orthodox associations were registered in the Ministry of Justice's NGO database at the end of 2015.

Of course, the charitable sector and the importance of charity work are only now being recognized by the public; two or three years ago, even the powerful "Give Life" Foundation, whose advertising is now in nearly every branch of Sberbank Russia, was known to only 5% of respondents according to the Public Opinion Foundation (FOM).[32] Nevertheless, my experience from nearly ten

---

32 "Otnoshenie k blagovroritel'nosti i blagotvoritelyam," FOM, November 27,

years of attending the Church's "Christmas Readings" educational conference speaks to the fact that the church community is not built for efficiency: for example, the same things regarding the "Foundations of Orthodox Culture" were reiterated year after year at the Readings, but a mechanism was never developed to solve the problem of teaching them—achieving this required state intervention. The government took on the task of training the teachers who now teach (albeit poorly) "religious cultures." If the church really intends to organize a "network" of drug treatment rehab centers, where will it hire staff for this work? Or is it yet again pinning its hopes on the government for this endeavor?

In pursuit of scale, which is directly related to applications for public money, it is possible to ruin the whole venture, as a number of cases have demonstrated, including the Temple of the Cover of the Virgin in the village of Yerino (Podolski district, "Old World" Rehab Center) and the St. Innocent of Irkutsk Orthodox Center of Pastoral Counseling (Irkutsk).

The Costs of "Strict Hierarchy"

Patriarch Kirill's dreams of a social church also encountered difficulties created by the Primate's own policies. The authoritarian course the Patriarch has taken within the church since his accession does not promote the development of initiatives by lay Orthodox citizens. Priests have long complained about the regulation of parish life and the bureaucratic paperwork that archpriests or abbots are forced to deal with—how could an NGO develop here? After all, NGOs need at least some elements of democracy—or, as it is customary to say in the church, *sobornost*—to function. If parishioners cannot do anything without seeking the priest's blessing (and he, in turn, must go to the dean or even the bishop for permission), what regular and coordinated work can we talk about? After all, NGOs require constant hard work. So it turns out that most of the registered church associations exist only on paper or are barely

---

2013, http://soc.fom.ru/posts/11215.

functioning, remembering their stated objectives only sporadically, usually when a reporting deadline is approaching.

The aforementioned lack of transparency also gets in the way—each church's ledger is as opaque as the general church budget. Yuri Belanovsky has stated about the effect of this dynamic:

> Basically, the church community follows the habits they have when it comes to church-building. The construction of churches is a non-transparent process. But the level of trust on this topic is so high that people are ready to donate without understanding what is going on. When something else develops in the church, the organizers rely on this model: give us money, and we will do something good. But even in that very same parishioner who donated to build the church, there is a kind of internal 'switch' that clearly flips when he thinks, 'Here I donated to the priest to build a church, but now I donated for this other thing and I don't know what for, so tell me how my money was spent. If you wanted to buy a washing machine for a poor family, show me this washing machine.

Donors follow the same logic. In mid-February 2016, the Russian Orthodox University hosted a roundtable, "Religious Charity in Russia: Modern Forms and Mechanisms of Partnership and Collaboration." Foundation representatives who spoke at the roundtable cited fears that financial relations would not be sufficiently transparent as one of the primary obstacles to supporting religious organizations. As experience shows, the "you give to us, and we will pray for you" approach will not work with the foundations.[33]

In addition, NGOs need financial independence to succeed. And with the financial order prevailing in the church, there is no guarantee that the archpriest or abbot, whether he is the head of the NGO or the chairman of the board of trustees (a situation where the archpriest or abbot is not involved in the governance of a church NGO is, in my opinion, unimaginable), will be able to refrain from sticking his hand into the "common" purse in a time of need.

---

33 Krugly stol "Religioznaya blagotvoritel'nost' v Rossii: sovremennye formy i mekhanizmy partnerstva i vzaimodejstviya." Itogi, Forum donorov, February 12, 2016, http://www.donorsforum.ru/reports/kruglyj-stol-religioznaya-blagotvoritelnost-v-rossii-sovremennye-formy-i-mekhanizmy-partnerstva-i-vzaimodejstviya-itogi/.

Charity as a School of Citizenship

Nevertheless, the segment of the Orthodox community actively involved in charity is a serious force that is increasing its professionalism and strengthening its solidarity. Experts say that the situation in Russian orphanages has changed dramatically, thanks in large part to Orthodox (though, of course, not only Orthodox) volunteers and sisters. Government Regulation 481 came into force, setting new standards for orphanages: they must look like ordinary homes with conditions similar to those in a family situation; each child's individual developmental plan must be reviewed every six months; the separation of siblings in orphanages is banned; and orphanages must help children find families as soon as possible. Community organizations (including Orthodox ones) played a huge role in these changes, pushing hard to end the *internat* (state-run residential care facility) system and replace it with something more human. According to Natalia Starinova, a senior lawyer in the Synodal Department for Charity,[34] the church is trying to amend the law on guardianship and custody to change the situation where the administrators of the *internat* (state-run residential care facility) where, say, people with intellectual disabilities live are also the guardians of these people and themselves bill the state for taking care of their charges. According to the Synodal Department, external guardians are needed.

When there is a danger that what small achievements have been made are under threat, civically engaged Orthodox are ready to present their demands to the authorities. In 2014, a wave of suicides of cancer patients who died because of the inaccessibility of painkillers swept through Russia, and Roskomnadzor, frightened by the scope of the discussion of this topic in the press, tried to go after publications for allegedly promoting "suicide propaganda." The web portal "Pravoslavie i mir" also landed in Roskomnadzor's

---

34 "Na smenu "optovomu obsluzhivaniyu" v internatakh dolzhen pridti individual'ny podkhod," Interv'yu so starshim yuristom sinodal'nogo Otdela po tserkovnoj blagotvoritel'nosti i sotsial'nomu sluzheniyu N. Starinovoj, Interfax Religion, February 4, 2016, http://www.interfax-religion.ru/?act=interview&div=429.

sights and was ordered to edit a news piece on the death of Rear Admiral Vyacheslav Apanasenko to remove language about the causes of his suicide. Then the web portal, together with the "Vera" Foundation for Assistance to Hospices, arranged a roundtable and invited the censorship agency's officers to it, raising the question point-blank: will Roskomnadzor's demands not lead to a complete ban on mentioning the causes of a given suicide? The roundtable participants categorically objected to the question being posed this way, and it was precisely thanks to wide publicity of the "Apanasenko case" that the Ministry of Health revised the rules for prescribing painkillers to make them more reasonable.

The Orthodox now often join forces with secular charities, at least in the capital region. The aforementioned roundtable and, for example, the cooperation of Miloserdie with the charity "Live Now," created by ALS patients, is evidence of this. "Our collaboration with Miloserdie developed naturally," says Maria Ilchenko, the foundation's executive director. "Our foundation was created by people being assisted by Miloserdie. That is, we belong to the so-called patient movements, which are common all over the world: patients with a certain diagnosis often unite to protect their interests. As a foundation, we aim to help Miloserdie develop in this area—to find new ways to help, new medical practices. For example, it is already obvious that ALS patients receive enormous emotional support from music therapy and art therapy. We were then confronted with the task of finding volunteers who could learn these techniques and visit families to work with patients. It so happened that Miloserdie provided us with these volunteers, already selected, verified, and reliable. The foundation's experts conducted workshops and training sessions with them, and we can now send them to visit patients with confidence. That is, thanks to this collaboration, we were spared unnecessary hassle and Miloserdie had an opportunity to develop its assistance programs."

"In Moscow, quite a few of the social workers know each other and collaborate with each other," confirms Elena Alshanskaya, head of one of the largest social work projects, the Volunteers for Orphaned Children Foundation. "Especially close cooperation has developed in shelters for mothers with children. There are Catholic shelters (in fact, they appeared first), and Orthodox, and secular ones, and within this field we have developed a good collaboration; almost all of us know and communicate with each other. However, it is difficult to say whether the result would be the same if you looked at cooperation in the field as a whole. To get an overall picture, it would probably be necessary to conduct a study that no one has done. I know that in some places the situation is different and church projects see themselves as being outside the general sphere of social work organizations and do not communicate with their secular colleagues. Every situation is different. Even in Moscow, it is difficult to say how optimal our communication is, because you suddenly learn about some church projects happening literally next door about which you had not heard anything until the last minute. Nevertheless, there is certainly collaboration; there is even joint management of some clients."

The Russian church still has a long way to go to achieve the title of "social" church, and the church authorities' grandiose plans may interfere with, rather than accelerate, its transformation into such. However, we can already say that charitable projects in the Orthodox community not only have a humanizing effect on society, but also help Orthodox citizens to gain self-confidence and defend their position even in unfavorable circumstances.

Case of Dissernet: The Volunteer Network Community's Experience of Survival in an Aggressive Political Environment

Sergei Parkhomenko

In the three-and-a-half years since the "Law on Foreign Agents" took effect, Russia has earned a reputation for being a country where the government is systematically on the trail of the independent and self-organized public activity of its citizens.[1] Any activities intended for the collective application of civic energy in any of its forms that might seem useful to people has become the subject of intensive—and, in the best-case scenario, disapproving—attention from various law enforcement agencies. In the end, the Russian government considers to be harmful and dangerous to it any work that people undertake by means of collective efforts of their own will and under their own guidance, by organizing and advancing themselves, independently attracting new participants, and independently giving the public an account of the results of this work — if such work does not adhere to the clearly established goal of gaining some sort of understandable material advantage.

In short, from the point of view of the government, if people gather together in order to make a living, that is more or less acceptable, but if they start something just because it is interesting or important to them, then that is very suspicious. In other words, the government seeks to monopolize any activity that determines the

---

1   The full name of the "law on foreign agents" is Federal'ny zakon №121-FZ "O vnesenii izmenenij v otdel'nye zakonodatel'nye akty Rossijskoj Federatsii v chasti regulirovaniya deyatel'nosti nekommercheskikh organizatsij, vypolnyayushchikh funktsii inostrannogo agenta"." In May 2015, there appeared another tool to drive NGOs from Russian soil—the "Zakon o nezhelatel'nykh organizatsiyakh" (Law on Undesirable Organizations)." This law, however, was intended for use against foreign organizations trying to function on Russian territory, so the scope of its application has so far remained comparably smaller.

quality of life of its citizens, regulating to a significant extent the very content of that life.

The Russian Government against NGOs: Scorched Earth Tactics

The involuntary designation of Russian NGOs as "foreign agents" under an offensive law has turned out to be the most effective and widely used instrument of government repression of self-organized civic activity in recent years. Bureaucrats of various ranks — from minor provincial department heads to ministers and Kremlin administration officials — regularly cite that "the status of foreign agent does not assume any prohibition of their activity."[2] This is as if to say that, legally speaking, the status of "agent" is nothing but useful "honest information" for the public about an entity's sources of financing, and in and of itself this information in no way threatens the work of the NGO.

In reality, when an NGO receives the decision that it has been entered into the registry of "foreign agents," if it does not disband, then a large portion of the personnel of such an organization becomes occupied with the endless and meaningless collection and presentation of documentation demanded by the mockingly meticulous queries of a multitude of audit and oversight bodies. Since this accounting must be presented on paper in printed form (which, by the way, clearly means that the supervisory agencies never had any intention of analyzing this material), the list of documents is often meters long; sometimes the pile of paper gathered is the height of a person. All this is reminiscent of the traditions of camp punishment through meaningless work: in the morning, dig a hole, and after lunch, fill it in.

Any contact with government agencies becomes impossible for the "foreign agent," in particular in the sphere of education or with any information companies that are supervised or financed by

---

2   "V Kremle sozhaleyut v svyazi s likvidatsiej fonda "Dinastiya", kotoromu nikto ne meshal rabotat'," TASS, July 8, 2015, http://tass.ru/politika/2102370.

the authorities, either federal or local. This leaves absolutely no possibility for such NGOs to function in the Russian provinces: regional and municipal authorities, and more often than not private companies as well, avoid any contact with "agents."

By the beginning of 2016, 113 organizations were included in the official "Registry of NGOs Functioning as Foreign Agents" published on the website of the Ministry of Justice of the Russian Federation.[3] Twenty-one of them were later removed from the list, but the damage inflicted on the activity of such organizations by that time most often turned out to be catastrophic: in the majority of cases, it would prove impossible to resume normal work.

Among these 113 legal entities, there was not one single political party, political movement, voter association, or voting bloc — not one organization whose work could be called political in the normal understanding of the word, where its work was intended for its own political goals.

Do not think, however, that the Russian legislature lacks a rational definition of the term "political activity." Such a definition has long been hammered out and is used, in particular, in the regulatory documents that determine the status of certain government officials whose function is incompatible with an active role in politics, including judges, prosecutors, and investigators. In these laws, the definition of political activity is reduced to two points: 1) participation as a candidate in elections to any government body, and 2) offering support to other candidates in such elections (either directly or indirectly in the form of criticizing their opponents).

Such simple and intelligible criteria are not applied to civic organizations, and because of this, the registry of "foreign agents" is filled with organizations that focus on rights, education, and charity that never had any political ambitions.

Among the 113 organizations formerly or currently listed as "foreign agents" are six regional branches of the international "Memorial," the oldest society of NGOs in Russia defending human

---

3   "Svedeniya reestra NKO, vypolnyayushchikh funktsii inostrannogo agenta," Informatsionny portal Ministerstva yustitsii Rossijskoi Federatsii, http://unro.minjust.ru/NKOForeignAgent.aspx.

rights, which are involved mostly with historical research and memorialization of the victims of political repression in the USSR and Russia. The list also consists of the largest regional branch (St. Petersburg) of "Soldiers' Mothers of Russia." In addition, five legal entities of the federal or regional level of the Golos network of civic organizations, which undertakes the collection and analysis of information on violations of election procedures, are listed. The registry further includes a whole host of organizations that provide legal assistance to citizens in the event that their rights are violated by officials from security agencies, courts, or the penitentiary system ("Public Verdict," "Lawyers for Constitutional Rights and Freedom," "The Committee Against Torture," "Agora," and others). Also included are ten societies of ecologists and defenders of the environment, two groups fighting for consumer rights, three volunteer scientific research organizations, and more.

Conferring the title of "foreign agent" on the charitable fund "Dinastia" received a huge amount of attention. The fund was bankrolled by the personal money of the family of Dmitri Zimin, one of the founders of the Russian mobile network industry. That capital was created in Russia, and taxes paid on it in Russia. The Ministry of Justice did not deny that Dinastia supported exclusively educational programs, research and publishing projects, and individual support of exemplary scholars, teachers, and authors of popular science books. But that did not prevent the ministry from making an unfair and offensive decision against Dinastia, after which the fund immediately announced that it would cease its activity.

The authors and interpreters of this repressive law — and, most importantly, those who are putting it into practice — often claim in the pro-Kremlin semiofficial press that it is as simple as can be to avoid being placed on the registry: it is sufficient to refrain from any financial activity with foreign NGOs. But in reality, among those organizations named by the Ministry of Justice as "foreign agents," there are more than a few who have never received a single cent of their budgets from foreign donors, partners, or customers. There are also those who, from the moment they were formed, worked exclusively through the volunteer work of their participants and supporters, which is to say completely without financing.

There is the example given above of Dinastia, where the founder of the charitable fund financed the work with his own money but held that money in a foreign bank. There is an anecdotal case where "foreign financing" was determined from the fact that the organization received a prestigious international award (which consisted not only of a certificate of achievement, but a financial award as well) and the laureate was not even spared from being included in the registry by thinking ahead and refusing to accept the award.[4]

There is simply no practical way to guarantee that one will not be accused of receiving foreign financing. Since the time that the "Law on Foreign Agents" went into effect, any Russian non-commercial organization that has attempted to avoid minute-by-minute control and oversight of its activities by official bureaucrats has been at risk.

Do you want to collect some small donations on a website, and for this purpose you install the usual "payment gateways" so that visitors to the site can conveniently make their deposits? Here in the record of your transactions are several micro-transactions completed using a credit card issued by a bank outside of Russia, ostensibly proving that you have received "financial means from foreign sources."

Are you ready to receive cash donations from people who visit the office of your NGO in person? Or do you send them to the bank with your bank details? But here your donor, even half a year later, makes a slip of the tongue while making an official statement or testimony on some other issue completely unrelated to you, saying that he brought the money at the request of his friend who lives abroad, and now you are faced with an unexpected and impossible-to-predict "foreign source of financing." In both cases, this will put you on the registry of "foreign agents."

There are many such traps in the path of Russian NGOs. As a result, the risk of receiving the moniker "foreign agent" ceases to

---

4   Metelitsa Ye. "'Golos' oshtrafovan za otkaz priznat' sebia inostrannym agentom" Slon.ru. April 25, 2013, https://slon.ru/fast/russia/golos-oshtrafovan-za-otkaz-priznat-sebya-inostrannym-agentom-936485.xhtml; "'Golos' ne smog ubedit' Minyust v otsutstvii inostrannogo finansirovaniya," Interfax, November 27, 2014, http://www.interfax.ru/russia/409757.

depend on the desire of the organization to have foreign partners and is connected exclusively with the degree of its loyalty: an NGO that is "detrimental" from the government's point of view will certainly become an "agent" sooner or later, while a "useful" one can afford not to worry about such unpleasantness.

Formation of an Aggressive Environment: Pressure on the Press

Enacting the laws on "foreign agents" and on "undesirable organizations" did not change the government's approach to controlling civil society; it just broadened and strengthened a method that had been used many times before in relation to an independent (and at least to a certain degree outside the control of the government) press. The title of "foreign agent" was not created especially for journalists, but the task was the same: limit access to "uncontrolled" financing. The goals were twofold: 1) not to allow for independent earning based on their own work under their own efforts, and 2) to remove the possibility of receiving anyone's help—that is, to scare away potential partners and punish potential charitable donors.

Among other circumstances negatively affecting the ability of the Russian press to earn enough to exist, we note the fact that the Russian legislature successively reduced the advertising market for electronic and print media over the course of 15 years, either cutting whole segments from it (tobacco products and alcoholic drinks, medications, bio-active food additives, and medical services) or imposing strict limitations on the content of advertisements (as in the case of financial, legal, and educational services). All of this is done under the banner of "defense of consumer rights," however the legislation is formulated in such a way as to maximize damage to the advertising market.

Retail chains that are prepared to work with the press are systematically being reduced. In large cities—especially in Moscow and St. Petersburg—hardly any of the once-common newspaper kiosks remain today: city administrations refuse to offer them rental incentives for the space needed to set up trade pavilions (such incentives existed in the 1990s) and therefore, under these conditions, the owners turn to types of commerce more profitable for them, from flowers to fast food.

Also well-known is the law that went into effect on January 1, 2016, imposing a 20-percent limit on foreign capital in companies that own Russian media outlets. The new restriction affected several large publication houses that work in Russia and predominantly publish magazines and newspapers from the quality segment of the market (Sanoma Independent Media, Burda, Bauer Media, etc.).

In addition to these large-scale government solutions that affect the interests of the media industry as a whole, from time to time certain "spot" measures can be observed, directed toward the destruction of the economic foundation of concrete media outlets — for example, the independent television station "Dozhd'." In February 2014, over literally two to three days, there was a sudden and completely coordinated loss of commercial interest of several dozen cable operators who had previously broadcast it on the basis of contracts that they considered quite profitable to them. In the blink of an eye, the audience of the channel was reduced by 80%, which forced the loss of practically all its advertising contracts. The mass refusal of broadcasters to cooperate was preceded by a hysterical propaganda campaign in the semi-official press and on state television channels: Dozhd' was accused, under completely false pretenses, of offending the memory of the victims of the Leningrad Blockade during the Second World War.

The Education of an Entrepreneur: Supporting Civic Activity is Lethal for Business

It was a single process: on the one hand, the enslavement of the media environment, taking control of the information industry and systematically limiting freedom of speech; on the other, frightening Russian businesses so that they completely refused to support any political, social or civic initiative that was "separate from the authorities."

As a result, the government managed to create an almost impenetrable wall between entrepreneurship and civic activity. We will not dwell here on the history and technology used by the government to construct this wall. We note only that the chronicle should begin with the dismantling of Vladimir Gusinsky's "Media-Most" (which took place largely from 1999 to 2001). The second very important episode was the looting of the oil company YUKOS (in 2003-2004) and the dismantling of the YUKOS-financed "Open Russia," an organization that stimulated the development of civic initiatives and various forms of social activity.

As a result of these two operations (and a whole array of analogous though less shocking ones), it was made clear to ordinary Russian entrepreneurs that contact with nongovernmental organizations and civic "independent action" carried a direct risk to the existence of their businesses. Incautious activities (that is, those not discussed with authorities and directly approved of) made the company an object of acute interest to the police; the district attorney; investigators; the FSB; tax, customs, and anti-monopoly authorities; and fire, health, environmental, and labor inspections.

Thus, already in 2005, the concern "Neftyanoi," which belonged to one of the richest Russian entrepreneurs at that time, Igor Linshits, was subjected to a massive coordinated attack by certain oversight and law enforcement bodies, and ended up on the brink of closure and bankruptcy after its appointment of Boris Nemtsov, the disgraced ex-Deputy Prime Minister of the Russian government and one of the best-known leaders of the democratic opposition movement, to the post of vice president. After Nemtsov was fired, all of Neftyanoi's difficulties quickly and painlessly dissolved.

In 2011, the Alfa Financial Group chose to part ways with Vladimir Ashurkov, who had held a senior management post in one of its companies, after he stopped hiding the fact that he spent his free time helping Alexei Navalny's Anti-Corruption Foundation. In April 2012, one of the owners of Alfa, Mikhail Fridman, explained directly in his interview:

> that Ashurkov had the right to choose: either not to be involved in politics or to leave the business... We live in Russia, and it goes without saying that

such an active political life is not entirely acceptable under current Russian circumstances.[5]

In April 2014, the well-known Russian entrepreneur and financier Alfred Kokh announced that a criminal case had been opened against him and a warrant issued for his arrest. Kokh was accused of "smuggling works of art" — namely, attempting to take out of the country a painting valued by experts at the equivalent of $200. His house and office were searched and papers were seized. He has announced that he does not intend to return to Russia from abroad. As early as the beginning of the 2000s, he worked closely with the Kremlin and power structures, and, in particular, was one of the ideologues and leaders of an operation that sought the destruction of Media-Most. However, after the massive rise in civic activity in Russia in 2011-2012, it became known that he had on multiple occasions provided financial assistance to various types of civic initiatives and NGOs, including the *"Rus' sidyashchaia"* Foundation, the "Agora" Association, and several groups that were organizing election observation and uncovering voting fraud. The list of such cases goes on.

The Third Term: Tightening Control

From the beginning of Putin's third presidential term, the implementation of this system of total government oversight became even more sophisticated. Putin has repeated the formula "the one who pays is the one who chooses the music" many times in his public speeches and interviews. Today, that basic principle of authority has taken on a somewhat more refined form: it is not important that no one can feed themselves, but that we feed from our own hand all who should be fed.

The Putin government insists that only it has the right to be the "source of life" in terms of both information and civic activity.

---

5   A. Kreknina, Yu. Yarosh, "X5 rasstalas' s menedzherom iz-za ego politicheskikh vzgliadov," Vedomosti, April 13, 2012, http://www.vedomosti.ru/management/articles/2012/04/13/216915-x5-rasstalas-s-menedzherom-iz-za-ego-politicheskih-vzglyadov.

Theoretically, any civic activity is possible, however only the government has the right to provide the material and organizational foundation for it or to refuse such support. This approach has become increasingly universal, cutting across the entire practice of cooperation between the government and society on all levels. The standard answer of a bureaucrat of any level to any question posed is, "Is it allowed?" This means that maybe it is allowed and maybe it is not—we ourselves will decide—but keep in mind that even if it is allowed, you still have to ask for the money for it from us.

This is an incredibly important element of the system of oversight over civic life constructed by the Putin government and its main hope for a fundamental and final solution to the uncomfortable question of civic initiatives. Does this mean that a community of activists in Russia who have come up with a socially significant project and feel that they have the energy and desire to bring it to fruition have no chance to survive in such a barren region constructed specifically for them?

No, it does not. In today's Russia, as before, dozens of interesting and really effective civic organizations have been able to preserve activism and, in a number of cases, to noticeably grow and broaden it. As before, there is an entire group of NGOs that offer legal aid to the population in spite of the continual pressure and unending lawsuits and fines that they endure for refusing the offensive moniker of "foreign agent." Thousands of volunteer observers are present at elections, recruited and trained by several powerful groups that continue their work in spite of the necessity of re-registering, changing their names and sometimes even going into "underground" forms of work (the most famous story of malicious pursuit is that suffered by the largest organization in the sphere of elections, the Russian Golos Association). New communities are created, ready to register various and disparate kinds of civic initiatives in order to optimize the work of volunteers, increase fundraising intensity, and use the money they collect more rationally—these include the project *"Nuzhna pomoshch'"* [Help is Needed] and the charitable collective *"Vse vmeste"* [All Together].

But here it is worth pausing on one specific and very important factor that enables this community to stand against the government structure. That is its readiness to depart from traditional forms of being "solid" and "real" NGOs. Several qualities that are inevitably inherent to such traditionally structured organizations are well known:

- Institutionalization by means of typical legal frameworks;
- Formation of a familiar centralized structure;
- Financing managed through widely accepted corporate principles;
- Management through traditional administrative structures.

What would happen if all these demands were consciously abandoned? What if, instead, the emphasis were on the desire of a large number of individual activists to unite in a movable, flexibly organized community in which the common goals — sometimes quite large-scale and complex — were established and implemented through the effective distribution of efforts and the creation of a network structure along the principles of crowdsourcing?

In my opinion, a particularly interesting and successful example of such a collective answer to the challenge presented by the government "order" in contemporary Russia can be seen in the creation of the volunteer community network Dissernet.

"Factory of Troubles": Why Does a Bureaucrat Need a Dissertation?

"A voluntary community network of experts, researchers and reporters dedicating their work to exposing those involved in fraud, falsification, and lies" is how the founders of this civic project, one of whom is the author of the present chapter, define the essence of their initiative. In effect, it began its activity at the very end of 2012, but the date of the full public "launch" is considered by the founders to be April 1, 2013, when the site www.dissernet.org was made publicly accessible.

The founders' page of the Dissernet site features four individuals: three scholars and one journalist. It is these "physical personages" who have taken it upon themselves to represent the community in all external contact, to make statements in its name, to provide contact with the press, and, when necessary, to answer for its activities in court.

However, in reality, the community today includes several hundred activists, who vary in the intensity of their participation in the group's work and who maintain their anonymity. Almost all these people are connected to the research and educational sectors and they are geographically dispersed. Many of them live outside Russia, working in well-regarded think tanks in the United States, Canada, Germany, Great Britain, France, Italy, Spain, Finland, the Czech Republic, Israel, and Australia. All of them are people of means, having achieved notable professional success. And each of them has a reserve of energy for society, a desire to take part in the public life of Russia and in the development of its educational and research sectors in particular. The manifesto of Dissernet states:

> Participants of the community combine their collective efforts through the principles of network distribution of labor and use of modern computer technology to act against the unlawful machinations and fraud in the area of scholarly research and educational activity, in particular in the process of defending dissertations and awarding academic degrees in Russia

But the work of the community is not limited to interest in the internal life and activities of a narrow group of professional researchers. Among representatives of the Russian political and parapolitical establishments, the conferring of false scholarly degrees has become a common occurrence. Governors, senators, members of the government, deputies of the State Duma and local legislative bodies, judges, prosecutors, police, members of the military, lawyers, doctors, businessmen, party functionaries, priests, and journalists—if you study the resume of any even somewhat notable figure in Russia today, you will discover that they hold a Master's or PhD in some field.

A significant majority of dissertations defended to receive these degrees were falsified in one way or another. Sometimes they are prepared to order by one of thousands of "consulting firms" that actively advertise their services on the internet and in newspaper classified ads. Sometimes they are purchased as-is. Sometimes they are independently stolen wholesale or copied from the work of others. It is also clear that these falsified degrees are no less widespread in academia itself, among rectors and administrators of universities, school principals, leaders of think tanks, and laboratory researchers.

The scale of the phenomenon forces us to speak of an entire industry of falsified dissertations that exists in Russia: an industry with its own large production centers and small artisanal workshops, with movable market conditions, with technological innovation, with a developed infrastructure of advertisement, marketing, market demand studies, and promotional services. And like any other large service industry, "dissertation manufacturing" does not passively await client interest but actively promotes its services and goods, intensively broadening the circle of potential purchasers, offering them ever more focused and individualized service, using an incentive system for loyal clients, wholesale discounts, and promotional deals.

The success of this industry is huge. Its rapid growth took place from the 1990s to the 2000s, when the libraries and academic repositories organized a massive digitization of scholarly material and dissertations from previous years, making it easy to search for the necessary "raw materials" and to compile new, falsified works.

An analysis of the data collected over Dissernet's three years of operations shows that around four percent of dissertations defended in Russia should be considered falsified. And those that are plagiarized—which is to say stolen—comprise:

- more than 17% of works defended by Moscow school principals;
- more than 21% of dissertations from rectors of institutions of higher learning throughout Russia;
- more than 29% of dissertations of governors of Russian regions;
- more than 41% of dissertations of State Duma deputies.

Some four or five years after the appearance of a significant digitized mass of dissertations and academic sources, having a higher degree took its place among the necessary attributes of "a truly successful person," alongside a fancy car, a luxury watch, and tailor-made, expensive Italian suits. This twisted prestige and vulgar "fashion" can, in the majority of cases, explain why people who have had not a minute of contact with either science or education suddenly want to decorate themselves with the title of *kandidat* or *doktor* in various areas (usually humanities or social sciences). However, there are other reasons for this epidemic.

In a number of different areas of professional activity, having an academic degree is informally an indispensable factor for success in moving up the career ladder. One such area is law enforcement: regional judges who want to move up to the city level must have a Candidate of Juridical Sciences degree. The same is true for a police officer trying to become the head of a city police department or a regional prosecutor who is trying to move a step up the career ladder. It also happens in medicine: a doctor intending to take the post of department head in a hospital should have a Candidate degree, and when the goal is to be the head doctor of a clinic, then a Doctorate is necessary. The situation is no different in the appointment of principals of general education schools, departments in regional and municipal administrations, etc. None of these "qualification demands" are written down anywhere, but they are known to all and are adhered to without fail. In some way, this situation is reminiscent of the Army practice of *dedovshchina* [or codified abuse of lower ranking officers including physical beatings] — the senior member says to his subordinate, "When I was young, I suffered; now you will also suffer, just like everyone else."

In addition, working as an instructor remains one of the last types of "side activity" permissible for deputies and government officials under the law and administrative rules. And the honoraria for mysterious "lectures," "consultations," and "help in preparing methodological resources" are often a convenient and safe way for the recipient to engage in corruption. These factors — broad demand from people able to pay; support from current trends and corporate ways of doing things; administrative rules; and the rapid development of high-tech, massive offerings on the "dissertation market" — combine to create what Dissernet activists describe as a "reputational catastrophe." This refers to the massive, complete domination of various spheres of government, business, and public life in Russia by people with false reputations. That is to say, these people are not in reality who they portray themselves to be.

In this way, the work of Dissernet, which at first seemed a very specific and narrowly focused fight against false dissertations, quite quickly took on a much broader and more universal meaning, becoming a war against falsified reputations.

From here it is but one short step to the main "political slogan" that has taken shape in the Russian political system, one that is not at all trivial and even quite innovative, built in large part on the total irresponsibility of the elite in a context where there was not even the idea of oversight by the electorate—the citizen—of the deeds of the politician or leader: "REPUTATION MEANS SOMETHING."

It turns out that investigation of dissertations to determine whether they contain plagiarized text or possible intentional violations of the regulations for the preparation of scholarly papers (for example, the falsification of publications of scholarly articles in specialized journals, and sometimes the inclusion of false citations of entire monographs necessary to receive the doctorate degree) can be conducted through a very simple and reliable technological method called "express analysis" of the business, professional, and moral qualifications of the owner of a work under investigation. Note here the use of the word "owner," as Dissernet tries not to use the word "author" in any case.

Experts at Dissernet often analogize such an analysis of dissertations to blood analysis: in taking a drop of blood from the finger, the doctor is not interested in the blood as such but tries to determine based on its components the condition of the internal organs and life support systems of the body. In exactly the same way, when a dissertation and the circumstances surrounding how it was obtained are investigated, it becomes possible for Dissernet to make a judgment about the key qualities of the person who put his or her name on the title page.

Here, the experts of Dissernet do not take it upon themselves to evaluate the content and meaning of the text being investigated. Dissernet does not try to differentiate a "good" dissertation from a "bad" one, a "smart" one from a "stupid" one, or an "innovative" one from an "empty" one. That is the realm of the academic community and specialists in the given field of scholarly knowledge, and Dissernet does not attempt to place itself above them or to represent itself as an expert authority in all areas of study that exist. Dissernet's attention is concentrated only on formal criteria of conscientiousness, honesty, and correct preparation of a scholarly work and procedures for its defense.

"The Anthill Principle": The Network Builds Itself

The circle of participants within the community formed gradually, by the snowball method, which in this case rolled along in no great hurry: a new member of the general team could appear only through direct recommendation of colleagues who already worked there. Incidentally, the total number of participants and even their geographical distribution quickly ceased to be common knowledge even to the project's founders. And this is not due to an excessive penchant for conspiracy. As it grew, the structure of the community began to be built on the "nest" principle: some of its members began to hand out a volume of work each day that it was clearly impossible for one person to complete. This means that certain "subgroups" were hidden behind them: who these people were, how many of them there were, and where they were located, along with details of organized division of responsibilities among them, all remained unknown, and colleagues working on a common project preferred not to take an interest in these details. In the end, it is not of great importance, but it is significant that the "front-men" of those sub-groups that recommended themselves bear all the responsibility for the quality and reliability of the group work that they add to the common pot and on which they sign off.

Thus, the network of participants in the community grows organically and builds on itself in proportion to the degree of difficulty and the volume of work tasks. Nevertheless, the work of the community as it grew was gradually organized into a fairly complex technological chain, which provided a high degree of effectiveness, speed, and reliability in conducting expert analysis and working up the results. This structure is built around the site and server of dissernet.org, which has a significant "non-public" part that is accessible only to members of the community. It is here that a mass of texts awaiting testing is assembled, and from here authorized participants of the community can take a portion of the work that needs to be done, complete it, and post the results of their work.

The work is organized by the "anthill" method, where each member of the community drags along his or her small bit, transforming it from a formless pile of uncompleted work into a streamlined construction of completed work. The duties of various participants may vary greatly: some undertake the search for and collection of material for analysis, others develop and perfect the programming products that are used in comparative examinations, still others complete these examinations, others oversee and recheck completed work, others prepare analytic results and formal legal documents about the results of the completed investigations, others prepare information for publication and place them on the site, and the final group of participants publish material important to the public on social media, pushing it forward and promoting it.

A critical characteristic of Dissernet's work remains the fact that all the work, from the initial collection of information to the expert investigation to the analysis of results is conducted by living people and not by machines. Programmed, automatized analysis is used only in the early stages of work in order to indicate to the experts directions for further search, which is then completed by "hands and eyes."

The results of expert investigations are rendered through model diagrams in which each page of the examined work is given a color marking independent or plagiarized (in part or in full) work taken from one source or another. Each of these stolen pages is clickable—anyone who wants to see for themselves can compare the examined text with the source it was stolen from. The form of such "brand"-style table diagrams has gradually become readily recognizable to the public.

The first few months of work for the community were accompanied by loud, incriminating scandals in the press and information networks. Each new investigation of a false dissertation of some very famous public figure became almost a sensation and was effusively discussed by journalists and bloggers alike. Dissernet began to be called "the ideal trolling project," meant to deliver systematic blows to all kinds of well-known politicians in a kind of desacralization of the powers-that-be, mercilessly ridiculing government authorities.

The founders of the community and those who take on public speaking in its name, who announce their current work on blogs and in the press and who publish the results of expert investigation and analysis, have invested no small amount of effort in convincing readers that the work of the community was not inspired by any political groups and does not have as its goal the discreditation of any "political opponents." But given that the first objects of Dissernet's attention were people in notable governmental "leadership" posts, the overall tone of the publications turned out to be plainly critical of the Russian authorities.

At the same time, the program group at Dissernet worked up a simple search program bot that allowed the use of production line methods to discover and systematically investigate dissertations selected by criteria chosen in advance. Blanket checks were done on people of a certain kind who had academic degrees: for example, all the scholarly works written over the last ten years by all deputies of legislative bodies throughout the Russian Federation were examined, as well as those of all judges of all levels of the courts, from the very lowest of the regional levels, and of all regional governors and chairs of electoral committees. Thorough review was also conducted on all works defended within certain scholarly fields, in certain academic institutions, under certain professors, on a certain group of topics containing key ideas established ahead of time, etc.

Obviously, such universal testing was conducted with the use of machine sorting in the early stages: bots first scoured the internet to make a complete list of persons of a predetermined type, then selected from among them those who had ever defended a dissertation, then narrowed it down to those who had defended one within ten years, then determined a group of works that had broad levels of coincidence with other texts. And only these last, "suspicious" works were given to experts for further examination.

Thanks to this method of universal testing, Dissernet soon began to compile a huge database of works that had been examined, which also included notes on how they came to be: the places they were defended and the names of academic advisors, opponents, and members of the dissertation committee who allowed the "falsification" to pass all the regulatory filters. In this way, they gradually began to compile information not only on the dishonest "purchasers" of the scholarly falsifications, but also on those who put them on the dissertation market and ensured demand for them. This information was later put to further analysis, allowing for the study of the industry behind the production and trade of falsified dissertations. In turn, this analysis became the basis for concluding that the existing system for attestation of scholars was unable to defend the academic environment from the dishonesty, abuse, and sometimes outright fraud that discredited the very idea of awarding academic degrees.

In addition to expert analysis, Dissernet was able to place direct pressure on participants in the dissertation market. Practically every falsified work, in cases where the time limit for filing a complaint has not run out at the time the analysis is conducted, provides a reason for lawyers in the community to prepare a formal "Statement on the Removal of an Academic Degree," which is then sent to the State Commission for Academic Degrees and Titles under the Ministry of Education of the Russian Federation. A special section appeared on the Dissernet site in early 2015 that was dedicated to a chronicle of happenings on this "bureaucratic front," where all the stages through which such statements must pass are followed and the results of the decisions recorded. In many tens of cases, such processes end in the owners of falsified dissertations being stripped of their illegally obtained academic degrees.

There are even some cases where the owners of discovered plagiarism have voluntarily refused academic degrees, hoping to avoid the embarrassment that unavoidably awaited them if formal charges were filed by Dissernet. This formal-bureaucratic side of Dissernet's activities necessitated the inclusion of new "specialties" among the participants of the community. First, the expanded volume of legal work needed to prepare the statements forced the community to seek the help of a large number of qualified jurists. Second, they needed to gather an entire support group made up of authoritative scholars from various academic fields who had academic degrees that were beyond doubt and who were prepared to sign off on all of Dissernet's formal petitions. Dissernet turns to this group each time that it is necessary to start legal proceedings on a statement of complaint for a dissertation in a field corresponding to their expertise: both the Federal Bureau of Anti-Corruption and members of dissertation committees where these cases will later be examined are more attentive to Dissernet's statements if, for example, there is a signature under the demand for the removal of a legal degree from someone who holds a doctorate in jurisprudence, for the removal of a history degree signed by a doctorate in history, etc.

It is curious that the tactic of self-defense for those holding dubious (from the point of view of independent work) dissertations has been built largely around a battle over the regulations from the Federal Bureau of Anti-Corruption on the statute of limitations for presenting any grievances or petitions for action. The statute of limitations for petitions regarding dissertations was itself introduced in 1989, at which time it was determined to be ten years. However, in 2009, the Federal Bureau for Anti-Corruption shortened that to just three years. This created an awkward situation where even if a dissertation was copied word for word from another author, at the end of three years it was as though the work was of good quality and it was impossible to rebuke the author for submitting it.

In 2013, the Ministry of Education made a ruling through the government of the Russian Federation that the statute of limitations be returned to ten years, but with a "proactive caveat" that all dissertations that had been defended before January 1, 2011 (that is, those for which three years or more had passed at the moment this ruling went into effect), would remain "under amnesty." It is clear that such a caveat defies the basic norms of "one law for all" and creates a sort of unexplained benefit for plagiarizers from 2006 to 2010. In addition, there is a much more serious legislative collision at hand here: the statute of limitations itself is in conflict with statutes 208, 1228, 1250, 1251, 1265, and 1267 of the Civil Code of the Russian Federation, all of which defend copyright without time limitations.

In the fall of 2015, three State Duma deputies (Dmitri Gudkov, Ilya Ponomarev, and Oleg Smolin), trying to retain their right to independent action and not cave to the complete "discipline" demanded by the president's administration, became the sponsors of a bill that would remove all statute of limitations restrictions. However, the bill was voted down due to the solidarity of the Edinaia Rossiia deputies. Almost immediately after this vote, the economists Oleg Monogarov and Sergei Kalinovsky, both stripped of their Candidate degrees after Dissernet found massive borrowings in their works and submitted a formal complaint to the Federal Commission for Anti-Corruption, filed suit against the Russian Federation, demanding the return of the three-year statute of limitations for all dissertation-holders. This created a paradoxical situation in which officials of the Ministry of Education, the leadership of the government of the Russian Federation, and members of the Dissernet community suddenly found themselves on the same side of a legal case. Of course, it is clear that the government was not fighting to uphold the right of Dissernet to continue its activity but simply against the attempt to impugn its own competence and the worthwhile nature of the decision the government had made.

Kalinovsky and Monogarov took their case all the way to the Supreme Court of the Russian Federation, but on March 16, 2016, their demands were definitively rejected. The ten-year period stood, and Dissernet retained the ability to continue its systematic search for dissertation fraud, developing a massive production of ZOLUSes, an acronym for "Statement for Removal of Academic Degree" that became internal slang among activists.

Thanks to daily updates to the section for new expert investigations, to the flow of news concerning the submission of

ZOLUSes, and to the newly opened section called the "Disseropedia of Russian Institutes of Higher Learning," which included information formatted for easy search and analysis of the "Dissernet Proceedings" in several hundred Russian universities and institutes, the Dissernet site became a valued resource containing a truly significant volume of regularly updated and expanded original data. It gradually became quite popular with journalists, especially those from regional and specialized publications and information portals. Information from the Dissernet site is offered to all at no cost, so it is of particular interest to regional journalists because they can return regularly to the Dissernet material in search of information on "their own" notables; deputies of regional parliaments, judges, prosecutors, bureaucrats, local businessmen, and leaders and professors of local academic institutions become followed insiders.

To this point, between two and three new personal expert investigations have appeared on the Dissernet site daily, including analytical overviews, diagrams, and thematic selections and portfolios of material.

"If There is No Head, there is Nothing to Cut Off": The Network Tries to Become Impervious

This entire technological structure, which offers up a huge volume of information for further use and dissemination, has, despite its size, turned out to be fairly inexpensive. Dissernet continually needs funds only for the wages of hired specialists: some of the lawyers, technicians, and editors who develop and support the site. Notable budget lines are for obtaining and copying portions of texts necessary for the expert analysis from various fee-based storage sites and information banks. In addition, it is becoming more expensive for representatives of Dissernet to travel to participate in commissions where they are reviewing Statements for Removal of Academic Degree filed by the network community's experts.

By the way, it is specifically this newly appearing part of their work — participation in public hearings and commissions — that has forced Dissernet to gradually broaden the circle of community members that represent it openly, without hiding their names or their involvement in the work of the group. Nonetheless, Dissernet's budget remains extremely meager. In the early stages, a small amount of "initial capital" was raised with the help of an internet crowdfunding portal that organizes such public actions. Later, the budget began to receive systematic contributions from private individuals.

The system for attracting volunteers to set up fee-based services and accounts in internet libraries has turned out to be quite successful, and from there they get the majority of the raw material for the expert analysis: by using Facebook and other social media networks, they can regularly expand the circle of volunteer helpers who agree to open personal accounts in the information storage portals and help Dissernet to collect information. This also helps to drastically reduce the overall budget. The network community does not have a general bank account or single "register"; the collection of donations happens simultaneously on several personal accounts of physical individuals on various electronic payment systems like YandexMoney, Web-money or PayPal, and also through regular banks. From here, money is sent to cover various expenses: payment for the server and work on the site; transport and postal costs; honoraria for specialists who contribute regularly (mainly lawyers) and others who provide various services; and payments for accounts providing access to information databases and fee-based internet services.

Such a spread-out financial structure, in the opinion of the participants, is best suited for work organized around the Cheshire Cat principle, just as in Alice's classic phrase that she "had seen cats without smiles, but not smiles without cats...."

In truth, when there is no head, there is nothing to cut off. This is the best guarantee of the stability and security of the organization's work. It is clear that Dissernet, which is a continually functioning factory of unpleasantness for a huge number of influential and sometimes powerful figures in the circles of Russian government, would not last a week if it could be localized in a concrete structure. But Dissernet has no place of work, and therefore that place cannot be closed. It has no stationary server, and therefore the server cannot be confiscated. It has no bank account, and therefore the account cannot be blocked. It has no accounting or employment documentation, and therefore these things cannot be seized.

Even the Dissernet domain and the virtual server that holds the database that the community has built is registered to a physical person through an international registrar that does not release the names of its clients.

Since the participants of the network community work over a broad geographic area and a number of time zones, they maintain contact with one another through email and several internet messenger services. Nor does Dissernet have any single center for collection or distribution.

In the general sense, Dissernet is organized in such a way that it is spread over as large an area as possible and has no weak spots that could be used to block or delete and thus paralyze its work. The loss of any individual participant will in no way impede the movement of the general "conveyor," as each individual specialist can be easily replaced by a large number of other community members who perform analogous functions.

In essence, this is a flat, single-level network that has no hierarchical structure or center of control. This example of a crowdsourced construction is able to support its work function through rational internal division of tasks and the ability to continually expand and build outward depending on the complexity of the common goals. Of course, the success of such a structure in the organization was based on a lucky combination of many factors that is not always easy to put together around a creative idea.

First of all, there is a high level of motivation among the participants. As has already been said, the majority of the community's activists are professional scholars and researchers: they share a special interest in and empathy for the state of the academic sciences, an exclusively responsible relationship to their profession. Many of them sincerely worry a great deal when they see the sciences used as fodder for furthering low and shameful human vices such as vanity, hypocrisy, and readiness to achieve career success through dishonest methods. It is precisely this "offense on behalf of domestic sciences" that becomes their main motivation to dedicate, day after day, a significant amount of time and effort to a collective activity that will not benefit them financially and will certainly not gain them any fame.

Certain professional qualities of people who have dedicated their lives to scholarly research have turned out to be quite valuable. They are very stubborn, intellectually resilient, and able to concentrate for long periods of time on completing meticulous work that demands focus and methodical work. They have experience participating in large, collective research projects that assume a division of general tasks among many individuals, all of whom independently oversee their own work schedule and are responsible for the quality of their contribution to the whole. They are able to independently optimize their labor, develop useful habits, and share them with partners in the general process of ongoing work. At the same time, there is no doubt that such a single-level structure does create additional difficulties for its organizers.

First and foremost, the confusing (at least from the outside) system, built largely on mutual trust and the decentralization of financing for individual tasks and functions, adds great difficulty to general fundraising. Potential contributors not infrequently refuse to participate in financing an organization that is unable to describe its internal budgeting or present any clear picture of financial responsibilities. Cooperation with many organizations that do follow exacting internal corporatized rules on choosing partners and participating in common activities with them can also become impossible when potential grant recipients do not have a clearly described organizational and legal format. Contractual relationships are almost impossible (in Dissernet's activity, for example, there have been many cases when large research and educational institutions were prepared to join the community as partners in order to make use of its services as a continually acting outside auditor of outgoing scholarly works, but they rejected the idea because there was no legal entity with which they could sign a formal contract).

The single-level system of communications among the participants also turns out to be not always the most efficient and convenient in the ongoing flow of work. Writing from everyone to everyone else produces a huge volume of mail and demands serious efforts on the part of participants not to lose track of messages significant to them in this flow of informational noise. But nevertheless, it does seem that such an approach to forming an activist community has turned out to be efficient and reliable in conditions where the government is enacting new limitations all the time and where law enforcement takes on something of a sardonic nature.

Arguments about the power and efficacy of network civic communities have raged heatedly ever since modern means of communication, and predominantly social media, began to make it technologically possible to organize them. Dissernet is one example of a successful creation and lengthy and fruitful functioning. It has become a convincing illustration of how a social organism can adapt to a dangerous and aggressive environment—in complete accordance with Darwin's theory.

Territory Free from the State

Maria Eismont

There are around 80,000 registered media outlets in Russia, the vast majority of which are non-state run. Of these, only a few adhere to standards of quality journalism and have the ambitious goal of enlightening and uniting local communities. The economic decline of recent years has reduced the size of the advertising market, especially in small towns; as a result, media outlets have been confronted by the necessity for serious cutbacks, and some are teetering on the edge of existence.

This article is about those publishers and journalists who, even in unfavorable economic and political conditions, have continued to work and see sense in doing so. In this stubbornness, it is difficult to say what predominates—the inability to take up any other occupation, the unwillingness to give up and feeling of pity for a life spent in the media, the sense of responsibility to the audience, or the hope of lasting until a new upturn.

The most active publishers connect this latter hope with the development of internet media. Those who are managing to find a way to earn and stay afloat talk about the necessity of strengthening the professional community and searching together for new forms of quality journalism.

Reduced Income, Reduced Editorial Staff

Before releasing an issue containing a long interview with Aleksey Navalny at the end of March 2017,[1] the editor and owner of the newspaper *Zhukovskie Vesti*, **Natalya Znamenskaya**, together with

---

1 Znamenskaya E. Po urovniu zhitelei Zhukovskogo vlast' dolzhna byt' v tri raza umnee i v vosem' raz chestnee, Interview with Aleksey Navalny, Zhukhovskie vesti. 2017. 28 March, http://www.zhukvesti.ru/blogs/detail/39918/.

her daughter, commercial director of the newspaper Ella Znamenskaya, called everyone who had placed advertisements to warn them of the possible risks:

> We thought that many would pull their ads, because Navalny is an opposition politician and a red flag for our officials. But quite the opposite happened: only one business pulled their advertisements, but many others came. They made the decision not for noble reasons, but simply because they had decided that it would be a popular story.

Those advertisers turned out to be correct: the entire printing of the newspaper sold out. Readers in this science town took a liking to Navalny's words, featured in the headline, that "judging by the level of the residents of Zhukovsky, the local government should be three times smarter and eight times more honest." For the first time in many months, an issue not only sold out but also yielded a small profit.

But from the very next issue, all returned to the previous crisis situation. *Zhukovskie vesti*, which celebrated twenty-five years just last year, has been in the red for the past year: debts for typography are growing, and there is often nothing with which to pay the rent. "For now, local merchants are helping me," admitted the elder Znamenskaya. "Among them are idealists and those who just have a good relationship with me, respect me, and pity me." On the editorial staff, which until recently could have been considered one of the strongest journalism teams in the area around Moscow, only four people are left: one writes only about sports, another is 75 years old, the third is an aviation expert, "because it is impossible not to have an aviation column in the paper," and the fourth is the commercial director, Ella Znamenskaya. Natalya has not paid herself a salary for almost two years and is supported by her husband; he also sometimes gives them money to help pay the rent.

In Znamenskaya's evaluation, the advertising market in the city has shrunk by more than 50 percent over the past two years. Every week, some business or other closes, replaced by companies that are considered to be affiliated with regional governmental structures and are therefore not interested in advertising.

Both mother and daughter admit that they often consider closing the newspaper, but each time they stop themselves. "It's not just that I feel sorry to lose the project because it is a part of my life," says Znamenskaya senior, who was once elected to the local town council. "But I also think: what will they [town residents] do without a newspaper? But if this [economic decline] continues much longer, we will have to close. Maybe we will just leave the website."

Zhukovskie vesti is not just a private publication that has been in opposition to local officials since 2009, when it supported the between 3,000 and 5,000 protesters (of the town's 100,000 population) who took to the streets to protest against the falsification of the mayoral election. For many years, it has played the role of a center for civic resistance, as when residents fought against cutting down part of the Tsagovsky forest to build a new highway.[2]

The forest proved impossible to protect, but ever since, almost all activities of the local civil society have been conducted on the basis of *Zhukovskie vesti*, with the direct participation of the skeleton editorial staff. Several activists from among the defenders of the Tsagovsky forest, among them Ella Znamenskaya, ran for town council seats in September 2014. Judging by log books remaining in the hands of observers, people from the team of forest defenders won a minimum of six of the 25 seats, but the official election system input completely different data. (A falsification lawsuit filed by the Moscow Oblast' Investigation Committee never made it to court.)[3] Recently, Znamenskaya relates, a former official of the mayor's office with whom the newspaper had always had a confrontational relationship approached her at an event and said:

> He hated our newspaper, and here he comes up to me and says, 'You berated me back then, but now you are the only one left. Hang in there, Natasha.' I told him, 'So help us, if we are to hang in there!' He said he would think about it.

---

2 P. Lobkov, "V Tsagovskom lesu snosyat lager' ekologov," Telekanal 'Dozhd', May 14, 2012, https://tvrain.ru/teleshow/here_and_now/v_tsagovskom_lesu_snosyat_lager_ekologov-257701/.

3 M. Eismont, "Falsifikatsiya radi falsifikatsii", The New Times, September 14, 2014, http://newtimes.ru/stati/xroniki/4d0efe3eb96d117fc981cc6f4a8fb251-falsufukacuya-radu-falsufukacuu.html.

In recent years, independent publishers in many small towns in Russia have been going through a crisis due to the collapse of the advertising market. Editorial staff from local papers that were fairly firmly on their feet just five years ago are now cutting down their number of columns and laying off workers; sharp declines in income force them to turn away from additional projects and, in the worse cases, from print editions that only a short time ago helped to feed the online versions. Valeriy Bespyatykh, the publisher of several local newspapers stated:

> We can last for another year. If during that time some economic miracle happens and the multi-year drop in the market suddenly reverses, then we will make plans. We have one real problem—the dismal condition of our local small businesses, whose advertisement used to provide more than 80% of our income... Options? Reformat ourselves, search for new sources of income, make further cutbacks. Without changes, nothing is possible. This especially concerns our Pervouralsk publication.

Bespyatykh is the publisher of the newspapers *Gorodskie vesti – Revda* and *Gorodskie vesti – Pervouralsk*, which are issued in Sverdlovsky District. Issuing a social-political newspaper in the neighboring larger town (by population, Pervouralsk is exactly twice the size of Revda), and right in the middle of the 2008-2009 crisis, was a source of pride for Bespyatykh all the more so because the new publication turned out to be just as high-quality as the main paper and became influential in its first weeks. *Gorodskie vesti – Pervouralsk* was never profitable, but there was enough money in the media group "Gorodskie vesti" to support what was, by local standards, a quality journalism project. Now that money is gone. "There is a feeling that the print business is ending in small towns," admits Bespyatykh. "The decline isn't stopping."

The newspaper *Courier. Wednesday. Berdsk*, from Novosibirsk Oblast', this year reduced its number of print columns from 32 to 24. There are three salaried positions and just two journalists remain. The third journalist left, not for financial reasons but because she was not prepared to write about problematic topics. "She said to me, 'I want to write positive material,'" says the publisher and editor of the newspaper, Galina Komornikova. "'Not about poor grandmothers who are beaten by their alcoholic sons, not about why there is only one cardiologist working at the hospital, but about how good everything is.' I told her, 'But that wouldn't be journalism!' And she said to me, 'No, Galina Vladimirovna, it would be real journalism.'" Komornikova placed an ad for the vacancy, but now doubts whether the publication can support another salary.

"To be in the media business in Russia today, you have to be suicidal," says Komornikova, who recently celebrated the fourteenth anniversary of the newspaper that used to be called *Berdsk Courier*. The publication first belonged to one of the city's businessmen, but then the editor-in-chief had a conflict with the owner: he demanded the removal from the front page of material about a millionaire he knew who had beaten an old lady who swept the courtyard and went by the nickname Baba Yaga because she said something reproachful to his son. Komornikova, as editor, removed the material at the time, but a few weeks put it back in again,[4] and the whole staff supported her decision to create her own independent newspaper. (This is where the strange name comes from: it was thought up on the fly in order to guarantee that the paper would pass registration checks for unique status.) Ten years ago, *Courier's* journalists won a competition for investigative journalism. Now, according to Komornikova, "there is simply no one to do this. For fourteen years, you do something, build it, plan to grow it, and here one year ago, when everything started to crumble, I was going crazy, and now I understand: nothing depends on your efforts, emotions, knowledge, or ideas anymore."

One source of financial assistance for publications — albeit not consistent and not enough to survive on — is grants from Rospechat'. For several years in a row, the agency has provided state financial assistance for socially significant projects in print media, including regional publications. It is possible to receive government grants for material on social topics — ecology, health and education, historical and regional studies, and projects supporting families or a healthy lifestyle: Rospechat' reimburses newspapers for

---

4   Rudnev M. "Gazeta.ru" o sluchae v Berdske: Izbitaya dvornichikha popala pod tsenzuru. Taiga.Info.2006, 19 oktyabrya, http://old5.tayga.info/92733.

honoraria, workers' salaries, printing services, paper, and distribution expenses.

In 2017, *Courier. Wednesday. Berdsk* and *Zhukovskie vesti* between them received aid for three projects. All publishers who receive grants from Rospechat' affirm that Rospechat' never made any political demands. Media with a wide variety of political alignments, from pro-regime to opposition, appear on the list of those receiving grant monies.

Subsidies and Other Forms of State Aid

In April 2017, a media forum called "Truth and Justice" was held in St. Petersburg by the All-Russia People's Front (ONF).[5] This is the name of a foundation that supports independent and local mass media and organizes an annual competition for them. As a result of the contest, dozens of journalists from regional publications receive significant monetary prizes (up to 300,000 rubles) for works that "call public attention to themes of anticorruption, the effective distribution of budget resources, or the implementation of 'May orders' and assignments from the president."

The winners are gathered at a Petersburg media forum, the central event of which has become a meeting with Vladimir Putin. At the April forum, the first question of the meeting was given to Yury Purgin, founder and leader of "Altapress," one of the largest regional media holdings in Russia; president of the Alliance of Independent Regional Publishers (AIRP);[6] and a recent member of the public council foundation in support of media in the ONF.

Yury Purgin is a legendary figure in publishing circles. A first-wave democrat, he founded Russia's first independent newspaper, *Svobodnyi Kurs*, back in 1990 in Barnaul, and in the mid-1990s was among the first to grasp the idea that in order to survive in the media industry, it would be necessary to learn to earn money. He became one of the largest taxpayers in the region and one of the larg-

---

5   See http://pravdaispravedlivost.onf.ru/.
6   The alliance was created in 2005 to unite publishers of private print media in Russian regions. See http://anri.org.ru/about/about.php.

est media managers in Russia. At various times, his holding has included business magazines, "yellow" publications, two radio stations (which Purgin recently sold in order to invest in internet projects), free newspapers with advertisements, internet portals, a chain of distribution kiosks, and his own printing press. The office building was constructed by special permit, in the shape of a ship, which symbolizes the "idea of freedom and independence." Purgin in a conversation with Putin stated:

> From this year, the Russian Post Office is raising its base fees by 10 percent. And another 10 percent will be cut from benefits to socially significant publications, coming to a total of 20 percent. You understand that for us this means the following situation: it will not be very good for any of us... We propose returning to the topic of subsidizing subscriptions for regional and local media.

"You have started with yourselves, dears," smiled Putin in response. "Well, that's as it should be."[7]

Later, Purgin explained in a private conversation why he chose to ask the president about subsidized subscriptions and not about an issue that concerned an active part of Russian society — Russian participation in wars, political prisoners, or the anti-corruption protests that had taken place just a week before the forum and the subsequent arrest of their participants:

> Because that is a different form of communication. This is a space for regional media in which the problem can be solved or at least brought to the fore. AIRP is trying to bring [to the president] those regional problems that usually remain unheard. Other questions demand a different format.

The president of AIRP has reason to believe that the Russian president listened to his words. At the very least, the 18 different orders that the president signed at the conclusion of the media forum included a directive to the government to, by July 1, 2017, provide publishers of regional and local media with special subsidies for the distribution of printed products to subscribers in far-off and hard-to-reach territories, and also to adopt a list of categories for

---

[7] "Altapress.ru: Yury Purgin zadal vopros Vladimiru Putinu," YouTube, April 3, 2017, https://www.youtube.com/watch?v=xIDVBwXAAmY.

socially vulnerable citizens who are eligible for distribution subsidies.

Another decree from Putin came as a result of a question from a journalist from Berezovsky, in Sverdlovsk Oblast', who told about an improvised landfill of sludge deposits in his town. The president ordered that the government present proposals by July 15 to strengthen responsibility for the breakdown of norms in the solid waste management sphere.

Natalya Kalinina, the content director for *Vechernyi Krasnotur'yinsk*, a newspaper with a 6,600-copy print run in the eponymous monocity in the Northern Urals, which has a population of some 60,000, is one of those who submitted an application for the ONF competition. For several months, she helped an oncology patient in her town fight for life, and in so doing discovered why local clinics buy medicines at much higher prices than in other regions and why residents of three cities are served by only one oncologist. This resulted in what was, in Natalya's opinion, a rather discombobulated but important text that she wrote at night in order to meet the competition deadline. Her application was not selected. She subsequently issued the following quote:

> Generally speaking, the very fact that only after a question to Putin does anything change is very degrading. But I had to get there in order to ask him about the oncology center and hospice in our areas. Yes, [I have] a tortuous choice. What is important to me is not only the problem of a lack of oncology treatment and hospice in my city, but also protests, arrests, investigations of the Federal Banking Commission. And at the same time it is understood after all: if you ask, for example, about Sentsov or Navalny, you'll get likes and a lot of flack (in our city, more likely the latter), and not a darned thing will change. And with the problem for oncology patients, it may be miserly, but there is a chance that something locally will begin to stir...

Kalinina's 39-year-old ward passed away. Thanks to help from people who answered the call on the internet and provided the city with the necessary oxygen concentrators, she barely suffered. But the theory of on-the-spot help through addressing the president proved its effectiveness just two months later: another oncology patient, a young woman from Apatity, who managed to speak to Putin through *Direct Line*[8] and complain about the condition of medicine in Murmansk District was transferred to Moscow for treatment after her conversation with the head of state.[9]

In addition to the fact that cooperation with ONF offers a chance to directly address the president at the media forum and possibly solve concrete local issues, just participating in an event attended by the first person becomes a kind of security certificate that boosts the recipient's immunity to pressure from local bosses. That is the opinion, in particular, of Komornikova, who publishes the newspaper *Courier. Wednesday. Berdsk*. In 2015, the speaker of the Berdsk city council sent a letter to the editor, calling it an "inquiry from a deputy," with a request to provide information on the foreign travels of journalists from the year 2000 to the present. The speaker hinted at the multi-year participation of the newspaper in educational programs of the New Eurasia Fund for journalists and publishers who received aid from USAID.[10] The editorial office refused to comply with the request from the head of the council, and a month later there appeared on the walls of the building where the editorial office was located the words "USA Agent" and "5th Column."[11] The police could not determine the author of the graffiti. Several months later, the Metropolitan of Novosibirsk and Berdsk contended that the Novosibirsk media were "waging an information war against the church" and publicly accused *Courier. Wednesday. Berdsk* of being affiliated with the U.S. State Department. In response, the editorial office sent the Novosibirsk bishop

---

8   V. Kondrashov, "Pryamaya liniya s prezidentom. Apatity, Darya Starikova," YouTube. June 15, 2017, https://www.youtube.com/watch?v=8-5eywso7Xk.
9   "Spetsbortom MChS v Moskvu na lechenie dostavili Dar'yu Starikovu, u kotoroi vovremya ne raspoznali rak," Pervy kanal, June 19, 2017, https://www.1tv.ru/news/2017-06-19/327322-spetsbortom_mchs_v_moskvu_na_lechenie_do stavili_daryu_starikovu_u_kotoroy_vovremya_ne_raspoznali_rak.
10 K. Gorelova, Nadpisyami "Agent SShA" i "Pyataya kolonna" ispisali ofis redaktsii "Kur'er. Sreda. Berdsk". Kur'yer. Sreda. Berdsk. May 4, 2015, http://www.kurer-sreda.ru/2015/05/04/180628-nadpisyami-agent-ssha-i-pyataya-kolonna-ispisali-ofis-redakcii-kurer-sreda-berdsk.
11 The author of this chapter from 2006 through 2013 headed the New Eurasia Foundation's program "Russian Independent Print Media" funded by USAID. Many media outlets mentioned here took part in that program's training events: professional competitions, conferences, seminars and internships.

a statement from the Uniform State Register of Legal Entities proving that the publication had been established by Russian citizens. But after Komornikova's participation in ONF events, harassment ceased. "My interaction with ONF influenced the situation here at home," indicates Komornikova, "and they stopped 'manhandling' us."

Political Pressure: The Case of TV-2—Right Up to Destruction

Authorities have long used accusations of connections with Western (especially American) organizations to fight not only against political opponents, but also against various types of groups and citizens not under their control, in particular independent regional media outlets. In March 2016, television channel NTV broadcast the latest in a series of "exposing" materials on secret State Department agents.[12] On that day, the traitors were determined to be those media companies that had at one time received credit from the American NGO MDLF (Media Development Loan Fund, which changed its name to Media Development Investment Fund in 2013; the fund issued credit at low interest rates to independent media in many countries around the world, including Russia. In 2016, MDLF was listed in Russia as an "undesirable organization.") Among them were Yury Purgin's "Altapress," as well as *Yakutsk vechernyi*, *Chelyabinsk rabochii*, and the Tomsk news agency TV-2 (in the recent past, TV-2 had been a media holding that included one of the best regional television stations of the same name. In 2014, the television station TV-2 suffered serious pressure over the course of several months; the leaders of the holding claimed that the harassment was of a political nature.[13] In the beginning of 2015, the station was taken off the air and then had its license revoked.[14]

---

12 "ChP. Rassledovanie": "Dolzhniki Gosdepa". NTV, March 4, 2016, http://www.ntv.ru/video/1265547/.
13 N. Rostova, "U nas est' primerno mesyats," Interv'yu s prezidentom TV-2 Arkadiem Mayofisom, Slon.ru. May 21, 2014, https://republic.ru/russia/tv_2_tomsk-1100897.xhtml.
14 I. Gerasimov, G. Naberezhnov, "Tomskaya telekompaniya TV-2 prekratila

The fact of having received loans from MDLF was the only truth in the television drama. All of the rest was intentional discrediting, according to the Public Collegium for Complaints against the Press, to which the aggrieved publishers turned for help. In its conclusion, the Collegium states that the NTV story was "a veiled attempt as the result of some kind of 'journalistic investigation' to publicly accuse a number of Russian publishing houses, media and specific people that created them and that continue to lead them, in essence, of a serious state crime: betrayal of the Homeland."[15] The Collegium called the attempt to denigrate people presented in this film as "anti-heroes" "categorically unacceptable in the legal and moral sense, shameful for both its initiators and executors, throwing a shadow on the entirety of the Russian 'media guild.'"[16] Representatives of NTV did not appear at trial, instead sending word of their position: the publishers should have addressed them directly and only as a last resort in court.

Having obtained the Commission's decision, regional publishers went on the offensive. At first, Leonid Levin, creator of the regional newspaper *Yakutsk vechernyi*, which had one of the largest print runs in the area (he also figures in the NTV story, in that at one point he received credit from MDLF to obtain his own printing press), announced that the pages in his publication bearing the weekly television schedule would now be accompanied by a banner with the warning: "Be careful! Information shows on TV often allow distorted and false information. The channels most noted for this are 'Rossiya' and NTV." Soon after this, several of Levin's AIRP colleagues (including those at the above-mentioned *Vechernyi Krasnotur'yinsk*, *Gorodskie vesti*, and *Zhukovskie vesti*) decided to support

---

veshchanie v kabel'nykh setyakh," RBC, February 8, 2015, http://www.rbc.ru/technology_and_media/08/02/2015/54d7bcfa9a794718956b381a.

15 Obnarodovano reshenie po zhalobe na fil'm "Dolzhniki Gosdepa," Obshchestvennaya kollegiya po zhalobam na pressu, May 12, 2016, http://www.presscouncil.ru/index.php/novosti/5308-film-ntv-dolzhniki-gosdepa-lozhnyj-donos-kotoryj-pozorit-avtorov-i-brosaet-ten-na-mediatsekh-v-tselom.

16 Zaklyuchenie Obshchestvennoi kollegii po zhalobam na pressu o fil'me NTV "Dolzhniki Gosdepa", PlanetaSMI.Ru, May 23, 2016, http://planetasmi.ru/ofitsialno/44269-zaklyuchenie-obshchestvennoj-kollegii-po-zhalobam-na-pressu-o-filme-ntv-dolzhniki-gosdepa.

the effort and printed similar warnings in their daily papers — though without mentioning the "Rossiya" television channel. "Well, it was NTV that went after us, so let it be NTV [that we go after]," the publishers explained to me, agreeing that propaganda exists on a variety of state channels, but that the goal of this particular action was more to "defend and support our colleagues." The protest action turned out to have some resonance, and many federal media outlets wrote about it.

These examples of attacks on regional media outlets, though disgusting, can nevertheless be considered relatively harmless manifestations of a general anti-Western information campaign: in the end, it seems that all opposition political and social public figures, and somewhat independent social organizations and civic groups, managed to attain the stamp of "State Department agent." The story of TV-2, however, shows that everything could be significantly more serious.

In February 2016, the Federal Supervision Agency for Information Technologies and Communications received a letter from one Evgeny Semyonovich Vinnik — all attempts to contact him at the e-mail indicated in the document were to no avail — in which he cited "information he possessed" that Tomsk media group founder Viktor Muchnik "often traveled outside Russia, from which it was possible to draw the conclusion that he held dual citizenship."[17] The author asked that the agency "take this into consideration when processing the license for the media outlet." The agency took Vinnik's letter seriously and refused to extend the group's license for on-the-air media — radio and cable television.

The absurdity of the situation was worsened by the fact that the burden of proof for not having dual citizenship was placed on Muchnik himself. The agency let him know that he had to present documents regarding the lack of any citizenship from a foreign state, any foreign state — after all, Vinnik did not precisely indicate

---

17 Roskomnadzor podozrevaet glavnogo redaktora TV-2 v dvojnom grazhdanstve iz-za pis'ma tomicha Evgeniya Vinnika. ТВ-2. 20 December, http://tv2.today/TV2Old/Sud-vchetvertyy-raz-perenes-rassmotrenie-dela-po-licenzi i-radiostanciievropa-plyus-tomsk.

which country might have given the founder of TV-2 a second passport. In the end, Muchnik wrote requests to the embassies of all countries that had diplomatic representation in Russia, and so far he has yet to receive answers.[18] "The only government to immediately confirm that I am not a citizen was Estonia, and many thanks to them for this," he explains. "The others mainly suggest some other mechanism for confirming this."

The break-up of a large media holding on the basis of a letter from a person whom it is unknown whether he actually exists or was invented, and who stated without any evidence that the founder held dual citizenship, is an extremely alarming precedent. As absurd as this story might sound to a lawyer, or really to any right-minded individual, it worked. The team at TV-2 is well known, but Muchnik says that they increasingly come across government officials who explain their refusal to give information to the site's journalists on the grounds of the founder's supposedly indeterminate citizenship.

The formula for incapacitating objectionable media outlets tested on the Tomsk media holding demonstrated its effectiveness and will possibly be used again. According to Muchnik, several other founders of media outlets who have "encountered similar situations" have recently approached him, but they are not yet ready to go public.

"Nothing will happen in the foreseeable future. Under the current political regime, we will never be given a license," Muchnik assures us. He says that he knows well (from several sources) the contents of the report on TV-2 that was given to the president's administration. In it, claims the main editor of TV-2, the leadership of the media holding was accused of, first, planning to use Khodorkovsky money to put out a satellite broadcast throughout the country; second, propagandizing separatism; and third, meddling in the historical politics of Russia, trying to undermine one of

---

18 "Idiotskoe dejstvie: Tomskij telekanal obratilsya v posol'stva 144 stran mira izza Roskomnadzora," NEWSru.com, September 5, 2016, http://www.newsru.com/russia/05sep2016/tomsk.html.

the main ties that bind—the memory of the Great War for the Fatherland. The reference is to the "Immortal Regiment" campaign that was conceived of and first organized by staff members at TV-2. Evidently, the campaign had become too popular and uncontrollable, such that the authorities preferred to terminate the activity of TV-2 and take over the "Immortal Regiment" name and initiative to conduct their own public campaign.

At the first stages of the persecution of the Tomsk media holding, ONF wrote letters in its defense, Muchnik says, "but later they let us know that nothing would help, 'you yourselves understand why.'"

Now there remains of TV-2 only an online news site, where once it included a television station, cable television, and four radio stations; of more than 100 staff members, only 15 remain, working on temporary contracts and understanding that at any moment this work could end. Muchnik calls the situation "life after death," saying that now the company has essentially been destroyed, it "can do almost anything. I have never felt to such an extent that my hands were untied. All of our journalists are limited only by their own imagination."

The Newspaper as Center of Civic Activity

The owner and editor-in-chief of the newspaper *Parma-Novosti*, Yana Yanovskaya, received two loans from MDLF and is still paying one of them, though she did not end up on the NTV show "In Dept to the State Department." "We are too small for them," she explains. Yanovskaya owns the newspaper, which puts out a 5,000-copy printing in the town of Kudymkar (population 30,000). Once the capital of the Komi-Permyatsk Autonomous Okrug, it became a part of the Perm District in 2005.

The former director of the ethnic cultural center of the Komi-Permyatsk Okrug, Yanovskaya bought the newspaper, in which she had held the position of commercial director, from its founder and editor-in-chief. That was what her second loan was used for (the first was for her own office). On the newspaper she said:

> Probably this is melodramatic and wrong, but it's just my life. That's how it turned out, that I don't want anything else, don't know how to do anything else... Here I feel free. I don't answer to anyone, no one gives me orders from above. What, how, and when to do things I decide for myself. I like that we can ask any question of anyone—bureaucrats, deputies, prosecutors—everyone.

Three years ago, several mothers whose newborns or young children had died in a local hospital—according to them, at the fault of the doctors—found each other through the *Parma-Novosti* newspaper and came together to organize a protest in the center of Kudymkar, the first in the history of the town.[19] Yanovskaya was one of the people calling for the protest, which was held in spite of the fact that the city administration refused to approve it. The police decided not to drive the women away as they held posters and photos of their dead children in their hands, but after it was over, the leader was arrested and the court issued administrative fines to Yanovskaya and another organizer, the grandmother of a small girl who had died in the hospital. Subsequently, on the recommendation of the local prosecutor, who reminded the mayor about Article 31 of the Constitution, the "lawbreakers" were acquitted.

The second protest in the history of Kudymkar took place a year later and was regarding the lack of action by local authorities during a flood. The entire organization was conducted in the same way: through the *Parma-Novosti* newspaper, with the direct participation of members of the editorial staff. "Because they all come to us for help," explains Yana.

At the end of July 2017, Yanovskaya and her colleagues organized a rally in memory of people from Kudymkar who were repressed in the years of the Great Terror. The list of those who died was given to the Perm branch of "Memorial." For the first time in the history of Kudymkar, the names of the local victims of Stalin's repressions were read aloud.

Elena Khorosheva, the head journalist from *Parma-Novosti*, in a summary of the rally on Facebook wrote:

---

19 "Telekanal "Dozhd'". Miting mertvykh detej. Istoriya odnogo protesta v Kudymkare," YouTube. December 6, 2014, https://www.youtube.com/watch?v=vV5zkEk9E1U.

Not many people came, unfortunately. But that's probably not the most important thing... I remember once, the former Chair of the Writers' Union of Perm District, Tatyana Sokolova, said to me: over the course of her life, a writer can write just one phrase that is worthwhile, and that will be enough. Working in journalism, it's the same... Even if what you do helps just one person, that means you didn't do it in vain. And so, after the rally, an elderly townswoman came up to me and began to thank me. When the participants of the rally read the names of the deceased from Kudymkar during the years of the Great Terror, she heard the name of her uncle. He disappeared when he was 18, and they didn't know anything of his fate up to that point. Now she had found out.

When Yanovskaya accepted the loan from MDLF, it seemed like a good deal due to the low interest rate and the stability of the exchange rate. After the sharp decline of the ruble rate, the foundation reached out to her and restructured the loan, but the responsibility to pay it back remained, and this seriously disrupted the economic situation of the publication. If she had not taken the loan, things would not be altogether bad, thinks Yanovskaya. "Because the miserly advertising that we had remains about the same, and if we had almost no money before, we have none now either. It's a bit simpler for us than for our colleagues in larger cities."

Legal Training for Farmers

It is also simpler in some ways for the publishing house "Krestyanin" from Rostov-on-Don, with its flagship weekly paper of the same name, than for its colleagues, though in a completely different sense. For all of its more than a quarter-century history, it has occupied a special place among regional publishers: its audience is made up of the peasants and farmers of the south of Russia. The 16,000-copy print run newspaper is distributed in three southern regions: 70 percent in Rostov Oblast', 20 percent in Krasnodar, and 10 percent in Stavropol.

"Agriculture," explains the owner and director of the publishing house Irina Samokhina, "is that segment of society that, as the authorities say, is showing growth." But, she adds, "Growth is a bit over the top, and I would rather say that this segment is somehow still alive." Advertisers are largely federal; they include manufacturers of harvesters, fertilizers, etc., and they still place ads. *Krestyanin* has no debts to the printing press (though the press belongs to the publishing house, it was decided from the beginning that the newspaper should keep separate accounts with the press so that it was more transparent and clear for accounting purposes), the staff receive their salaries on time, and there is no need to fire anyone. "True, we can't pay out bonuses or raise salaries," says Samokhina, "but so far we have been able to avoid cutbacks. The main problem is that before I had a strategic five-year plan, and now I don't try to look further ahead than a month. We live in a state of continual stress."

Samokhina sees her mission as undertaking the enlightenment and legal training of farmers, clarifying news from the legislature, helping solve various problems, and finding ways out of crisis situations. *Krestyanin* correspondent Viktor Shostko is the author of one of the best investigations from the regional press on the tragedy in the Kushchevskaya stanitsa (for that story, he was awarded the 2012 Andrey Sakharov prize "For Journalism as an Act of Conscience"). And quite recently, *Krestyanin* covered an attempt to organize a protest "tractor march": farmers from the south of Russia intended to drive their tractors to Moscow with demands to cease raids seizing lands and to clear up corruption in the local legal system. The march did not take place due to the interference of security forces, so *Krestyanin* also covered the consequences of the "march" for its organizers.

Samokhina says that she does not notice any particular political pressure, but she does admit that after the passage of new federal laws intensifying responsibility for various types of statements, the editors of the publication began to look at texts in a different way. Journalists are not allowed to state their opinions too much, and the text undergoes a thorough review before publication: "of course, we work with the text like never before, testing to make sure there is not a hint of any kind of extremism."

Trench Warfare

One of the loudest publications of 2016 was an investigative piece about ChVK Wagner, a private company that hires soldiers to participate in military operations in Syria.[20] The story was unearthed by Denis Korotkov, one of the leading journalists of the St. Petersburg internet publication *Fontanka.ru*. Earlier, his colleague Irina Tumakova, also from *Fontanka.ru*, had investigated a story about the deaths of Pskov paratroopers in eastern Ukraine together with a journalist from the St. Petersburg *Novaya Gazeta*.[21]

If St. Petersburg can be considered not the capital and therefore the provinces, then *Fontanka* has a good chance to top the charts for quality regional publications. "Media in St. Petersburg feel completely free," answers the editor-in-chief of *Fontanka*, Alexander Gorshkov, to the question of the political atmosphere in which the St. Petersburg publications are working. "The whole difference is whether or not a media outlet is financially stable or needs to go begging, which is to say, to serve someone's narrow interests."

Fontanka, founded in 2000 by four investigative journalists (one of whom was Gorshkov), has been profitable almost from the very beginning. It did not even find itself in the red in the hard economic years of 2015-2016, though according to Gorshkov, growth did stop at that point. The publication has 250,000 visitors per day, and its main source of income is advertising, both banners and native advertising. Another source of income is special projects like the international festival FontankaSUP [Stand up paddle] along the rivers and canals of St. Petersburg. Upcoming plans include biking along the Zapadnyi Skorostnoi Diameter with 10,000 people. Such projects are playing the long game, Gorshkov says: they won't pay off immediately, but with time they are sure to.

---

20 D. Korotkov, "Oni srazhalis' za Pal'miru," Fontanka.ru. March 29, 2016, http://www.fontanka.ru/2016/03/28/171/.

21 I. Tumakova, "Gvardejskaya diviziya nesyot poteri v mirnoe vremya," Fontanka.ru. August 26, 2014, http://www.fontanka.ru/2014/08/26/030/.

In a conversation about the limits of what is allowed for a journalist in Russia—the so-called "double yellow line"[22]—Gorshkov formulates his position in the following way:

> It is possible to raise an attack and send in the troops, or it is possible to conduct drawn-out trench warfare and come out with a victory." Each time, in making a decision, says the editor-in-chief of *Fontanka*, the editorial staff reviews all possible consequences. In the majority of cases, the decision is to publish: "It is extremely rare that we encounter a situation where we say that we have to put aside a topic and return to it later."

In 2017, *Fontanka* joined AIRP. At the 2017 AIRP summit in Sochi, a strategic decision had been made to change the criteria for membership: the alliance opened its doors to informational internet projects.

"Today, to answer the question of who is an independent publisher is not simple, since any internet user can become a publisher at any point," says the AIRP website under the "mission statement" tab. "In this context, we recognize as publishers only those for whom the creation of content in various media spheres is not a hobby, but a professional activity, a business. A business of a particular sort, with clear ethical categories, with responsibility for each written word or each on-air statement. Journalism and its basic values lie at the foundation of our craft, and economic independence at the foundation of the formation of our professional association."

In addition to *Fontanka.ru*, the alliance has added as members the young St. Petersburg media outlet *Bumaga* and the news site TV-2, the executive director of which is one of the minds behind "Immortal Regiment," Sergei Lapenkov.[23] AIRP also plans to invite into

---

22 The phrase "double yellow line" came into general use of Russian journalists from the case of Igor Trosnikov, who had replaced the team of Elizaveta Osetinskaya as the leader of the RBK editorial staff. It is in these terms that Trosnikov explained to the journalists of RBK that their professional freedom was limited. See "Esli kto-to schitaet, chto mozhno priamo voobshche vse - eto ne tak". Vstrecha sotrudnikov RBK s novym rukovodstvom: rasshifrova, Meduza.io, https://meduza.io/feature/2016/07/08/esli-kto-to-schitaet-chto-mozhno-pryamo-voobsche-vse-eto-ne-tak.

23 Prinadlezhashchej telekompanii TV-2 radiostantsii otkazalis' prodlit' litsenziyu," RBC, May 11, 2016, http://www.rbc.ru/rbcfreenews/573374309a7947221ac956d9

its ranks *7x7*, one of the youngest and most rapidly developing regional internet projects. To the question of whether it is easy for independent regional journalists to work in Russia today, one of the leading correspondents of *7x7*, from Karelia, Gleb Yarovoy, answers, "Of course it is easy, when you have your main editorial office in Syktyvkar and the local authorities can't lay a hand on you, when you don't depend on the regional government for either money or orders, or if you have no business money issues. It's easy when editorial policies are worked through, if not by consensus, then at least collectively, together, and when difficult questions are decided based on the interests of both the leadership and the journalist collective."

Gleb Yarovoy and his wife, Anna Yarovaya, split a single correspondent's position on the project; in addition to that, Yarovoy teaches at the Petrozavodsk State University, where he was recently reinstated by court decision after being fired "for absence." The reason for his firing, as it came out during the trial, was an inquiry from the FSB on trips abroad that the instructor had made without properly formatting business travel documents. It is difficult to say which of his activities were the reason for heightened interest from the special services: his journalism or his work as coordinator for the regional division of the "Golos" movement.

The following paragraph is highlighted in bold on the *7x7* site under the "about" tab: "'7x7 — Horizontal Russia' is a space free from the government. We have set an ambitious goal for ourselves — to draw together in cooperation all the living forces of civic society."

"We are convinced that the most important value is the initiative of ordinary citizens," explains project director Pavel Andreev. "The Russian government, alas, often crushes initiatives. We want to show that even in our reality there are many examples where citizens have joined together and changed life around them."

In 2009, the last independent newspaper in Komi closed, and a group of members of the republic's branch of "Memorial" decided to found their own media outlet, in order, according to Andreev, to "fulfill the idea." The first investors were local entrepreneurs, the now deceased Alexander Ostrovsky and Leonid Zilberg, the main initiator of creating the site. Instead of printed media, it was decided to put out a website that would present journalistic material and blogs equally.

The successful launch of *7x7* in Syktyvkar in 2010 encouraged organizers to broaden the geography of the project. "We thought that technology would allow us to speed up the site," says Pavel Andreev. "And we started to go to different forums making presentations."

Today, the *7x7* team is working in Komi, Ryazan, Kirov, Kostroma, Orlov, Voronezh, and Yaroslavl districts, plus Karelia and Mariy El.[24]

"We want *7x7* to write about real problems in every region and serve as an instrument to introduce and unite independent activists," says Andreev. In Karelia, Gleb Yarovoy is writing an investigation into a billion-ruble business on the island of Valaam, where the monastery is squeezing out the local population. His wife, Anna Yarovaya, is the author of the first large piece on the matter of Yuri Dmitriev from the Karelian "Memorial," who dedicated his life to the search for buried victims of the Great Terror and is now under criminal indictment for sex crimes.[25] In Komi, *7x7* journalist Elena Solovyova published an article about the connections between nationalists and the government of the republic in the period from 2008 to 2016, for which she was awarded the "Redkollegia" prize.[26]

"It is clear what is to be done," says "Altapress" head Yuri Purgin. "The future is an infinity of multimedia." So far, his intuition has not let him down: not in the very beginning of the 1990s, when he was one of the first to react to the passage of the Law on

---

24 Project 7x7 has staff correspondents in Komi, Kirov, Karelia, Mariy El, Kostroma. The project also covers events in a number of other regions, in Arkhangelsk, Murmansk, Ryazan, Oryol, Voronezh, Kaluga, Yaroslavl, Chuvashia, drawing, in part, on freelancers.
25 A. Yarovaya, "Delo Dmitrieva". Spetsial'ny reportazh o dele arestovannogo karel'skogo istorika", 7x7. Respublika Karelia, March 1, 2017, https://7×7-journal.ru/item/92393.
26 Project Redkollegia is an independent prize founded by the charitable organization Sreda Foundation for the support of free professional journalism in Russia. On its site redkollegia.org the organizers of the prize write that their goal is "to help those who maintain high standards of the profession in Russia at a time when free and quality journalism is under pressure from the state."

Print, founding his own publication, nor in the middle of that decade, when he felt that he needed to learn how to earn money from advertising, nor in the beginning of the 2000s, when he began investing in the internet.

The crisis did not pass "Altapress" by. The holding was forced to lay off around 30 percent of its staff (including around 25 percent of its journalists). On the other hand, "Altapress" performance indicators are growing on the internet at a rate of 30 percent per year. Of the top three leaders of "innovative internet" in Barnaul, altapress.ru occupies the first place.

The second part of Purgin's plan for the future is to make sure his publication becomes the moderator of public discussions. The first step on that path was the new and successful Altapress project, a course of paid lectures from the best entrepreneurs of the Altai region: "Something like an MBA, but based less on theory and more on the personal experience of the lecturer," describes Purgin. "At first we thought that only 10-12 people would sign up, but there was a crush. Assistant directors came, directors, from the generation of 30-somethings."

Purgin is sure that those who want to change will survive. "This is very similar to the 1990s, with the exception of the level of freedom that is at zero. But new possibilities are emerging that we just can't miss."

Narrative Journalism in Russia: A Tentative History

Alexander Gorbachev

The revival of narrative journalism in the West could not help but influence Russian media as well, especially considering that by the beginning of the 2010s a new generation of journalists had taken shape who had grown up under conditions of virtually unlimited access to the internet and who existed in a global context. Before speaking about how to describe the history of the development of narrative journalism in Russia, it is necessary to understand the history of the term in the context in which it was born—the US. "Journalism that reads like a novel." In 1973, Tom Wolfe thus defined what he called "new journalism," a way of writing characteristic of a broad group of American magazine contributors of the 1960s, ranging from Gay Talese and Joan Didion to Hunter Thompson and Truman Capote. Wolfe's foreword to the weighty volume *The New Journalism*, in which the most colorful texts springing from this tentative movement were gathered, became its manifesto. In a characteristically pathetic-elitist (and in its own way irresistible) manner, the author proclaimed that virtuously written journalism based on facts stole the thunder from fading realistic prose; Wolfe claimed that reporting was the new literature, which was valuable in that it was not inclined to falsehood.

The future author of *Bonfire of the Vanities* never shied away from self-exaltation, and it goes without saying that in introducing the term "new literature," Wolfe had in mind not only to declare his place in literature, but also to distance himself from non-new journalism and designate the principal innovation of his generation. In this sense, he was seriously dissembling, as journalism based on narrative and storytelling did not first appear in America only in the 1960s. As early as the beginning of the 20th century, reporters like Upton Sinclair and Jacob Riis, involved in what was nicely called muckraking (literally, grubbing around in manure), gave their texts a more narrative tone than was typical of newspaper journalism at the time. It is indicative that these materials were frequently printed in magazines that were only just appearing on the scene at that time: *Collier's, McClure's*, etc. Then, not long before the First World War, a definitive professionalization of journalism took place and the first ethical standards were established. The first department of journalism in the US appeared at the University of Missouri in 1908, and from then on reporting became not merely a job, but a specialization. The profession of journalism was taught in universities, and media that had earlier served as a weapon for direct political influence began to care about the principles of objectivity. Thus, it is to the beginning of the 20th century that narrative journalism is traced by modern researchers of this type of writing.[1]

1925 saw the release of the first issue of *The New Yorker*, which remains to this day perhaps the main example of narrative journalism, which it had successfully published before Wolfe's generation. As a matter of fact, the "new" journalism of Wolfe and his colleagues was in relation to the "old" traditions of *The New Yorker* and a group of the magazine's authors, whose discursive models could look, in the era of pop-culture and sexual revolution, too demure and simply old-fashioned. There were also economic reasons for the appearance of "new journalism."[2] America's post-war prosperity and the growth of city populations led to citizens having a good deal more free time; it was now possible to spend it not only on dry newspaper announcements of the latest important events, but also on more fanciful, engaging, and in some sense more "entertaining" journalism printed in magazines like *New York* and *Esquire*. A new public also helped the flowering of narrative: the intellectuals and the creative class demanded high-quality writing. Finally, "new journalism" offered the authors themselves the possibility to achieve economic independence in a relatively short period of time:

---

1   See, for instance, J.A. Hartsock, A History of American Literary Journalism: The Emergence of a Modern Narrative Form (Amherst (MA): University of Massachusetts Press, 2000)

2   J.J. Pauly, The Politics of the New Journalism (Sims N. (Ed.) Literary Journalism in the Twentieth Century. New York: Oxford University Press, 1990)

since such texts were more literary, they could often provide reporters with lucrative book contracts. Wolfe's own creative career is quite telling in this respect, as he went from being a magazine writer to one of the leading American novelists.

It is generally accepted that "new journalism," as a specific type of reporting discourse (which among other things not infrequently includes personalization and significant involvement of the author in the fabric of the reality that he or she is describing), had on the whole retreated to the periphery of the journalism profession by the beginning of the 1980s, whereas narrative journalism remains virtually the most reputable reporting genre. As paradoxical as it might seem, there is no generally accepted definition of "narrative journalism," and moreover, there is not even a universal term that could be used to discuss the genre. Today, both within the profession and in academic texts, the words "literary," "narrative," and "longform" are used to define one and the same thing. Some researchers studying the theory and practice of journalism have even suggested that the term "narrative journalism" is principally "epistemologically flexible" — that is, constantly changing and eluding a clear definition.[3]

In speaking about the principles of "new journalism," Wolfe distinguished several of its basic elements: the construction of material through a montage of scenes that relate to the topic of the material (ideally, the author should observe these scenes with his or her own eyes, though reconstructed scenes are also allowed); dialogues and conversations of the heroes; third-person narration; and "status details," or a particular accent on descriptive elements that reveal the social circumstances of what is taking place. With a few additional broadening elements, these criteria can be considered adequate for narrative journalism as a whole. Thus, it is obvious that along with third-person narration, first-person narration is also possible (and was practiced by representatives of new journalism themselves, for example Joan Didion). In addition, along with

---

3 See J.A. Hartsock, "Literary Journalism» as an Epistemological Moving Object within a Larger 'Quantum' Narrative," Journal of Communication Inquiry Vol. 23, №4. (1999): 423–447.

strictly "status" details, narrative journalism can be characterized by attention to detail in general, and it is precisely these details that create a sense of the authenticity of the described phenomena, people, or events. In the majority of research on narrative journalism, some of the most significant characteristics are, in one way or another, "depth" of immersion in the topic and maximally complete coverage; attention to dramaturgy, narration, and the literary quality of the text; particular attention to such categories as characters and authorial voice; and the adherence of materials to professional journalistic standards of exactitude and factual correctness.[4]

If in the American tradition there is difficulty with an exact terminological definition of narrative journalism, in the Russian tradition there is, for the most part, not even an understanding of the concept. In this text, I use the phrase "narrative journalism" taken directly from the English, with the understanding that it adequately transmits the general meaning of the term in Russian. It is indicative that another word often used to refer to this type of material — longread — is a literal transliteration from the English. The non-existent, or in any case thus far non-existent, history of narrative journalism in Russian is a large and difficult topic that deserves separate professional research. In this text, I offer my own insights into this problem, unavoidably superficial both in the volume of my analysis and in that I am myself more of a practitioner than strictly a researcher.

It goes without saying that it would be incorrect to begin this history with the post-Soviet period. For all the ideological bias of Soviet journalism, it was in large part built on narrative — or, more specifically, on a broad collection of narrative devices from which texts were constructed. The mechanics of the creation of such texts is graphically described in the novella *Compromise* by Sergey Dovlatov, which consists entirely of stories about these very compromises — about how living journalism, once issued, becomes notes that are filled exclusively with ideological clichés. (*Compromise* is,

---

[4] These basic criteria form the foundation and working definition of the genre that I proposed in my master's dissertation, defended in 2016 at the University of Missouri.

of course, a work of fiction, but it seems to rather exactly transmit both the process of the death of language itself and the relationship of the first generation of the post-Soviet journalistic elite to Soviet journalistic discourse). Alexei Yurchak, in his brilliant *Everything Was Forever, Until It Was No More*, vividly shows how in the post-Stalin USSR there occurred a process of washing sense out of official discourse, which allowed citizens of the country to take a position of "outsideness" in relation to the government and formally introduce completely foreign meanings into its language. It would seem that Yurchak's analysis is applicable to Soviet journalism as well: though less formal than the rhetoric of the state, it was still closely connected to it. It goes without saying that this does not mean that in Soviet times there was no journalism that was not reduced to ideological clichés, but it seems to be possible to say that by the time the Soviet world fell apart and a new media industry was created, the very concept of journalistic narrative was closely associated with an ideologized approach to reporting that was unacceptable to a new generation of authors, editors, and publishers. The rejection of all things Soviet, characteristic of the culture of perestroika and early post-perestroika, not infrequently led to a denial of literariness in journalism.

The flagship of post-Soviet journalism was the groundbreaking newspaper *Kommersant*. It is generally understood that *Kommersant*, which appeared in December 1989, virtually created its own audience, inventing an image of the Russian businessperson before the new social class even had time to recognize itself as such. *Kommersant* also reworked the language under which reality was organized. (This bold strategy in post-Soviet conditions, when reality and its discourses where virtually remade anew, turned out to be shockingly productive — it would later be used by *Afisha*, for example.) This language, of course, fundamentally differed from the language of Soviet journalism, in which the very word "business" seemed foreign and hostile. It is typical that the first issue of *Kommersant* was put out under the name of "Fact" — it was precisely this dry, harsh, almost unequivocal language that the creators of the newspaper were betting on. As its founder, Vladimir Yakovlev, later recounted, the publication "was very informative, harsh, very impersonal and with the absolute idea of guaranteed information that the reader was receiving."[5] In this way, Soviet discourse, in which direct emotionality somehow softened the required ideological bias, is contrasted against the new style, in which there was essentially no room for emotions. With the help of this dry language of facts and figures, *Kommersant* was trying to organize the chaos of post-Soviet reality, acting to a certain extent as a kind of therapist: in an extremely unstable world, the newspaper created the illusion of normalcy. "We painted the picture of a respectable Western life, as it was understood by the Moscow liberals for thirty years," explained Alexander Timofeyevsky, who used to work at *Kommersant* also stated:

> Part of that world was, for example, protocol. The newspaper outlined this very clearly. The world consisted of newsmakers, their comings and goings, appointments and firings, birthdays and funerals. The natural cycle of life was underscored in order to create the sensation of a normal flow of life, the way things should be.[6]

In this sense, the rejection of storytelling, which by definition promotes the dramatization of reality, is even more logical. *Kommersant* set the standard for new, post-Soviet social-political journalism, and did so essentially by removing narrative from its collection of devices.

It is interesting that when a culture section appeared in *Kommersant*, it began to play by completely different rules than the "serious" part of the paper. As Timofeyevsky recalls:

> the culture section allowed everything: there, complete, hard-hitting freedom reigned. Those who were usually putting a spoke in the wheel—'be closer to the people'—here to the contrary were pulling it out. The goal was the exact opposite: to be further from the people.

As a result, the culture section of the early *Kommersant* became a triumph of literary journalism in the most direct sense of the word

---

[5] A. Gorbachev, O. Kashin, I. Krasilschik, N. Rostova, et al. "Chto my nadelali? Istoriya russkikh SMI 1989-2011," Afisha, July 6, 2011, https://www.afisha.ru/article/mediahistory/.

[6] Kommersant-Daily, September 1992. A. Gorbachev, O. Kashin, I Krasilschik, N. Rostova, et al., Op. cit, https://www.afisha.ru/article/mediahistory/page7/.

"literary": they published complex, exquisite texts, maximally aestheticized and filled with quotations, sometimes seemingly intentionally obtuse. This strict division of jurisdiction and language between "serious" and culture journalism became a kind of standard for Russian media of the 1990s, as similar stories were repeated in the pages of the newspapers *Today* and *Russian Telegraph* (the culture columns by Vyacheslav Kuritsyn in the newspaper *Today* were used in 2016 in a visual arts piece called "Garage," and now they are, in their lack of compromise, truly like a kind of performance art). In this way, an important structural watershed was created: "beautiful" writing was essentially set at odds with fact-based writing; narrative was positioned not as a function of journalism in general, but of only one of its segments.

This state of affairs reinforced the appearance at the end of the 1990s of publications on various sides of the thematic spectrum. On the one hand, there was the business newspaper *Vedomosti*, which quickly became *Kommersant*'s main competitor and one of the most respected publications in the country. In one of *Vedomosti*'s fundamental documents, "Dogma," the main demands concerned exactness, clarity and simplicity: "Dogma" fairly strictly prescribed both the style and the structure of the newspaper texts, and in this way unavoidably achieved the very "authorless" effect that Yakovlev had sought earlier.[7] On the other hand, in the same year (1999), a magazine called *Afisha* appeared that combined the tabloid press with the intellectual approach and refined writing of the abovementioned sections on culture. *Afisha* presented a new view on culture, understanding it more broadly and, if you will, more liberally (that music, film, and theater existed in the magazine on the same level as restaurants and fashionable shops was an obvious policy), but at the same time nurtured a high, literary style that overflowed with quotations, references, and calculated narrative experiments.

Here it should be clarified that this version of the history of post-Soviet journalism is of course consciously superficial—and to a large extent subjective. As we are interested first and foremost in

---

7   See the text: https://www.khodorkovsky.ru/images/editor/File/dogma-Vedomosti.doc.

the adventures of journalistic narrative, there is no room here for an exhaustive and multi-sided analysis of the discursive practices that appeared in print media in the 1990s. Nevertheless, it is impossible not to mention several significant phenomena. The above-mentioned "humane" Soviet style was transformed in a curious way into the stylistics of new tabloids, popular and populist media of social-political character, whose continuity with the previous discourse was underscored even in the names of the publications. In the writing style of the largest papers of the 1990s — *Komsomolskaia pravda, Moskovskii komsomolets, Argumenty i fakty* — it is possible to detect all of the same stylistic accents that were visible in the Soviet press. In the low register, these practices put out "yellow" tabloids like *Ekspress-gazeta* and *Megapolis-ekspress*, but it is also interesting that *Novaya gazeta*, a publication that consistently maintains a combination of emotionality, didacticism, and investigative journalism, was created by a collective that split off from *Komsomolka*.

Yet another type of writing was created by tabloid publications, ranging from *Cosmopolitan* to the magazine *Domovoi*. It undoubtedly deserves separate analysis. For our purposes, it is important to mention that such magazines first and foremost occupied a position of conversation partner with the reader. Characteristically, many of them addressed the audience using the informal pronoun for "you," such that the publications seemed to have a heartfelt conversation with the reader rather than tell them a story. Lastly, it is impossible not to talk about the Russian tradition of weekly magazines, from Sergey Parkhomenko's *Itogi* to Leonid Parfyonov's *Russian Newsweek*. It goes without saying that elements and aspects of narrative journalism in them existed in an almost unavoidable way — it was the magazine that was first connected with the appearance of the genre. However, it is worth mentioning here two additional circumstances. First, the weekly news magazine was never really developed as a media type in Russia: by the beginning of the 2010s, only *Russian Reporter*, which continued in the discursive sense the tradition of "humane" Soviet writing, remained (of course, the print weekly magazines gradually entered a deep crisis with the appearance of the internet). Second, attempts to put out a "Russian *New Yorker*," as made by, for example, the publications *Novyi ochevidets* and *Russkaia zhizn'*, inevitably met with failure (in the first case, both by way of content and financially; in the second, only financially).

The conceptualization given above is grounded in my own personal experiences. In 2005, I began to work at *Afisha*, in large part consciously choosing this approach to journalism out of all those that existed (I say "in large part" because it is probably not worth evaluating the depth of my own reflections from twelve years ago). I was interested in journalism predominantly from the point of view of writing; I wanted to create texts that would develop the language of speaking about culture and understanding culture, texts that one would want to read again and again. There were no such publications from social-political houses in those years—in 2007, working on material about the situation surrounding the Madonna concert in Moscow for *Russian Newsweek*, I tried to write more simply and dryly than I was used to doing for *Afisha* (I leave it to others to judge my success at this). It goes without saying that this does not negate the fact that in a wide variety of publications— from the *Vlast'* magazine put out by *Kommersant* to the aforementioned *Russkaia zhiz'*—narrative journalism was regularly practiced; however, in the general discursive hierarchy of social-political media, it occupied a rather sidelined, marginalized position.

It appears that this situation began to change at the end of the 2000s or the beginning of the 2010s. There were several reasons for this: for one, a silent social contract that proposed a distinct division between the spheres of politics and recreation gradually began to break apart. Culture began to become an inexorable part of politics, and politics part of culture; this, in turn, led to the convergence of previously diversified media discourses. It goes without saying that the most striking example here is the protests of 2011-2012, which at a certain point turned into just such "fashionable leisure" as going to a concert or to the theater, possibly even more in demand, with staff from media like *Afisha* participating in their organization (a borderline case from the point of view of journalistic ethics, but illustrative of the integration of various media and social segments. See Mikhail Idov's article in *New York Magazine*, published in January 2012).[8] In this same period, *Afisha* itself began to change. It became clear that to the target audience of the publication, *Afisha*'s main subject of interest—namely the urban environment—was also rapidly becoming politicized. The previous trend-setting approach, based mainly on keeping track of and developing cultural fashions in the broad sense of the word, was gradually replaced with a phenomenological one. The magazine began to analyze all aspects of the urban environment; urban reforms, the state of education, the lives of sexual minorities in Russia, and the above-mentioned protests became equally legitimate topics as film or literature.

Nevertheless, *Afisha*'s general approach to language and journalism remained unchanged—and in this way, narrative devices and storytelling began to be applied to topics more common to social-political publications (be it the state youth camp on Lake Seliger or the activities of the leader of the Moscow Department of Culture, Sergei Kapkov). It goes without saying that I am speaking here specifically about *Afisha* because I was myself involved with changing the discourse there, but that in no way means that *Afisha* was solely responsible for the demarginalization of storytelling as a device for social-political, "serious" journalism. *Afisha* is just one example that seems to illustrate how narrative methods gradually won a place in Russian journalism comparable to the one they occupy in English-language journalism. Similar processes took place in other editorial offices, for example, in *Snob*, which tried to return the old term "sketch" to professional usage, or *Bolshoi Gorod* and *Lenta.ru*, which became the inarguably central internet media sources in Russia at exactly the time that they introduced a section for special correspondents that practiced predominantly the storytelling approach, for events both within the realm of the everyday and beyond. The efforts of various individual reporters also played a significant role in strengthening the influence of narrative journalism (for example, Olesya Gerasimenko and Svetlana Reiter from

---

8   M. Idov "The New Decembrists," New York Magazine, January 22nd, 2012, http://nymag.com/news/features/russian-revolutionaries-2012-1/.

Kommersant), as did those of editors (for example, Nikolai Kononov from *Forbes* and *Secret Firmy*; he in particular seems to have helped fix the term "longread" in the professional lexicon).

Another important factor for the development of narrative journalism in Russia seems to have been its globalization, based on the development of the internet and corresponding global trends. Before the end of the 2000s, the media industry in the US was dominated by a pessimistic consensus that the new digital medium and new means of media consumption were deadly for the traditions of narrative journalism. There are many examples of alarmist publications lamenting the fact that distracted attention and other issues connected with internet usage would unavoidably lead to the death of their respected genre.[9] However, in the 2010s, the situation changed. This was facilitated by the appearance of new methods of digital storytelling (notably the *New York Times* project "Snowfall," a multimedia project created by the editorial staff around the narrative of an avalanche that caused the deaths of 16 people; in spite of the resulting ambiguity, this publication showed how "long" journalism could use multimedia in the internet and the spread of smartphones as instruments for reading long texts.[10] These, combined with other factors, led to the renaissance of narrative journalism in America. This renaissance was also expressed in the appearance of individual curated projects, daily selected from the best examples of the genre (for example, Longform, Longreads, and The Browser), and in the rise of a whole generation of publications dedicated in whole or in part to the genre, both in print and on the internet.[11]

---

9   See, for instance, Candy Cooper's article tellingly titled "The Death of Slow Journalism," American Journalism Review, June/July, 2009, http://ajrarchive.org/Article.asp?id=4789.

10 See John Branch, "Snow Fall. The Avalanche at Tunnel Creek," The New York Times, 2012, http://www.nytimes.com/projects/2012/snow-fall/#/?part=tunnel-creek.

11 My master's dissertation, defended in 2016 at the University of Missouri, was dedicated to the latter—more specifically, to theory business models; as I was able to establish as the result of an interview with the managers of the publication, narrative journalism almost never pays for itself financially, however it not infrequently pays for itself in the sense of reputation and is monetized in indirect ways: for example, through the sale of platforms for digital storytelling,

At any rate, the rebirth of narrative journalism and the confirmation of its status as the apotheosis of a reporter's work could not help but influence Russian media as well—especially considering that by the beginning of the 2010s, a new generation of journalists had taken shape, one that had grown up under conditions of practically unlimited access to the internet and that existed in a global context. Consequently, Russia also began to see the appearance of publications that claimed storytelling as their main approach or presented narrative texts as their most valuable type of content. In the first category, we can name *Baten'ka, da vy transformer* [Old chap, but you are a transformer] (a type of internet *samizdat*, or self-publishing) and *Takie dela*. It is indicative that this last piece is built on a unique economic model in which the reputational value of narrative content is transformed into emotional, trying to motivate the reader to participate in good works. In the second category are *Snob*, which has undergone several conceptual iterations, *Sekret firmy*, and *Meduza*, which was founded by the core of the *Lenta.ru* team after the editor-in-chief of the publication was fired for political reasons in spring 2014.[12]

The development of storytelling is also especially important for media outlets by virtue of the specific role of journalism in Russia. In the US, for a number of historical-cultural and legal reasons, mass media is the most important instrument of public control over the authorities—and in some sense, storytelling can be called a superstructure over the more principal and basic function of journalism. Roughly speaking, in order for journalistic investigation to lead to formal results such as, for example, the firing of a person in power or investigation into his activities by law enforcement agencies, the most important component of the piece is the facts, not the literary narrative. The present-day Russian government is structured in a different way: the result of an anti-corruption investigation could be suits filed against the media outlet that published it

---

the sale of film rights to studios and directors, through off-line events, etc.
12   It was at "Meduza" that I began to work as editor of special correspondents section (the main "narrative" department of the publication) in the summer of 2016.

(see, for example, the suits by the head of Rosneft, Igor Sechin, against *Novaya Gazeta* and *RBK*), but almost never real consequences for those featured in the pieces. In essence, the state in Russia is neither audience nor partner for the independent media; far more often, it becomes their active opponent. Thus, a realistic measure of the effectiveness of journalism as a democratic instrument becomes its ability to bring significant information to the attention of the public — to "hook" its audience. And in this sense, the value of storytelling as a type of journalistic discourse is difficult to overestimate — to return to Tom Wolfe's definition, "journalism that reads like a novel" is capable of reaching a far larger number of people than journalism that reads like a quarterly report.

The Art of Complexity Surrenders to the Government of Simplicity

Yulia Bederova

Two cultural events which occurred in early spring 2016 in Moscow demonstrated unheard-of growth in the consumption of cultural production: the now-famous Serov exhibit in the Tretyakov Gallery and the market launch of subscriptions to the new season of the Moscow Philharmonic. In just forty-eight hours, a million rubles' worth of tickets were sold to concerts in 2016-2017, and individual concert series were completely sold out. The tempo of sales did not fall the following week until almost all of the assorted subscription ticket packages had sold out. At a time when the political atmosphere was growing more charged and there was a deficit in public trust regarding the maintenance of everyday life, citizens agreed to stand in line for academic art—the plastique of the noisy but precise expectation effectively visualized the demand that swept over Muscovites to interact with eternal values and deep meanings. It would seem that such a reaction on the part of society is due to the investment opportunity for the cultural production sphere, to the point that the latter could confidently count on the money and time of the public, and shortly thereafter on the favor of the state as well.

Return on Investment and Self-Identity

According to announcements from Minister of Culture Vladimir Medinsky and program documents of the Ministry of Culture (primarily "Foundations of State Culture Policy"), the state is interested in the return on investment in the cultural sphere. This effectively boils down to the idea that "Culture should work and earn," if we take into account the ideological dimension, the main idea of state culture policy. The reality appears to be that the budget is being swiftly cut, and new principles of finance for the cultural sphere suggest a paradoxical ideal—whoever earns more by themselves will receive more from the state. In essence, the governmental customer operates as a credit establishment: when the order has been put into production, culture returns the subsidy to the state on its product. And if in cinematography, understood as a commercial art, such a mechanism is provided for in contracts upon receipt of government subsidy (the share of monies returned is on average 40 percent, but promises to grow higher), in performing arts (academic music, dramatic theater, opera, ballet) this principle so far works only unofficially[1] Whoever racks up more points for efficacy, is evaluated by considering, among other things, such indicators as quantity of premieres, number of shows on home stages and on tours, the extent to which the hall is filled, and revenue from ticket sales) receives the next subsidy, all the way up to prizes for the leaders for exceeding the plan for attracting extra-budgetary means.[2]

As far as cultural rush is concerned, no matter how you explain its inflation of meanings in society, it is of primary importance that both sensational lines took place in the capital. In the regions, massive buying-up of all academic musical or artistic offerings a year in advance was not noted.

Even more importantly, the two events that triggered this speculation noticeably differ from one another in both structure and character. The Serov exhibit became the flagship project of the Strategy for Optimization of Production in the Field actively promoted by the Ministry of Culture. Medinsky in an interview with TASS:[3]

> Earlier the main yardstick for museums was the number of exhibits and not the number of people coming to them. So they would have an exhibit of one

---

[1] Vandenko A. "Ya chelovek beskonfliktnyi. No upertyi." Interview with Russian Minister of Culture Vladimir Medinsky, TASS. April 27, 2016, http://tass.ru/opinions/top-officials/3236070?page=1.

[2] Kakovy kriterii otsenki effektivnosti deyatel'nosti oblastnykh gosudarstvennykh teatrov. Spravochnik rukovoditelya uchrezhdeniya kul'tury, February 7, 2016, http://www.cultmanager.ru/question/6635-kakovy-kriterii-otsenki-eff ektivnosti-deyatelnosti-oblastnyh-gosudarstvennyh-teatrov. A scoring system of criteria for evaluating the effectiveness of culture enterprises was introduced by the Ministry of Culture in 2015 as an addition to the system of "effective contract" that had been introduced by government directive in 2012.

[3] Vandenko A., Op cit.

item that was open for one day... We are changing the system. Why practice self-deception? Better one Serov exhibit than 355 showings of who knows what and for whom.

In other words, we are talking about setting up for the production of cultural blockbusters of mainstream artistic content, at the same time as offerings that are not expected to see massive demand are cut back. The subscription package to the Moscow Philharmonic, by contrast, is a seriously thought-out collection of diverse possibilities: programs that are both simple and complex in their content, relation to the performance mainstream, and the innovativeness of their repertoire.

Under the pressure of crisis, some alteration of the season — making it shorter or more expensive — occurs, but without lowering the quality. The subscription cycle is preserved, with its elegant premiere events (from modern academic music to the Russian premiere of Handel's operas) and irregular weekday concerts; the philharmonic's repertoire includes, in one way or another, early, classical, and new music; import substitution is reflected in the programs of Russian musicians, who become as inventive as they once were on the road; and foreign musicians, though in more modest numbers, continue to come, not only with solo performances, but to participate in collective works, which are the most interesting.

However, the Moscow Philharmonic seriously differs from other concert organizations in the country, not only — and not even primarily — in terms of the amount of financing it receives. Here we are dealing with a rare example of the ideas of cultural development and the multi-layered quality of the cultural field. The Moscow Philharmonic is skillfully adapting to the proposed strategies of optimization in the field and is not hurrying to follow the newest principle of "better one event for a hundred people than a hundred events for one."

Another important event happened at the end of 2014, when the president signed the order "On the confirmation of the Foundations of State Culture Policy," which did not receive considerable attention, but nevertheless became quite significant for culture.[4]

---

4   "Utverzhdeny osnovy gosudarstvennoj kulturnoj politiki," Prezident Rossii.

The "Foundations" do not include a mechanism for the administration of culture or the principles of its functioning; they are more of an ideological manifesto and conceptual base for further decisions coming from the Ministry of Culture. Nevertheless, until the "Law on Culture" has passed (it has been much discussed, but its formulation is always postponed), the "Foundations" remain the only programmatic document on which the ministry bases its decisions and according to which the entire field of culture is to live—the independent, non-governmental segment of the field has been destroyed, especially in the performing arts.

In the "Foundations," culture is spoken about in general categories: a course is proclaimed to "increase the social status of culture, to have a cultural influence on all spheres of state policy and public life." But there is also a concrete description of the goals: culture is "the instrument used to transfer to the new generation a corpus of moral and ethical values that comprise the basis of national identity." Referring to the text of "Foundations," the Ministry of Culture supports (or closes) a production or institution on the basis of their own understanding of "values" and "national identity." Sources familiar with the situation confirm that concepts and grant proposals that underscore the "inclusion of Russian art in a global context" engender undisguised annoyance in the Ministry of Culture. Immoral "acidic aesthetics and a twisted image of man in shows oriented toward Western experience" express the anti-state intentions of their creators. In a discussion of the summary of the yearly Report on the State of Culture of the Ministry of Culture in 2014, the contents of which the author of this article managed to obtain access to, it read:

> From the point of view of content, the general direction of 'new drama' and theater innovation could be characterized as provocative, anti-state, facilitating the subversion of traditional Russian culture, and contradicting the spiritual and moral values of Russian society.

December 24, 2014, http://kremlin.ru/events/president/news/47325.

The increase in the level of self-identity is expressed in the predominance of a domestic repertoire in all areas, for example the increase in the proportion of domestic films for rent (they now comprise 50 percent of the total). Incidentally, it is precisely in film that the market makes direct quotas impossible—the greatest box office successes are the foreign (Hollywood) films. In theater, it seems to the Ministry of Culture, the elimination of styles and forms "borrowed from the West" (such as postdramatic theater and other unconventional theater practices), together with an increase in the proportion of domestic classics, would in no way impede the extant market form of culture. The fact that the mechanisms for placing quotas on the repertoire are not in the hands of this ministry is another question.

State Pressure on Complexity

On the one hand, the protective pathos of the "Foundations" does not contradict either the "line for the Serov" or the complete public buy-out of classical music tickets, especially given that they are not legally fixed by concrete mechanisms of pressure on culture. Of course, it is not this pathos that accounts for the sudden growth in cultural demand, and it cannot directly influence the process of broadening or reducing the assortment of cultural products offered.

On the other hand, not only is there a noticeable general decline in this area, but we can also see a change in the structure of offerings: forms of productions that are aesthetically complex, unconventional, and new in content and language are gradually squeezed to the periphery of the market, with a noticeable impulse from the government. And when, say, the Committee for Culture in St. Petersburg refuses to finance (thus essentially shutting down) not only the elegant, significant, and serious ReMusic festival of new music (one of the main festivals in the sphere of modern academic music in Russia), but also the Obraztsova youth vocal competition, it is difficult to detect any ideological motive for this. However, the number of rejections received by non-mainstream festivals and programs that are not sufficiently "self-identifying" is growing, thus limiting access to what is sought after and included in the current global art sphere.

At the same time, not only innovative but also academic performing arts as a whole are going through not the best of times. Over the past two decades, there has been a steady decline in growth (the success of the Moscow Philharmonic is the result of prior growth not only in the volume of financing, but also in freedom and competency).

Simultaneously, the crisis and a harsh political climate have intensified the already palpable deficit of quality systematic reforms. The cultural sphere looks increasingly like a blurred field with unclear outlines within it, where there are complex interwoven tendencies pulling in different directions, not only adding to one another, but underscoring one another. Among them is economic censorship, the source of which — the economic crisis — is impersonal and therefore it is impossible to make any deals with it. Another key factor is psychological pressure from the Ministry of Culture, which comes across in the rhetoric of public speeches and documents, the manipulation of finances, unpredictable staffing decisions, and even, as journalists relate, in articles written to order that are directed against certain institutions or productions.

Thus far, the explosive growth of the beginning of the 2000s is still noticeable, since it broadened the borders of repertoire, international and interregional connections, and performance competency. To a significant extent, individual regions are still living on the contacts established in the past. For example, without the Krasnoyarsk "Festival of Asian-Pacific Countries of the Region," the artistic and performance level of programs of academic music and opera would be lower. The musical life of Yekaterinburg would be more bland without the "Symphonic Forum of Russia," and that of Perm without the Diaghilev Festival. All these events are of outstanding quality, feature non-local additions, and display a variety of performance and repertoire content.

That being said, the government's lack of a systematic approach to this sphere has begun to be felt, and it is not clear how the authorities are leading, providing support or, conversely, refusing to pay attention to the field, ignoring its goals and specifics and placing bets on the simplification of its content and mechanisms of functioning. The dichotomy between the formal artistic freedom of theaters and philharmonics and their simultaneous dependence not only on the political leadership (federal, regional, or municipal, depending on the organizational structure of the facility), but also on the tastes of the public has become more noticeable.

However tangled the spool of tendencies discernible in the cultural sphere might be, they can be divided into two opposing groups. On the one hand, there is pressure from the state as it rids itself of paternalism, forcing the field to work according to new rules and new administrative schematics and to make money. (Experts differ in their opinions as to whether reform is happening in the cultural sphere and whether it is possible to speak of general economic or ideological policy having an influence on that sphere.) In addition, state pressure to become less paternalistic means that culture is burdened with the function of serving the state ideology in order to receive a share of the limited money available.

On the other hand, the state demonstrates a particular lack of attention to the specifics of complex arts not for mass consumption. In other words, the ideological supervisory agency that the Ministry of Culture is today proclaims its goal to be instilling values through academic art, which is reflected in the structure of government support for enterprises and projects in a surprisingly straightforward way. "Instilling" is to be understood to mean not enlightenment (liberation), but ordering (suppression); in this context, sufficiently values-instilling classic works are from conservative genres and take conservative forms. Under such conditions, it might be expected that the symphony, opera and ballet would be rushing toward development, but nothing of the kind is taking place.

The state, which acts as the customer for any cultural product created using state budget funds, understands academism not as a space for complexity, but as a field for simplicity. Using available administrative, ideological, and financial instruments of influence, it has created a situation in which the proper upbringing of the population is thought of as adherence to simple meanings and ideas of faithfulness, the fixity of values—and such upbringing can only be achieved by the routinized classics. The real development of modern academic arts, meanwhile, answers the spirit of modernity in a completely different way, demanding from both producer and consumer not only a certain level of education and mental responsiveness, but also the ability to comprehend the complex, changing, unstable, and multi-layered, to see a multiplicity of historical perspectives and variations of aesthetic norms and positions.

Thus, the Moscow Philharmonic wins the competition by including in its repertoire the rarely performed Handel or organizing the "Another Space" contemporary music festival—that is, by broadening the repertoire. Vladimir Yurovsky's State Orchestra is leading due not only to the quality of its sound, but also to a large degree to the beauty, complexity, intellectual value, emotional richness, and aesthetic multi-dimensionality of its programs and concepts. Only thanks to that can such (by the standard of our times) improbable events take place, like the now-famous multi-day "Military Cycle," which turned out to be not a grand parade, but a complexly structured anti-totalitarian research experiment and artistic manifesto.

The freedoms of the Moscow Philharmonic were protected by public attention and the non-verbal character of the production, coupled with its academic status. Where the public is not ready to take interest in the complex, by contrast, academism is swiftly returned to the routine. The state's ideological pressure against complexity per se noticeably deforms the field of culture, though no one is currently talking about direct, systematic censorship of content or of total control over who can participate in the cultural process. The directors of philharmonics and theaters, critics from the capital and the regions, and also directors, conductors and actors deny in chorus any suggestion of censorship. Then what is happening with the symphonies—why are they, in all their diversity, not heard "from every steam iron", or the opposite, not reduced to one generalized Tchaikovsky, since the Ministry of Culture demands that the domestic repertoire take priority?

Prohibition of Freedom of Interpretation

In words, the ministry declares that the planned repertoires of theaters and philharmonics need to be corrected:

> In our view, there are certain problems with the repertoire, but it is not such a rapid process, it cannot be changed in one season, and we are trying to avoid directly dictating. Instead, we patiently await changes, quietly pushing the line indicated in the Foundations for State Culture Policy.

In this statement, Medinsky phrases his expectation of change.[5] As yet, the state does not have direct levers of influence on theater advertising and the content of specific programs, or else they are very limited. For example, the Perm Opera Theater and Ballet was forced to put on only one opera, one ballet, and one children's show due to the government assignations for 2016, on the basis of which the amount of state financing is determined. (A separate tragi-comic nuance is that the state finances subordinate jurisdictional institutions by the year, and philharmonics and theaters plan and work by the season.) Three shows a year, it goes without saying, is a laughably small amount for a leading theater that had become a brand with worldwide recognition and regularly staged works of global significance, including receiving international musical prizes. Furthermore, it is stipulated in the government assignment that in terms of theater repertoire, domestic repertoire should predominate (at least, the regional ministry made a public statement to that effect), but in the documents, this stance is nowhere to be found on the record.

The problem is that, for example, in the opera genre, domestic scores make up only a small part of the world operatic canon. And as wonderful as Mussorgsky's "Boris Godunov," Borodin's "Prince Igor," Tchaikovsky's "Iolanta" and "Eugene Onegin," or Rimsky-Korsakov's "Snegurochka" are (these are the hit-parade, but in the sense of repertoire also the Russian opera iceberg, only the very top of which ends up on theater stages), no Russian theater could exist on Russian opera alone. The public demands Verdi's "La Traviata,"

---

5   Vandenko A., Op cit.

Donizetti's "The Elixir of Love," Puccini's "La Boheme." In addition, the majority of Russian scores are so complex in terms of performance and aesthetics that they simply cannot play the role of repertoire blockbusters. In the same way, it is impossible to imagine the culture of the symphony only in a domestic framework — the disappearance of Mozart, Beethoven, and Chopin from the concert stage would call into question not only the adequate representation of world artistic culture on the local stage, but also the very idea of the inviolability and importance of the classics. The classics as such would then cease to exist as a full canon and a gathering together of immutable values. The government is not going for this, even in rhetorical terms.

In exactly the same way as there are no levers of influence on repertoire that would allow for substantive censorship to be carried out, there are no legal mechanisms of systemic control over staffing. Thus, for example, even after the grand scandal of the staging of the opera "Tannhäuser" by the Novosibirsk Opera and Ballet Theater, no one besides director Boris Mezdrich received even a tacit "Berufsverbot". The scandal became the only case in the history of music in the country in recent decades when the director of the theater was removed from his post due not to any administrative issues, but to the outrage of a conservative public against the content and form of a show. Religious people who did not see the show in Novosibirsk, but who had obviously heard about it, publicly reported their wounded feelings (the trial, by the way, did not find anything objectionable in the show and dismissed their case). By all appearances, the reason that Mezdrich was punished, and remains out of work to this day, was that he offended the minister himself by refusing to apologize to those offended and insisting on defending the freedom of directorial interpretation (you can hear this in the words of Medinsky, who called Mezdrich's answer to the complaints "loutish").

As far as the central figure of the scandal is concerned, director Timofei Kulyabin had, according to complainants, incorrectly staged a classic (one in low demand until him: Wagner's opera "Tannhäuser" had been staged in Moscow by Andrejs Zagars in the Stanislavsky and Nemirovich-Danchenko Academic Music Theater for the first time in many decades just a year before the Novosibirsk case), but he was not blacklisted. In the spring of 2016, his production of the opera "Don Pasquale" was staged in the Bolshoi Theater, and negotiations are now under way for new work. It is another question that aside from the Bolshoi, no one in Russia is currently out hunting for Kulyabin's operas, in spite of the screaming deficit of director hands on opera scaffolds, with the same five recognized masters putting up everything throughout Russia, repeating and just slightly adjusting their concepts.

However, the fact that the theaters are not interested in new directors is not so much the fault of blatant censorship or control as general state pressure and the corresponding self-censorship of theaters that are becoming concerned about insufficiently famous directors and aesthetic unpredictability. The ideal premiere is structured in such a way that the state does not notice it, but the public, on the contrary, keeps going and going to it.

The only real lever of control on the working hands in culture is the possibility that the minister could order the removal of ineffective administrators or strip financing from a project the artistic director of which causes him frustration. Medinsky speaks of this directly:

> I have questions regarding the civic position of this director (Vitaly Mansky — Iu. B.). To feed from the hand of the state while biting and spitting on it is, in my opinion, indecent... He can put it on here again if he finds the money. But the ministry will not give any grant money for such activities [referring here to the Artdokfest Festival — author's note], since, I repeat, the position of the festival organizers contradicts the "Foundations of State Culture Policy of the Russian Federation.[6]

Despite closing projects due to personal insights that the social-political views of the project's leadership do not correspond to state ideology and removing directors and administrators from their posts on the grounds of "ideological differences," the ministry does not interfere in the content of the production directly and has not introduced artistic councils (though this idea has been actively

---

6   Ibid.

discussed in the last two years.[7] It does, however, undertake to discredit the institution of independent expertise. At least, that is how things stand in the sphere of theater and music criticism. This can be seen, in particular, in the attack on the professional theatrical prize "Golden Mask," which is based on the independent selection of active critics rotating in the staff of the Expert Councils: this year, the ministry used the threat of pulling funding to place its own experts on the "Mask" Council.[8] The idea is that in the event that a favorable situation arises for the introduction of art councils in one form or another (for example, one made up of critics), the reputation of the entire current professional society will be discredited and there will be no one to defend the independent point of view. The current equivalents of art councils are the Expert Councils of the ministry itself, where they choose loyal critics on whom grant support depends.

To replace certain critics with others is to reformat criticism into a service industry and not analysis to which not only the state bureaucrats in the ministry, but also the heads of theaters and philharmonics agree. Their enterprises today exist under such conditions that independent analytics only harm, and the only form of journalism that is in demand becomes hidden PR. Though the content is not literally censored, a creeping taboo is happening in freedom of interpretation — in which a noticeable role is played not only by state pressure, but also by public pressure. It would seem that the sacral status of academic classics that combine linguistic inaccessibility to the public at large with a high level of intention should contradict the idea of earning for themselves, but in the opinion of the state, there is nothing strange in the combination. The sacral should and can bring not only reputational but actual revenue to the treasury, and besides, the custodians of the sacral (in essence, the censors) can be the audience.

---

7   "Tangeyzera" obsudili v Obshchestvennoj palate," Dni.ru. April 1, 2015.
8   See Elena Fanailova's interview with theater critic Marina Davydova in issue four of "Kontrapunkt", www.ponarseurasia.org/sites/default/files/Davydova_counterpoint4_0.pdf, — editor's note.

In preaching the principle "the one who pays the piper calls the tune" and in frightening artists with taking away money and directors with removal from their posts, the purveyors of the state policy inform the public of something important: when the state distributes money, it distributes not its own money, but that of the people. That means that the public *is* the contractor (in the same general sense as the money is d "people's" property), therefore they have the right to be offended by complexity and to demand for themselves clear, simple products.

Signs of Stagnation

Insofar as the entire sphere of academic musical and musical-theater arts in Russia is located in the public domain, the processes in it are influenced not so much by the ideology of "Foundations of State Policy in the Sphere of Culture" as they are by concrete mechanisms of cultural control. Here, experts have differing points of view on what is happening. A version of important reforms is popular — ones that are being introduced into the field, possibly not using the best methods, but which are capable of providing culture with a future. Defenders of the concept of existing reforms believe that Medinsky forced the field to work, convinced the leadership that culture should earn and provide for itself, introduced new criteria for the evaluation of effectiveness in the workings of cultural institutions, raised wages, forced philharmonics and theaters (and also art institutes that provide a scholarly basis for creative organizations) to get rid of ballast (not only coworkers who cannot use a computer well enough, but also exceedingly elderly professors still working, even if they are among the main authorities in their sphere), and influenced what was taken to be most necessary for the field, a law on patronage.

Other experts disagree, noting, for example, that the president's order on increasing salaries (not only in culture, but in education and science as well) is in no way provided for financially, and therefore the institution is forced to cut staff in order to raise salaries for the rest of the workers. Thus, legendary professor Vadim Gayevsky, founder of the school for ballet studies, was fired from the State Institute for Art Studies, and from the Moscow Conservatory the main specialist on Stravinsky and the Russian 20th century, Professor Svetlana Savenko, was let go. Optimization and cutbacks in turn lead to volunteer staffing solutions. Thus, legendary professor Vadim Gayevsky was fired from the State Institute for Art Studies, founder of the school for ballet studies, and from the Moscow Conservatory—the main specialist on Stravinsky and the Russian 20th Century, Professor Svetlana Savenko.

Many also find it doubtful that the system of evaluating the efficiency of cultural institutions—on the basis of which the budget is determined—has modernizing potential. At the moment, the system amounts to a voluminous list of criteria; by next summer, their number is to be reduced to five main ones: the fullness of the halls, the number of premieres, the number of shows and concerts on home stages and on tour, the extent to which the website is updated, and the number of tickets sold. Already, however, many regional and area philharmonics function according to such requirements, an example being the Samara Philharmonic. In general terms, their schedule assumes a limited personnel base dominated by collectives and actors that satisfy the taste of the masses (orchestras and choirs of folk instruments, pop music acts with a national component, and also charismatic recitals of poetry), a relatively low level of staff (who will not expect large salaries), and the possibility of rolling out the same repertoire in cities and culture houses far from the regional center. There are strong philharmonics like those in Yekaterinburg, Nizhny Novgorod, or Novosibirsk that draw full houses not only in village locations, but also on their home stages in the city. However, the more developed the idea of self-providing culture becomes, the more it narrows the repertoire in these philharmonics as well. Observers confirm that the Yekaterinburg Philharmonic's ability to sell out its concerts is such that if it had a house with two thousand seats, it would swim in gold. But there is a nuance: 80-85 percent of the performances on the concert programs of such philharmonics are Russian classic symphonic works that are popular with the audience. First and foremost, this means a limited selection of works by Rachmaninov and Tchaikovsky. Interesting musical strategies are possible here, on the basis of nothing more than a residual model. If there is no Rachmaninov, the public will not come, and that means the evaluation of efficiency will be poor, as a result of which the level of government subsidies will drop and the philharmonic will not even be able to show Rachmaninov's Second Piano Concerto. In other words, the contemporary system of administration of culture plunges academic arts into an insular, albeit beautiful, Rachmaninov circle, not demonstrating either systemic support or systemic pressure.

After the active growth of the 2000s, when opera theaters began to noticeably broaden their repertoires and the possibilities for interpreting the works (complex conductor solutions, elegant musical interpretations, guest performers and producers), signs of stagnation are now noticeable.

Accountability demands an increase in the number of philharmonic concerts at the same time as the repertoire options are narrowing. Even with the development of inter-regional contacts and skills in touring, some places have seen a notable decrease in the number of musicians participating in tours. Forced to earn for themselves, philharmonics compete for the right to invite those artists capable of filling halls—and that is a limited circle of television stars: Matsuyev, Repin, Gergiev, Bashmet, Spivakov. Over the course of one season, the only competition that they have are the laureates of the most recent Tchaikovsky competition, and the latter are taken as a group. It is interesting that philharmonics are capable of providing huge honorariums to such performers, given that the expenses for the concert and the income from ticket sales appear on different lines in accounting reports and are summarized as points in a system of criteria for effectiveness. As a result, a small philharmonic can do nothing more than fill in the lines for the number of concerts with a non-stop rollout of a single program by the Cossack choir on staff around the various houses of culture in the region, and then pay a big star once and rake in a good amount from that.

Though some production decisions in opera and ballet are beautiful, the long-term repertoire plans are being cut back at theaters. For example, in the vigorously developing Yekaterinburg Opera Theater, which has staged some striking premieres in recent years, there is only evidence of one new opera-related development for next season (albeit a significant one): the world premiere of Mieczysław Weinberg's "The Passenger," a legendary score dedicated to the theme of the Holocaust. But the project began some years ago, and it is already unclear what sort of artistic breakthroughs the theater will see from this point on.

One of the main arguments made by proponents of cultural reform is the Law on Patronage. However, the long-awaited document was passed in a truncated form. It contains a licensing part, but no incentivizing part: the principle of preferential taxation for sponsors did not actually make it in, since to achieve that, it would be necessary to introduce changes to the tax code. As a result, spheres of cultural activity that count on private investment (modern dance, new music, chamber festivals, etc.) are limited in their possibilities, exist without rehearsal venues, or are unique examples of success outside the system. One such example is the private "Kolyada Theater" in Yekaterinburg, which exists on the copyright royalties received by its artistic director for plays that are put on across the country. In Perm, a private philharmonic, "Triumph," is opening, and the modern dance troupes of Olga Pona and Tatyana Baganova are being replicated and adapted to state theaters. In the meantime, private festivals (like the Levitan Festival in Plyos, an intellectually refined and programmatically elegant festival the renewal of which for next season is already uncertain) are all under threat of reformatting: philanthropists and sponsors are too dependent on governors, and those governors may have their own artistic aspirations. And in the event of a difference of politics between the program facilitators and the governors, the difference in artistic positions becomes especially stark.

Outside the System

The general cutbacks to financing are making themselves known. To take one example, the recently built Astrakhan Opera Theater, grandiose in both look and equipment, lost one hundred percent of financing for new productions in 2016. But the consequences of the rapid growth, literally a boom in the area of academic music and opera, are still palpable, and in certain places oases of flickering state support for academic culture can still be found. Along with the Yekaterinburg Theater and Philharmonic, which have come to an arrangement with local authorities, or the Perm Opera Theater, which, conversely, lost part of its funding but has managed to remain afloat, and a few other sanctuaries, one of the brightest examples is the State Academic Symphonic Orchestra of the Tatarstan Republic. The orchestra functions under the personal guardianship of the head of the republic, and in a few short years, its new artistic director, Aleksander Sladkovsky, has managed to achieve an orchestra and programs that are fully capable of competing with many of the orchestras in the capital. But neither the model "favorite toy of the governor," nor the plan "we play Rachmaninov better than everyone, but every day without weekends or holidays," nor the principle "we put on shows that become artistic events of global significance on major world record labels, we have become a major brand, the locals don't count, and to remove us would be a great risk to anyone's reputation" can replace systemic solutions.

In a situation that is reminiscent of, as they say in the provinces, a combination of a collective farm and economic accountability (an enterprise is in the hands of the government and is required to provide work for the staff and a certain number of shows and concerts per year, all while earning its own keep), public figures in the arts do not expect any swift results from reforms, such as growth in the popularity of domestic classics or increased interest in culture in general on the part of the population.

The best, most complex, freshest, most unconventional things almost always find their place outside the system. For example, the orchestra "Performance" — which just received a "Mask" award for a rearrangement show of the constructivist music of the early Soviet avant garde — collected money on Planeta.org for the restoration of museum instruments for its show in order to compete for a Mask award. The "Vozvrashchenie" [Return] festival is the best chamber music festival in Russia, one that would be a credit to any European city, with a twenty-year history, yearly world premieres, intellectually composed programs, and phenomenal music performance quality, and it exists without patronage or a rehearsal space, regularly playing premieres and making sure to have performances not only at modernist festivals, but in the opera calendar as well: it is simply impossible to premiere a complex modern opera like those that have recently taken place without it. The composition academy in the city of Tchaikovsky (in the Perm krai, project on the level of European analogues in both teaching and performance) is also successful outside the system, as are nearly all exploratory practices in the area of academic music. Among other premieres, there is the composition competition for the creation of a ballet for the one-hundredth anniversary of the Likhachev Auto Factory, with a prize of five hundred thousand rubles and a theme of Russian constructivism that was announced in the framework of the competition. The auto factory itself has nothing to do with the competition; the Cultural Center ZIL (an independent enterprise not directly connected with the factory) is responsible for ordering the music and the show with rather *Kulturträger* goals. Here, repertoire breakthroughs in opera can be noted, such as "The Passenger" in Yekaterinburg or, also there, the sensational Russian premiere of the opera of a classic of American minimalism of the twentieth century, Philip Glass's "Satyagraha," on the theme of nonviolent civil resistance. None of them are the result of any kind of state program to support a search for new repertoires, but the consequence of non-systemic enlightening efforts by individuals. The premiere of "The Passenger," which the entire musical world is looking forward to in September (Weinberg posthumously became one of the most performed composers in Europe), was conceived with the participation of critic Andrei Ustinov, and in the case of "Satyagraha," minimalism and India (the main hero of the opera is Mahatma Gandhi) had been interests of theater director Andre Shishkin since his youth.

But if a couple of years ago it seemed that the efforts of individuals and non-systemic innovations were influencing the modernization of the system, there is now noticeable apathy in the field. The cultural situation is increasingly frozen. Signs of stagnation are noticeable both in the capitals and in the provinces. The menu of repertoire from which symphony orchestras can choose is decreasing, the long-term plans of opera theaters are growing poorer, the list of names of performers whose concerts the philharmonics can justify organizing is growing shorter, the number of tours by foreign performers is being minimized, and the programs of festivals are being deformed.

It is interesting that at the same time, the dissatisfied are disappearing from the ranks of cultural administrators. The economic crisis is broadening, and it seems logical that there would be massive cutbacks in financing provided to cultural institutions that are under the oversight of both federal and regional bureaucratic structures.

Paradoxically, directors of theaters and philharmonics are no longer talking about lack of attention from the state, lack of financing, or even unfair distribution of resources, as they had been not long ago when the system of grand supplements gave the main orchestras and theaters a chance for an expressive life and the rest had to envy and waste time searching for local-level patronage that did not at all compare with the support given by the center. There were, of course, exceptions: with financing amounting to 32 percent of the regional budget, the Perm Opera created over several years dozens of shows of global significance and became the center of refined innovation in academism, while developing such mechanisms for the education and attraction of the public as are absent not only in the provinces, but also in the capital. But the model of the Perm Opera included relying on the strength of guest performers. And it proved impossible to create a convincing plan according to which the theater would function both as a provincial one and an international one at the same time—far from a trivial task. The lack of balance between guest and local performance strength was reflected in the size of their salaries, and that always provoked great opposition and in the end resulted in cutbacks to regional government support.

One way or another, the theme of unfairness in the cultural narrative of leadership is no more, since the distribution itself is being cut back. In part, such resignation stems from the fact that keen attention from the state in the cultural sphere has led to some large problems over the course of recent seasons. All it takes is for the state to notice what exactly a theater is staging and, most importantly, how the public is talking about it, and then you can expect disaster.

It is characteristic that behind every scandal in which public outrage acts as an instrument for aesthetic censorship, there is some sort of administrative intrigue. In 2012, American director Christopher Alden's production of Benjamin Britten's "A Midsummer Night's Dream" provoked audience dissatisfaction (in the form of a letter supposedly signed by a disgruntled mother of a child from the children's choir of the theater, though neither the mother herself nor her child were ever found). The Stanislavsky and Nemirovich-Danchenko Theater is under the auspices of the city of Moscow; the theater supposes that the letter appeared as a result of internal intrigue and was directed against the leadership of the theater. That conflict was extinguished by Sergei Kapkov.

Those responsible for searching out reasons for moral danger in the show "Ruslan and Liudmila" by Dmitri Chernyakov at the Bolshoi were trying to remove theater director Iksanov (many believe that Vladimir Kekhman, who replaced the fired Mezdrich as head of the Novosibirsk Opera Theater, had a hand in the attacks on Iksanov). However, Ikanov managed to defend himself for a time: he was sent into retirement later, not in the wake of the scandal, so it is formally impossible to say that it happened due to concrete incorrect repertoire decisions. But the campaign against Tannhäuser had already met with success and scared many people.

In not resenting the lack of financing and accepting reality as it is, regional institutions today demonstrate panicked anticipation of utter homelessness. It seems that just a bit more, and the state will leave the academic philharmonics and theaters alone with the people, who are subjected to ever-increasing government propaganda in the spirit of anti-enlightenment. It is precisely with the complete synchronization of state assignments, volume of financing, and simplification of audience demands that are formed not by art but directly through state ideology—a request it does not behoove art to simply follow—that the main expectations of the cultural sphere are connected. And they are not rosy.

"Russia, Don't Tear Your Soul to Pieces: I'm the Same as You"

Alexander Gorbachev

Mainstream Russian hip hop interacts with politics principally through its rejection of it, which involves a conscious alienation from social and daily news, as well as a relationship to the government that treats it as something profoundly external.

A crowd of inspired young people—garbed in colorful hoodies, jean jackets, black glasses, and other attire marking people who have freed themselves from the travails of hard economic times—jump in unison to a wild beat, surrounded by dingy city walls. A mobile stage appears from somewhere, and on it are three young men who look markedly anti-Soviet, sporting leather jackets and Mohawks or tousled hair. They are rapping, addressing the public: "You should decide everything to get rid of the problems / Who can give you freedom, and who can take it from you / Dot all the i's cause it's time for you to choose." In the background, artists paint graffiti: the Russian tricolor flag next to a portrait of the first president of Russia, Boris Yeltsin.

Thousands of musicians of all genres participated in the "Vote or Lose" campaign, which in 1996 used what were (for these towns) revolutionary political spin methods to get young people to come to the polls and vote for the future of Russia, in the person of its current present. But the hymn of the movement was entrusted not to distinguished artists, but to a raunchy rap trio called "Malchishnik," which specialized in tracks about sex that were unusually explicit for the period. At that time, Russian hip hop still seemed exotic and was considered the sound of a new time, the symbol of a Western cultural path down which, the song hinted, Russia would triumphantly set off under the president's leadership. In a curious paradox, the picture, aesthetics, and sound of "Vote or Lose" were all lifted from director Spike Lee's video for the Public Enemy song "Fight the Power," turning what was in the American context a harsh manifesto of opposition to power in the name of the oppressed African American population into a declaration of support for the direction of the government.

Three years later, some very different lines were heard on the channel MTV. The teenage Detsl in the song "Nadezhda na zavtra" (Hope for Tomorrow), along with his mentors Vlad Valov and Ligalaiz, new superstars of the genre who had been run up the flagpole by the channel, rapped:

> I only believe those who say and do. Who don't throw their words into the wind, follow their idea. I've never seen such politicians in all my years. I only see gossip and licentious snouts... They're the same old thugs, just now in power. I didn't go to vote, I know New Hitlers sit among them.

In the chorus, they stated clearly: "We are new people, Russia outside of politics." There are many myths surrounding this track: many people think that this was Detsl's producer and father Alexander Tolmatsky's way of responding to a government order, planting the idea in the head of young people that Vladimir Putin was not a politician, but someone who "says and does." The rapper himself claimed that the song was ordered by the Yabloko Party, though it is not quite clear precisely what they had to gain from it.

One way or another, the relationship to politics that was expressed in "Nadezhda na zavtra" soon spread everywhere: it was best to stay far away from all aspects of it, including the voting booth. These two opposing songs—which came out of what were, for the 1990s, rare displays of hip hop to a broad Russian audience—created the poles around which the genre would cluster in the future: the hard-fought fatalism of Russian rappers alternates with an activist message, without almost any shades of gray in between.

This collection of assertions does not pretend to be all-encompassing, not least due to the limitless material available. As things stand in 2016, hip hop is the most lively musical environment in Russia: it has its own industrial and informational infrastructure, only indirectly connected with traditional labels and media (the most important territory for hip hop has been the internet as a whole and the social media network VKontakte in particular); its own methods of building hierarchy and producing heroes; its own schools and traditions; its own internal slang; and its own chronology. Below, I will only talk about the most visible and, in my view, indicative manifestations of political consciousness in Russian-language hip hop, taking a broad understanding of the political as all that is in one way or another related to the interactions between a person and the state.

It is interesting to look at how politics manifests itself in rap from the socio-cultural point of view. A comparison of hip hop with chanson has become commonplace in social and political journalism, and generally not unconsciously. Like chanson, the primary function of hip hop is to describe daily life. On the one hand, the form lends itself to lifting reality into a higher, poetic realm; on the other, a more historically important category for rap is authenticity, the genuineness of the speaker and of the spoken. Thus, rap becomes an optimal way to translate homespun life "truths" of the new millennium, which from the point of view of language and theme are too broad for the chanson genre. Characteristically, the thematic evolution of Russian rap is in many ways similar to the development of chanson—from self-validation through street and criminal themes to broader and more everyday events, both emotional and social. Built on strict, conservative, traditional masculine values (strength, loyalty, family, Homeland with a capital H), cheap to produce, and appealing mainly to personal rather than collective experience, hip hop is good material for studying the Russian collective unconscious, as the "silent majority" — or at least its younger half — sees itself and the surrounding world.

The degree to which this material is representative is also supported by numbers—although the local music industry is stingy with them, there is decent access on the internet. For example, the public circle of one of the leading rap labels, "Gazgol'der," has a million and a half subscribers on VKontakte; the "Noize MC" vK page has over a million; and other leading representatives of the genre have similar numbers. For comparison, Zemfira, who is deservedly considered the most in-demand artist in the country, has only 300,000 subscribers. All the remaining statistics indicate the same impressive gap, which is not yet seen in the concert industry only because hip hop listeners (the majority of whom are young and not infrequently underage males) have a lower ability to purchase tickets than do rock listeners. Nevertheless, the rappers are gaining ground: in 2015, Basta was the first representative of the genre to fill the hall at the Moscow Olympic Stadium; new superstars of the subculture, like Oxxxymiron, regularly draw standing-room-only crowds at the largest venues.

In other words, Russian rap is in and of itself a kind of aesthetic sociology, and certain conclusions can be drawn about society from how it interprets this or other aspects of public life. Several years ago, Vasily Vakulenko, one of the most popular and productive Russian rappers, who performs under the name of Basta, told me in an interview, "The state should pay us a premium for being the mirror and monitoring system in the country."[1]

To put it very simply, within the general body of Russian rap texts, it is possible to detect three more or less distinct types of political interaction. I will examine each of these in turn.

Politics as Justice

One of the genre-defining songs for American hip hop was "Fuck the Police" by the Los Angeles group NWA, directed at the police as a repressive force that oppressed African Americans. Indeed, the entire fighting energy of the genre of gangster rap was born of the idea, not entirely without foundation, that a criminal career was the only possible social elevator for people with a certain skin color (interestingly, hip hop itself later became such an elevator, transforming into one of the most lucrative sectors of American pop culture, producing role models and fashion trends at industrial scale, and providing music that emanates from every other car). A difficult, if not outright hostile relationship with the law is the logical legacy of the genre, which was welcomed with open arms in Russia, where the police are also historically not well loved. In local hip hop, of course, the racial factor is absent, replaced by the cultural context

---

[1] "Gosudarstvo dolzhno nam priplachivat', Interview with Basta and Guf, Afisha. № 325. July 13, 2012, https://daily.afisha.ru/archive/volna/archive/basta-i-guf/.

of prison folk lyrics (yet another parallel with chanson). In addition, as in the US, rap as a lifestyle is often connected with the use—and not infrequently the sale—of illegal substances, which itself attracts a certain amount of criminal prosecution. For example, in the early 2000s, rap superstar Guf (legal name Aleskey Dolmatov), according to his own statements, spent a short period in prison for violating Article 228 (possession and distribution of narcotics), which is quite often mentioned in the texts of Russian rap. Last year, the staff of State Narcotics Control more than once arrested him and his colleagues after concerts in various cities across the Russian Federation. One of the most influential Russian underground rap groups, Kunteynir, was forced to cease creative work after its leader was imprisoned for four years under the same article. Already this year, members of "Rynochnie otnosheniya" (Market Relations) have been arrested for possession of 18 kilos of hashish.

A chronicle of daily criminal life made up a significant portion of the Russian rap mainstream in the early days—the early and mid-2000s—and continues to be a notable theme. Some ensembles built their image entirely on crime (for example, the Stavropol group "Krestnaya sem'ya," while others approached it from a comical-postmodern position (for example, Noggano or the group "Krovostok"). Moreover, it is possible to say that it is one of the primary plots of the genre. In the 1990s, during the earliest stages of development of Russian rap, one of the pioneers of Russian hip hop, the group Bad Balance, rapped the following in their album with the indicative title "Vishe zakona" (Above the Law): "There is fear on the street, cash in the restaurants, darkness in the hotels, people sit at home <... But the dear police are making a plan: where is your alibi, think one up yourself." As in many other texts of the same type, the self-definition and self-justification of the hero happens through the delegitimization of the law; the actions of the police are described as essentially unfair, thus sanctioning exit from the legal system. There are many examples of this implicit logic. In last year's "A.C.A.B.," Guf raps:

> I don't know any good trash [cops]. And I'm willing to bet that there are a million like me. Since we were raised by our neighborhood. Not to trust the

cops from childhood, Vovan, sorry. Vovan, you take the lead without doubt. But there will always be too little smoke for these blocks.

By Vovan, he obviously means Vladimir Putin, framing the latter as some kind of mob boss, the creator and arbiter of the system from which the hero wants to escape. In another text from Guf, the same paradigm of his relationship with the law is embodied in a still more concrete narrative: "People get two and a half for vacation. Somewhere in Mordovia the soft black bun. The newly-baked guy from SWAT. Just finished building his house in Barcelona."

Interaction with the law can be rhetorically colored in various ways. Sometimes it is a tragedy, as in Basta's song characteristically titled "Solntsa ne vidno" (Can't See the Sun): "For these hounds in blue we're nothing but rabble / And the choice isn't great — shut up or be killed." Sometimes it is open aggression, as in a composition attributed to the above-mentioned "Rynochnie otnosheniya": "How much blood of those close to me has been spilled. How many bucks taken from my pocket. I just want the trash cops to suck. In the burning sun and the pouring rain." Sometimes it is taunting satire, as in "Kuri bambuk" (Smoke Bamboo) from Noize MC (Ivan Alekseev), where the whole song is a monologue from the point of view of a member of law enforcement: "I was the stupidest kid in the class. My classmates didn't like me and that's why I dropped out ... What could be worse than skinheads and bulls? …. [not a hard] question: Me, only me, and one more time me." (*To comply with instructions from the Federal Supervision Agency for Television and Communications, we were forced to replace some words in the original text due to their obscene and expletive nature – Ed. Note*). Alekseev was sentenced in 2010 to ten days of administrative arrest after performing this song in Volgograd, as the court considered it to publicly debase police personnel.

It is important to note that in the last two cases, as in many others, there is no longer any context for criminal opposition. Specifically, in the passage from the "Rynochnie otnosheniya" song quoted above, the aggression against police officers ("I want the trash cops to suck...") comes not from personal experience of coming into contact with them, but from a general despair over police excesses. The nature of how Russian hip hop perceives the law can, of course, be linked both to gangster rap and to traditional criminal songs, but there is a decidedly negative relationship with and disregard for the law enforcement agencies: the sense is that the state is not protecting citizens, but rather is predominantly a source of threat and violence, such that the best strategy for interacting with them is to avoid all contact.

Politics as Routine

Precisely this strategy of existence *outside* politics defines another way of relating to the state that is widespread in Russian-language rap. Here it is possible to see the continuation and intensification of the logic of the above-quoted song "Nadezhda na zavtra," which, generally speaking, can seem paradoxical, especially the line "I didn't go to vote, I know: among them are new Hitlers" — really, why not vote and try to get someone else in office? Yet the refusal to participate in the election makes sense if we accept that the very procedure is part of a game that cannot be won. As Vasily Vakulenko said in our interview, "The fight against the system is already a system." Similar political behavior looks like a logical consequence of a silent social contract that, it is often believed, the Russian government agreed with the populace in the 2000s: in exchange for economic stability, the government received a mandate for an existence separate from the citizenry, while citizens were given the chance to live their lives without fear of state interference. Politics was essentially marginalized and stigmatized, driven from the public consciousness as something empty, dirty, and uninteresting.

Another factor in this stigmatization of the political in Russian popular culture is the memory of the perestroika boom of Soviet protest rock, which for a long time beat back any desire among the new generation of musicians to make frank statements or public messages (loosely, few wanted to be Shevchuk). Symptomatically, politics is just as absent from Russian indie culture, among young groups that try, in one way or another, to react to and engage with the newest international musical trends. The allergy to politics, making it taboo and suffering it like something deeply unfashionable and bad, is to a certain extent a matter of age — and of course, it also reflects the success of the state's efforts to edge the political out of the zone of the actual.

The formation of such an indifferent discourse is helped by the fact that small groups are inherent to hip hop (think "party scene" or "neighborhood"). Unlike in Russian rock, if the word "we" appears in rap, then it usually refers to a narrow circle of "ours" and hardly ever to society at large. It is precisely within these narrow circles and between them that hip hop's internal politics — with its own economy and system of loyalty and conflict — exists, compensating for the lack of politics in the broader sense of the word. The strategy of relations with the government becomes very simple: a more or less active refusal to interact, in contrast to a focus on their own mission, which exists apart from the current agenda.

In general, the idea of "doing your own thing," whether against social realities or in parallel, is quite widespread among Russian rappers. Take the example of "Pis'mo iz Rossii" (Letter from Russia), from the Urals group "Triagrutika":

> And it seems like my homeland: careful, vomit. Clever Mavrodi, stolen melody. On the street some strange kind of drugs are in style. Images of Volodya. Uproar among the people. But nevertheless, we will be in your city this Saturday, on a plane again. Coming right from the studio to the people to rap.

Or a recent track from the "Centr" group, "Porosya" (Piglet): "While you ... [use for sexual satisfaction] moms at the battle. Your country is... [roasted] on cash. We also stamp out our garden."[2] The track "Shtora" (Curtain) is likewise typical of the group: "It's a pun, a village of idiots. A parade of monsters, Cirque du Soleil. Through the cable a modern hole punch. Hammers the electorate of voters." Participation in the government's democratic system is seen as the result of brainwashing. In Basta's "Solntsa ne vidno" (the track that the musician usually refers to when he is asked why he does not

---

2   Here "battle" implies the hip hop rhetorical battle in which one of the most common insults used is chest-thumping about sexual interaction with the mother of the opponent.

write about the situation in the country), the same motif is present, though in a slightly more tragic light:

> Can't see a way out, I didn't go and vote. It's all the same to them what you swear on, the Constitution or the Bible. They shout about freedom at rallies. Looking at the country like a company, counting the profits... And so far carrot and stick, shoulder boards with a seal. Rap music that we are ready to answer for. And so far we haven't gone wild, gone for good. We sway to our own beat. That's right, chief.

It is worth noting that in this last quote, there is an obvious hint that all figures on the political field are equally corrupt, other, and uninteresting. As the group "Kaspiiskii gruz" sings, "I wish the thoughts in my head were smarter, guys / But I'm so dumb I should be elected deputy." Russian rap's everyday relationship to the state is most clearly revealed in such minor, ostensibly insignificant mentions of it.

Another quote from the group "Triagrutrika" perhaps best expresses the mild indifference typical of this discourse: "Moscow was burning sometime back in July. And while we were blowing, gran's house burned down. In the news fires, fires, fire. I shrugged my shoulders and said: I'm sorry." Here, the social agenda is analogized to the weather: it is impossible to affect the government, and that means that at most it is worth acknowledging.

In this regard, it is worth mentioning the song "Voprosy" (Questions), which now often draws attention to Timati, a rapper who has in recent years has become one of the most active supporters of the current regime in the artistic community (more on this later). "Questions" was written at the very beginning of Timati's career, in 2006, and at first it could truly almost be taken as a protest song: "Why is there no money in the provinces. And all the bucks go to Moscow? Why are we at war with Chechnya? Who is behind this campaign, I can't understand," and so on, referencing the injustices of the imprisonment of Khodorkovsky and of *dedovschina*[3] (we will leave aside the fact that at the moment that the song was written, there was no ongoing war with Chechnya). Nevertheless, any view of these issues as claims against the government breaks down

---

3 The practice of hazing new military recruits with cruel beatings—trans. note.

in the chorus: "How many questions, how many will there be. You can't understand Russia with your mind. Or measure it with a stick. Russia should be known and believed." In this way, there is an admission of problems, although this leads not to action, but to its own kind of informational fatalism.

Of course, such fatalism is usually voiced in a more expressive or even tortured way. In a sense, it is yet another variation on the widespread theory of the inescapability of Russia's historical fate. Almost along the lines of Dostoevsky, pain over this inevitability becomes the required companion of love for it, since the circumstances that cause this pain are inborn, unavoidable, and unremovable. The same Detsl who in 1999 rapped about Russia outside of politics now sings about something entirely different: "Difficult childhood, poor old age. Everything as it once was remains the same. Faces on the street, tired and wilted. Hungry faces, full men of the regime / In this country, nothing has changed."

Perhaps one of the most striking examples of such hard-fought fatalism is the Omsk group "25/17," the most colorful people in the populist *pochvennik* hip hop circles. Almost all of their album from last year, "Russkii podorozhnik" (Russian Plantain), talks in one way or another about the depth, complexity, and tragedy of Russian fate. In much rap, this is no longer the function of chanson, but of rock, with its inclination toward historiosophy and messianism; also typical in this sense are collaborations between "25/17" and Dmitry Revyakin from "Kalinov most" or Konstantin Kinchev from "Alisa." The apotheosis of the album is the track "Poslednii iz nas" (The Last of Us), in which they sing with complete ruthlessness about the characteristics of the Russian people: "We are a people bearing a religious mission. We are a people of conquerors. We will cut each other. And you will watch." A remark from the leader of "25/17," Andrey Bledny, in an interview with "Afisha" is telling:

> For people who believe, who are often called religious in Russia, the album was inspiring. They saw hope in it. For atheists and nominal believers, for those who don't go to church except on holidays, 'Russian Traveler' is

gloomy and bleak. It is possible that they are seeking happiness in the material world, where there is little to be had. Here there is war, disease, death, envy, hatred, and so on down the list.[4]

No less typical is a piece titled "Topory" (Hatchets) that did not make it onto the album (it is telling that the writer Zakhar Prilepin, a good friend and fan of the collective, appears in the music video for "Topory"): "They drink oil like blood, we drown in tears. In closed offices they wind the threads of fates. Those dissatisfied rot in jail. That's how it was, is, and will be." The recognition and acceptance of historical-ethnic trauma, emancipation from which comes to a certain extent from the state itself, becomes the first step to obtaining a political consciousness, even if that consciousness consists of admitting, making peace with, forgiving, and spiritually overcoming. But not necessarily. Somewhat later in "Topory," there appears the line, "But every Ivan has a hatchet in the garage"—and here we cross over to politics in its active form, as civic action.

Politics as Activism

Essentially, we are facing a paradox. On the one hand, hip hop is historically and genetically connected with social problems; as a genre that arose as the voice of the streets and belonged to the oppressed minority (or to those who felt oppressed), it made a political statement by definition. The current Russian reality, however you look at it, provides a huge number of reasons for such statements. On the other hand, the Russian rap mainstream is a rejection of the political, a conscious alienation of itself from the news and social agenda, and an attempt to exist outside of government concerns.

Yet Russian hip hop is multifaceted enough to encompass some notable figures whose image and reputation are largely built on the manifestation of one political belief or another.

---

4   "Andrey Bledny iz '25/17' o "Russkom podorozhnike", "Fizruke" i nacionalizme," Afisha—Volna, December 15, 2014, https://daily.afisha.ru/archive/volna/heroes/andrey-blednyy-iz-2517-o-russkom-podorozhnike-fizruke-i-nacionalizme/.

Right Rap

It is important to examine "Topory" in the context of the ideological trajectory of the "25/17" group. The song effectively provides a sarcastic answer to those who think of the group as supporting a radical right-wing worldview. You cannot call such a point of view entirely baseless: we know that representatives of right-wing movements did in fact love the group and attend their concerts at one point. The early repertoire of "25/17" includes such compositions as "Bud' belym-2" (Be white-2) ("And a white Russian teenager will never look like black-skinned bandits. Even if he spends all summer on the beach. Be yourself. Be white. Value that"), which also strengthens the hypothesis. But the ideology of "25/17" was always more complex than vulgar nationalism — it is instead the populist *pochvennik* movement, mixed with a kind of hard-won patriotism, conservative values, and Orthodox spirituality. Even in the composition mentioned above, the emphasis is on the fact that imitation of foreign hip hop is inappropriate, not on race.

Right rap is undoubtedly a phenomenon, however. Its dominant ideological features are a negative relationship to migrants; criticism of drunkenness, drug use, and other aspects of an unhealthy lifestyle; and opposition to the state, which (it claims) does not recognize the rights of Russians. Here we see a paradox: is it not strange to agitate for the white race within a framework invented and formed by the black race? Obviously, however, racial antagonism is far from the dominant theme for Russian nationalism; moreover, in this view African Americans and Russians are typologically similar, because both groups consider themselves the object of oppression, having had their basic rights and social identity taken away. In fact, Russian right rap specifically includes the need to cultivate this identity — mainly through physical training, and not infrequently through violence against "others" and the state. A characteristic example is a collaboration between "Grot" and "25/17" called "Sila soprotivleniya" (Strength of Resistance):

> Well, we're not to blame. Let's just pretend. That none of this exists. Or that it's really nothing to do with you... Maybe then it's not you that will be raped, cut. Mashas, Natashas, Lenas, Ivans and all the Vasyas ... Two-eight-

two for the self-protection of the ethnic group.[5] The system will start to tempt you, offer to sell itself. But you go and refuse, wreaking more havoc. Resistance is self-protection.

Another, still harsher theme can be seen in the "Tyazhkie telesnye" (Grave Bodily Injury) album by "Proyect Uvech'e" (Project Mutilation), which was released in 2011 during a particular historical peak of Russian nationalism — or at least of the social concern connected with it that was called forth by the Moscow nationalists' protests after the murder of Spartak fan Yegor Sviridov in December 2010. The track "Ne Frantsiya" (This Isn't France) explicitly links the anti-migrant and revolutionary narratives:

> They hoisted their totem right here, get it. Can't tell where you live — Istanbul or Beijing. They chafe on the TV... those kind have no faith. The stakes are high: either they will drown you, or you will do the drowning. Even schoolkids don't like babes that wear a hijab. Rap is not a genre, it's a protest, not shoved in a box ... The homeland will get up off her knees to throw off both ... Judgment day is right around the corner, fear doesn't hold you down...

The theme of unavoidable retaliation is still more clear in the composition "A.S.A.B.": "The last rays of the sunset will shine, the press will be left out of the shot. The anger of the people, showing how stupid another provocateur is. From a fire downtown, the suburbs outside the ring will flame up." It must be said, however, that a purely political narrative nevertheless occupies a less significant place in right rap than the narrative of values regarding ethnic Russians' rejection of the bad habits that are destroying it. As the group "Grot" sings: "Those who can't tell the difference between the Homeland and an outhouse. Will be reeducated or deported the ... [heck] out." Artist Misha Mavashi made his name on the propaganda of healthy lifestyle as the only way to raise up the country:

> The opinion of the yawners is this: they spit on all that is native. All the habits of stepping in ... [excrement] with bare feet. A Russian person is only associated with vodka. [Nothing] to do, except smoke up, pouring out swallows? ... Leave the protests to those who have plenty of time. They could give a ... [care] about our exhaling and inhaling ... I could care less about

---

5   This refers to Article 282 of the Legal Code of the Russian Federation — A.G.

their politics generally and in general. I'm for the human, you should remember!

Noteworthy in this case is the same explicit rejection of the political as a compromised arena that exists outside morals and generally outside the environment of the lyrical hero. Right rap is also interesting for its historical perspective. Some form of the genre undoubtedly exists to this day, but generally speaking, it's breakthrough into the hip hop mainstream coincided with the above-mentioned peak in the activity of Russian nationalists and came to an end in the late 2000s or early 2010s. All those right rap groups that made up the genre's avant garde are now disavowing such rhetoric, either like "25/17," which continues to make its ideology more nuanced, or like "Grot" and the leader of "Proyect Uvech'e," Luperkal' (who changed his name and now goes by Horus), who have shifted from social problematics to more abstract philosophical issues. Over the past five years, the government has been unable to suppress the activity not only of radical right political organizations, but also of their aesthetic cover.[6]

Patriotic rap

Picturesque smoke blankets Red Square; two bearded men in expensive leather jackets strike confident poses against a backdrop of the cupolas of St. Basil's Cathedral. A refrain sounds, "My best friend is President Putin," the first line of the first verse of the song "Moi beliy vladyka" (My White Lord). Released on October 6, 2015, the eve of Vladimir Putin's birthday, the joint video by Timati and newcomer Sasha Chest became the apotheosis of the pro-government discourse that Timati and, to a lesser degree, his colleagues on the Black Star label have been building over the past few years.

The song is telling in many respects. From his very first compositions, the main narrative of Timati's body of work has been a declaration of personal success and presentation of the material

---

[6] On the crisis of radical Russian nationalism, see Alexander Verkhovsky, "Natsional-radicaly ot prezidentstva Medvedeva do vojny na Donbasse" . Kontrapunkt №2 http://www.ponarseurasia.org/sites/default/files/documents/verkhovsky_counterpoint2.pdf

proof of that fact. It is hard not to consider it semiotic that whereas at the beginning of his career those proofs consisted of expensive goods, women, and clubs, the main evidence of his success is now the admiration of bureaucrats ("The main gentleman called me in for a visit. A train of black horses carries me to the White House. The president has my album playing in his office"). This is particularly true if you consider the broader cultural context: in choosing role models for himself, Timati clearly focuses on his American colleagues, not infrequently borrowing their music and even their texts. But if for the Americans the manifestations of being on the right path in life are mainly money and drugs, for Timati "reputational currency" has become connected with the government. In some sense, this substitution is not a bad description of the difference between the American and Russian versions of capitalism.

That being said, Timati's ideology is not altogether different from the principles voiced in right rap. For example, in his text, as in some from the "right," there is a line promoting a healthy lifestyle. However, for Timati, unlike in right rap, this is directly tied to love of the state, presumably one that is undergoing a period of rebirth. In some sense, political will and subjectivity can be obtained only within the government system of values, as shown in a text from the artist L'One, also with the Black Star label: "Love your country, not only when it's in bad shape. And take part always, don't pretend that you don't give a ... [care]." In Timati's vision, the general situation in the country corresponds with the one broadcast by official media outlets and looks something like this:

> Khorodorkovsky is free and it seems everyone has left from the Maidan. And we lost a brotherly people. Maybe for a long time, thanks to Obama! But the Russian man stood up and said—Enough! And the country believes him It won't be easy, but we will gather together. The shards of the Russian Empire. And you know, I get that besides showing off. There are things much more important: A healthy people, a clear goal. The strength of a national idea.

Later in the text of "I'll tell you in the end," there is a description of how the author beat up a seller who offered him drugs—behavior that would undoubtedly call forth sympathy from Misha

Mavashi and his associates. Pro-government hip hop is not exclusively the province of Timati and his team, but the rest of the examples are largely curiosities, like the son of the director of the Federation Foundation, Vladimir Kiselev, whose name is connected with a number of scandals.[7] Recently, Yuri Kiselev (pseudonym YurKiss) recorded an obsequious and not very skillful track "Letter to the President" (quote: "Comrade President, all my friends and I and even my girl don't need any changes. Dear President of mine, having lived 15 years with you. I sing this rap for you"; the remaining text demonstrates a similarly low level of poetry).

However, against the background of events of recent years and the Ukrainian crisis, some sharpening of the patriotic theme has nevertheless occurred—mainly along the lines of confrontation with representatives of the opposition. Judging by his songs, Ukraine native Tipsi Tip truly believes in the existence of the Dulles Plan, and mentioned the leader of the Russian opposition in an unfriendly way in one of his tracks: "Don't pile on, Navalny, don't worry the worrisome agency much, or you'll end up on the end of a fork, Navalny." The rapper Drago, of Ukrainian heritage, composed a song praising the Russian weapon "Babay" that is dedicated to one of the Donetsk People's Republic's militia leaders:

> The dogs wanted to set a course for Russia even. But it won't work, just like Napoleon, Hitler, and Conchita Wurst. And once more the rapid pulse, the taste of smoke from the powder. With a Babay you can't fail, it's a tough guy, I swear.

Lastly, the writer Zakhar Prilepin, who sometimes enters the territory of hip hop, joined with two rappers to record a track with an unambiguous refrain:

> It's time to shove off those who say 'Time to shove off,' time to forget those who forgot to shut their traps. Pragmatic vampires who are used to setting

---

[7] See, for example, A. Chernykh, O. Kashin, A. Voronov, " Vladimiru Putinu isportili pesnyu," Kommersant №39., March 9, 2011, http://www.kommersant.ru/doc/1597361.

aside. Everything that isn't about their own personal interests. People-subscribers, passive demons. It's time to be proud of what it's customary to be ashamed of.

Here, the question logically arises as to whether the above-described phenomena are evidence of a goal-oriented government policy aimed at coopting youth culture. This hypothesis appears to be reinforced by the fact that former Kremlin ideologue Vladislav Surkov was famous for his love of American hip hop in general and gangster rapper Tupac Shakur in particular. It is difficult to be certain: on the one hand, Timati really does have a friendship with Ramzan Kadyrov and was an authorized delegate of Vladimir Putin in the last presidential election; on the other, as we have already said, connections are a sort of reputational currency for this rapper that he himself is interested in accumulating even without the additional efforts of bureaucrats. On the whole, there is no sense that the government is currently seeking to control or curate Russian hip hop to any extent, which is logical enough: in the end, rap culture exists in a very specific media zone, control of which, it seems, is not a task of primary importance for the authorities.

In addition, it would be unfair to consider that patriotic hip hop can only be exclusively pro-government or anti-liberal. Rap from "25/17" is undoubtedly patriotic, though love is interwoven with unavoidable pain and the recognition of the heavy burden of one's own land (the group has a statement about Ukraine in "Rakhunok" (Score), a cathartic track on the fratricidal war that mentions "commandant Yarosha"). In general, the theme of love for the homeland despite its tortuous nature is a leitmotif of Russian hip hop just as it is of Russian rock. One of the classic tracks of Russian rap, in its own way genre-defining, is "Na poryadok vyshe" (Next-Higher Order), from the Rostov group "Kasta," which is structured as a conversation with a potential emigrant and speaks directly to this:

> What, you want to eat till you're full? You want to sleep soundly? Then what the ... [heck] are you thinking, it's long time to split. It's just that I've seen those rough faces, you will wither up there. And if you look inside, you'll

die from nostalgia. It's empty there, and you're a bro—Russian. That's important for you, and the ... with the rest. Understand this ardent confession, sincere sincerity. The soul at sunset is like a pure drop of vodka.

And further: "Russia, don't tear your soul to shreds. I'm the same as you, and on that it ends."

Protest Rap

The above-mentioned stigmatization of the political in Russian popular culture related to protest songs to an even greater degree than the rest. They are often deliberately perceived, by the artists themselves as well as their audiences, as the sort of commonplace banality that is beyond the limits of aesthetics. It is unsurprising that the gravity of this kind of protest rap in Russia is not great, and fairly often it is seen as sporadic statements rather than an entire creative strategy. Among compositions of this type it is possible to note, say, Perm rapper-conceptualist Syava's track in support of Pussy Riot ("What's with all the chumminess. Serve time for sacrilege. When girls are singing against the kingdom of the devil") or a birthday greeting for Vladimir Putin composed in 2011 by the artist Khaski, who would go on to write "Pora valit" (Time to Get Lost) with Prilepin:

> Sniffs with rejection, the womb stuffed with carrion. Teddy bear Medvedev, deceased by the throne. The keeper of the crown, favorite of the tsar. And oppressor of the people. But Caesar is pleased that he commanded all these swine. With all of this ... That the miners are still digging up. Everything will be great.

It is noteworthy, however, that in the last case the political statement exists in the mode of allegory and not open advocacy. Open advocacy had its place in the RapInfo project conducted by the editorial offices of RIA Novosti in conjunction with Moscow rappers Dino MC47 and ST (neither are first-tier stars, but nor are they outsiders) in fall 2011. Every few weeks, the two MCs, sometimes joined by guests, would retell the recent news, from Vladimir Putin's divorce to the Universiade in Kazan, in the form of hip hop, not shying away from difficult topics like the Bolotnaya affair or the trial of Aleksey Navalny. Strictly speaking, this is more a kind of infotainment than a strictly musical project, something in between rap and journalism. One way or another, the tone of RapInfo was mostly restrained, and only in extreme cases sarcastic ("It's a strange regime they have there in the USA. That each time they go to the polls, there's a new candidate"), due in all likelihood to the fact that RIA Novosti is the main state information agency. At the end of December 2014, when RIA was remade into MIA "Russia Today," the hip hop project also came to an end. During its existence, the "news" clips received more than 13 million views on YouTube, which is not few, but also not a very high number for Russian rap: Timati's Baklazhan (Eggplant) got 73 million, while an average video from Basta receives no less than two million on its own.

It is typical that those representatives of hip hop that are the most deliberate and open in their political statements are almost always a little (and sometimes entirely) foreign to the rap community. We already spoke about "25/17," who relate to other rappers with skepticism but collaborate with rock musicians. The musician Vasya Oblomov, who performed the tragi-comic couplets about the horrors of the Russian social sphere and who nominally also performs hip hop — that is, music based on rapping to a beat — falls entirely outside the rap context from any point of view, be it media or audience. He is closer to the entertaining opposition advocacy, along the lines of the "Mr. Good" project from Dmitry Bykov and Mikhail Yefremov.

Ivan Alekseev, aka Noize MC, is the person who is perhaps most steadily associated with opposition hip hop by the public at large, yet he also has a borderline status in this regard. He is undoubtedly one of the most popular and in-demand Russian rappers; at the same time, there is much that pushes him closer to a rock context, be it his sound, his social network, or the venues where his songs are played (Noize can often be heard on "Nashe Radio" radio station). And it is curious that the vast majority of Alekseev's most resonant statements are answers to external political stimuli. The raucous track "Mercedes S666," which accuses public officials and top managers of state corporations of being unaccountable, was precipitated by DTP with the participation of the Vice

President of Lukoil, Anatoly Barkov, and friends of Alekseev. The track "10 sutok v rayu" (10 Days in Heaven), which is a sarcastic story of the spurious benefits of the Russian penal system, was the result of his above-mentioned jail term in Volgograd. The sharply anti-clerical piece "Vo imya otsa" (In the Name of the Father) was inspired by the Pussy Riot affair. And so on.

Thus, in a significant number of cases, the political exists for Alekseev in the paradigm of reaction, counteracting. In this sense, the rapper is similar to the Russian opposition, which also has certain problems with a positive narrative. Nevertheless, songs with social criticism and political messages do not appear from Noize without reason, whether it is "Vliyatel'nye pokroviteli" (Influential Benefactors) or "Temnuyu storonu sily" (The Dark Side of Strength) on the corruption of means of social mobility ("I really value freedom of speech and freedom of will. I live in a free country... [what of it?] I'm happy the world is harmonious, just, simply wonderful. When you have an influential backer behind you") or "Goi esi" (God Be With You) on the church as a business corporation ("God be with you, Noize MC, praise throughout Rus'. Talk crazy, howl and spend a wad of cash") or the anti-military "Na Marse klassno" (It's Cool on Mars) or the harshly anti-fascist manifesto "Edem 14/88." It is also impossible not to mention one interesting circumstance: almost all of the compositions listed here exist in a paradigm of role play, where the author, exposing the absurdity and depravity of a given social practice, performs from the point of view of the subject of these practices. This exclusive inclination toward sarcasm and relating to the political as invariably ludicrous could be written off as the character of the author, but there is no shortage of serious texts about love or family in Alekseev's repertoire either. Obviously, carnivalization here becomes a means for overcoming the stigma inherent in the topic. In other words, politics is too unpleasant a matter to be taken seriously.

In rare cooperation with rap artists, it must be said that the state willingly demonstrates its unpleasant character. In the direct political sense, it is Noize MC who has suffered most of all. In 2014, performing at the Kubana Festival in Krasnodar, the rapper informed the audience that he had been in Lvov and seen fascists there. Alekseev's microphone was cut off; in an act of protest, a short time later he came out onto the stage during the performance of another friendly group completely naked. Soon after that, the Communist Party of the Russian Federation suggested banning performances by Alekseev (and Andrey Makarevich) in Russia all together, and in the middle of the group's Fall tour of Russia, several concerts were unexpectedly canceled. Still later, the Kubana Festival had to relocate to the Baltics. Of course, it is hardly the case that instructions from the Kremlin had anything to do with this; rather, local officials and organizers were reacting to the general emotional mood surrounding the conflict in Ukraine. Nevertheless, the situation is telling and in many ways unique—more often, interactions between the state and rappers are a result of the enforcement of Article 228. This, too, can take on an ideological overtone: the campaign against Guf was headed by LDPR Duma deputy and leader of the "Anti-dealer" movement Dmitry Nosov, who accused the rapper of promoting narcotics among underage people. But here it is possible to speak of an exception more than a rule, especially considering how widespread songs about illegal substances are in Russian hip hop. Here another rhyme comes up: selectivity regarding the prosecution of rappers is like the way that, unsystematically but persistently, the state wages its fight against opponents in the political field.[8]

The end of 2015 became, to a significant degree, a turning point for Russian hip hop. Undoubtedly, by that time rap had already taken shape in mass culture and created a full-fledged industry. However, two records released almost simultaneously raised the creative stakes, proposing new and much more complex, engaging, and independent types of sounds and narratives. And if Skriptonite's "Dom s normal'nymi yavleniyami" (House with Normal Ways), which is something of a psychedelic chronicle of alcoholic and emotional delirium, is important from the point of view of music and language, then Oxxxymiron's "Gorgorod" (Citcity)

---

8   See the ideas of Gleb Pavlovsky on the essential unpredictability of the so-called "'Systema.rf'": Zhizn' posle Sochi. Vlast'. Afisha. №362, http://mag.afisha.ru/stories/zhizn-posle-sochi/vlast-gleb-pavlovskiy/.

can be interpreted as a breakthrough in the realm of political statements.

Having spent his childhood in Germany and studied at Oxford, Oxxxymiron (legally, Miron Fyodorov) is a rare kind of musician in Russia, as successful with the elite audience, by which I mean critics and public intellectuals, as he is with the masses. First, he made people respect him for his education and exceptional rap technique, and second, because cultural erudition does not interfere with drive, aggressive charisma, or trustworthy conversation about what is important, the result is box office success even at some of the largest venues in the country. Having grown up on rapid-fire English grime with its fixation on alliteration and multi-tiered rhymes, Fyodorov himself builds impressive phonetic numbers, turning to the least obvious sources (like Blavatskaya and Lautreamont) and using word combinations that are a kind of "change of paradigm." Purely linguistically, he seriously raised the bar for his rivals even in his early songs; in this sense, Gorgorod is the next step, because here, aside from his own language, Oxxxymiron is creating his own macrocosm.

Formally, Gorgorod is a conceptual album about how the writer, somewhat too big for his britches and living in an invented city-state, became entangled in a scheme. The story is told in part through the songs themselves and in part through cutaways that are presented as calls from a literary agent. Trying unsuccessfully to finish writing yet another text for a deadline and burning the candle at both ends, the main hero falls in love with a girl he met at a party honoring the town's mayor, and she opens up to him an underground political world prepared to rise up against the repressive authorities. This allegorical frame is extremely typical. As it is presented, it performs a dual carnivalizing function, simultaneously diverting the listeners (the album is disguised as a non-current statement) and engaging them (understanding the tricky gossip requires a separate effort from the audience to delve into the texts). In essence, then, Gorgorod is an array of comments on the most burning issues of the day, a newsreel of self-cannibalism by a creative person who finds himself a public figure in a space of lethal symbolic conflict where he does not want to belong to either side.

There is a track on the value-based responsibilities of the poet ("Why, when walls are growing here, are prisoners dying. Sentenced for a couple of caricatures of the mayor, they lie blindly. And for you it's suddenly taboo to reflect back society to itself. Are you a coward or have you just caved in ... [pretty much]?") and there is a track about how, in a reality where all institutions are compromised, those responsibilities lose meaning ("If the authorities are a bunch of clowns, and fighting them is gibberish, [why] should I work and sweat?"). There is a manifesto of revolution ("If we're lucky, the garrison will be broken and taken. The Rubicon crossed, the clock run down. You will read all about it in the news") and there is a monologue from a representative of the authorities that presents an argument in favor of an authoritarian consumer society:

> What will happen if I leave? Neighboring towns, having cleared out their despots, suffer and die. For comparison here. Mountain air, sport and health, resort. A gaming house, a house of trade, a food court... My people don't want reform when they've been fed again.

In essence, the entire album is a many-branched tree of commentary made to himself. Thanks to this narrative structure, Oxxxymiron manages to absorb and rework the entire spectrum of political meanings that traditionally existed in Russian rap: he raps for the patriots and for the opposition; for the fatalists and for the rebels. At the same time, the author himself is not above the fray, but in the midst of it, and takes hits from both sides (or, rather, fights for each of them): "Some think that I'm super ... [cunning]. Others see in me the naive world of games and books. Understand this: I'm a hybrid, I grew up both one way and the other." The result of this multi-layered internal discussion becomes the principal lack of result; the paradox of this reality is exactly its eternal polyvalence, in that it raises objections to its every argument. Insofar as there is no exit from this crazy infinity and none in sight, language becomes the only optic that allows a view of the whole picture, or at least the only way to ask the right question. "Your city—it was also a lampoon. You would swim away, but it's not right over there. And you along the way really landed in it. Gorgorod, Gorgorod—home, but a steep trap."

Gorgorod is a surprising example of a very personal and very directly political statement, the author of which (fairly successfully) avoids with all his might both directness and personalization. In principle, it is from this recording that it makes sense to become acquainted with the political consciousness of Russian hip hop. In essence, it is possible to end with it as well.

SOVIET AND POST-SOVIET POLITICS AND SOCIETY
Edited by Dr. Andreas Umland | ISSN 1614-3515

1   *Андреас Умланд (ред.)* | Воплощение Европейской конвенции по правам человека в России. Философские, юридические и эмпирические исследования | ISBN 3-89821-387-0

2   *Christian Wipperfürth* | Russland – ein vertrauenswürdiger Partner? Grundlagen, Hintergründe und Praxis gegenwärtiger russischer Außenpolitik | Mit einem Vorwort von Heinz Timmermann | ISBN 3-89821-401-X

3   *Manja Hussner* | Die Übernahme internationalen Rechts in die russische und deutsche Rechtsordnung. Eine vergleichende Analyse zur Völkerrechtsfreundlichkeit der Verfassungen der Russländischen Föderation und der Bundesrepublik Deutschland | Mit einem Vorwort von Rainer Arnold | ISBN 3-89821-438-9

4   *Matthew Tejada* | Bulgaria's Democratic Consolidation and the Kozloduy Nuclear Power Plant (KNPP). The Unattainability of Closure | With a foreword by Richard J. Crampton | ISBN 3-89821-439-7

5   *Марк Григорьевич Меерович* | Квадратные метры, определяющие сознание. Государственная жилищная политика в СССР. 1921 – 1941 гг | ISBN 3-89821-474-5

6   *Andrei P. Tsygankov, Pavel A. Tsygankov (Eds.)* | New Directions in Russian International Studies | ISBN 3-89821-422-2

7   *Марк Григорьевич Меерович* | Как власть народ к труду приучала. Жилище в СССР – средство управления людьми. 1917 – 1941 гг. | С предисловием Елены Осокиной | ISBN 3-89821-495-8

8   *David J. Galbreath* | Nation-Building and Minority Politics in Post-Socialist States. Interests, Influence and Identities in Estonia and Latvia | With a foreword by David J. Smith | ISBN 3-89821-467-2

9   *Алексей Юрьевич Безугольный* | Народы Кавказа в Вооруженных силах СССР в годы Великой Отечественной войны 1941-1945 гг. | С предисловием Николая Бугая | ISBN 3-89821-475-3

10 *Вячеслав Лихачев и Владимир Прибыловский (ред.)* | Русское Национальное Единство, 1990-2000. В 2-х томах | ISBN 3-89821-523-7

11 *Николай Бугай (ред.)* | Народы стран Балтии в условиях сталинизма (1940-е – 1950-е годы). Документированная история | ISBN 3-89821-525-3

12 *Ingmar Bredies (Hrsg.)* | Zur Anatomie der Orange Revolution in der Ukraine. Wechsel des Elitenregimes oder Triumph des Parlamentarismus? | ISBN 3-89821-524-5

13 *Anastasia V. Mitrofanova* | The Politicization of Russian Orthodoxy. Actors and Ideas | With a foreword by William C. Gay | ISBN 3-89821-481-8

14 *Nathan D. Larson* | Alexander Solzhenitsyn and the Russo-Jewish Question | ISBN 3-89821-483-4

15 *Guido Houben* | Kulturpolitik und Ethnizität. Staatliche Kunstförderung im Russland der neunziger Jahre | Mit einem Vorwort von Gert Weisskirchen | ISBN 3-89821-542-3

16 *Leonid Luks* | Der russische „Sonderweg"? Aufsätze zur neuesten Geschichte Russlands im europäischen Kontext | ISBN 3-89821-496-6

17 *Евгений Мороз* | История «Мёртвой воды» – от страшной сказки к большой политике. Политическое неоязычество в постсоветской России | ISBN 3-89821-551-2

18 *Александр Верховский и Галина Кожевникова (ред.)* | Этническая и религиозная интолерантность в российских СМИ. Результаты мониторинга 2001-2004 гг. | ISBN 3-89821-569-5

19 *Christian Ganzer* | Sowjetisches Erbe und ukrainische Nation. Das Museum der Geschichte des Zaporoger Kosakentums auf der Insel Chortycja | Mit einem Vorwort von Frank Golczewski | ISBN 3-89821-504-0

20 *Эльза-Баир Гучинова* | Помнить нельзя забыть. Антропология депортационной травмы калмыков | С предисловием Кэролайн Хамфри | ISBN 3-89821-506-7

21 *Юлия Лидерман* | Мотивы «проверки» и «испытания» в постсоветской культуре. Советское прошлое в российском кинематографе 1990-х годов | С предисловием Евгения Марголита | ISBN 3-89821-511-3

22 *Tanya Lokshina, Ray Thomas, Mary Mayer (Eds.)* | The Imposition of a Fake Political Settlement in the Northern Caucasus. The 2003 Chechen Presidential Election | ISBN 3-89821-436-2

23 *Timothy McCajor Hall, Rosie Read (Eds.)* | Changes in the Heart of Europe. Recent Ethnographies of Czechs, Slovaks, Roma, and Sorbs | With an afterword by Zdeněk Salzmann | ISBN 3-89821-606-3

24 *Christian Autengruber* | Die politischen Parteien in Bulgarien und Rumänien. Eine vergleichende Analyse seit Beginn der 90er Jahre | Mit einem Vorwort von Dorothée de Nève | ISBN 3-89821-476-1

25 *Annette Freyberg-Inan with Radu Cristescu* | The Ghosts in Our Classrooms, or: John Dewey Meets Ceauşescu. The Promise and the Failures of Civic Education in Romania | ISBN 3-89821-416-8

26 *John B. Dunlop* | The 2002 Dubrovka and 2004 Beslan Hostage Crises. A Critique of Russian Counter-Terrorism | With a foreword by Donald N. Jensen | ISBN 3-89821-608-X

27 *Peter Koller* | Das touristische Potenzial von Kam"janec'–Podil's'kyj. Eine fremdenverkehrsgeographische Untersuchung der Zukunftsperspektiven und Maßnahmenplanung zur Destinationsentwicklung des „ukrainischen Rothenburg" | Mit einem Vorwort von Kristiane Klemm | ISBN 3-89821-640-3

28 *Françoise Daucé, Elisabeth Sieca-Kozlowski (Eds.)* | Dedovshchina in the Post-Soviet Military. Hazing of Russian Army Conscripts in a Comparative Perspective | With a foreword by Dale Herspring | ISBN 3-89821-616-0

29 *Florian Strasser* | Zivilgesellschaftliche Einflüsse auf die Orange Revolution. Die gewaltlose Massenbewegung und die ukrainische Wahlkrise 2004 | Mit einem Vorwort von Egbert Jahn | ISBN 3-89821-648-9

30 *Rebecca S. Katz* | The Georgian Regime Crisis of 2003-2004. A Case Study in Post-Soviet Media Representation of Politics, Crime and Corruption | ISBN 3-89821-413-3

31 *Vladimir Kantor* | Willkür oder Freiheit. Beiträge zur russischen Geschichtsphilosophie | Ediert von Dagmar Herrmann sowie mit einem Vorwort versehen von Leonid Luks | ISBN 3-89821-589-X

32 *Laura A. Victoir* | The Russian Land Estate Today. A Case Study of Cultural Politics in Post-Soviet Russia | With a foreword by Priscilla Roosevelt | ISBN 3-89821-426-5

33 *Ivan Katchanovski* | Cleft Countries. Regional Political Divisions and Cultures in Post-Soviet Ukraine and Moldova| With a foreword by Francis Fukuyama | ISBN 3-89821-558-X

34 *Florian Mühlfried* | Postsowjetische Feiern. Das Georgische Bankett im Wandel | Mit einem Vorwort von Kevin Tuite | ISBN 3-89821-601-2

35 *Roger Griffin, Werner Loh, Andreas Umland (Eds.)* | Fascism Past and Present, West and East. An International Debate on Concepts and Cases in the Comparative Study of the Extreme Right | With an afterword by Walter Laqueur | ISBN 3-89821-674-8

36 *Sebastian Schlegel* | Der „Weiße Archipel". Sowjetische Atomstädte 1945-1991 | Mit einem Geleitwort von Thomas Bohn | ISBN 3-89821-679-9

37 *Vyacheslav Likhachev* | Political Anti-Semitism in Post-Soviet Russia. Actors and Ideas in 1991-2003 | Edited and translated from Russian by Eugene Veklerov | ISBN 3-89821-529-6

38 *Josette Baer (Ed.)* | Preparing Liberty in Central Europe. Political Texts from the Spring of Nations 1848 to the Spring of Prague 1968 | With a foreword by Zdeněk V. David | ISBN 3-89821-546-6

39 *Михаил Лукьянов* | Российский консерватизм и реформа, 1907-1914 | С предисловием Марка Д. Стейнберга | ISBN 3-89821-503-2

40 *Nicola Melloni* | Market Without Economy. The 1998 Russian Financial Crisis | With a foreword by Eiji Furukawa | ISBN 3-89821-407-9

41 *Dmitrij Chmelnizki* | Die Architektur Stalins | Bd. 1: Studien zu Ideologie und Stil | Bd. 2: Bilddokumentation | Mit einem Vorwort von Bruno Flierl | ISBN 3-89821-515-6

42 *Katja Yafimava* | Post-Soviet Russian-Belarussian Relationships. The Role of Gas Transit Pipelines | With a foreword by Jonathan P. Stern | ISBN 3-89821-655-1

43 *Boris Chavkin* | Verflechtungen der deutschen und russischen Zeitgeschichte. Aufsätze und Archivfunde zu den Beziehungen Deutschlands und der Sowjetunion von 1917 bis 1991 | Ediert von Markus Edlinger sowie mit einem Vorwort versehen von Leonid Luks | ISBN 3-89821-756-4

44 *Anastasija Grynenko in Zusammenarbeit mit Claudia Dathe* | Die Terminologie des Gerichtswesens der Ukraine und Deutschlands im Vergleich. Eine übersetzungswissenschaftliche Analyse juristischer Fachbegriffe im Deutschen, Ukrainischen und Russischen | Mit einem Vorwort von Ulrich Hartmann | ISBN 3-89821-691-8

45 *Anton Burkov* | The Impact of the European Convention on Human Rights on Russian Law. Legislation and Application in 1996-2006 | With a foreword by Françoise Hampson | ISBN 978-3-89821-639-5

46 *Stina Torjesen, Indra Overland (Eds.)* | International Election Observers in Post-Soviet Azerbaijan. Geopolitical Pawns or Agents of Change? | ISBN 978-3-89821-743-9

47 *Taras Kuzio* | Ukraine – Crimea – Russia. Triangle of Conflict | ISBN 978-3-89821-761-3

48 *Claudia Šabić* | „Ich erinnere mich nicht, aber L'viv!" Zur Funktion kultureller Faktoren für die Institutionalisierung und Entwicklung einer ukrainischen Region | Mit einem Vorwort von Melanie Tatur | ISBN 978-3-89821-752-1

49 *Marlies Bilz* | Tatarstan in der Transformation. Nationaler Diskurs und Politische Praxis 1988-1994 | Mit einem Vorwort von Frank Golczewski | ISBN 978-3-89821-722-4

50 *Марлен Ларюэль (ред.)* | Современные интерпретации русского национализма | ISBN 978-3-89821-795-8

51 *Sonja Schüler* | Die ethnische Dimension der Armut. Roma im postsozialistischen Rumänien | Mit einem Vorwort von Anton Sterbling | ISBN 978-3-89821-776-7

52 *Галина Кожевникова* | Радикальный национализм в России и противодействие ему. Сборник докладов Центра «Сова» за 2004-2007 гг. | С предисловием Александра Верховского | ISBN 978-3-89821-721-7

53 *Галина Кожевникова и Владимир Прибыловский* | Российская власть в биографиях I. Высшие должностные лица РФ в 2004 г. | ISBN 978-3-89821-796-5

54 *Галина Кожевникова и Владимир Прибыловский* | Российская власть в биографиях II. Члены Правительства РФ в 2004 г. | ISBN 978-3-89821-797-2

55 *Галина Кожевникова и Владимир Прибыловский* | Российская власть в биографиях III. Руководители федеральных служб и агентств РФ в 2004 г.| ISBN 978-3-89821-798-9

56 *Ileana Petroniu* | Privatisierung in Transformationsökonomien. Determinanten der Restrukturierungs-Bereitschaft am Beispiel Polens, Rumäniens und der Ukraine | Mit einem Vorwort von Rainer W. Schäfer | ISBN 978-3-89821-790-3

57 *Christian Wipperfürth* | Russland und seine GUS-Nachbarn. Hintergründe, aktuelle Entwicklungen und Konflikte in einer ressourcenreichen Region| ISBN 978-3-89821-801-6

58 *Togzhan Kassenova* | From Antagonism to Partnership. The Uneasy Path of the U.S.-Russian Cooperative Threat Reduction | With a foreword by Christoph Bluth | ISBN 978-3-89821-707-1

59 *Alexander Höllwerth* | Das sakrale eurasische Imperium des Aleksandr Dugin. Eine Diskursanalyse zum postsowjetischen russischen Rechtsextremismus | Mit einem Vorwort von Dirk Uffelmann | ISBN 978-3-89821-813-9

60 *Олег Рябов* | «Россия-Матушка». Национализм, гендер и война в России XX века | С предисловием Елены Гощило | ISBN 978-3-89821-487-2

61 *Ivan Maistrenko* | Borot'bism. A Chapter in the History of the Ukrainian Revolution | With a new Introduction by Chris Ford | Translated by George S. N. Luckyj with the assistance of Ivan L. Rudnytsky | Second, Revised and Expanded Edition ISBN 978-3-8382-1107-7

62 *Maryna Romanets* | Anamorphosic Texts and Reconfigured Visions. Improvised Traditions in Contemporary Ukrainian and Irish Literature | ISBN 978-3-89821-576-3

63 *Paul D'Anieri and Taras Kuzio (Eds.)* | Aspects of the Orange Revolution I. Democratization and Elections in Post-Communist Ukraine | ISBN 978-3-89821-698-2

64 *Bohdan Harasymiw in collaboration with Oleh S. Ilnytzkyj (Eds.)* | Aspects of the Orange Revolution II. Information and Manipulation Strategies in the 2004 Ukrainian Presidential Elections | ISBN 978-3-89821-699-9

65 *Ingmar Bredies, Andreas Umland and Valentin Yakushik (Eds.)* | Aspects of the Orange Revolution III. The Context and Dynamics of the 2004 Ukrainian Presidential Elections | ISBN 978-3-89821-803-0

66 *Ingmar Bredies, Andreas Umland and Valentin Yakushik (Eds.)* | Aspects of the Orange Revolution IV. Foreign Assistance and Civic Action in the 2004 Ukrainian Presidential Elections | ISBN 978-3-89821-808-5

67 *Ingmar Bredies, Andreas Umland and Valentin Yakushik (Eds.)* | Aspects of the Orange Revolution V. Institutional Observation Reports on the 2004 Ukrainian Presidential Elections | ISBN 978-3-89821-809-2

68 *Taras Kuzio (Ed.)* | Aspects of the Orange Revolution VI. Post-Communist Democratic Revolutions in Comparative Perspective | ISBN 978-3-89821-820-7

69 *Tim Bohse* | Autoritarismus statt Selbstverwaltung. Die Transformation der kommunalen Politik in der Stadt Kaliningrad 1990-2005 | Mit einem Geleitwort von Stefan Troebst | ISBN 978-3-89821-782-8

70 *David Rupp* | Die Rußländische Föderation und die russischsprachige Minderheit in Lettland. Eine Fallstudie zur Anwaltspolitik Moskaus gegenüber den russophonen Minderheiten im „Nahen Ausland" von 1991 bis 2002 | Mit einem Vorwort von Helmut Wagner | ISBN 978-3-89821-778-1

71 *Taras Kuzio* | Theoretical and Comparative Perspectives on Nationalism. New Directions in Cross-Cultural and Post-Communist Studies | With a foreword by Paul Robert Magocsi | ISBN 978-3-89821-815-3

72 *Christine Teichmann* | Die Hochschultransformation im heutigen Osteuropa. Kontinuität und Wandel bei der Entwicklung des postkommunistischen Universitätswesens | Mit einem Vorwort von Oskar Anweiler | ISBN 978-3-89821-842-9

73 *Julia Kusznir* | Der politische Einfluss von Wirtschaftseliten in russischen Regionen. Eine Analyse am Beispiel der Erdöl- und Erdgasindustrie, 1992-2005 | Mit einem Vorwort von Wolfgang Eichwede | ISBN 978-3-89821-821-4

74 Alena Vysotskaya | Russland, Belarus und die EU-Osterweiterung. Zur Minderheitenfrage und zum Problem der Freizügigkeit des Personenverkehrs | Mit einem Vorwort von Katlijn Malfliet | ISBN 978-3-89821-822-1

75 Heiko Pleines (Hrsg.) | Corporate Governance in post-sozialistischen Volkswirtschaften | ISBN 978-3-89821-766-8

76 Stefan Ihrig | Wer sind die Moldawier? Rumänismus versus Moldowanismus in Historiographie und Schulbüchern der Republik Moldova, 1991-2006 | Mit einem Vorwort von Holm Sundhaussen | ISBN 978-3-89821-466-7

77 Galina Kozhevnikova in collaboration with Alexander Verkhovsky and Eugene Veklerov | Ultra-Nationalism and Hate Crimes in Contemporary Russia. The 2004-2006 Annual Reports of Moscow's SOVA Center | With a foreword by Stephen D. Shenfield | ISBN 978-3-89821-868-9

78 Florian Küchler | The Role of the European Union in Moldova's Transnistria Conflict | With a foreword by Christopher Hill | ISBN 978-3-89821-850-4

79 Bernd Rechel | The Long Way Back to Europe. Minority Protection in Bulgaria | With a foreword by Richard Crampton | ISBN 978-3-89821-863-4

80 Peter W. Rodgers | Nation, Region and History in Post-Communist Transitions. Identity Politics in Ukraine, 1991-2006 | With a foreword by Vera Tolz | ISBN 978-3-89821-903-7

81 Stephanie Solywoda | The Life and Work of Semen L. Frank. A Study of Russian Religious Philosophy | With a foreword by Philip Walters | ISBN 978-3-89821-457-5

82 Vera Sokolova | Cultural Politics of Ethnicity. Discourses on Roma in Communist Czechoslovakia | ISBN 978-3-89821-864-1

83 Natalya Shevchik Ketenci | Kazakhstani Enterprises in Transition. The Role of Historical Regional Development in Kazakhstan's Post-Soviet Economic Transformation | ISBN 978-3-89821-831-3

84 Martin Malek, Anna Schor-Tschudnowskaja (Hgg.) | Europa im Tschetschenienkrieg. Zwischen politischer Ohnmacht und Gleichgültigkeit | Mit einem Vorwort von Lipchan Basajewa | ISBN 978-3-89821-676-0

85 Stefan Meister | Das postsowjetische Universitätswesen zwischen nationalem und internationalem Wandel. Die Entwicklung der regionalen Hochschule in Russland als Gradmesser der Systemtransformation | Mit einem Vorwort von Joan DeBardeleben | ISBN 978-3-89821-891-7

86 Konstantin Sheiko in collaboration with Stephen Brown | Nationalist Imaginings of the Russian Past. Anatolii Fomenko and the Rise of Alternative History in Post-Communist Russia | With a foreword by Donald Ostrowski | ISBN 978-3-89821-915-0

87 Sabine Jenni | Wie stark ist das „Einige Russland"? Zur Parteibindung der Eliten und zum Wahlerfolg der Machtpartei im Dezember 2007 | Mit einem Vorwort von Klaus Armingeon | ISBN 978-3-89821-961-7

88 Thomas Borén | Meeting-Places of Transformation. Urban Identity, Spatial Representations and Local Politics in Post-Soviet St Petersburg | ISBN 978-3-89821-739-2

89 Aygul Ashirova | Stalinismus und Stalin-Kult in Zentralasien. Turkmenistan 1924-1953 | Mit einem Vorwort von Leonid Luks | ISBN 978-3-89821-987-7

90 Leonid Luks | Freiheit oder imperiale Größe? Essays zu einem russischen Dilemma | ISBN 978-3-8382-0011-8

91 Christopher Gilley | The 'Change of Signposts' in the Ukrainian Emigration. A Contribution to the History of Sovietophilism in the 1920s | With a foreword by Frank Golczewski | ISBN 978-3-89821-965-5

92 Philipp Casula, Jeronim Perovic (Eds.) | Identities and Politics During the Putin Presidency. The Discursive Foundations of Russia's Stability | With a foreword by Heiko Haumann | ISBN 978-3-8382-0015-6

93 Marcel Viëtor | Europa und die Frage nach seinen Grenzen im Osten. Zur Konstruktion ‚europäischer Identität' in Geschichte und Gegenwart | Mit einem Vorwort von Albrecht Lehmann | ISBN 978-3-8382-0045-3

94 Ben Hellman, Andrei Rogachevskii | Filming the Unfilmable. Casper Wrede's 'One Day in the Life of Ivan Denisovich' | Second, Revised and Expanded Edition | ISBN 978-3-8382-0044-6

95 Eva Fuchslocher | Vaterland, Sprache, Glaube. Orthodoxie und Nationenbildung am Beispiel Georgiens | Mit einem Vorwort von Christina von Braun | ISBN 978-3-89821-884-9

96 Vladimir Kantor | Das Westlertum und der Weg Russlands. Zur Entwicklung der russischen Literatur und Philosophie | Ediert von Dagmar Herrmann | Mit einem Beitrag von Nikolaus Lobkowicz | ISBN 978-3-8382-0102-3

97 Kamran Musayev | Die postsowjetische Transformation im Baltikum und Südkaukasus. Eine vergleichende Untersuchung der politischen Entwicklung Lettlands und Aserbaidschans 1985-2009 | Mit einem Vorwort von Leonid Luks | Ediert von Sandro Henschel | ISBN 978-3-8382-0103-0

98 Tatiana Zhurzhenko | Borderlands into Bordered Lands. Geopolitics of Identity in Post-Soviet Ukraine | With a foreword by Dieter Segert | ISBN 978-3-8382-0042-2

99 *Кирилл Галушко, Лидия Смола (ред.)* | Пределы падения – варианты украинского будущего. Аналитико-прогностические исследования | ISBN 978-3-8382-0148-1

100 *Michael Minkenberg (Ed.)* | Historical Legacies and the Radical Right in Post-Cold War Central and Eastern Europe | With an afterword by Sabrina P. Ramet | ISBN 978-3-8382-0124-5

101 *David-Emil Wickström* | Rocking St. Petersburg. Transcultural Flows and Identity Politics in the St. Petersburg Popular Music Scene | With a foreword by Yngvar B. Steinholt | Second, Revised and Expanded Edition | ISBN 978-3-8382-0100-9

102 *Eva Zabka* | Eine neue „Zeit der Wirren"? Der spät- und postsowjetische Systemwandel 1985-2000 im Spiegel russischer gesellschaftspolitischer Diskurse | Mit einem Vorwort von Margareta Mommsen | ISBN 978-3-8382-0161-0

103 *Ulrike Ziemer* | Ethnic Belonging, Gender and Cultural Practices. Youth Identitites in Contemporary Russia | With a foreword by Anoop Nayak | ISBN 978-3-8382-0152-8

104 *Ksenia Chepikova* | ‚Einiges Russland' - eine zweite KPdSU? Aspekte der Identitätskonstruktion einer postsowjetischen „Partei der Macht" | Mit einem Vorwort von Torsten Oppelland | ISBN 978-3-8382-0311-9

105 *Леонид Люкс* | Западничество или евразийство? Демократия или идеократия? Сборник статей об исторических дилеммах России | С предисловием Владимира Кантора | ISBN 978-3-8382-0211-2

106 *Anna Dost* | Das russische Verfassungsrecht auf dem Weg zum Föderalismus und zurück. Zum Konflikt von Rechtsnormen und -wirklichkeit in der Russländischen Föderation von 1991 bis 2009 | Mit einem Vorwort von Alexander Blankenagel | ISBN 978-3-8382-0292-1

107 *Philipp Herzog* | Sozialistische Völkerfreundschaft, nationaler Widerstand oder harmloser Zeitvertreib? Zur politischen Funktion der Volkskunst im sowjetischen Estland | Mit einem Vorwort von Andreas Kappeler | ISBN 978-3-8382-0216-7

108 *Marlène Laruelle (Ed.)* | Russian Nationalism, Foreign Policy, and Identity Debates in Putin's Russia. New Ideological Patterns after the Orange Revolution | ISBN 978-3-8382-0325-6

109 *Michail Logvinov* | Russlands Kampf gegen den internationalen Terrorismus. Eine kritische Bestandsaufnahme des Bekämpfungsansatzes | Mit einem Geleitwort von Hans-Henning Schröder und einem Vorwort von Eckhard Jesse | ISBN 978-3-8382-0329-4

110 *John B. Dunlop* | The Moscow Bombings of September 1999. Examinations of Russian Terrorist Attacks at the Onset of Vladimir Putin's Rule | Second, Revised and Expanded Edition | ISBN 978-3-8382-0388-1

111 *Андрей А. Ковалёв* | Свидетельство из-за кулис российской политики I. Можно ли делать добро из зла? (Воспоминания и размышления о последних советских и первых послесоветских годах) | With a foreword by Peter Reddaway | ISBN 978-3-8382-0302-7

112 *Андрей А. Ковалёв* | Свидетельство из-за кулис российской политики II. Угроза для себя и окружающих (Наблюдения и предостережения относительно происходящего после 2000 г.) | ISBN 978-3-8382-0303-4

113 *Bernd Kappenberg* | Zeichen setzen für Europa. Der Gebrauch europäischer lateinischer Sonderzeichen in der deutschen Öffentlichkeit | Mit einem Vorwort von Peter Schlobinski | ISBN 978-3-89821-749-1

114 *Ivo Mijnssen* | The Quest for an Ideal Youth in Putin's Russia I. Back to Our Future! History, Modernity, and Patriotism according to Nashi, 2005-2013 | With a foreword by Jeronim Perović | Second, Revised and Expanded Edition | ISBN 978-3-8382-0368-3

115 *Jussi Lassila* | The Quest for an Ideal Youth in Putin's Russia II. The Search for Distinctive Conformism in the Political Communication of Nashi, 2005-2009 | With a foreword by Kirill Postoutenko | Second, Revised and Expanded Edition | ISBN 978-3-8382-0415-4

116 *Valerio Trabandt* | Neue Nachbarn, gute Nachbarschaft? Die EU als internationaler Akteur am Beispiel ihrer Demokratieförderung in Belarus und der Ukraine 2004-2009 | Mit einem Vorwort von Jutta Joachim | ISBN 978-3-8382-0437-6

117 *Fabian Pfeiffer* | Estlands Außen- und Sicherheitspolitik I. Der estnische Atlantizismus nach der wiedererlangten Unabhängigkeit 1991-2004 | Mit einem Vorwort von Helmut Hubel | ISBN 978-3-8382-0127-6

118 *Jana Podßuweit* | Estlands Außen- und Sicherheitspolitik II. Handlungsoptionen eines Kleinstaates im Rahmen seiner EU-Mitgliedschaft (2004-2008) | Mit einem Vorwort von Helmut Hubel | ISBN 978-3-8382-0440-6

119 *Karin Pointner* | Estlands Außen- und Sicherheitspolitik III. Eine gedächtnispolitische Analyse estnischer Entwicklungskooperation 2006-2010 | Mit einem Vorwort von Karin Liebhart | ISBN 978-3-8382-0435-2

120 *Ruslana Vovk* | Die Offenheit der ukrainischen Verfassung für das Völkerrecht und die europäische Integration | Mit einem Vorwort von Alexander Blankenagel | ISBN 978-3-8382-0481-9

121 *Mykhaylo Banakh* | Die Relevanz der Zivilgesellschaft bei den postkommunistischen Transformationsprozessen in mittel- und osteuropäischen Ländern. Das Beispiel der spät- und postsowjetischen Ukraine 1986-2009 | Mit einem Vorwort von Gerhard Simon | ISBN 978-3-8382-0499-4

122 *Michael Moser* | Language Policy and the Discourse on Languages in Ukraine under President Viktor Yanukovych (25 February 2010–28 October 2012) | ISBN 978-3-8382-0497-0 (Paperback edition) | ISBN 978-3-8382-0507-6 (Hardcover edition)

123 *Nicole Krome* | Russischer Netzwerkkapitalismus Restrukturierungsprozesse in der Russischen Föderation am Beispiel des Luftfahrtunternehmens „Aviastar" | Mit einem Vorwort von Petra Stykow | ISBN 978-3-8382-0534-2

124 *David R. Marples* | 'Our Glorious Past'. Lukashenka's Belarus and the Great Patriotic War | ISBN 978-3-8382-0574-8 (Paperback edition) | ISBN 978-3-8382-0675-2 (Hardcover edition)

125 *Ulf Walther* | Russlands „neuer Adel". Die Macht des Geheimdienstes von Gorbatschow bis Putin | Mit einem Vorwort von Hans-Georg Wieck | ISBN 978-3-8382-0584-7

126 *Simon Geissbühler (Hrsg.)* | Kiew – Revolution 3.0. Der Euromaidan 2013/14 und die Zukunftsperspektiven der Ukraine | ISBN 978-3-8382-0581-6 (Paperback edition) | ISBN 978-3-8382-0681-3 (Hardcover edition)

127 *Andrey Makarychev* | Russia and the EU in a Multipolar World. Discourses, Identities, Norms | With a foreword by Klaus Segbers | ISBN 978-3-8382-0629-5

128 *Roland Scharff* | Kasachstan als postsowjetischer Wohlfahrtsstaat. Die Transformation des sozialen Schutzsystems | Mit einem Vorwort von Joachim Ahrens | ISBN 978-3-8382-0622-6

129 *Katja Grupp* | Bild Lücke Deutschland. Kaliningrader Studierende sprechen über Deutschland | Mit einem Vorwort von Martin Schulz | ISBN 978-3-8382-0552-6

130 *Konstantin Sheiko, Stephen Brown* | History as Therapy. Alternative History and Nationalist Imaginings in Russia, 1991-2014 | ISBN 978-3-8382-0665-3

131 *Elisa Kriza* | Alexander Solzhenitsyn: Cold War Icon, Gulag Author, Russian Nationalist? A Study of the Western Reception of his Literary Writings, Historical Interpretations, and Political Ideas | With a foreword by Andrei Rogatchevski | ISBN 978-3-8382-0589-2 (Paperback edition) | ISBN 978-3-8382-0690-5 (Hardcover edition)

132 *Serghei Golunov* | The Elephant in the Room. Corruption and Cheating in Russian Universities | ISBN 978-3-8382-0570-0

133 *Manja Hussner, Rainer Arnold (Hgg.)* | Verfassungsgerichtsbarkeit in Zentralasien I. Sammlung von Verfassungstexten | ISBN 978-3-8382-0595-3

134 *Nikolay Mitrokhin* | Die „Russische Partei". Die Bewegung der russischen Nationalisten in der UdSSR 1953-1985 | Aus dem Russischen übertragen von einem Übersetzerteam unter der Leitung von Larisa Schippel | ISBN 978-3-8382-0024-8

135 *Manja Hussner, Rainer Arnold (Hgg.)* | Verfassungsgerichtsbarkeit in Zentralasien II. Sammlung von Verfassungstexten | ISBN 978-3-8382-0597-7

136 *Manfred Zeller* | Das sowjetische Fieber. Fußballfans im poststalinistischen Vielvölkerreich | Mit einem Vorwort von Nikolaus Katzer | ISBN 978-3-8382-0757-5

137 *Kristin Schreiter* | Stellung und Entwicklungspotential zivilgesellschaftlicher Gruppen in Russland. Menschenrechtsorganisationen im Vergleich | ISBN 978-3-8382-0673-8

138 *David R. Marples, Frederick V. Mills (Eds.)* | Ukraine's Euromaidan. Analyses of a Civil Revolution | ISBN 978-3-8382-0660-8

139 *Bernd Kappenberg* | Setting Signs for Europe. Why Diacritics Matter for European Integration | With a foreword by Peter Schlobinski | ISBN 978-3-8382-0663-9

140 *René Lenz* | Internationalisierung, Kooperation und Transfer. Externe bildungspolitische Akteure in der Russischen Föderation | Mit einem Vorwort von Frank Ettrich | ISBN 978-3-8382-0751-3

141 *Juri Plusnin, Yana Zausaeva, Natalia Zhidkevich, Artemy Pozanenko* | Wandering Workers. Mores, Behavior, Way of Life, and Political Status of Domestic Russian Labor Migrants | Translated by Julia Kazantseva | ISBN 978-3-8382-0653-0

142 *David J. Smith (Eds.)* | Latvia – A Work in Progress? 100 Years of State- and Nation-Building | ISBN 978-3-8382-0648-6

143 *Инна Чувычкина (ред.)* | Экспортные нефте- и газопроводы на постсоветском пространстве. Анализ трубопроводной политики в свете теории международных отношений | ISBN 978-3-8382-0822-0

144 *Johann Zajaczkowski* | Russland – eine pragmatische Großmacht? Eine rollentheoretische Untersuchung russischer Außenpolitik am Beispiel der Zusammenarbeit mit den USA nach 9/11 und des Georgienkrieges von 2008 | Mit einem Vorwort von Siegfried Schieder | ISBN 978-3-8382-0837-4

145 *Boris Popivanov* | Changing Images of the Left in Bulgaria. The Challenge of Post-Communism in the Early 21st Century | ISBN 978-3-8382-0667-7

146 *Lenka Krátká* | A History of the Czechoslovak Ocean Shipping Company 1948-1989. How a Small, Landlocked Country Ran Maritime Business During the Cold War | ISBN 978-3-8382-0666-0

147 *Alexander Sergunin* | Explaining Russian Foreign Policy Behavior. Theory and Practice | ISBN 978-3-8382-0752-0

148 *Darya Malyutina* | Migrant Friendships in a Super-Diverse City. Russian-Speakers and their Social Relationships in London in the 21st Century | With a foreword by Claire Dwyer | ISBN 978-3-8382-0652-3

149 *Alexander Sergunin, Valery Konyshev* | Russia in the Arctic. Hard or Soft Power? | ISBN 978-3-8382-0753-7

150 *John J. Maresca* | Helsinki Revisited. A Key U.S. Negotiator's Memoirs on the Development of the CSCE into the OSCE | With a foreword by Hafiz Pashayev | ISBN 978-3-8382-0852-7

151 *Jardar Østbø* | The New Third Rome. Readings of a Russian Nationalist Myth | With a foreword by Pål Kolstø | ISBN 978-3-8382-0870-1

152 *Simon Kordonsky* | Socio-Economic Foundations of the Russian Post-Soviet Regime. The Resource-Based Economy and Estate-Based Social Structure of Contemporary Russia | With a foreword by Svetlana Barsukova | ISBN 978-3-8382-0775-9

153 *Duncan Leitch* | Assisting Reform in Post-Communist Ukraine 2000–2012. The Illusions of Donors and the Disillusion of Beneficiaries | With a foreword by Kataryna Wolczuk | ISBN 978-3-8382-0844-2

154 *Abel Polese* | Limits of a Post-Soviet State. How Informality Replaces, Renegotiates, and Reshapes Governance in Contemporary Ukraine | With a foreword by Colin Williams | ISBN 978-3-8382-0845-9

155 *Mikhail Suslov (Ed.)* | Digital Orthodoxy in the Post-Soviet World. The Russian Orthodox Church and Web 2.0 | With a foreword by Father Cyril Hovorun | ISBN 978-3-8382-0871-8

156 *Leonid Luks* | Zwei „Sonderwege"? Russisch-deutsche Parallelen und Kontraste (1917-2014). Vergleichende Essays | ISBN 978-3-8382-0823-7

157 *Vladimir V. Karacharovskiy, Ovsey I. Shkaratan, Gordey A. Yastrebov* | Towards a New Russian Work Culture. Can Western Companies and Expatriates Change Russian Society? | With a foreword by Elena N. Danilova | Translated by Julia Kazantseva | ISBN 978-3-8382-0902-9

158 *Edmund Griffiths* | Aleksandr Prokhanov and Post-Soviet Esotericism | ISBN 978-3-8382-0903-6

159 *Timm Beichelt, Susann Worschech (Eds.)* | Transnational Ukraine? Networks and Ties that Influence(d) Contemporary Ukraine | ISBN 978-3-8382-0944-9

160 *Mieste Hotopp-Riecke* | Die Tataren der Krim zwischen Assimilation und Selbstbehauptung. Der Aufbau des krimtatarischen Bildungswesens nach Deportation und Heimkehr (1990-2005) | Mit einem Vorwort von Swetlana Czerwonnaja | ISBN 978-3-89821-940-2

161 *Olga Bertelsen (Ed.)* | Revolution and War in Contemporary Ukraine. The Challenge of Change | ISBN 978-3-8382-1016-2

162 *Natalya Ryabinska* | Ukraine's Post-Communist Mass Media. Between Capture and Commercialization | With a foreword by Marta Dyczok | ISBN 978-3-8382-1011-7

163 *Alexandra Cotofana, James M. Nyce (Eds.)* | Religion and Magic in Socialist and Post-Socialist Contexts. Historic and Ethnographic Case Studies of Orthodoxy, Heterodoxy, and Alternative Spirituality | With a foreword by Patrick L. Michelson | ISBN 978-3-8382-0989-0

164 *Nozima Akhrarkhodjaeva* | The Instrumentalisation of Mass Media in Electoral Authoritarian Regimes. Evidence from Russia's Presidential Election Campaigns of 2000 and 2008 | ISBN 978-3-8382-1013-1

165 *Yulia Krasheninnikova* | Informal Healthcare in Contemporary Russia. Sociographic Essays on the Post-Soviet Infrastructure for Alternative Healing Practices | ISBN 978-3-8382-0970-8

166 *Peter Kaiser* | Das Schachbrett der Macht. Die Handlungsspielräume eines sowjetischen Funktionärs unter Stalin am Beispiel des Generalsekretärs des Komsomol Aleksandr Kosarev (1929-1938) | Mit einem Vorwort von Dietmar Neutatz | ISBN 978-3-8382-1052-0

167 *Oksana Kim* | The Effects and Implications of Kazakhstan's Adoption of International Financial Reporting Standards. A Resource Dependence Perspective | With a foreword by Svetlana Vlady | ISBN 978-3-8382-0987-6

168 *Anna Sanina* | Patriotic Education in Contemporary Russia. Sociological Studies in the Making of the Post-Soviet Citizen | With a foreword by Anna Oldfield | ISBN 978-3-8382-0993-7

169 *Rudolf Wolters* | Spezialist in Sibirien Faksimile der 1933 erschienenen ersten Ausgabe | Mit einem Vorwort von Dmitrij Chmelnizki | ISBN 978-3-8382-0515-1

170 *Michal Vít, Magdalena M. Baran (Eds.)* | Transregional versus National Perspectives on Contemporary Central European History. Studies on the Building of Nation-States and Their Cooperation in the 20th and 21st Century | With a foreword by Petr Vágner | ISBN 978-3-8382-1015-5

171 *Philip Gamaghelyan* | Conflict Resolution Beyond the International Relations Paradigm. Evolving Designs as a Transformative Practice in Nagorno-Karabakh and Syria | With a foreword by Susan Allen | ISBN 978-3-8382-1057-5

172 *Maria Shagina* | Joining a Prestigious Club. Cooperation with Europarties and Its Impact on Party Development in Georgia, Moldova, and Ukraine 2004–2015 | With a foreword by Kataryna Wolczuk | ISBN 978-3-8382-1084-1

173 *Alexandra Cotofana, James M. Nyce (Eds.)* | Religion and Magic in Socialist and Post-Socialist Contexts II. Baltic, Eastern European, and Post-USSR Case Studies | With a foreword by Anita Stasulane | ISBN 978-3-8382-0990-6

174 *Barbara Kunz* | Kind Words, Cruise Missiles, and Everything in Between. The Use of Power Resources in U.S. Policies towards Poland, Ukraine, and Belarus 1989–2008 | With a foreword by William Hill | ISBN 978-3-8382-1065-0

175 *Eduard Klein* | Bildungskorruption in Russland und der Ukraine. Eine komparative Analyse der Performanz staatlicher Antikorruptionsmaßnahmen im Hochschulsektor am Beispiel universitärer Aufnahmeprüfungen | Mit einem Vorwort von Heiko Pleines | ISBN 978-3-8382-0995-1

176 *Markus Soldner* | Politischer Kapitalismus im postsowjetischen Russland. Die politische, wirtschaftliche und mediale Transformation in den 1990er Jahren | Mit einem Vorwort von Wolfgang Ismayr | ISBN 978-3-8382-1222-7

177 *Anton Oleinik* | Building Ukraine from Within. A Sociological, Institutional, and Economic Analysis of a Nation-State in the Making | ISBN 978-3-8382-1150-3

178 *Peter Rollberg, Marlene Laruelle (Eds.)* | Mass Media in the Post-Soviet World. Market Forces, State Actors, and Political Manipulation in the Informational Environment after Communism | ISBN 978-3-8382-1116-9

179 *Mikhail Minakov* | Development and Dystopia. Studies in Post-Soviet Ukraine and Eastern Europe | With a foreword by Alexander Etkind | ISBN 978-3-8382-1112-1

180 *Aijan Sharshenova* | The European Union's Democracy Promotion in Central Asia. A Study of Political Interests, Influence, and Development in Kazakhstan and Kyrgyzstan in 2007–2013 | With a foreword by Gordon Crawford | ISBN 978-3-8382-1151-0

181 *Andrey Makarychev, Alexandra Yatsyk (Eds.)* | Boris Nemtsov and Russian Politics. Power and Resistance | With a foreword by Zhanna Nemtsova | ISBN 978-3-8382-1122-0

182 *Sophie Falsini* | The Euromaidan's Effect on Civil Society. Why and How Ukrainian Social Capital Increased after the Revolution of Dignity | With a foreword by Susann Worschech | ISBN 978-3-8382-1131-2

183 *Valentyna Romanova, Andreas Umland (Eds.)* | Ukraine's Decentralization. Challenges and Implications of the Local Governance Reform after the Euromaidan Revolution | ISBN 978-3-8382-1162-6

184 *Leonid Luks* | A Fateful Triangle. Essays on Contemporary Russian, German and Polish History | ISBN 978-3-8382-1143-5

185 *John B. Dunlop* | The February 2015 Assassination of Boris Nemtsov and the Flawed Trial of his Alleged Killers. An Exploration of Russia's "Crime of the 21st Century" | ISBN 978-3-8382-1188-6

186 *Vasile Rotaru* | Russia, the EU, and the Eastern Partnership. Building Bridges or Digging Trenches? | ISBN 978-3-8382-1134-3

187 *Marina Lebedeva* | Russian Studies of International Relations. From the Soviet Past to the Post-Cold-War Present | With a foreword by Andrei P. Tsygankov | ISBN 978-3-8382-0851-0

188 *Tomasz Stępniewski, George Soroka (Eds.)* | Ukraine after Maidan. Revisiting Domestic and Regional Security | ISBN 978-3-8382-1075-9

189 *Petar Cholakov* | Ethnic Entrepreneurs Unmasked. Political Institutions and Ethnic Conflicts in Contemporary Bulgaria | ISBN 978-3-8382-1189-3

190 *A. Salem, G. Hazeldine, D. Morgan (Eds.)* | Higher Education in Post-Communist States. Comparative and Sociological Perspectives | ISBN 978-3-8382-1183-1

191 *Igor Torbakov* | After Empire. Nationalist Imagination and Symbolic Politics in Russia and Eurasia in the Twentieth and Twenty-First Century | With a foreword by Serhii Plokhy | ISBN 978-3-8382-1217-3

192 *Aleksandr Burakovskiy* | Jewish-Ukrainian Relations in Late and Post-Soviet Ukraine. Articles, Lectures and Essays from 1986 to 2016 | ISBN 978-3-8382-1210-4

193 *Natalia Shapovalova, Olga Burlyuk (Eds.)* | Civil Society in Post-Euromaidan Ukraine. From Revolution to Consolidation | With a foreword by Richard Youngs | ISBN 978-3-8382-1216-6

194 *Franz Preissler* | Positionsverteidigung, Imperialismus oder Irredentismus? Russland und die „Russischsprachigen", 1991–2015 | ISBN 978-3-8382-1262-3

195 *Marian Madeła* | Der Reformprozess in der Ukraine 2014-2017. Eine Fallstudie zur Reform der öffentlichen Verwaltung | Mit einem Vorwort von Martin Malek | ISBN 978-3-8382-1266-1

196 *Anke Giesen* | „Wie kann denn der Sieger ein Verbrecher sein?" Eine diskursanalytische Untersuchung der russlandweiten Debatte über Konzept und Verstaatlichungsprozess der Lagergedenkstätte „Perm'-36" im Ural | ISBN 978-3-8382-1284-5

197 *Alla Leukavets* | The Integration Policies of Belarus and Ukraine vis-à-vis the EU and Russia. A Comparative Case Study Through the Prism of a Two-Level Game Approach | ISBN 978-3-8382-1247-0

198 *Oksana Kim* | The Development and Challenges of Russian Corporate Governance I. The Roles and Functions of Boards of Directors | With a foreword by Sheila M. Puffer | ISBN 978-3-8382-1287-6

199 *Thomas D. Grant* | International Law and the Post-Soviet Space I. Essays on Chechnya and the Baltic States | With a foreword by Stephen M. Schwebel | ISBN 978-3-8382-1279-1

200 *Thomas D. Grant* | International Law and the Post-Soviet Space II. Essays on Ukraine, Intervention, and Non-Proliferation | ISBN 978-3-8382-1280-7

201 *Slavomír Michálek, Michal Štefansky* | The Age of Fear. The Cold War and Its Influence on Czechoslovakia 1945–1968 | ISBN 978-3-8382-1285-2

202 *Iulia-Sabina Joja* | Romania's Strategic Culture 1990–2014. Continuity and Change in a Post-Communist Country's Evolution of National Interests and Security Policies | With a foreword by Heiko Biehl | ISBN 978-3-8382-1286-9

203 *Andrei Rogatchevski, Yngvar B. Steinholt, Arve Hansen, David-Emil Wickström* | War of Songs. Popular Music and Recent Russia-Ukraine Relations | With a foreword by Artemy Troitsky | ISBN 978-3-8382-1173-2

204 *Maria Lipman (Ed.)* | Russian Voices on Post-Crimea Russia. An Almanac of Counterpoint Essays from 2015–2018 | ISBN 978-3-8382-1251-7

205 *Ksenia Maksimovtsova* | Language Conflicts in Contemporary Estonia, Latvia, and Ukraine. A Comparative Exploration of Discourses in Post-Soviet Russian-Language Digital Media | With a foreword by Ammon Cheskin | ISBN 978-3-8382-1282-1

206 *Michal Vít* | The EU's Impact on Identity Formation in East-Central Europe between 2004 and 2013. Perceptions of the Nation and Europe in Political Parties of the Czech Republic, Poland, and Slovakia | With a foreword by Andrea Pető | ISBN 978-3-8382-1275-3

207 *Per A. Rudling* | Tarnished Heroes. The Organization of Ukrainian Nationalists in the Memory Politics of Post-Soviet Ukraine | ISBN 978-3-8382-0999-9

208 *Kaja Gadowska, Peter Solomon (Eds.)* | Legal Change in Post-Communist States. Progress, Reversions, Explanations | ISBN 978-3-8382-1312-5

209 *Paweł Kowal, Georges Mink, Iwona Reichardt (Eds.)* | Three Revolutions: Mobilization and Change in Contemporary Ukraine I. Theoretical Aspects and Analyses on Religion, Memory, and Identity | ISBN 978-3-8382-1321-7

210 *Paweł Kowal, Georges Mink, Adam Reichardt, Iwona Reichardt (Eds.)* | Three Revolutions: Mobilization and Change in Contemporary Ukraine II. An Oral History of the Revolution on Granite, Orange Revolution, and Revolution of Dignity | ISBN 978-3-8382-1323-1

211 *Li Bennich-Björkman, Sergiy Kurbatov (Eds.)* | When the Future Came. The Collapse of the USSR and the Emergence of National Memory in Post-Soviet History Textbooks | ISBN 978-3-8382-1335-4

212 *Olga R. Gulina* | Migration as a (Geo-)Political Challenge in the Post-Soviet Space. Border Regimes, Policy Choices, Visa Agendas | With a foreword by Nils Muižnieks | ISBN 978-3-8382-1338-5

213 *Sanna Turoma, Kaarina Aitamurto, Slobodanka Vladiv-Glover (Eds.)* | Religion, Expression, and Patriotism in Russia. Essays on Post-Soviet Society and the State. ISBN 978-3-8382-1346-0

214 *Vasif Huseynov* | Geopolitical Rivalries in the "Common Neighborhood". Russia's Conflict with the West, Soft Power, and Neoclassical Realism | With a foreword by Nicholas Ross Smith | ISBN 978-3-8382-1277-7

215 *Mikhail Suslov* | Geopolitical Imagination. Ideology and Utopia in Post-Soviet Russia | With a foreword by Mark Bassin | ISBN 978-3-8382-1361-3

216 *Alexander Etkind, Mikhail Minakov (Eds.)* | Ideology after Union. Political Doctrines, Discourses, and Debates in Post-Soviet Societies | ISBN 978-3-8382-1388-0

217 *Jakob Mischke, Oleksandr Zabirko (Hgg.)* | Protestbewegungen im langen Schatten des Kreml. Aufbruch und Resignation in Russland und der Ukraine | ISBN 978-3-8382-0926-5

218 *Oksana Huss* | How Corruption and Anti-Corruption Policies Sustain Hybrid Regimes. Strategies of Political Domination under Ukraine's Presidents in 1994-2014. With a foreword by Tobias Debiel and Andrea Gawrich | ISBN 978-3-8382-1430-6

219 *Dmitry Travin, Vladimir Gel'man, Otar Marganiya* | The Russian Path. Ideas, Interests, Institutions, Illusions. With a foreword by Vladimir Ryzhkov | ISBN 978-3-8382-1421-4

220 *Gergana Dimova* | Political Uncertainty. A Comparative Exploration. With a foreword by Todor Yalamov and Rumena Filipova | ISBN 978-3-8382-1385-9

221 *Torben Waschke* | Russland in Transition. Geopolitik zwischen Raum, Identität und Machtinteressen. Mit einem Vorwort von Andreas Dittmann | ISBN 978-3-8382-1480-1

222 *Steven Jobbitt, Zsolt Bottlik, Marton Berki (Eds.)* | Power and Identity in the Post-Soviet Realm. Geographies of Ethnicity and Nationality after 1991 | ISBN 978-3-8382-1399-6

223 *Daria Buteiko* | Erinnerungsort. Ort des Gedenkens, der Erholung oder der Einkehr? Kommunismus-Erinnerung am Beispiel der Gedenkstätte Berliner Mauer sowie des Soloveckij-Klosters und -Museumsparks | ISBN 978-3-8382-1367-5

224 *Olga Bertelsen (Eds.)* | Russian Active Measures. Yesterday, Today, Tomorrow. With a foreword by Jan Goldman | ISBN 978-3-8382-1529-7

225 *David Mandel* | "Optimizing" Higher Education in Russia. University Teachers and their Union "Universitetskaya solidarnost'" | ISBN 978-3-8382-1519-8

226 *Daria Isachenko, Mykhailo Minakov, Gwendolyn Sasse (Eds.)* | Post-Soviet Secessionism | Nation-Building and State-Failure after Communism | ISBN 978-3-8382-1538-9

227 *Jakob Hauter (Ed.)* | Civil War? Interstate War? Hybrid War? | Dimensions and Interpretations of the Donbas Conflict in 2014–2020. With a foreword by Andrew Wilson | ISBN 978-3-8382-1383-5

228 *Tima T. Moldogaziev, Gene A. Brewer, J. Edward Kellough (Eds.)* | Public Policy and Politics in Georgia | Lessons from Post-Soviet Transition. With a foreword by Dan Durning | ISBN 978-3-8382-1535-8

***ibidem**.eu*